Made in Britain

Made in Britain

Nation and Emigration
in Nineteenth-Century America

Stephen Tuffnell

UNIVERSITY OF CALIFORNIA PRESS

University of California Press
Oakland, California

© 2020 by Stephen Tuffnell

Library of Congress Cataloging-in-Publication Data

Names: Tuffnell, Stephen, 1987– author.
Title: Made in Britain : nation and emigration in
    nineteenth-century America / Stephen Tuffnell.
Description: Oakland, California : University of
    California Press, [2020] | Includes bibliographical
    references and index.
Identifiers: LCCN 2020010936 (print) | LCCN 2020010937
    (ebook) | ISBN 9780520344709 (cloth) | ISBN
    9780520975637 (ebook)
Subjects: LCSH: Americans—Great Britain—History—
    19th century. | United States—History—19th century.
Classification: LCC DA125.A6 T84 2020 (print) |
    LCC DA125.A6 (ebook) | DDC 941/.00413009034—
    dc23
LC record available at https://lccn.loc.gov/2020010936
LC ebook record available at https://lccn.loc
    .gov/2020010937

Manufactured in the United States of America

28 27 26 25 24 23 22 21 20
10 9 8 7 6 5 4 3 2 1

For Hilary Monkman

Contents

Tables and Figures

Acknowledgments

Among the most enjoyable parts of this project has been to reflect at its end on the generosity, collaborations, and friendships that shaped the endeavor.

I am deeply indebted to Jay Sexton, who set me on this track and triggered a passion for US history as a first-year undergraduate. It has been a tremendous privilege to have the benefit of his guidance and good judgment since then. His mentorship, wisdom, unflagging support, and instinct for when to push me further have propelled this project. But above all, his sense that intellectual discussion should be fun while remaining rigorous made the journey a real pleasure.

Without a Research Preparation Masters Studentship and a Doctoral Studentship from the Arts and Humanities Research Council (AHRC) I would not have been able to take up postgraduate study, and I am profoundly grateful for their support. In Oxford I am also indebted to the support of a Senior Scholarship from Wadham College; to the Rothermere American Institute for awarding me a Graduate Studentship and essential financial support from the Academic Programme Fund; to the President and Fellows of Corpus Christi College where I was welcomed as a research assistant and later as a British Academy Postdoctoral Fellow; and to the O'Connor Fund at St Peter's College. I am also grateful to the AHRC's International Placement Scheme, which supported indispensable research at the John W. Kluge Center at the Library of Congress, and to Mary Lou Reker from the Kluge for her warm welcome and support throughout my visit. Funding from the Peter J. Parish Memorial Fund of the British American Nineteenth Century Historians (BrANCH); the British Association of American Studies; the Phillips Library of the Peabody Essex Museum, Salem, MA; the Royal Historical Society; and the Society for Historians of American Foreign Relations made this book possible.

This book emerged from my doctoral research, but has been transformed by the wisdom of others. A frenzy of rewriting was inspired by Gareth Davies, David Sim, Daniel Kilbride, Nicole Phelps, and Andrew Heath, who attended a Monograph Workshop for an earlier draft of the manuscript; all forced me to make crucial decisions about the book and suggested ways to make the chapters clearer and more compelling. Thank you to Martin Conway and the Oxford History Faculty for providing support to host the workshop. I owe further debts to Daniel Bender, who encouraged me to be bolder in some of my arguments, and to the anonymous readers who took the time to read the whole manuscript and suggest ways to strengthen and clarify the argument. Special thanks also to Richard Carwardine, Benjamin Mountford, John Watts, Kristin Hoganson, Brooke Blower, Gary Gerstle, and Martin Crawford. Huge thanks to the whole community at St. Peter's College, where this book took its final shape through numerous small interventions in tutorials, lunches, walks in Italy, and snatched conversations which forced me to see the problems it tackles in fresh perspectives. The generosity of the Harmsworth family, who support my tutorial fellowship, is unmatched and sincerely appreciated. The friendly comments and questions from the members of BrANCH sharpened many of the arguments presented here, but their welcome into the community of British Americanists resonated most to a bewildered postgraduate. The friendship and comradery of Huw David, Sebastian Page, Ed Adkins, David Sim (again!) and the US History graduate community in Oxford was always thought-provoking. Since 2005 the intellectual and personal generosity of Jane Garnett has been an inspiration.

I would also like to thank all the archivists and librarians on both sides of the Atlantic who helped me to navigate and understand the materials in their collections—and who despatched my requests with patience and expertise. I thank, in particular, Tal Nadan at the New York Public Library, who helped me through the United States Sanitary Commission files; Andrew French and Kathy Flynn at the Phillips Library; Moira Lovegrove at the Barings Archive; Jane Rawson at the Vere Harmsworth Library; the David Bruce Centre at Keele University;

and the staff at the Library of Congress Manuscript Reading Room, the National Archives at College Park, and the Huntington Library, Pasadena. It has been a real pleasure to collaborate with Niels Hooper and Robin Manley at the University of California Press who have been terrific stewards and supporters of the book, and Catherine Osborne has improved it immeasurably with her interventions.

Parts of this book have been reproduced from the following journal articles: "Expatriate Foreign Relations: Britain's American Community and Transnational Approaches to the U.S. Civil War," *Diplomatic History* 40, no. 4 (2016): 635–63, with the permission of Oxford University Press; and "Anglo-American Inter-Imperialism: US Expansion and the British World, c.1865–1914," *Britain and the World* 7, no. 2 (2014): 174–95, with the permission of Edinburgh University Press.

Especial thanks go to my friends and a family who enriched the research and writing of this book. Mike Kelly probably now knows more about Anglo-American relations than he ever cared to and will be as relieved as I am to see this in print: I owe you a drink or two. Joe Dunlop: you're the best. Annie Sylvain has been a great host and a great distractor on research trips to Pittsburgh and Washington, DC. A long time ago Pete Morgan sparked the revelation that I might pursue history at university and deserves particularly heartfelt thanks. My brothers Rob and Ben not only lent me spaces on floors, sofas, and spare rooms in London and New York, but taught me never to take it too seriously. My parents, Elaine and Andrew Tuffnell, are both great history lovers and require special thanks for all their support, encouragement, and enthusiasm for my studies—I'm sorry that this book is about neither the Tudors nor the Vikings. From my nana, Hilary, to whom this book is dedicated, I inherited the "Yorkshire gene," which it turns out can be weaponised to great effect in the archives. My greatest debts are to Joanna and Aoife: they are the best incentive to down tools.

Introduction

American Invaders

The "American Invasion" preoccupied many Britons in 1902. Against the backdrop of Queen Victoria's death, the British Army's parlous performance in the Boer War, and a fierce debate over "national efficiency" raised by the mass poverty of Britain's slums, several influential books sounded the alarm at the threatened American economic competition. William T. Stead, Frederick MacKenzie, John Hobson, and Benjamin Thwaite described the transformation of British domestic life by American consumer goods, industrial materials, the power of its "trusts," and superior managerial organization.[1] "America has invaded Europe not with armed men, but manufactured products," declared MacKenzie.[2] At the vanguard were emigrant salesmen, financiers, and advertisers, who cultivated new tastes for American products amongst British consumers. "With these Americans who settle in our midst," wrote Stead, "the Old Country will become the new home of the American colonists."[3] For all these writers, the anxiety over Britain's dependence on the United States ran deep. "We are absolutely spoon-fed from day to day by the Americans," Stead exclaimed.[4]

How was it that by the turn of the twentieth century Britons had come to fear Americanization, when for much of the nineteenth US citizens feared Anglicization? Historians of nineteenth-century Anglo-American relations arm us with a formidable set of frameworks for understanding this diplomatic shift: a "great rapprochement" laid the groundwork for the "American Century," underwrote a global imperial transition, and opened the way to the "Americanization" of the world. These models tell us more about the perceived centrality and disproportionality of US power and expansion to global affairs after 1945 than they do the United States' place in the nineteenth-century world. They are models of US projection into, not interaction with the world.[5] But to immerse oneself in the mechanics of the "American Invasion" is to uncover a new perspective on Anglo-American relations. Beneath reports of the onward march of American exports is a hidden world of Americans overseas. This was a world of travelling salesmen, merchants, and financiers working hard to drum up interest in US investments and commerce; a world of socialites and genteel Americans joining headlong the rush of the London social "Season" and seeking introductions to a foreign sovereign; a world of social clubs and national celebrations at which to debate the meaning of residence abroad and the global role of the United States.

LEAVING THE UNITED STATES

At first glance, telling the history of American economic development, nationalism, and imperialism from the vantage point of American emigrants may seem puzzling. The United States is, after all, generally perceived as a migrant destination, not a departure point. US emigrants have only a minor role, if any, in the major narrative histories of the nineteenth-century United States. Taking center stage instead are the massive and dramatic human influxes of immigrants that convulsed American politics, transformed its cities, and "peopled" the North American continent. Recent scholarship suggests that only a small—less than 1 percent—although steadily increasing proportion of American citizens travelled abroad between 1820 and 1900.[6] Of what significance could a handful of elite migrants be?

More puzzling is the assumption that American citizens were static against this backdrop of human crossings and connections. Powerful national tropes upholding the United States as a nation built by immigration, settlement, and assimilation have left little room to even consider that those who emigrated could have anything to do with its national development; they had, after all, left the national-territorial framework of the American past.[7] One piece of the puzzle is the transformation in the concept of expatriation since the nineteenth century, when it was synonymous with *becoming* American. The ability to transform British subjects into citizens was central to American claims to independence, which meant countering arguments that subjects owed "perpetual allegiance" to their sovereign.[8] As one lawmaker put it, "emigration and expatriation are practical declarations of independence of the individual citizen."[9] The United States repeatedly reaffirmed this stance while around Europe an "Exit Revolution" lifted restrictions on citizens' right to leave in one country after another.[10] Yet American opinion on the expatriation of US citizens was far from settled. Throughout the century, the State Department struggled to establish the principles of expatriation, rarely kept reliable records of its citizens overseas, and was at times hostile to Americans resident abroad.[11] According to one consul in Central America, expatriated American citizens represented a "class of persons who have never become identified in spirit and feeling with the ideas our government represents," contributed "little or nothing to its welfare," and lent "nothing to its support."[12] It was not until the 1907 Law of Expatriation that the United States made explicit the conditions under which Americans could lose their citizenship overseas, part of a proliferation of treaty- and law-making in which the state policed the boundaries of citizenship across borders through extradition, extraterritoriality, and exclusion.[13]

As American consular officials found, pinning down American emigrants is challenging. The term "emigrant" was rarely employed by Americans overseas in the nineteenth century, but it better captures the subjective experiences and shifting political valences attached to transatlantic mobility than the more delimiting legal status "expatriate." Many Americans overseas moved into and through the categories of traveler, settler, and serial migrant, and are not easily separated by occupation, as with professionally itinerant sailors or soldiers. Emigrant communities contained men and women in the professional and service trades, such as merchants, sales agents, and financiers; state employees found in consulates and legations; enterprising entrepreneurs and inventors; and restless journalists, socialites, and reformers. Some hoped to return home, while others enjoyed long lives overseas and threw themselves into organizing social clubs and celebrating national anniversaries; still other Americans, black and white, hoped to use their presence overseas to exert moral pressure on domestic institutions. Placing emigrants center stage unambiguously focusses attention on their ongoing connection with the United States, their offshore creation of national communities and spaces, their relationships with foreign elites, and how those relationships affected Anglo-American relations. This ongoing interplay between residence overseas and nation-building at home is best characterized as "emigrant foreign relations." Although they had left the United States, emigrants kept in touch via correspondence, journal articles, travelogues, and the wealth of goods and money they remitted to family, friends, and customers. They did not simply sever ties with the nation, but connected it to the world and to foreign peoples in new ways. Their offshore lives were sometimes viewed as a form of informal ambassadorship, sometimes feared as a dangerous method of denationalization or vector of moral and anti-republican contagion, and at others denounced as a drain of valuable human capital and an evasion of the obligations of citizenship. Through their conspicuous presence abroad, as we shall see, emigrants raised troubling questions about the relationship between nationhood, nationality, and foreign connection.

American emigration is only surprising if we think in terms of contrasts with the incoming nineteenth-century mass migrations to the United States. If we relocate our point of comparison, American emigration is neither surprising nor unique. In fact, American emigrants resemble the many internationally mobile professionals, officials, and sojourners who worked in a variety of specialist occupations in ports and capital cities around the world and who ensured the smooth operation of commercial, communication, and transportation networks between nations.[14] Foreign merchant communities populated the United States' own cities, like New York, Philadelphia, New Orleans, and San Francisco.[15] A steadily growing body of scholarship has shown that the variety of American communities abroad was wide. American merchants directed international trade from port cities around the globe;[16] European capitals hosted American artists, socialites, businessmen, and sojourners;[17] students acquired new learning at European technical schools and ancient universities;[18] entrepreneurs and engineers scoured the world for profitable opportunities;[19] and evangelists proselytized among the peoples of the Americas and the Pacific World.[20] The presence of manifold emigrant enclaves around the world does not equate to a mass movement, but their distribution does reveal the disproportional role of emigrants in determining the scope of the United States' overseas and overland connections. Recently, historians of the United States' continental empire have linked emigration directly to the colonization of the west and to a longer history of American settlement of non-US spaces.[21] Throughout its history, Brooke Blower has strikingly argued, the United States has been a "nation of outposts," connected to a multitude of non-American territories by continental and globetrotting migrants whose travels laid the pathway for the United States' twentieth-century empire of military bases.[22]

By leaving the United States for Britain, this book argues, American emigrants became the necessary counterpart of American nation-building and identity formation, and integral to its foreign relations. American overseas emigration is best understood in the light of the ongoing and open-ended development of the American Union and the British Empire. Just as American historians have begun to recapture how US nation-building was shaped by the pressures of other empires and the industrial revolutions that took place in the world economy, so British imperial historians now depict a sprawling, improvised British imperial world of permeable external borders, exposed to world trade and indigenous and non-British cultural movements.[23] Contemporaries thought deeply about the entangled development of these unfinished empires. In the United States, controversy was aroused over almost every facet of this entanglement. As historians we might ask on what axes of race, class, party, and gender discussion of these entanglements turned. How did transatlantic political, social, and commercial exchanges work in practice, and how did this change over time? Did Americans simply use pre-existing networks, or were they central to the creation and management of new mechanisms of transnational exchange? How could the United States maintain its independence when so many of these networks were dominated by an expansive and ambitious British Empire? How might British power be co-opted or leveraged to the advantage of different groups of migrant Americans? And, in a society dominated so extensively by British cultural production, how could one maintain an American identity? *Made in Britain* takes up these questions.

TRANSNATIONAL CONNECTORS IN A BRITISH WORLD

American emigrants in Britain generated, managed, and sustained many of the United States' foremost transnational linkages and were the front-line of the relationship with its largest trading partner and the world's most powerful empire. In their daily working lives, they acted as intermediaries in Atlantic commerce and finance by inspecting goods and assessing credit-worthiness; they were key brokers of commercial and political intelligence; and they managed the mechanisms that shaped the movement of goods, capital, and people across the Atlantic. They were, in short, connectors.[24] These activities anchored the United States *in* the world, expanding the scale of the nation's trade, information, and communications networks and its integration with the commodity and capital markets of Britain. In turn, patterns of American emigration were sensitive to the changing nature of the world's transnational networks and especially to the dramatic technological changes that characterized the final third of the century.

American emigration to Britain began as an anxious outflow to reconnect the lifelines of Atlantic trade and capital so central to the new nation's prosperity and security.[25] The leading role in restoring Atlantic trade was played not by the government in Whitehall nor by the provisions of the Articles of Confederation, but by transatlantic migrants who travelled between both nations as sales agents, and founded and managed the overseas branches of merchant and financial houses. Shortly after peace was concluded in 1783, David Ramsay reported from Charleston, South Carolina that "The genius of our people is entirely turned from war to commerce. Schemes of business & partnerships for extending commerce are daily forming."[26] Migrants were responsible for a wide range of daily activities required to keep trade flowing, such as loading cargoes and organizing payment, sending commercial intelligence to partners in the United States, and opening new lines of transatlantic credit. American migrants were active in trade organizations such as Liverpool's American Chamber of Commerce, founded in 1801 by the American tobacco merchant and United States Consul James Maury to lobby Parliament in the interests of Atlantic commerce and mitigate the risk of war. Through regular correspondence and the relationships they forged with fellow merchants, American emigrants continually reinforced the underlying community of trust so essential to the smooth operation of long-distance trade. The transformation these migrants oversaw was as rapid as it was dramatic. By 1790–92, the total tonnage of American trade with Britain was perhaps 50 to 80 percent above what it had been before the Revolution.[27] By the end of the eighteenth century, the United States was the most significant consumer of British goods in the world.[28] Migrants also reinforced the economic interdependence of the United States and Britain, raising troubling questions for nationalist political economists. As Edmund Morford put it in his 1806 *Inquiry into the Present State of Foreign Relations of the Union:*

> Although three thousand miles of boisterous waters divide us from Europe, yet, the events of one continent affect the concerns of the other so intimately, that space is swallowed up in the mutuality and comixing of wants, dependencies and interests. Nothing is now done in any quarter of the globe, which does not bear upon its farthest limits; and it behoves the people of the United States, composing as they do the great division of the political world, and ranking second among commercial nations, to keep a steady, watchful eye

upon the restless potentates of Europe . . . . We cannot exist an isolated member of the grand community of nations. Our commerce touches the jealous rivals of the old world at every point, and they are always ready to find or to make reasons, which, to rapacity, are sufficiently just for plundering and abusing us.[29]

This ongoing dualism between independence and interdependence (to be "isolated" or a part of the "mutuality" of trade and connection, as Morford portrayed it) was central to how migration was understood throughout the nineteenth century.

By the 1830s, what began as a movement to restore transatlantic lifelines and tastes became one to sustain booming transatlantic traffic. Britain's American-born population grew steadily, to almost eight thousand by 1861, as merchants and financiers, socialites and travelers flocked to the world's commercial and financial hub. The four decades between 1830 and 1870 were the critical phase of Britain's transformation from a sprawling web of mercantilism, old plantation colonies, and treaty-ports into the world's banker and shipper. British exports rose in value from £38 million in 1830 to £60 million in 1845 and, following the repeal of the Corn Laws in 1846, to £122 million by 1857.[30] Just as important was the world-changing cotton revolution in the American South. In the mid-1780s, the United States produced less than 0.2 percent of the raw cotton imported into Britain.[31] By the late 1850s, this figure had risen to 77 percent of the 800 million pounds of cotton consumed annually by British mills.[32] American emigrants were at the center of these transformations and, by managing the international networks of the American economy, sped its integration into Britain's worldwide empire of commerce.[33] Two partnerships were of paramount importance. The first was between cotton and Liverpool, home to 2,800 Americans in 1861, and the second was between credit and London, with an American-born population of 1,910 in the same year.[34]

Liverpool, gateway of the Atlantic, was the epicenter of the overlapping Empires of Cotton and Free Trade (see figure 1). The Stars and Stripes were "prominent among the dock's foremasts, pleasing proofs of the increasing commerce of the rising empire of the United States," in the estimation of one visitor's guide.[35] Roughly four of every five tons of shipping arriving from the Northern United States in Liverpool was carried by US-registered ships, and the figure for Southern ports was not far behind.[36] Thousands of American sailors landed in Liverpool every year, but alongside these transient workers was a permanent community of US merchants and cotton brokers, mostly from the Northern states.

FIGURE 1. This image of St George's dock encapsulates the sheer volume of Liverpool's commerce and the forest of masts that dominated its docksides. Image: Glass lantern slide of St George's Dock, Liverpool, c. 1874, courtesy National Museums Liverpool.

Liverpool merchants were the master link in the commodity chains of the global cotton industry: they traded raw cotton arriving from New Orleans and New York and exported finished goods around Britain's imperial markets, while financing both cotton agriculture in the South and cotton manufacturing in nearby Lancashire.[37] The Americans among them also traded in gossip and commercial intelligence with planters at home who waited eagerly, or, as Matthew Carey would have it, "hung in suspense," for the arrival of regularly scheduled transatlantic packet services and set their economic life to the "price in Liverpool."[38] These connections did not operate solely along a Southern axis, however. By 1845, fifty-two transatlantic packets sailed regularly from New York, or three regular sailings a week, giving the port control over the flow of Atlantic business knowledge.[39] It was little wonder that the nationalist political economist Henry Carey, looking back in 1865, surmised that "Liverpool had been becoming daily more and more the centre round which revolved our whole societary system."[40]

The international credit system headquartered in the City of London facilitated this traffic. The United States, a debtor nation, craved London's capital, while its short-term credit market lubricated transatlantic trade. In the square mile of streets, byways, and alleys of the City could be found the headquarters of the world's most important banks, merchant houses, insurance brokers, shippers, and imperial corporations—not to mention the Bank of England and the Stock Exchange. American emigrants established or managed powerful transatlantic merchant banks, including Brown Brothers, Phelps, Dodge & Co., George Peabody & Co., and Barings. Emigrant bankers, like George Peabody and his partner Junius Spencer Morgan and Joshua Bates and Russell Sturgis at Barings (all New Englanders), were attracted to the "inner city" of high finance and mastered specialist trading in US railroad stocks, government bonds, and state securities. Commodity trades like wheat and cotton—staple American exports to Britain—relied on the advance of credit, which was negotiated by emigrant financiers and brokers from the Liverpool branches of London's financial powerhouses. These banking houses were never far removed from the cotton economy, as they underwrote paper scrip, invested in regional banks, and brokered state bonds.[41] Through these transactions the United States and Great Britain became closely inter-related parts of a dynamic web of global credit and commercial enterprise centered on the City of London.

The combined impacts of new technologies and the American Civil War transformed many of these transnational linkages and the role that emigrants played in managing them. The collapse of time and distance across the Atlantic that resulted from new technologies of travel and communication had simultaneous and contradictory results. American oceanic tourism boomed after the Civil War as steam eclipsed sail, fares became cheaper, and steamship companies synchronized their services with overland rail services, at the same time adding far greater numbers of passenger cabins. In 1885, American foreign travelers reached an estimated one hundred thousand people for the first time—still a tiny fraction of the booming US population.[42] It was at this point too that the American-born population of Britain, and London especially, grew rapidly, as indicated in the table below.

Yet this same combination of factors, operating in conjunction with the damaging impact of the American Civil War on the nation's Atlantic

TABLE 1   TOTAL AMERICAN RESIDENTS IN BRITAIN BY DECADE, 1861–1911

	1861	1871	1881	1891	1901	1911
Total	7,861	7,370	17,767	19,740	16,668	14,236
Male	5,056	4,298	9,226	9,726	9,832	7,961
Female	2,805	3,072	8,451	10,014	6,836	6,275
			London			
Total	1,910	2,787	4,301	4,903	5,561	5,352
Male	1,126	1,397	2,255	2,450	3,100	2,675
Female	784	1,390	2,046	2,453	2,461	2,677

SOURCES: Compiled by the author from sources available at http://www.histpop.org/ohpr/servlet: "Table XXVII. England and Wales number and country of birth of all foreigners, in registration divisions," *Census of England and Wales 1861, Volume II, Part 1: Population Tables* (London: George Edward Eyre and William Spottiswoode, 1863), lxxv; "Table XXIII. Number and country of birth of all foreigners, in registration divisions," *Census of England and Wales 1871, Volume III: Population Abstracts* (London: George Edward Eyre and William Spottiswoode, 1873), li; "Table 9. Country of birth of all foreigners enumerated in England and Wales," *Census of England and Wales 1881, Volume III: Ages, Condition as to Marriage, Occupations and Birth-Places of the People* (London: Eyre and Spottiswoode, 1883), xxiv; "Table CVIII. Number of Foreigners of Various Nationalities, and Proportion to Total Foreigners, 1891, 1901, and 1911," *Census of England and Wales 1911, General Report with Appendices* (London: HM Stationery Office, 1917), 219.

maritime industry, caused the dramatic decline of Liverpool's American emigrant community, which by 1881 had fallen by 2,000, to just 801. Atlantic networks of trade dominated by cotton merchants had been destroyed by the war, prompting merchants, manufacturers and government bureaucrats to search furiously for new sources of land and labor—in Britain's case in India, which already produced large amounts of cotton for the world market, and Egypt, to produce inexpensive raw cotton. In the final third of the century the United States itself became one of the world's major cotton manufacturers and consumers of its own domestic production until, by 1900, it was second only to Great Britain.[43] Following the successful laying of the transatlantic cable in 1866, cotton factors traveled less frequently to meet buyers and creditors, inspect goods, and assess market conditions. Cotton purchasers and speculators adjusted their demands quickly in response to instantaneous (albeit costly) news received remotely through the cable.[44]

London, by contrast, continued to entice migrants as a hub of the new mechanisms of connectivity and world trade, whose value rose tenfold between 1850 and 1913.[45] A huge proportion of the world's trade depended on London for the financial instruments that commerce required: sterling was the currency of international trade, the "Bill on

London" the usual form of payment, and the gold standard the pillar of commercial stability. It was also the "listening post for commercial opportunities in every continent."[46] It had tentacular reach, thanks to the cabling of the globe with roughly 115,000 undersea and 650,000 overland miles of telegraph wires by the late 1880s.[47] Reflecting these new sources of financial information, London's Stock Exchange diversified its business to railway shares and loans to foreign states, in addition to the sale of government bonds that had dominated its trade until mid-century, during the careers of emigrants like Peabody, Bates, and Sturgis.[48] American emigrants—numbering almost five thousand by 1891—continued to work in the dynamic City, seeking to refinance the United States' Civil War debt, and aggressively marketing US mines and railroads, sometimes unscrupulously, to British investors.[49]

By the 1890s, American entrepreneurs were migrating to Britain to found factories, headquarters, and retail outlets. American firms including utility companies, insurance brokers, pharmacists, confectioners, machine manufacturers, and advertising agencies arrived steadily on British shores, enhancing the web of connections that bound the two Atlantic powers (see figure 2). Adding to this "invasion" was an array of American products and machinery that found their way into the homes, stores, and factories of Britons. To share know-how on breaking into British markets—both domestic and imperial—leading migrants established the American Society in London in 1895 as a social club through which to build new social networks among British investors and officials from the Foreign Office and Board of Trade. "The American invasion has turned into an army of occupation," quipped *Harper's Weekly*.[50] Amidst this highly visible "invasion" came anxieties that Great Britain would become, in the words of London's *National Review* in 1902, "a mere annex of the United States."[51] Between 1900 and 1902, many American commentators celebrated this symbolic role reversal when, faced with the tremendous cost of fighting the Boer War, Great Britain paused its own foreign lending and borrowed $227 million on the New York securities market. "The 'debtor nation' has become the chief creditor nation," declared Secretary of State John Hay, and "the financial center of the world, which required thousands of years to journey from the Euphrates to the Thames and the Seine, seems to be passing to the Hudson between the daybreak and the dark."[52] Perhaps, some Britons began to wonder, "Americans were going to buy out the empire itself."[53] The moment was short-lived; by 1903 Britain had repurchased most of the bonds sold in the United

THEY CAN'T FIGHT.

FIGURE 2. At the height of the war-scare surrounding the Venezuela Crisis, Frederick Opper captured the social, cultural, and economic entanglements that restrained a third Anglo-American war. Such entanglements were not uncontentious, on either side of the Atlantic, and were hotly contested in the ongoing debate over the extent of US independence and the desirability of Atlantic interdependence—for Britons and Americans alike. Image: Frederick Opper, "They Can't Fight," January 15, 1896, *Puck,* Library of Congress Prints and Photographs Division.

States during this period, but it was a clear sign of the United States' emerging economic independence.

This framing reveals emigrant foreign relations in their most expansive sense: as the history of the human activity of creating transnational connections. Historians should resist the assumption that the United States existed in a world of pre-existent, boundless connection.[54] Focusing on the individuals in this story highlights the practical ways connections formed, operated, and changed over time. Telling this history requires close attention to the transnational spaces organized and occupied by American emigrants, to the dense web of social connections they forged with one another and with their British hosts, and to the material exchanges of correspondence, information, and goods they oversaw. This history of transnational connection shows the production of the Atlantic capitalist economy in process. Working under the banner of the "New History of Capitalism," historians have undertaken to denaturalize capitalism and show that "the market" itself was an artifice, or the invention of those who administered it.[55] Scholars have reimagined the business of tabulating prices and inventory, monitoring the shifting values of stocks, and drawing up promissory notes, drafts, or bills of exchange for transmission across the Atlantic as part of an extensive commercial "knowledge economy" through which the market was produced.[56] Alongside the more dramatic revolutions in transportation and the expansion of printing and publishing in this period, the commercial knowledge created by American migrants, examined closely in chapters 1 and 5, was foundational to capitalism in the Atlantic world.[57] But the influential role of this small economic elite in shaping the United States' transnational linkages to the world, and their integration with the economic infrastructure of Britain's empire, poses further questions. How integral were US emigrants to the development of ideas about American nationalism, political economy, and empire? How were they related to the US diplomatic and consular service? What was their place in British society, and how were they viewed by their fellow Americans?

EMIGRANT AMBASSADORS

In recent years, historians have expanded the definition of "foreign relations," looking beyond state-to-state negotiations to the non-state actors who enlarged the nation's overseas presence. The awe and chauvinism of American tourists, missionaries, and sailors (recently dubbed "ambassadors in the forecastle") who acted as conduits for information about race, nation, gender, and class between the United States and the outside world have been vividly described.[58] In contrast, the concern of this volume is how Americans overseas integrated themselves within foreign societies and how that integration shaped American foreign relations.

Emigrant lives were not consumed solely by the business of managing transnational connection described above. In Liverpool and London, they enjoyed rich social lives, founded their own clubs to dine, dance, and drink together in celebration of national anniversaries, and published their own newspapers and directories. Emigrants in London also entertained travelling Americans, while keeping a close eye on those deemed too rough-hewn for presentation at the Court of St James. "It gave us much pleasure to meet with a large number of our fellow-citizens, from different states in the Union, while we were in London," reflected one tourist on a visit to Britain in the 1850s.[59] The offices of American bankers overseas often included reading rooms filled with American newspapers, offering both respite and a lifeline to events at home. But what was good for the souls of travelers was also good for business—tourists needed to exchange foreign currencies and extend lines of credit. American bankers could even vouch for a customer's passport and as a result have been called "adjunct consulates" by one historian.[60] In the antebellum period, this social world was largely ad hoc and dependent on the grace of the emigrant social elite; by the mid-1890s these functions had been institutionalized and organized into "a complete little pocket edition of the USA . . . dropped into the midst of the Queen's capital."[61] The constant interplay between these two impulses—to be both an integral element of British social life and to remain distinctively American—is one of the central themes of this book.

These spaces are absent from most accounts of American foreign relations, which depict the infrastructure of diplomacy—the legations, embassies, and consular offices—in purely transactional terms. The men laboring in these spaces are only animate when major crises erupt or when treaty negotiations are concluded. Ministers shuttle back and forth between the legation and Foreign Office with messages from the Secretary of State while the response of the Foreign Secretary is patiently transcribed for return to Washington. Historians' view of US diplomatic space in the past has been shaped overwhelmingly by our understanding of American embassies as architectural embodiments of US power in the present.[62] Built to advance foreign policy objectives, isolated behind security barriers, armed guards, and proudly fluttering flags, they are now designed to keep foreign influences (and threats) out rather than

FIGURE 3. In this satirical take from *Puck*, a fictive US Ambassador serves the nations of the world a dinner of baked beans and iced water, while bottles of root beer and ginger ale cool in a bucket of still more ice. In the background, his wife prepares the next course. *Puck* was not praising the Spartan simplicity of the republican ambassador, but mortified that the US Ambassador must "live on his salary." Image: Carl Hassmann, "The United States Abroad," May 6, 1908, *Puck*, Library of Congress Prints and Photographs Division.

being incorporated into the social world of their host countries.[63] In the nineteenth century, by contrast, American diplomatic buildings were not purpose-built and were spaces where the boundary between state and non-state was blurred. In London, the Legation, and by 1893 the Embassy, was a social venue—more domestic than diplomatic—where Americans overseas gathered to socialize and the Minister's diplomatic household hosted public receptions and private dinner parties as part of the flow of the fashionable world (see figure 3). The Minister's wife was also expected to adapt quickly to the role of political hostess and, as one American newspaper recognized, "become *au fait* in duties which in their infinitesimal demands of every branch of social etiquette far exceed those which he will be called upon to become the master of."[64]

In Britain, this diplomatic work depended on the advice, support, and continuity offered by American emigrants. The worlds of American diplomats and emigrants were closely intertwined. American emigrants enjoyed friendships with the staff of the legation and consulate, who were often resident overseas for much longer periods than the Minister and took an active role in emigrant society. The United States' anemic diplomatic system suffered from this constant rotation of office. Ministers and their wives barely had time to create a notable diplomatic household, forge close relationships with British elites, or achieve social prominence among the diplomatic corps in London. On arrival, diplomats were presented with the immediate difficulties of finding a home at a fashionable address, procuring the correct court dress, and mastering the elaborate customs of presentation at court and the Queen's diplomatic levees. American emigrants initiated American diplomats in London's frenetic social calendar and fastidious etiquette. In Liverpool, emigrant merchants welcomed new Ministers to Britain with lavish public receptions organized by the American Chamber of Commerce. As long-term residents, leading emigrants provided letters of introduction to British business and political elites, secured tickets to fashionable balls, parades, and operas, advised on the game of invitation and counter-invitation that maintained the Season, and brokered meetings with prominent hostesses and politicians out of hours. As one diplomat observed of Peabody, he "generally *bags* the *new* American Minister for his own purposes and shows him up around town."[65] "Bagging" the American minister and hosting public receptions was, in turn, a costly but effective way of cultivating social standing and signifying to potential investors that his credit and political intelligence were sound (see chapter 2).

In London, the Season, active from the recall of Parliament in February but peaking from the beginning of May to the end of July, dictated the rhythm of social life. Independence Day celebrations fell directly in the Season's most frantic month. Prominent emigrants, and later the American Society in London, hosted elaborate public banquets with guest lists that stretched to more than one hundred Americans and Britons. When one emigrant financier encouraged Louis McLane to host public Fourth of July banquets during his first stint as Minister between 1829 and 1831, he was aiming "to fix the character which the Am' [sic] Minister shall sustain in future."[66] While the Minister's meager salary did not stretch far enough to cover the expense of these spectacular and sumptuous events, the social standing and financial position of many American emigrants in British life rescued US diplomacy from that obscurity. As London's *Morning Post* reflected in 1854, the events hosted by the American emigrant community were "a sort of rallying point for all respectable Americans in the metropolis," and "tended to increase friendly intercourse between various classes in both countries."[67] Emigrant newspapers, including the *London American* (published 1860–63 and 1895–1901, after which it became the *Anglo-American Press*), recorded the speeches at these celebrations to maintain the sense of commonality among members of the offshore community.

The transatlantic connections formed by emigrant ambassadors were densest with the Northern states. Southerners travelled widely in the Old World both to publicly demonstrate membership in an elite class and to cultivate refined tastes.[68] But, although indigo and rice merchants from South Carolina and tobacco merchants from Virginia left home to tend networks of Atlantic trade, leading antebellum emigrants generally hailed from the Northeastern seaboard.[69] Southerners did not dally in Liverpool or London: for some Paris was their metropole and could be reached directly, and easily, from New Orleans, but others simply could not penetrate English society.[70] "Whether [it] be ascribed to the deficiency of my means, or the additional reserve of the English I will not decide," lamented one Virginian, "but I have made fewer acquaintances in England than anywhere else I have been."[71] It was not that elite emigrants excluded Southerners, but that they lacked the letters of introduction that would admit them to the inner circle of genteel Britain. Even in the maze of transatlantic connection, social power, knowledge, and influence accumulated along prescribed routes. This had direct consequence for Civil War diplomacy, as Confederate agents found themselves hamstrung by their limited social and political connections to British elites.

Though we think of "public diplomacy" as a set of practices developed in the Cold War to influence foreign public opinion through organized information campaigns and cultural exchange, almost every aspect of the diplomat's life in the nineteenth century had a public dimension to audiences at home and abroad.[72] As New York's *Daily Times* advised in 1853, American representatives should ensure that all their "energies be employed to represent a *true American* in principle, manners, and action."[73] American diplomats struggled to strike the right republican tone for audiences at home, without transgressing too far the sensibilities of the tradition-bound world of European diplomacy. At the beginning of his tenure as Minister in 1853, James Buchanan agonized that adopting simple court attire would impede his position in British high society, noting to the Secretary of State that "it is probable I shall be placed, socially, in Coventry, on the question of dress, because it is certain, that should Her Majesty not invite the American Minister to her Balls and dinners, he will not be invited to the Balls and dinners of her courtiers."[74] Although the Minister held a position in British society as a member of the diplomatic corps, American emigrants were often more prominent representatives and shaped perceptions of the young republic among Britain's political elite. The emigrant press also worked hard to change foreign perception on subjects as wide-ranging as American democracy, slavery, and literature, and to shape the policy of foreign statesmen at times of diplomatic crisis. The dinners and balls hosted by emigrants as part of the Season should rightfully take their place in the history of American foreign relations as the extraterritorial venues where the United States' international image was established through the interactions of Americans with foreign citizens—with scarcely any involvement from Washington.[75]

DENATIONALIZATION AND THE MORAL CONTAGIONS OF ATLANTIC MOBILITY

Precisely because emigrants exerted such disproportionate influence over the nature of the United States' transnational linkages and foreign relations, they were the subject of intense scrutiny. American nationalism was constructed transnationally in direct dialogue against emigrants, who collapsed the boundaries between the inside and out. Nineteenth-century Americans defined their nationality with particular reference to flexible notions of democratic political principle, Providence, the celebration of the American Revolution, and, for Southerners, slaveholding.[76] While at times these combined to form a robust amalgam, nineteenth-century Americans understood that their nationality was unproven and required constant and careful maintenance. For much of the century, Americans found themselves torn between multiple, co-existing strands of "invented" or "imagined" nationalisms; between allegiance to nation, section, state, and party; and between suspicion of central government and a commitment to Union that some scholars have described as mystical.[77] For a people struggling to understand the role of nation and nationality in their lives, Americans migrating overseas and across the North American continent blurred distinctions between those who belonged and those who did not. As historians have recognized, the nation was defined as much by exclusion—in this case, those quite literally on the outside—as it was a belief in shared values.[78]

Emigrants embody the entanglement between domestic and foreign affairs in the making of American nationality. From Britain, Americans looked backwards across the Atlantic and considered American nationhood in its international context. At emigrant Fourth of July parties and

Thanksgiving banquets, wrote Abbott Lawrence, Americans abroad "burnished anew our patriotism" and learned to become "better citizens, more devoted to the institutions of the country, than when they left their homes."[79] As another American in London wrote, "though the resident of another I love my country with an *increasing love.*"[80] Emigrant civic events were public spectacles charged with symbolic celebrations of Anglo-American connection. These events sparked fraught debates over the nature of the United States' contemporary connections to the British Empire and its so-called Anglo-Saxon descent.

Though a belief in Anglo-Saxon racial exceptionalism was widespread on both sides of the Atlantic by the 1850s, it was far from a unitary idea. Both the persistence and versatility of Anglo-Saxon discourse made it an important element of continuity in emigrant foreign relations, but this must be balanced by its dynamic remaking in the transnational spaces of Britain's American community. Historians have long understood Anglo-Saxonism as a form of transnational race-making.[81] Drawing on internationalist currents of "scientific" racialism—themselves the products of the age of slavery and imperialism—white Britons and Americans found the supposed essence of their race in Anglo-Saxonism, even while they struggled to say what exactly it was. Anglo-Saxon race theories proliferated in the Victorian Atlantic, travelling in any number of directions through different alchemies of blood, biology, language, kinship, Protestantism, civilizational genealogies, and nationality, in a host of different intellectual and popular spaces. By the final third of the century Anglo-Saxonism had become a transnational ideology of whiteness that was, in the words of Marilyn Lake and Henry Reynolds, "at once global in its power and personal in its meaning, the basis of geo-political alliances and a subjective sense of self."[82] In the 1898 formulation of former Secretary of State Richard Olney, "there is a patriotism of race, as well as of country."[83] At the same time, Anglo-Saxon "race patriots" demanded constant vigilance: against the external threats posed by the African and Asian races and the entropy produced by timorous over-civilization and ignoble peace.[84]

Anglo-Saxonism was both ubiquitous and, because it passed through so many hands, elusive. For this reason, historians of American foreign relations have emphasized, above all, Anglo-Saxonism's functionality to Anglo-American diplomatic rapprochement and to the dynamic creation of transimperial solidarities.[85] It also provided a language with which Americans and Britons constructed a self-conscious bond with one another and came to understand the widening and deepening social, familial, and commercial entanglements of the Atlantic. But at the same time Anglo-Saxonism proved problematic for American migrants who debated, amongst themselves and with incoming American nationalists, whether it was yet another form of debilitating colonial dependence, or a cosmopolitan internationalism through which the United States and the British imperial world might achieve a mutually beneficial interdependence. At emigrant celebrations, Americans in Britain tried to balance their pride in sharing a common ancestry, blood, language, and culture with fears of lingering cultural dependence, and grappled with the problem of celebrating an ancient racial ancestry alongside claims that American Anglo-Saxons were a unique branch of the race.

The racial valences of mobility were starkest for black travelers. African American travelers, for whom Britain was an imagined space of liberation, crossed the Atlantic as sailors, fugitives from slavery, activists nourishing the anti-slavery movement, preachers, and pleasure seekers. For African Americans fighting segregation, travel was viewed as a crucial component of citizenship. As the historian Elizabeth Pryor has written, African Americans "not only understood travel as a cog to geographic mobility but also imagined it as a type of currency. Access to travel opened up economic, political, and social possibilities."[86] As a result, white Americans constructed a system of legal and cultural proscriptions to surveil and curtail black travel. Black mobility was criminalized in the passage of so-called Negro Seamen's Acts, imprisoning all black mariners under threat of enslavement, by all Southern states with an Atlantic port; and circumscribed by the State Department, which refused to grant free black Americans passports for international travel between 1834 and the 1860s.[87] "With their known habits, feelings, and principles, animated and emboldened as they are by the philanthropy of the day," wrote one South Carolina editor in an attack on mobile African Americans, their free movement would "introduce a moral pestilence which is to destroy subordination in the slave, and with it the state itself. . . . It is a moral contagion. It is the Upas Tree, whose touch is death."[88] If the language of contagion underpinned the quarantine of black bodies, black Atlantic activists responded directly by working to maintain a *cordon sanitaire* around the pathologies of Southern slavery and Jim Crow through a strategic alliance with the British anti-slavery state. Through travel, moral contagion was transformed into moral capital. Working with British allies in the anti-slavery movement, black Americans used transatlantic travel to exert political pressure on the British state to internationalize abolition and, later in the century, to create new transatlantic racial solidarities. "No nation can now shut itself up from the surrounding world, and trot around in the same old path of its fathers without interference," Frederick Douglass famously asserted in 1852. "Oceans no longer divide us, but link nations together," he continued: "Space is comparatively annihilated. Thoughts expressed on one side of the Atlantic are distinctly heard on the other."[89]

Douglass was right: sectional, racial, partisan, and class divisions crossed the Atlantic with ease and were at the center of emigrant communities in Britain. American emigrants were confronted repeatedly over the terms of their nationalism by Anglophobic American travelers, exuberant nationalists determined to spread republican and revolutionary principles around the globe, and partisan diplomats. In the antebellum period, because emigrant sociability depended on the social capital of individual migrants, opposition to emigrant nationalism turned on the question of class. For observers at home, these events had little to do with patriotism, but indicated, according to the *New York Times,* "a morbid social ambition" (see figure 4).[90] As transatlantic ticket prices fell in the final third of the nineteenth century, Americans remained anxious over the vulnerability of their nationality to the "interchange of national customs" that arose from "the facilitated intercourse of our day . . . the intimacy begotten by inter-marriage, by commerce, by travel," as one writer in Boston's *Arena* expressed it. "But it is sad if we are to borrow more than we lend, and if the balance of trade is to be perpetually against us," the writer continued, "we must find or invent a remedy if republicanism is to survive."[91]

Throughout the nineteenth century, incoming migrants were critical foils against whom anxious political elites shaped purportedly scientific hierarchies of race and nationality, but many nationalists also used emigrants to clarify differences between white Americans and to sharpen the civic components of nationality.[92] By choosing to leave, it was claimed, they had cast off the political and cultural values of American nationality and excluded themselves from the nation. "Why do Americans live abroad?" asked the *Washington Post* in 1883. "An American "living abroad" remains always that—a person who is out of his own country and not adopted by the one in which he lives."[93] More strident critics complained bitterly, as *Life* magazine did, that they were "apostate patriots," or, as another middle class journal put it, "a felon to [their] nature."[94] At the American Legation in London, one diplomat pithily summarized the dilemma of foreign residence and American nationality, noting in his diary that, "this being of two nationalities at once don't do."[95] Emigrants, these critics claimed, were denationalized

FIGURE 4. The elite nature of foreign travel was targeted by domestic writers throughout the nineteenth century, many of whom viewed it as a sign of the United States' continued dependence on the customs and culture of the Old World—and elite travelers as poor representatives of republican self-government. Here, the American millionaire cuts a "ridiculous figure" in London, bowing to the Prince of Wales, and is a "person of small consideration" in Berlin society. Image: Frederick Opper and Samuel D. Ehrhart, "The American Millionaire at Home and Abroad; or, Why a Great Many of Our Rich Men Ought to Refrain from 'Crossing the Pond,'" *Puck*, May 12, 1897, Library of Congress Prints and Photographs Division.

Americans. The benefits of foreign residence to Americans overseas, claimed one analyst, were "more than counterbalanced by all they lose in the way of the Spartan virtues; in the love of humanity, of simplicity, of republicanism, and of their country—in short, by their denationalization."[96] This discussion intensified as the century progressed and the nation's transnational entanglements increased, breaking down clear distinctions between the domestic and the foreign—trends embodied by conspicuous American emigrants.

Denationalization encapsulates a key premise of this book: for insular nationalists and outward-looking patriots alike, nationhood and nationality were inescapably transnational.[97] Nowhere can this better be seen than in emigrant communities. "Almost all large cities now have an 'American Colony,'" observed New York's *Independent* in 1884, which consisted of "a permanent nucleus and a transient accretion." Dangerously severed from domestic life, it was "not always safe for genuine Americans to affiliate with the 'American Colony.'" "The nucleus," the *Independent* warned, "is thoroughly *anti-American*."[98] But in seeking to draw clear boundaries between the domestic and the foreign, the "genuine" and the "anti-American," the critics of American emigrants succeeded mostly in entangling them further.

Viewed in this light, it is clear that the history of the United States in the world is in many ways the history of emigration. This book is a history of how American migration shaped the nature of US overseas economic exchange, cultural encounter, social interaction, and diplomatic engagement. It examines the ways that linkages created by trade and travel were made and unmade by migrants, and how interconnection was understood and contested by their fellow Americans. American migrants did not travel only to Britain, but those that did mattered because the United States' unfinished revolution was so deeply entangled in the evolving commercial, cultural, and communications networks of the British Empire. Emigrants do not merely transplant our existing understanding of the United States' struggle for independence, economic development, and nation-building into an overseas setting, however. When we begin to think of the United States' overseas connections as being developed and maintained by migrants, we can begin to envisage the history of nineteenth-century American foreign relations as one of dynamic border crossings, ambivalent encounters with foreign societies, and close collaboration with foreign businessmen and bureaucrats. By shifting our attention to American migrants, historians can examine the collapsed boundaries and motion between "home" and "abroad," independence and interdependence, how these categories were understood in relation to one another, and how they came together in the world of emigrant foreign relations.

CHAPTER I

Independence and Interdependence

"If any man is excusable for deserting his country," wrote James Fenimore Cooper in his travelogue *Gleanings from Europe,* "it is the American artist."[1] "His studies require it," Cooper continued, "for there is little to gratify his tastes at home." Yet Cooper conceded that residence abroad was fraught with dilemmas. "The American who comes to this country" and is "forgetful of self-respect, of national pride, of the usages of society even, becomes the toad-eater of the great."[2] The dilemma of the American in Britain, Cooper argued, reflected the nation's relationship with its former imperial master. Of all the "burthens" [sic] of the nascent American nation, "the mental dependence created by colonial subserviency" is "the most difficult to remove."[3] "We must make up our minds, I fear," Cooper wrote elsewhere, "to live our time as inhabitants of a mere colony."[4]

With John Bull intruding into almost every realm of public life in the young republic, the true meaning and extent of independence was unclear. Postcolonial insecurities made the maritime connections of the Atlantic world suspect. "Every shipment, every consignment, every commission," wrote James Madison in a conspiratorial analysis of the United States' Atlantic connections in 1799, was "a channel" through which Britain's "Anglicizing" influence flowed. "Our sea-port towns are the reservoirs into which it is collected. From these, issue a thousand streams to the inland towns, and country stores," Madison continued, that allowed a "stock of British ideas and sentiments proper to be retailed to the people. Thus it is, that our country is penetrated to its remotest corners with a foreign poison vitiating the American sentiment, recolonizing the American character, and duping us into the politics of a foreign nation."[5] But ideological warnings alone would not help the United States navigate the fluid context of Atlantic political economy from which Americans made repeated declarations of independence.[6] Economically, Americans hoped to throw off the chains of their chief creditor and wean domestic consumers off British imports; culturally, American intellectuals struggled to overcome the derivativeness of American morals, literature, and culture.[7] Those seeking to sever the remaining ties that bound the new nation to the Old World could not escape the interdependence of the British Empire and the United States. As Henry Clay quipped ruefully in 1820, the United States were little more than the "independent colonies of England."[8] Recognizing the ongoing tension between decolonization and nation-building in Americans' interactions with the wider world, historians have strikingly reframed the antebellum era as "America's postcolonial period."[9]

Britain's own relationship with the Atlantic underwent a dramatic transformation of its own in the decades following the American revolution. The world wars of 1793–1815 and Britain's industrial revolution opened new colonial markets to British merchants who traded more widely than ever before, thanks to the abundance of credit in London. Over time, Britain dismantled the complex system of protections and privileges known as "mercantilism" and, in 1846, switched to international free trade. This commercial and industrial revolution created new demands for a variety of raw materials produced in the Americas, drawing the United States further into the orbit of Britain's imperial economy; so far, according to the historian A. G. Hopkins, that the United States became an "honorary dominion" of the British Empire.[10] The United States stood to benefit from these transformations—if its leaders could successfully balance the political imperative of securing independence and the nation's continued interdependence with the economic ascendance of the British Empire.[11] For the aspirational states of the New World, Eliga Gould reminds us, "independent nationhood was an interdependent condition."[12] The constant interplay between the demands of independence and interdependence was the central dynamic of the fragile republic's relationship with the Atlantic world, and to the patterns of American emigration examined in this chapter.

The history of the Atlantic world is the history of human crossings and connection.[13] Though we tend to think of this travel as westerly, eastward-crossing migrants created connections that bound the British Atlantic into a thriving community. Georgian London was the "Capital of America" and a magnet for mobile agents of the Crown, merchant apprentices, aspirational authors and artists, pious pastors, and improvident tourists who enthusiastically embraced metropolitan fashions.[14] By the eve of the Revolution, these patterns of mobility were powerful agents of Atlantic integration, so much so that the Revolution might be viewed best as a crisis over the pace and style of Atlantic integration rather than the outcome of widening differences.[15] The Atlantic world's age of revolution dramatically transformed these flows as liberty's exiles took to the oceans—North American Loyalists and fugitive slaves, Irish radicals escaping Britain's "Church and King" repression, French democratic republicans fleeing the terror, and Haitian exiles, free and unfree, were alike set in motion, often in sagas of recurring flight.[16] A burst of transatlantic migration followed the rapid demise of the indentured servant trade, too, as some 252,300 people left the Old World for the New between 1776 and 1800.[17]

As the nineteenth century dawned, then, the Atlantic was alive with the movement of people. American emigrants tend to get lost amidst these mass migrations because historians over-emphasize the insular quality of the new republic. "It takes many chords to draw such a multitude so far across the ocean," suggested one antebellum writer surveying American tourism, and this chapter begins with a panoramic view of the chords of migration that underlay the political economy of Atlantic interdependence.[18] The fracturing of the Atlantic community into two political entities in 1783 had little impact on the eastward movement of people. Migration resumed with remarkable speed after the Peace Treaty, as newly-made Americans rushed eastwards to "knit together the arteries slashed through by war and separation."[19] Transatlantic connections proved not only strikingly persistent, but grew in importance. Americans travelled to Britain for diverse reasons, but did not merely connect points on the map: they directed the transfers of goods, capital, and knowledge that embedded the United States in the Atlantic world. Tourists, preachers, sailors, diplomats, freed and fugitive slaves, reformers, artists, and authors participated in a series of exchanges—of a shared transatlantic travel culture, of religious and moral ideas, of expertise, of economic knowledge, and (as we will see in later chapters) of American businesses—that did not always overlap, but together contributed to Atlantic interdependence.

By 1861, Atlantic crossings were so extensive that the British census captured more than eight thousand American-born residents in the country—equivalent to one-third of US citizens travelling overseas at the time, but a simplistic snapshot of the patterns of Atlantic mobility of which they were a part.[20] Many of those recorded in the census were passing through Britain on larger itineraries that took them to Europe and North Africa, or were temporarily in British port cities as laborers in the Atlantic's maritime industries. Their mobility is reflected in their tendency to cluster in Liverpool and London, together home to half of the American-born in Great Britain: 2,800 in Liverpool and its surrounding counties, and 1,910 in London (an increase from 1,054 in 1851).[21] This American presence left its mark on the urban space of both cities, in the hotels, boarding houses, consulates, and social clubs that catered to American migrants and travelers. Amidst these mobile crowds, distinct American communities organized around trade and finance thrived. The final sections of the chapter sharpen focus from the panoramic view of Atlantic crossings to examine Liverpool's emigrant merchants and London's emigrant financiers.

Few British cities could match Liverpool and London for commercial and financial opportunities. As the emporium of transatlantic trade and the port of arrival for American visitors to Europe, Liverpool was the gateway of the United States' Atlantic connections. "London and New York stand in the same rank as Liverpool, as commercial cities," argued one journalist, "but in some respects, as a place of commerce, [Liverpool] surpasses even the great capitals of the Old and New World."[22] By 1800, Anglo-American merchants benefitted from the "demise of distance," a virtual collapse of time and space achieved by the introduction and spread of commercial newspapers, and from the infrastructure of banks, clearinghouses, insurance companies, and stock exchanges created in the eighteenth century.[23] All this dramatically altered the speed of information exchange, but was no substitute for human mobility. Posting a partner overseas remained the most effective way of gathering trustworthy information on market opportunities, prices, and creditworthiness—essential to the production of the knowledge economy on which transatlantic markets depended. This arrangement had been the organizing principle of trade in the pre-revolutionary Atlantic and continued to be so throughout the antebellum period, especially as the volume of trade and the demand for economic knowledge increased and partnerships began to specialize in specific commodities such as metals and cotton.[24] The letter, then, was the paper technology of transnational connection and integral to the material infrastructure of the expanding Atlantic economy. Until 1866, when the Atlantic cable was permanently laid, Edmund Burke's 1796 observation that the "correspondence of the moneyed and mercantile world' was a "kind of electric communication everywhere" remained true.[25]

Even after London ceased to be the "capital of America," it continued to be the capital of American credit. As one contemporary description put it, there was "scarcely a commercial transaction upon the face of the globe which is not more or less connected with, or represented by, London."[26] American merchant bankers migrated to Britain to be close to the financial instruments and commodity markets of the City of London, where they maintained the credit network that supported Anglo-American merchants, wholesalers, and producers, and marketed American state debt and railroad securities to credit-rich British investors. Although the economic interdependence created by this vast web of credit and commerce raised the specter of commercial slavery to many Americans, Britons recognized that interdependence was a two-way street. "The prosperity of the United States is so intricately interwoven with that of this country," opined *The Times* in 1851, that "for all practical purposes" it was "far more closely united with this kingdom than any one of our colonies."[27] Transnational currents and capitalist markets did not occur naturally; they required continual maintenance and management to thrive. The daily, and at times routine, work undertaken by emigrant financiers and merchants was essential to transnational connection. Throughout their residence in Britain, American emigrants navigated the "post-colonial predicament" of establishing the balance between independence and interdependence—the central dynamic of this chapter.[28]

AMERICANS WITHOUT NUMBER

Voyaging twenty days or more across the Atlantic, venturesome Americans had little else to do than travel in their imaginations to a romanticized Britain. On arrival, many were shocked instead at Liverpool's similarity to the United States.[29] "Liverpool in some respects appears more like an American city than any which I have previously seen," noted the Reverend John March of Salem at the start of his English tour. "This is owing in part to its being more modern," he wrote in his diary, "having commenced its existence about the same time as New York and in part to its important intercourse with America."[30] Benjamin Silliman, on his second trip to Britain after having studied at Edinburgh University in 1805, was likewise struck by the incredible likeness of the city's residents to "our own countrymen in our large cities." "Every body here talks, dresses and acts, and every thing looks, so much like America," he continued, "I can hardly believe I crossed the ocean."[31] For many, the disappointment was palpable. Arriving in the late 1820s, Nathaniel Wheaton found the city no more than "docks, fat men and fat women, coal-smoke, dirty streets, cast iron, mammon and mud."[32] To another, it was "dark, dingy, and mold-colored."[33] Harriet Beecher Stowe was crestfallen at finding the port a "real New Yorkish place."[34]

The evangelist, the student, the tourist, and the author: March, Silliman, Wheaton, and Stowe highlight the diversity of American travel experiences in the antebellum period but also its striking continuities with the colonial era. All four travelled to Britain along timeworn pre-revolutionary itineraries; all viewed Britain as anxious post-colonials, measuring the imagined refinement of the Old World against the crudity of the New (the "New Yorkish place") they found on arrival; and by crossing the ocean in search of careers and personal objectives, all four reveal the complexity of connection that underlay the interdependence of the Atlantic. They were just the tip of the iceberg. Networks of kinship and friendship, international trade, evangelicalism and reform, fugitive activism, maritime labor, and return migration crossed the ocean in dizzying array. But while for many Americans Atlantic crossings promoted profitable exchanges, for others they were the conduit of dangerous foreign imports.

With the conclusion of the revolutionary wars, the wide web of cultural, familial, religious, and other informal ties that knitted the Atlantic world together proved their resilience. Travel from the United States to Britain quickly resumed.[35] According to one estimate, between the 1818 inauguration of the Black Ball Line, the first transatlantic packet, and 1850, two to eight thousand Americans ventured to Europe each year.[36] As early as 1833, the stream of American visitors to Britain was so large that one American resident in London noted there were "Americans without number."[37] In the colonial period, elite Americans cultivated refined sensibilities, social standing, and transatlantic professional connections through travel. The colonial Grand Tour became the tourist trail of the 1830s, sparking the decade-long boom in Anglo-American travel writing.[38] American tourists followed well-trodden pathways around the cultural shrines and imperial monuments of the British Isles, where they found "much to admire and imitate."[39] After this, they took in the sites of antiquity in Rome, the world of Parisian fashion, and the romantic, natural sublime in Northern Europe. During the early years of the republic, Americans also crossed the ocean to restore pre-revolutionary professional and intellectual networks and to acquire specialized training and intellectual prestige unattainable in the newly-independent United States.[40] Artists trained in the studios that orbited the Court of St James; ambitious lawyers at the Inns of Court; and medical students, like Benjamin Silliman, in the anatomical theaters of the University of Edinburgh.[41] American authors travelled to Britain in search of inspiration and cultural refinement, even while they attempted to unburden the United States from the dominance of its literary models.[42]

By the 1840s, the increased affordability of the Atlantic crossing transformed the demographics of travel. Those traveling under sail could expect to spend between $120 and $155 (roughly $2,500–$3,000 today) each way for a cabin in the 1820s and 1830s, a portion of which covered the cost of food and wine, but by 1855 some fares had fallen to $75. Steam prices declined similarly between the late 1830s, when they were as high as $140, and the 1860s when they averaged closer to $100; still, at this time a needlewoman working full-time could at best make $91 per year.[43] Not only was a ticket now affordable to more of the "middling sorts," close to one-third of transatlantic passengers were women.[44] Anglo-American marriages peaked later in the century, though by 1836 one American correspondent in London reported "great numbers of American ladies in London" who "seemed to be a good deal in fashion."[45] Socially, these women were important points of inter-elite contact and, for diplomatic wives managing the chief American household overseas, integral to the social world of foreign relations, as discussed in the next chapter. Antebellum women's overseas travel did not attract the same ire that it would after the Civil War, but it was considered dangerous to expose young women to the "temptations of the capitals of Europe."[46] For nationalist Americans, such exchanges indicated a "humiliating deference" and "slavishness" to—or, as Cooper would have it, a "mental dependence" on—British cultural authority.[47]

The ocean was no barrier to the "ferment of reform" that gripped the Atlantic world in the antebellum period.[48] Independence did not sever the Protestant bonds created by Empire.[49] New revivalists and American evangelicals swelled the flow of transatlantic traffic, moving back and forth across the Atlantic, promoting international cooperation, spreading knowledge of the "New-Measures" revivalism fueling fervent evangelical awakenings across the United States among British congregants.[50] American social reformers integrated easily into British evangelical and reform networks, collaborating in what one historian has called "the Anglo-American world of humanitarian endeavour."[51] Energetic Britons and Americans successfully fused moral and social reform networks—on issues as varied as temperance, abolition, mental health, women's rights, and prisons—with longstanding religious connections, sharing the conception that sin lay at the heart of social problems.[52] Transatlantic cooperation flourished through the mass circulation of correspondence, journals, pamphlets, and speaking tours and through tangible tactical ties forged by male and female activists at international gatherings such as the World's Anti-Slavery Convention in London in 1840 and the World Temperance Convention in 1846.[53] In the same year, more than nine hundred evangelical churchmen from fifty denominations gathered in London for the Evangelical Alliance, the "climax to decades of increasing cooperation across the ocean" between Anglo-American religious, philanthropic, and reform movements.[54] This variety of reform connections laid the foundations for transatlantic social politics in the late nineteenth century, but, as revealed in later chapters, they also became key auxiliaries of Civil War diplomacy.[55]

Britain beckoned as a safe haven for American abolitionists under attack at home as dangerous foreign agents.[56] After West Indian emancipation in 1833, Britain not only projected great symbolic and ethical power across the Atlantic, but among African Americans especially, was prized as an avenue of escape and empowerment.[57] For some the move was permanent, for most a sojourn on a journey to spread liberty around the Atlantic world. Scholars of black culture have established the centrality of transatlantic mobility to black identity and political consciousness, characterizing it as the central process underpinning the transcultural production of the black Atlantic.[58] Reflecting on their own mobility as a "liberating respatialization" of the Atlantic, black activists extended their own political agency by harnessing the power of British imperial abolitionism against the Southern empire of slavery.[59] "I am here, because you have an influence on America that no other nation can have," Frederick Douglass told congregants at Finsbury Chapel in 1846, explaining that "the power I extend now is something like the power that is exerted by the man at the end of the lever; my influence now is just in proportion to the distance that I am from the United States."[60] Such processes are better viewed as integral to the ongoing debate over Atlantic interdependence than they are as an exercise in counter-networking, then. Still, completing the transatlantic crossing was an emotive, even "talismanic" moment for black travelers.[61] In April 1840, Charles Lennox Remond, a free black from Salem, Massachusetts, sat in a drawing room in Newport, Rhode Island, and recorded his great anticipation of crossing the Atlantic to "tread upon the soil which the poor slave has but to touch and become free" and "inhale the air which if the slave shall breathe his shackles fall off."[62]

Fugitives fled to Britain in great numbers after the passage of Fugitive Slave Act of 1850, which abolished habeas corpus and Fourth Amendment protections for free blacks. Once in Britain they lectured and performed in taverns, church halls, theaters, and private parlors, exploiting the new republic's vulnerability to international public opinion. Such trips were highly organized and efficient. Frederick Douglass alone gave three hundred speeches in just nineteen months between 1845 and 1847.[63] British audiences were deeply engaged in the anti-slavery struggle—*Uncle Tom's Cabin* sold perhaps more than half a million copies (mostly pirated) in Britain and its colonies in 1853—and were energized further by the performative aspects of the transatlantic campaign: some speakers included panoramas depicting the horrors of enslavement and others used theatrical processions through local towns, such as Henry "Box" Brown's dramatic re-staging of his own escape.[64] The Mother Country's moral capital hid sobering realities—Britain was scarcely a haven from racism—but few areas of the country went untouched by the lecture tours of black abolitionists, supported by slave narratives, autobiographies, and pamphlets. Almost every major black antebellum leader visited Britain as an emissary, managing the movement's relationship with British abolition and overseeing a "new phase of international cooperation" that gave the period's black radical identity a transnational quality.[65] Such action had direct domestic consequences. "Every steam-ship that now crosses the Atlantic is an Anti-Slavery packet, and comes here freighted with intelligence which serves to advance the cause of freedom," declared the delegates at one convention in Worcester, Massachusetts.[66]

The mobility of people of color in the Atlantic world posed challenging questions about the racial boundaries of Atlantic connection. Nowhere was this more the case than with merchant seamen.[67] Sailors kept the Atlantic economy afloat; an estimated 100,000, of whom one-fifth were African American, departed the republic each year during the antebellum era and have been called the nation's "international face."[68] But while white working-class seamen were valued as conduits of "knowledge" about foreign societies—and as often vilified by exasperated consuls for their violent encounters with the peoples in those places—their general right to sail was not questioned. This cannot be said of dangerously mobile free black seafarers. Southern lawmakers and editorialists feared the "moral pestilence" of free black mariners who were an "evil which comes from a distance" and embodied a subversion of the social order that threatened to destroy slavery's containment of black mobility.[69] Infectious abolitionism travelled Atlantic waters, claimed anxious Southerners in the wake of the Denmark Vesey conspiracy, resulting in the passage of Negro Seamen Acts to quarantine subversive black deckhands from gullible local slaves in southern seaports—first in South Carolina but quickly followed by North Carolina, Georgia, Florida, Alabama, Louisiana and Texas—by subjecting all black mariners, regardless of nationality, to imprisonment under threat of enslavement.[70] As the historian Edlie Wong has forcefully written, outlawing black freedom of movement was elemental to the "territorialization of freedom in the Atlantic world" and "part of the systematic containment of the physical, social, and political dimensions of black mobility that was fundamental to the logic of mastery."[71] Laws against black sailors were thus fundamentally about the threats of transnational interconnection and aimed not merely to prevent slave insurrection but to regulate a much greater menace: the black Atlantic.

Integral to the nineteenth-century black Atlantic was the "geography of freedom" created by British abolition.[72] Canada, the British West Indies, and the British Isles all provided maritime escape routes from servitude—if escapees could navigate these unpredictable waters.[73] Black American sailors jumped ship or discharged their berths on landing in Liverpool, Bristol, London, and Glasgow, havens of a sort for the diaspora of the black Atlantic world.[74] "In Liverpool," wrote the mariner-turned-novelist Herman Melville, "the negro steps with a prouder pace and lifts his head like a man; for here, no such exaggerated feeling exists in respect to him, as in America." Black sailors, stewards, sailmakers, and stevedores, Melville continued, enjoyed "unwonted immunities" in the port and were, therefore, "very much attracted to the place and like to make voyages to it."[75] In the dockside area of Toxteth, African Americans entered one of Britain's oldest black communities, composed of fugitive slaves, African traders, Caribbean seafarers, and discharged sailors and soldiers who worked in the port's booming maritime industries.[76]

The "hub" of the black Atlantic was London.[77] From the 1780s, the capital's black population has been estimated at 15,000, a large proportion of whom were recent arrivals from North American or West Indian colonies, many moving on to other locales in the Empire.[78] Britain, then, "served more as a crossroads for black people in the Empire and elsewhere rather than a site of permanent settlement," writes the historian Winston James of the nineteenth century.[79] Most arrived on trading winds. Merchants and sailors from the Gold and Windward Coasts and Kru, with a long heritage of seafaring from West Africa, were joined by

East Indian "lascars," servants of the East India Company, who numbered 1,336 by 1813.[80] London's black populations "integrated with considerable success" in the East End, where racial mixing was no longer exceptional.[81] Communities in the riverside slums of Wapping (where the London Dock Company and Tobacco Dock were situated), Shadwell, Poplar (home to the West India docks), Canning Town (housing the Royal Docks), Rotherhithe (where American trade docked at the East Country Dock, renamed the South Dock in 1850), and Limehouse (where cargoes were offloaded onto canal barges at the Regent's Canal Dock) were composed largely of transient seafarers, living in sailors' boarding houses before taking return berths to the Gold Coast or West Indies.[82] Along the West India Dock Road, the Stranger's Home for Asiatics, Africans and South Sea Islanders opened in 1857 to cater to these transient populations.[83] To the northwest in St Giles, London's blacks mixed freely with other immigrant groups (see figure 5). Cable Street, for instance, was the site of "common lodging houses occupied by English, Scotch, Irish, Welsh, Americans, Germans, Norwegians, Flemish, Chinese, West Indians, and others."[84] African Americans joined this diverse black community and were prominent in these dockside areas, as shipping remained one of the few expanding industries open to men of color.[85]

But docksides were not exactly the racial refuges depicted by Melville or imagined by many African Americans—and sometimes suffered from the importation of US problems that British observers took to be a sign of the moral contagion spread by American slavery, a striking reversal of Southern fears of mobile African Americans. In some ports, American ships were anchored for up to a month, giving sailors plenty of time ashore. In 1820 one French traveler recorded two hundred American vessels anchored at Liverpool's docks, along with which came a flood of American tars to the boarding houses and taverns that lined the port's wharves.[86] Often paid at the end of the trip, many seamen squandered their wages carousing onshore between voyages. In Liverpool, white American sailors were frequently hauled before the local magistrate after acts of racial violence.[87] In 1858, an American seaman named George Washington Dickson shot a black Liverpudlian in the arm, chest, and thigh, in what Dickson described as a "muss" on the street.[88] In a separate incident, two American sailors, "excited by the dark skin of their victims," beat a Hindu tract seller about the head in "a most dastardly manner," assaulted a passing black sailor, and beat the mother of a mixed-race child. The judge overseeing the case hoped that a £5 fine—equivalent to two and a half month's wages—for assault would

FIGURE 5. In this rare depiction of life in East London, brothers Isaac Richard and George Cruickshank depict black sailors and entertainers mixing with other poor drinkers in the "Holy Land," a slum in the district of St Giles, so-called because of the large number of Irish Catholic migrants in the area. Accounts of the "black poor" were part observation, part reification of the Georgian and Victorian racial imaginary. It was no coincidence that images of black mendicants presenting themselves with fawning propriety on the streets of London, as found in Henry Mayhew's three-volume *London Labour and the London Poor* (1851), and the exaggerations of black minstrelsy based in the theaters of Drury Lane and the Vauxhall Pleasure Gardens, were popularized as Anglo-Saxon racial ideologies took hold in Victorian Britain (Lorimer, *Colour, Class, and the Victorians*, 86; Dubrulle, "Britain, the Civil War, and Race"). Image: "Tom and Jerry 'Masquerading it' among the cadgers in the 'Black Slums' of the Holy Land," Peirce Egan, *Life in London* (London: John Camden Hotton, 1823), © British Library Board. All Rights Reserved / Bridgeman Images.

"convince such of our American visitors as venture to beat and kick a man because he has black skin, that the law is too strong for them." While "in general the American sailors are well behaved and as respectable as our own," he continued, "now and then . . . the curse which slavery brings appears."[89]

Life in Britain was precarious for those who raised the capital and courage to seek asylum across the Atlantic. William G. Allen expatriated himself to Britain in the late 1850s, but failed to prosper outside of the lecture circuit. In May 1859 he wrote home to Gerrit Smith that he was "in the midst of a desperate struggle with the wolves, who are trying to break in at the door."[90] In response, fugitives in London organized the short-lived association American Fugitive Slaves in the British Metropolis to help the destitute and were soon joined by the Ladies Society for the

Aid of Fugitive Slaves in England.[91] Not all fugitives became destitute. Some, like Moses Roper and Alexander Crummell, successfully enrolled as students with funding from philanthropic networks, while others found employment as footmen, coachmen, street sweepers, or army bandsmen.[92] Still, the dream of independence was difficult to realize for black migrants who found their access to already meager resources squeezed by increasing numbers of transatlantic migrants fleeing the Fugitive Slave Act.[93] Reporting back to the *Liberator* in July 1851, William Wells Brown, one of the few fugitives to achieve a significant degree of financial autonomy, noted that "already hundreds have landed on these shores; every week shows an increase in the number of fugitive slaves in London." Brown issued a stark warning, however: "I would say to our fugitive brethren, if you don't want to become beggars, don't come to England."[94]

Each of the pathways charted here was one avenue of the United States' continued interdependence with the Atlantic world. Antebellum Americans journeyed, lived, and worked abroad more often than their colonial forebears. Over the antebellum period, transatlantic travel costs and times shrank, swelling the volume of transatlantic traffic. "Time and distance must submit to comparative annihilation," declared one leading American periodical in 1849.[95] These transformations also helped to integrate further the transatlantic cultural, social, and economic networks participated in by travelers and migrants. The most extensive and resilient webs of connection were those created by American merchants in Britain. Emigrant merchants lived and worked overseas for long periods of time, collaborating closely with British merchants and financiers and with their partners in the United States to ensure the reliability of long-distance trade. At the same time as building their businesses, emigrant merchants worked hard to create and maintain trading routes, to keep open the flows of knowledge and credit across the Atlantic, and to establish strong social connections with fellow traders and elite Britons. But this integration was double-edged: for many Americans Atlantic interdependence was evidence of the United States' ongoing colonial dependence.

THE COMMUNITY OF TRADE

Writing home from London in 1785, Abigail Adams complained to her son, the future president John Quincy Adams, that "our countrymen have most essentially injured themselves by running here in shoals after the peace, and obtaining a credit which they cannot support." Seeking to restore American trade and revive its lost prosperity, American merchants had instead "shackld and hamperd [sic] themselves."[96] American merchants bound the United States in a transatlantic world of goods and credit that raised the specter of colonial dependence to US citizens every day through the material objects they handled, encountered, and desired.[97] Political independence seemed only to reaffirm the new nation's continued economic dependence. As one enraged Virginian wrote in 1787, "All is British! British customs, British manners, British dress, British fashions, British folly and British vice."[98] Contentious as they were, colonial patterns of trade persisted long after the Revolution. "Though emancipated from foreign political domination," complained one mid-century author, "the people seemed yet enchained in complete dependence upon the workshops of Europe."[99]

For American merchants, the best way to restore transatlantic trade and outmaneuver their Dutch and French rivals was to follow old passages of travel across the Atlantic. After the war, few Americans doubted the importance of commerce to the survival of the republic and hoped to "lead the world into a revolution in free trade" in which Britain would be one of many trading partners.[100] Yet, although American exporters travelled to a wider range of European ports than before the Revolution, Britain remained the United States' largest export market, its greatest creditor, the largest re-exporter of American goods, and the chief exporter of factors of production (labor, capital, and technical expertise) to the United States.[101] The early republic's merchants therefore worked ceaselessly to re-open, and then keep open, colonial patterns of direct trade with Great Britain and to maintain the social networks of Atlantic commerce—though their ability to rise above their own interests in the marketplace was doubted. The proper extent of merchants' role in securing the new nation's independence was contested by agrarian theorists and proponents of a national system of manufactures alike.[102] "For an independent nation, to depend wholly on the supply of others, for their clothing and every other manufacture, is quite a political solecism," wrote one economic nationalist in 1785; "such a people may please themselves with sounds, and their independence like a child's rattle, may tickle their fancy."[103]

But British goods did tickle the fancy of American consumers. Despite the readjustments of the Confederation Period, trade boomed in the British Atlantic. In 1784, imports of British goods to the United States totaled £3.6 million, the highest amount since 1771.[104] At the close of the Revolutionary War, American merchants rushed to restore prewar connections and mend the disrepair of Atlantic trade, and a new generation of "transatlantics all young and unknown" entered London's merchant community.[105] According to Connecticut merchant Silas Deane, writing in April 1783, American merchants poured into Britain "from every quarter of their late dispersions" and went "as far as their money or credit [would] carry them in the purchase of goods" to ship back to the former colonies.[106] Observers at the Bank of England noted that "very few of the parties who represent the American houses in our market can be looked upon as permanent residents because they are constantly changing."[107] As a result, trust and credit-worthiness had to be continually reestablished. Among the new "transatlantics" was the eldest son of Robert Beverley, a Virginian tobacco and wheat merchant, sent to cultivate new contacts at the close of the war. He was not alone: many American merchants, including Thomas Blount and John Hatley Norton, travelled to the capital hoping to establish social standing and lines of credit from investors at the Royal Exchange.[108] William Bingham, a Philadelphian merchant and privateer made rich by trade in the French West Indies, took up residence in London between 1783 and 1786 to rebuild his family's commercial connections with Baring Brothers bank. To do so he arranged lucrative marriages between the two families, merging their business interests in the process.[109]

Slowly, these commercial emissaries reestablished confidence in the Atlantic world's trading networks by restoring personal relations (established by marriage and religion) that extended back into the colonial period.[110] Freed from Alien's Duty, the total exports from the United States to Great Britain were 37 percent above their prewar level by the early 1790s.[111] By 1790, Britain received as much as half of the United States' exports, and the United States took four-fifths of its imports from Britain.[112] Disillusioned that the Revolution had not created a new world of free trade, James Madison complained as the First Congress met in May 1789 that Great Britain "has bound us in commercial manacles, and very nearly defeated the object of our independence."[113] Meanwhile, Federalist political economists, dismissed as "Anglomen" by their opponents, attempted to restore the United States' public credit and fund the national debt (then more than thirty times greater than the federal government's expected annual income) through a national bank and the mobilization of mercantile capital, all of which required close commercial ties to Britain and the City of London.[114] Bitter disputes over fiscal and foreign policy soon convulsed the Union.

For all the ferment at home, the United States' trade fared surprisingly well throughout the repeated international crises that began with the French Revolution in 1793. Between 1792 and 1795, customs duties collected in the four major ports of New York, Philadelphia, Baltimore, and Charleston totaled $18.1 million, compared to just $1.2 million in internal revenue.[115] 1795 brought the Jay Treaty, which guaranteed the "neutral rights" of American shipping, granted trade between the United States and Britain "most favored nation" status, reopened British ports to American merchants, and also opened a limited number of imperial markets. Propelled by the treaty's provisions, the export trade of the United States surpassed $90 million by 1801.[116] While the Embargo and the War of 1812 all but destroyed the nation's overseas commerce, it recovered dramatically after 1815, sped by European demand for grain and the quickening pace of British industrialization after the Napoleonic wars, only to stall once more with the Panic of 1819 and the ensuing depression that lasted until 1821.[117] Even Madison, who had warned of the Anglicizing impact of British trade more than twenty years earlier, mused in 1823 that the United States' continued dependence on Great Britain provided both prosperity and protection: "With the British fleets and fiscal resources associated with our own we should be safe against the rest of the World."[118]

Throughout this period of turbulence, emigrant merchants tried to build their businesses. Liverpool emerged as the emporium of Atlantic trade in the years after the Revolution. Visiting the city in 1800, Pennsylvanian paper manufacturer Joshua Gilpin recorded ten prominent American houses in the port—a number that continued to rise alongside the city's stature as the gateway to the British Empire.[119] At the time of Gilpin's visit, Liverpool was still a minor city, surpassed in population by more than forty other urban centers on the continent, but in the following four decades its population quintupled and the city became the sixth largest in Europe and the third largest in the Atlantic basin.[120] Residence in Liverpool was a necessity if merchants were to overcome the basic challenges of overseas trade—long delays in communication, vulnerability to market fluctuations, and the difficulty of attracting credit—that remained constant between the colonial and antebellum periods. In real terms, importer and exporter could be weeks apart, and an experienced go-between was vital. As one guide to business etiquette informed its readers, the merchant "can scarcely move without danger. He is beset on all sides with disappointments, with fluctuations in the current of business, which sometimes leaves him stranded on an unknown bar, and sometimes sweep him helpless into the ocean."[121] As the *Southern Cultivator* put it, merchants lived a life of "abject slavery" in which they were "dependent on their credit, dependent on the banks, dependent on their customers, dependent on their friends."[122] Although the invention of packet ships in 1818 regularized sailing schedules and the Cunard Line's Royal Mail steamship franchise of 1840 increased the speed and regularity of mail delivery, the exchange of information did not accelerate dramatically until the successful laying of the Atlantic telegraph in 1866. Until then, to expand the reach of their operations and maintain flows of accurate information between marketplaces, merchants established webs of interlocking partnerships between ports.[123]

Residence in Britain also meant closer proximity to a wider variety of stock. This was the case for the Boston-based brothers Nathan and Eben Appleton, who entered into partnership with Daniel E. Parker in 1810. Explicitly writing into the deed of partnership that it was "for the interests of the concern that one or more parties should reside in England," Eben departed for Liverpool within the next year.[124] Once in the port, Eben travelled through the manufacturing districts of West Yorkshire purchasing goods direct from the manufacturer, cutting out costly commission agents. "By going into Yorkshire I think you get the goods very low and very soon," Nathan wrote Eben, adding that "low priced woolens are at present in great demand & must be higher in the winter."[125] The American dry goods importers John Guest & Co. alighted on the same solution. While the firm's co-partners lived in Liverpool and Philadelphia, they also employed George Palmer, a native of Philadelphia, who described to one Parliamentary committee his role as a purchasing agent of finished wool and dyed cottons from Yorkshire textile mills, which enabled the firm to forgo costly commission merchants.[126]

With success dependent on merchant houses' reliance on trust and personal character, family and co-religious networks were central to international trade.[127] The wholesale grocer Daniel James rose rapidly through the merchant ranks thanks to the web of family contacts, partnership agreements, and business strategy that defined the careers of many transatlantic merchants.[128] In 1829, James married Elizabeth Woodridge Phelps, daughter of the wealthy New York merchant Anson Greene Phelps. Two years later, James replaced his father-in-law's existing partner in Liverpool, Elisha Peck, who wished to return to the United States after fifteen years on Merseyside. At the same time, Phelps entered into a second partnership with another son-in-law, William E. Dodge, to form Phelps, Dodge & Co., which operated from New York. Dodge imported tin plate, sheet iron, copper, and other metals through the Liverpool house, which in return received cotton from New Orleans and, soon, from the firm's regular packet ship between Liverpool and Charleston.

The two linked firms thus became some of the most prominent importer-exporters of cotton and metals in both countries, but their transatlantic partnership required constant attention to succeed. From Liverpool, James maintained a ceaseless vigil over the flow of transatlantic communication. "I am now without any of your favours to reply to & sometimes think you must be sick with my long epistling," James chided Dodge early in the partnership, "but I am fully of opinion [sic] that the interest of the business is greatly profited by a free and full communication & exchange of our opinions on these matters."[129] Regular contact helped to clarify market uncertainties, ease decision-making, and facilitate longterm planning—especially important at times of financial crisis, which soon hit the firm. "I want *exceedingly to know what are taken up and what are not,*" James wrote Dodge from Liverpool at the height of the Panic of 1837, since "next month I am going to see all the manufacturers & this information if I had it would do *us much good.*"[130] As long as transatlantic communication remained dependent on prevailing winds, regular correspondence detailing stock inventory, accounts, and analyzing local market information was highly valued.

Because merchants put great faith in trustworthy correspondents thousands of miles away to supply them with accurate information, their letters were replete with the language of "confidence."[131] James, for instance, underlined the veracity of intelligence and gossip with phrases like "all this Shipley told Banks in *entire confidence,*" "Browns has always made *confidant* of Banks," and passed information to his partner, "*in confidence and to you only.*"[132] Before the invention of credit-reporting agencies, merchant elites prized intelligence on personal character to generate confidence.[133] When James Brown, of the New York-based Brown, Brothers & Co., described Robert White to Joseph Shipley, his partner in Liverpool, as a "very bad tempered man and . . . too selfish," he was not engaging in idle gossip but sending a clear indication: White was not credit-worthy.[134] Confidence possessed the power to generate credit—and with it, risk. Confidence could itself be generated through the public demonstration of gentility and social status, key pursuits of the gentlemanly merchant-bankers explored in the next chapter. Character and reputation, then, were powerful cultural forces underlying the expanding, credit-dependent, and therefore risk-laden, transatlantic economy.

For traders, emigration brought an apprenticeship in the day-to-day practicalities of international commerce that the theorists of political economy could not. In July 1843, William E. Bowen wrote from the Philadelphia branch house of Brown Brothers that their former agent in the Gulf Coast cotton port of Mobile, George Cleveland, was on his way to Liverpool. Once there, Bowen wrote, "he will have an opportunity of learning how things are done on your side and will come back well posted up." In his letter of introduction to Shipley, Bowen included key details about Cleveland's character, noting that he was "a very honest fellow, though his first appearance may not strike you as prepossessing" and that he "devotes his best energies and services to promote our interests."[135] Cleveland followed in the footsteps of many leading US merchants who cut their commercial teeth in the counting houses of London and Liverpool before returning to the United States. Pursuing a commercial apprenticeship overseas could be a shrewd business decision, granting access to new areas of expertise, new lines of business, and additional sources of capital. As a result, it continued throughout the antebellum period and was integral to the professional identity of many merchants in the Atlantic world.

Merchants worked hard to create and strengthen the institutions sustaining Anglo-American trade. In Liverpool, the Exchange was among the most important of these institutions. Opened in 1754 as an expression of the port city's commercial self-confidence, the "change" was a place where Liverpool-based merchants and agents met to buy and sell goods, establish credit-worthiness, and cultivate social contacts. As the port's importance grew, its merchants formed the Liverpool Chamber of Commerce in 1774 as a political pressure group where prominent merchants coordinated their response to political crises. More informal, non-market centered spaces that were part business association, part social club such as the City Tavern, Pontack's Coffee House, and the Merchant's Coffee House, were arenas of business activity and spaces to measure the social standing of potential customers.[136]

As specialist trades and commodity markets multiplied, and the all-purpose trader who dominated the eighteenth century declined, so did the formal lobbies that provided advice and information for their members. The associations in Liverpool were organized around the port's expanding global interests, and included the African Committee (1777), West

FIGURE 6. Robert Salmon (1775–1845) painted more than one thousand maritime and seascapes in his career. Fittingly, he enjoyed a transatlantic career: in 1828 he migrated to Boston, where he thrived accepting commissions to paint ship portraits and harbor views. Here, a pair of American ships approach the Liverpool docks, obscured by a mass of flags and sails on the choppy waters of the Mersey. Image: Robert W. Salmon, *American Ships in the Mersey*, oil on canvas, 1811, courtesy National Museums Liverpool.

Indian Association (1799), and East India Association (1818), indicating the port's early integration into global markets.[137] Specialist lobbies for particular products developed later, such as the Cotton Brokers' Association in 1841 and the Corn Trade Association in 1853, and indicated the rise of American interests in the port (see figure 6). Such trade associations were mechanisms of network management, "absolutely necessary" to coordinating international trade in the assessment of one observer, a task that was "beyond the power of individuals."[138] Their members maintained "watch" or "superintendence" over the port's trade, gathered reliable information, and lobbied local authorities to improve the infrastructure of international trade.[139] These commercial associations, wrote the British journalist Thomas Baines, were "the public face of business," and because their trading networks were so stretched across time and space, merchants paid close attention to their operation.[140]

To support the growing volume of transatlantic trade, American merchants in Liverpool established the American Chamber of Commerce

(ACC), a cosmopolitan body drawn from the port's international merchant diaspora engaged in the American trade. Founded in July 1801 at the instigation of the US Consul at Liverpool and Virginian tobacco merchant, James Maury, the ACC aimed at "the redress of existing and prevention of future grievances" afflicting the North American trade.[141] The ACC was committed to maintaining Atlantic trade. "It takes cognizance of all questions affecting the American trade," reported one newspaper, adding that it had been "instrumental in effecting improvements of the mercantile law of this country."[142] Locally, the Chamber liaised with the Liverpool dock management to plan the expansion of harbor and warehousing facilities and the port's connections to canal and railway infrastructure. Nationally, it lobbied Parliament and the Board of Trade through petitioning and the energetic work of John Backhouse from its London office.[143] Between its founding in 1801 and the end of the US Civil War, just seven of the ACC's presidents were American citizens, with a similar number being drawn from the ranks of German and French traders.[144]

The Chamber also fulfilled important social functions essential to the smooth operation of long-distance trade. Just as many of London and Bristol's pre-revolutionary coffee houses acted as a "lifeline to America" for anxious colonists, the ACC enabled Americans in the city to preserve national connections through the exchange of news and gossip, and the reception of visitors.[145] The Chamber's committee acted as a delegation when new American consuls and ministers arrived in the port, extending hospitality in its role as diplomatic lobby.[146] In April 1842, the ACC also created a reading room where itinerant and resident Americans could find British and American newspapers along with Parliamentary, Congressional, and statistical papers.[147] In this respect, the ACC reflected the constant interplay between integrating with local professional and social customs and the creation of distinct national institutions and spaces that characterized the lives of many American migrants.

Atlantic traders operated in a series of overlapping national, international, and global social and professional networks. Transnational merchants traveled freely between distant cities and towns, corresponded regularly with like-minded people, and at times lived overseas for long periods of time.[148] American migrants in Britain were not exceptional in this respect. In the United States' major Atlantic ports, just as in European ports, British and European merchants established branch houses to coordinate trade and investment, reflecting a broader exchange of merchant talent between international ports.[149] The merchant and brokerage houses crowding Wall Street and Pearl Street in Lower Manhattan swelled with Britons and Europeans attracted by the variety of imports and exports landing at the wharves.[150] By the 1830s, British-based banks viewed the United States as an attractive longterm investment and provided direct investment in American firms expanding cotton and lumber production and constructing canal, turnpikes, and railways in the United States, in addition to underwriting the bond issues of states undertaking their own infrastructure projects.[151] Maintaining this complex financial network required careful, conscious efforts at collective organization. Major transatlantic markets did not emerge naturally, but were coordinated by the human infrastructure of overseas correspondents, agents, and go-betweens. In the words of one contemporary assessment, migration to Britain placed these individuals "at the very heart of a world-wide commerce—beholding and understanding the multiplied and intimate connections on which the vast interests of commercial credit and prosperity depend."[152]

But just as contemporaries recognized that transatlantic merchant and financial networks generated great wealth and prosperity, they were also anxious about exposure to the powerful economic headwinds that accompanied interdependence. As financial panic gripped the American economy in 1837, and no fewer than eight states and the territory of Florida defaulted on their debt, transatlantic merchants came under attack for their abuse of paper credit and disregard of the national interest. Anglophobic Democrats argued that merchants' international connections were an integral element of the "*entangling alliance*" between the "banking and mercantile class" and "the colossal money power of Great Britain."[153] The claim that merchants had engaged in "overtrading" and upset the constant struggle to balance the nation's fragile political economy was made repeatedly by the Democratic press.[154] "The people of the United States will now perceive more fully than could be learned from volumes of elaborate argument," charged the Jacksonian *Globe* at the height of the crisis, "the necessity of guarding inviolate the public faith, by disengaging the public finances from a groveling state of dependence upon the operations of private mercantile speculations."[155] As the cousin of Joseph Shipley wrote in an acerbic aside, "By the way, I think the *increases* of your Bank have greatly aided in producing the present *discord* by striking the first blow of that confidence which if it had been properly sustained might have enabled them [the American people], if not to ride the whirlwind, at least to have given discretion & greatly diminished the force of the storm."[156]

As the storm receded and the export economy revived, transatlantic merchants could not promise stability but, against familiar charges that they were too interested to make virtuous citizens, insisted they were the agents of American economic independence. Transatlantic merchants were as much economic nationalists as Democratic partisans, but viewed the dense web of social, economic, and cultural connection that knit together the Atlantic world as the surest route to restoring the health of the public finances and securing US independence. Writing to his partner in Liverpool in 1843, William Brown reflected that American citizens were "daily learning that we have the material within us which if properly worked up will keep us independent of the Old World."[157] Later in the decade, Brown told the same correspondent that he "never could doubt as to national feelings. We must agree in being Americans *first.*" Yet, in a measure of the ambivalence felt by many transatlantic merchants, he added that he had "too many ties to dear Old England to blot her out from my affections."[158] The decades between the Panic of 1837 and the onset of the Civil War only brought further degrees of interdependence between the US economy and the financial and commercial instruments of the British Empire. At the center of this new interdependence was the credit-thirsty processes of US state-building and the lucrative cotton trade.

ENTREPÔT OF COTTON, METROPOLIS OF CREDIT

In 1838, Liverpool's docks stretched an impressive two and a half miles in length and captured some ninety acres of water; twenty years later, they extended over nine and a half miles (see figure 7).[159] The chaotic port crowded the senses. Bundles of textiles from mills in Lancashire and Yorkshire, Indian calicos and teak, crates of Midlands metalwares, bars of Swedish iron, and dusty bushels of Australian wheat struggled for space on the wharves. The tang of spices from around the world, earthy tobacco from Virginia, and the smoky aroma of lapsang teas from Asia fought against the stink of tar and fish. And over everything, "like an evil spirit," hung a pall of sooty smoke from the steamers and the local soda and glass works.[160] Visiting Americans gazed in awe at the "bustle" of dockside traffic, the scale of its "towering warehouses," and the "tangled masts and yards" that reached still higher and gave the impression of "large forests destitute of foliage."[161] "The particolored flags of various nations, streaming gaily from the numerous masts," recorded Zachariah Allen, "became mingled together, as in the great race of mercantile

FIGURE 7. The scale of Liverpool's shipping is captured vividly in this panoramic map. Panoramic maps were a popular cartographic form for representing urban centers from above, usually from an oblique angle, so that street patterns, notable buildings, and the drama of urban life could be evocatively portrayed. Such maps, writes Susan Schulten, were "a form of civic promotion that combined art, advertising, and cartography" (*Mapping the Nation*, 157). Several panoramic maps of Liverpool were produced in the nineteenth century, including *Ackerman's Panoramic View of Liverpool* (1847) and the colossal *Illustrated London News*'s "View of Liverpool from the Mersey" (1865). (Both maps can be found in excellent quality and detail at https://historic-liverpool.co.uk/old-maps-of-liverpool.) Image: John Raphael Isaac and Vincent Brooks, "Liverpool, 1859, Part of Birkenhead, the docks, and Cheshire Coast," Library of Congress Geography and Map Division.

competition."[162] Amidst this throng, the docks themselves stood out as "noble," "magnificent," and "stupendous works," that demonstrated "in a most astonishing degree the power of science and art in overcoming . . . insurmountable obstacles."[163] American merchants loaded their ships at Prince's dock alongside the transatlantic packets. Completed in 1821, Prince's was the largest dock yet built. A pair of forty-five-foot wide locks guarded more than four hundred and fifty meters of landing space and eleven acres of water (equivalent to ten city blocks) from the Mersey's swells.[164] Through the eyes of one American tourist, they were the "glory of Liverpool," while to another, "nothing in the world is to be seen more magnificent in extent."[165]

After landing and negotiating the crowds of cab drivers and porters in "ragged garb" waiting outside the doors of the Customs House,

FIGURE 8. In the foreground stands the Anglo-American House, a dining room and boarding house, and Uncle Sam's Ale and Porter Vaults. In the background stands the United States Hotel. Image: William Gawin Herdman, "Waterloo Road, Liverpool, eastern side from Oil Street to Vandries Street," watercolor, 1859, courtesy of Liverpool Record Office, Liverpool Libraries.

American migrants found that the trade in goods and travelers between Liverpool and the United States shaped city spaces.[166] One of the first ports of call for newly arrived Americans was the US consulate on Paradise Street, which ran along the quayside of Steer's Old Dock. While the personnel changed, the consulate remained a fixed point, providing the services required by a wide cross-section of Americans overseas. For ship captains it was the place to register cargoes, and for travelers and migrants it was a place to read the latest American newspaper or request official documents. Washington Street was home to the United States Hotel and its "parade of American insignia" (see figure 8). Above the door perched an "American Eagle, and the national motto" to which, Silliman reported, Americans crowded "in great numbers" excited by "patriotic sympathy."[167] The offices of Brown, Shipley at 7 Union Court, Castle Street, were the headquarters for American ship captains, where they kept abreast of recent arrivals and market information.[168] Only a stone's throw from the Liverpool Exchange and Customs House was Mary Blodgett's guest house. Blodgett's was, in the assessment of one resident American, "the favorite resort of American sea captains and shipping men, and . . .

a sort of central point for all Americans in Liverpool."[169] It was briefly home to Nathaniel Hawthorne, after the celebrated author accepted the position of consul in the city, and also to the two consuls who preceded him, Robert Armstrong and the Kentuckian Thomas L. Crittenden. There was, concluded one writer, "perhaps no other city in England where America is more justly appreciated," where "our commerce fills its docks, and our merchants move in its society."[170]

Liverpool's American merchants not only moved in society, but shaped the port's priorities. In 1780, Liverpool imported no cotton whatsoever from North America. By 1833—once American slavery had taken command of cotton production—the port had captured 90 percent of the global trade, twenty times the amount landed in London.[171] With the arrival of power weaving after 1830 and the expansion into and conversion of the fertile lands of the Mississippi River valley to cotton production, cotton exports boomed. While in 1830 the United States' cotton exports totaled almost $27 million (41 percent of total US exports), by 1860 that figure had risen to almost $192 million (58 percent of the total).[172] The bags of "white gold" landed on Liverpool's wharves connected mill towns in Massachusetts and Lancashire more than three thousand miles and twenty-eight days' sail away; linked more than four million slave laborers with between one-fifth and one-quarter of British laborers; and enmeshed ports up and down the United States' Atlantic seaboard with Europe and onward to markets in Asia. For slaveholders and slavery's bankers in the American South, in the words of New York journalist Thomas Kettell, cotton "enveloped the commercial world, and bound the fortunes of American slaves so firmly to human progress, that civilization may be said to depend on the continual servitude of blacks in America."[173]

Cotton has become the preeminent global commodity for historians of nineteenth-century global capitalism, consumption, and the South's transnational connections alike.[174] The best of the new literature on cotton's centrality to global capitalism, by Brian Schoen, Sven Beckert, and Giorgio Riello, places the institutional structures of trade created by merchants at the center of analysis.[175] Beginning in the mid-eighteenth century, a new regime of consumption centered on cotton propelled a global realignment of agricultural labor regimes and a relocation of cotton production from Asia to Europe and the Americas.[176] Liverpool's eighteenth-century merchants enriched themselves both by trading in slaves and taking advantage of the port's close relationship with its industrial hinterland.[177] The textile industries of South Lancashire provided a large market for imported

Northern cereals and slave-grown staples, and Liverpool merchants established strong business alliances with Manchester textile merchants and financiers in London. As we saw in the previous section, the webs of credit, social connection, and trust at the heart of the cotton trade did not appear naturally. Instead, they relied on the business acuity of a vast network of skilled merchants for their economic vitality.[178]

Cotton's connective power created a mutually beneficial interdependence for those engaged in its transatlantic trade.[179] For Southern planters and factors, the ever-expanding British Empire would be the best means of extending the South's reach into global markets, but the cotton-carrying trade was equally lucrative to Northeastern bankers, merchants, and shippers. Most cotton arrived in Liverpool on ships from the Northeast, which by the mid-1820s carried 90 percent of the United States' total export trade.[180] Northern carriers rode trade winds that carried them on a triangular route between southern ports and Liverpool before they returned home to Northeastern ports laden with finished European manufactures.[181] The majority of Americans in the port were drawn from the merchant elites of New York, Philadelphia, and New England, who dominated the transatlantic carrying trade or ran the financial institutions servicing the cotton trade.[182] Specialist Liverpool-American merchants and brokers were twinned with London-American financiers and together constituted the principal conduits of the Atlantic economy.

The cross-sectional nature of the cotton trade cautions historians against the easy assumption that the port would naturally have been a stronghold of Confederate support. Despite Liverpool's centrality to the Atlantic slave trade before 1807 and the subsequent predominance of the American cotton trade, Liverpool-Americans' identification with the southern states was deeply ambivalent. Few Southerners engaged in the cotton trade resided in the port until the opening of the cotton broker Fraser Trenholm in 1856. In the decades before Fraser Trenholm's arrival, Southern interests failed to coalesce around the trade associations of the city, with an important consequence: Southerners were less well-connected in Britain than were Northerners engaged in trade and finance. Although one traveler complained early in the century that Liverpool's merchants "pray God, not to change the colour of the negroes," the port was, after all, the birthplace of the abolitionist George Thompson.[183] Many of the ACC's most prominent Quaker members were intimately connected with Liverpool's abolition movement. James Cropper, for instance, a founding signatory of the ACC, was president of the Liverpool Anti-Slavery Society and closely tied to the transatlantic anti-slavery network, even working alongside fugitive slaves and free blacks to discredit colonization schemes among the British public.[184]

Connections between Liverpool and the capital integrated the financial services of the City of London with the specialized markets of the Liverpool quayside, especially after the completion of the London and Northwestern Railway in 1846. Proximity to the hubs of information, contacts, associations, and capital of both cities prompted the formation of American communities. Liverpool was not simply the economic satellite of London, however. The process of economic integration was multidirectional. Established banking firms such as Kleinworts, Rothschilds, Barings, and Brown, Shipley grew rapidly in this period, consolidating their position as major transatlantic merchant banks. These firms relied on up-to-date intelligence about commodity markets in Liverpool and appointed a network of agents to maintain the stream of information.[185]

So lucrative was the cotton trade that some Liverpool merchants made the transition from trader to financier. The Baltimore-based W. & J. Brown & Co. opened their Liverpool branch in 1810, quickly establishing a foothold in Liverpool's merchant community as the port's premier cotton traders.[186] In 1825, William Brown joined with fellow Liverpool resident Joseph Shipley, of Delaware, who was the agent of the Philadelphian merchant John Welsh, to create Brown, Shipley & Co. While the Liverpool house continued handling cotton consignments in concert with the firm's Southern branches, the partners sought protection from the volatility of Atlantic markets and state debt defaults by the mid-1830s. Brown, Shipley, operating long-distance with James Brown at the New York branch, began to concentrate on the provision of financial services.[187] William offered numerous small lines of credit, according to the Bank of England's agent in Liverpool, "to different agents of American houses who travel through the manufacturing districts and order goods at Manchester, Birmingham, Sheffield and other places."[188] In doing so the firm connected its branches in Baltimore, Philadelphia, New York, and Liverpool with its agents in Mobile, Natchez, New Orleans, Charleston, and by 1849 San Francisco, creating an international trading network that connected the markets of the American continent to the commercial and financial emporiums of the British Empire.

More established English banking houses moved into the financing of American trade and securities by employing US expertise. Baring Brothers extended their interest in transatlantic finance by opening a Liverpool office in 1832, appointing the American Samuel S. Gair and the Briton Charles Baring Young as partners in the port.[189] The Liverpool branch was one point on a network connecting London, Liverpool, and Boston via Barings's investment capital, masterminded in part by Joshua Bates. Born in Weymouth, Massachusetts, Bates arrived in England in 1816 as the European agent of the Bostonian merchant William Gray, specializing in the Russian and Indian trades.[190] The New Englander successfully cultivated contacts with prominent merchants in London, from which he built a firm with John Baring in 1826. Soon after, the firm, with its client list of nearly three dozen firms trading in the East Indies and Far East including the Bostonian China house Bryant & Sturgis, was bought out by Baring Brothers.[191] The move placed Bates at the center of Anglo-American finance and was the most productive partnership between a British bank and American state-building. The British bank was partially responsible for doubling the size of the United States in 1803 by negotiating the Louisiana Purchase, and was subsequently appointed the United States' agent in London—"Jefferson's Empire" was made possible by the Federalist system of international high finance. After the War of 1812, Barings went on to finance state loans, American railroad building, and the United States' war against Mexico. Bates was made a senior partner after Alexander Baring's retirement in 1830.[192] The firm's American presence was cemented in 1851 after Russell Sturgis, another Bostonian, was promoted to senior partner. Convinced that "American business will be safer than any other and should be cultivated with the greatest care," Bates kept abreast of transatlantic political and economic conditions via these vast networks of familial and business correspondents.[193]

The chief rival to Bates's pre-eminence on the American securities market was another New England financier, George Peabody. The third-born of a family of eight siblings from South Danvers, Massachusetts, Peabody cut his commercial teeth as a dry goods merchant in the firm Riggs, Peabody, & Co., operating from Baltimore. Between 1827 and 1837, Peabody made several successful trips across the Atlantic on behalf of the firm, before establishing George Peabody & Co. amid financial panic in the Atlantic world. Taking advantage of the availability of funds in London, Peabody specialized in American state bonds before moving into the world of Anglo-American stock and commodity trading.[194] By mid-century, Peabody financed everything from American securities to railroad iron exports and the silk trade in China, amassing a $20 million fortune in the process.[195] Peabody took on the New Yorker Junius Spencer Morgan as his partner in 1854. Residence in Britain was a necessity for American financiers seeking proximity to London's global financial instruments and was key to the favorable conditions enjoyed by the United States within Britain's international financial system.[196] American emigrants were partners in major transatlantic banks, managed their branches in commercial hubs in Britain, and developed strong connections with British political and economic elites in London society (the subject of the next chapter).

As a result, after independence a consistent flow of British capital crossed the Atlantic and London became a bull market for US Treasury bonds, state and national debt, and American railroad securities.[197] By 1853, half of the United States' national debt was held abroad—nearly all of it in the hands of British investors.[198] Although the New York Stock Exchange was created in 1817, local capital markets were unable to sustain the United States' thirst for development capital. As a result, the republic's transatlantic financial connections deepened throughout the nineteenth century, as the City of London maintained an ongoing commitment to nation-building in the United States. In the estimate of economic historians Davis and Cull, by 1860 Britain accounted for nine of every ten dollars of foreign investment in the United States.[199]

Not only elite merchant bankers were attracted to London's global financial markets, as the biographies of a number of entrepreneurs and inventors in the capital bear out. New York-born Benjamin Franklin Babcock ran B. F. Babcock & Co., a branch of the Great Western Insurance Company, and naturalized as a British subject in 1857. Curtis Miranda Lampson, of New Haven, Vermont, arrived in London in 1830 as an agent of John Jacob Astor, before opening his own fur trading firm, C. M. Lampson & Co. On May 14, 1849, he was likewise naturalized a British subject. In 1856, Lampson was elected to the board of directors of the Atlantic Telegraph Co., and was later created a baronet. Similarly, after serving as the American commissioner to the Great Exhibition in 1851, Nathaniel S. Dodge settled in London in 1852, hoping to capitalize on the imperial market opportunities for vulcanized rubber. Jacob Perkins and his eldest son Ebenezer, engravers from Old Newburyport, Massachusetts, moved to London in 1819 in pursuit of a contract to print and engrave the banknotes of the Bank of England. These individuals are emblematic of the migration of enterprise that underwrote the Atlantic economy and the way in which migrants were the central actors in the construction of transatlantic interdependence.

Anglo-American interdependence centered on London's inner city of high finance. George Peabody & Co. stood at the heart of the City of London at 22 Old Broad Street—just a short walk from the Royal Exchange, nestled between Threadneedle Street and Cornhill. The Exchange's Hall of

Commerce was the center for trading in American railroad securities and was gripped by "Railroad mania" in the mid-1840s. It was here, observed the Massachusetts Congressman Benjamin Gorham, that "the barometer of the American money market hangs up."[200] Opposite the Exchange was the Bank of England, the offices of Britain's so-called "money power," to which many Americans traced all manner of domestic and foreign crises.[201] Next door to the Bank was the former New England Coffee House. In 1825 the Colonial Coffee House expanded into the premises next door and rebranded itself as the North and South American Coffee House, described by one contemporary as "the complete center for American intelligence."[202] Barings, and the office of Joshua Bates, stood just around the corner at 8 Bishopsgate. As Edward Everett described the work of emigrant financiers in the City of London, they were "all concerned in weaving the mighty network of mutually beneficial exchanges which enwraps the world."[203] No more than a square mile in size, this was the financial heart of the British Empire, the capital of American credit, and a principal workplace of American emigrants.

The American merchants, financiers, and agents who migrated to Britain worked within formerly colonial frameworks of commercial interconnection. Americans in Britain directed these links, reorienting them as the Atlantic world itself changed, but also reinforced the interdependence of the two transatlantic economies.[204] As interpreted by transatlantic financiers, these interconnections demanded the temporary co-option of British economic power. It was at this juncture in transatlantic economics that the function of American communities in Britain intersected with disputes over Atlantic political economy in the United States. In an era of rising nationalism, some, particularly amongst the New England Whigs where links with Britain's American community were strongest, argued that meaningful independence could only be achieved by a temporary collaboration with British capital.[205] Britain's American community was the social context in which this collaboration was rooted.

As American communities in Britain mediated commercial relations between Great Britain and the United States, they performed analogous social functions. In the chapter that follows, John Bull looms large in debates over American national character. Transatlantic cultural ties ran deep, but renewed fears of colonial dependency. As American nationalism and sectionalism at home became both more proscriptive and increasingly assertive, Americans in Britain participated in the clash between Anglophobia and Anglophilia from the "frontline." While resident in Britain, Americans engaged directly and immediately with the tensions of American nationalism in ways that ordinary Americans could not. American travelers and visitors attached their own meanings to the patriotic orations of Americans overseas and to the transatlantic relationship. Britain's American community found its national expression contested by partisan and sectional opponents, whose recourse to Anglophobia was swift and voluble. The processes of "unbecoming British" and becoming American did not give way seamlessly to one another. Instead, Americans grappled continuously with the challenge of reconciling fundamentally opposing aspirations: between independence and interdependence, between the desire to beat and to be like their former imperial parent, and between integrating with and remaining distinct from Britain's global commercial system. Nowhere was this more visible than in the social world of Britain's American emigrant community.

CHAPTER 2

Representative Americans

How should US democracy be represented in a world of aristocracy? Which national traits should Americans overseas embody in their interactions with foreign people? And who, of the diverse Americans abroad, should represent the republic when, as one diplomat reflected, "Englishmen often say to me that they often get their worst opinions of Americans from Americans themselves"?[1] American emigrants devised their own solutions to these questions. As visible representatives of American citizens overseas, the actions of American emigrants had a direct impact on the international reputation of the United States. Prominent emigrants worked hard to integrate American social life in Britain with the exclusive world of British high society where they could interact with, and shape the perceptions of, elite Britons. But this activity gave rise to further, more troubling questions: if it was beneficial, even desirable, to integrate with British society, what would be the cost to the nationality of individual migrants and to the creation of a national community overseas?

The London Season shaped the social lives of upper-class American emigrants. The Season began with the opening of Parliament in February and thereafter was a rush of Court levees, Royal "drawing rooms," and lavish private balls, dinners, and garden parties hosted by fashionable Britons. Political and social affairs were so closely entwined in the Season that many dinner parties were timed to begin when the House of Commons rose, and MPs left debates straight for the dining table where political discussion continued.[2] Participation in the Season was an accepted part of diplomatic culture; it was a key period during which foreign representatives displayed refined taste and gentility, gathered intelligence, and cultivated connections.[3] Although they did not always agree with the aristocratic symbolism that underlay the Season's social rituals, many Americans accepted that the United States' representatives'should participate in them nonetheless, since doing so was essential to demonstrating reciprocity among nations. As one popular middle class American journal described it, diplomacy was "the art of employing the most refined perceptions and feelings by which the ruling powers of states are governed."[4] Nevertheless, it presented two problems for American diplomats: it was costly and socially exclusive.[5] As one traveler noted in 1853, unless the Minister "be not as opulent as a prince, he will be obliged to live in comparative obscurity, and must cut a very sorry figure."[6] For American diplomats employed by a cost-conscious government, ill-disposed toward the aristocratic nature of European diplomacy, these problems were at times insurmountable without the material and social aid of American emigrants.[7] For this reason, the United States' relations with Britain in this period are best described as emigrant foreign relations.

In contrast to American diplomats, many American emigrants were both wealthy and connected. By lending their reputation as men of social standing to the diplomatic service, American emigrants maintained the United States' credibility among prominent Britons during the Season—the key moment at which elite Britons would judge the republic's representatives. Throughout the Season, the blurred boundaries between political and social life meant that the "theatre of politics" extended into the drawing rooms and salons of private individuals.[8] The public celebrations of Joshua Bates and George Peabody brought together diverse Americans to demonstrate the qualities of American nationality and the credibility of the United States to elite Britons. The proliferation of seating plans, menus, after-dinner speeches, and newspaper clippings in the archives of elite emigrants reveals the significant energy they invested in creating a space where Anglo-American elites could come together. During a European tour in 1851, the American author Pliny Miles wrote to Peabody that his "munificent hospitalities tend greatly to exalt our nation and our people in the opinion of Englishmen."[9] Miles's observations neatly encapsulated the entanglement between publicly reaffirming American nationality overseas and demonstrating national standing to foreign representatives.

These recognizably American spaces shaped transatlantic travel. Daniel Kilbride has persuasively demonstrated that travel reinforced nationalism through sociability. Chance encounters and self-conscious efforts made by tourists to seek out fellow Americans were a "source of comfort in foreign lands."[10] In the words of one traveler, they "produced a community of feeling" among countrymen.[11] More than providing opportunities for socialization, Britain's community of American residents structured the way Americans travelled. "The traveller—often the friendless traveller—stands greatly in need of good offices in a foreign land," reflected Edward Everett, minister to London between 1841 and 1845. Through his "large scale" hospitality, Everett continued, Peabody extended a service that "had hitherto been done to a very limited extent by our diplomatic representative abroad."[12] Americans overseas built and sustained the infrastructure that enabled these moments of national recognition to take place with regularity, be it through private dinners or lavish national celebrations. Although guidebooks empowered travelers to plan their own itineraries and book their own lodgings, they did not make it any easier for Americans to access British social circles. Elite emigrants, by contrast, possessed the standing to guarantee entry into British high society. As one traveler remarked of an American resident in London, "he is a connecting link between our countrymen and the great institutions of the British metropolis."[13]

Peabody's lavish entertainments represented just one vision of American nationhood to elite Britons at a time when a wider variety of nationalist emigrants pursued their own economic interests overseas. In the 1850s, cheaper transoceanic travel brought many non-elite migrants and travelers to Britain. At the same time as making larger public celebrations possible, these travelers diversified the number of voices claiming to be representative Americans, each on their own sectional and partisan terms. Perturbed by the Anglophilia and social exclusivity of elite migrants, these migrants founded the *London American* newspaper and the American Association in London to draw clearer distinctions between British society and the American community overseas. Among them were hot-headed Young Americans appointed to diplomatic posts in the Pierce and Buchanan administrations, who attacked elite emigrants as denationalized "place men, and place hunters."[14] While Democratic partisans in London scoffed at Whig emigrants' inclination toward the "tinsel of rank," in Manchester their Southern counterparts launched (from the offices of the American consulate) the *London Cotton Plant,* a combative newspaper lauding the alliance between the Empires of Cotton and Free Trade.[15]

In this era of nascent nationalisms, creating a national community overseas was the best means of achieving two complementary objectives. The first was to establish the standards of behavior expected of American citizens overseas. Nested within was the second objective of displaying to foreign publics that the United States was a harmonious and fully independent nation—if only these rival claimants to the title of representative Americans could agree on what values best represented American nationhood.

STRANGERS IN LONDON:
GENTILITY AND FOREIGN RELATIONS

The size, sounds, smells, and smog of London confounded American visitors. "If London could be cut up," wrote one traveler in 1857, "and taken in twelve separate, distinct doses, the effect might perhaps be pleasant and helpful, but as it is, swallowed whole, it nearly kills one."[16] Georgian and Victorian London was expanding rapidly. In 1800, the population of the city was close to one million people; by 1851 it had reached three and a half million and expanded to cover fifty square miles.[17] It was, reflected the youthful American traveler Theodore Witmer, a "grand crucible of humanity."[18] Its streets were snarled with cabs and omnibuses and the pavements choked with "the currents and eddies of human beings ever rushing," all enveloped in the thick coal-smoke fogs or "pea soupers" for which the capital was famous.[19] "It is difficult to conceive of *any* colour except black, which can long preserve its identity, in an atmosphere perpetually charged with coal-smoke, which would speedily tarnish a palace of gold," remembered Nathaniel Wheaton, whose sojourn in London was beset with a "violent catarrh" for the same reason.[20] Amidst the cacophony and fogs, "you are insensibly inclined, every now and then, to make a full stop, in order to realize the fact that you are actually in possession of your mind," advised the New Yorker George Wilkes.[21] For all that, London seemed to defy simple comparison. "It resembles Boston in its tortuosities; New York in its activity; Philadelphia in its magnificence," wrote Henry McLellan at the end of his first day in the city.[22]

After navigating the traffic, American visitors habitually checked into Morley's Hotel, on the eastern side of Trafalgar Square.[23] The hotel parlor was the scene of regular dinners, the guestbook was a reference directory of current residents, while on the ground floor was a Post Office, which provided transient Americans with a permanent address. London's resident Americans shared information with their visiting compatriots, extended invitations into the high society gatherings of the British aristocracy, and shared reflections on the differences between

British and American societies. Morley's was also home to two of the city's most prominent Americans, the Vermont-born brothers Henry and Benjamin Franklin Stevens, and the place from which they coordinated their transatlantic book trade. Safely checked in, visitors were not guaranteed a good night's sleep. "The first night in London I heard everytime I awoke a rushing sound which at first I thought was the river . . . It sounds like the falls of Niagara. This was the noise of the streets; the steady flow of carriages along the streets around you, rises and falls, swells and sinks, but never ceases day or night."[24]

A short cab ride along Regent's Street from Morley's brought visitors to the American Legation, at 45 Portland Place. At the head of the diplomatic household was the Minister's wife, who was the public face of the United States overseas. A great deal of labor fell on ministers' wives, who were responsible for managing the domestic servants, entertaining the diplomatic corps, and navigating the complex social customs and personal relationships of the court. Public and private space was collapsed in the diplomatic household—at any one time, it might also include foreign visitors and the legation's staff of attachés and secretaries as they conducted official business.[25] In the winter of 1846 Elizabeth Bancroft arrived in London with her husband George and within only a few short weeks found herself "in the full career of London society."[26] Elizabeth was responsible for finding accommodation for the family, hosting the customary first visits of the diplomatic corps, and arranging the purchase of new outfits fit to represent the United States in British high society.[27] In George's absence from the capital, Elizabeth represented the United States in London socially and acted as his political partner by keeping him abreast of the opinions she gathered at these public events.[28] In order to socialize freely with the diplomatic corps Elizabeth practiced French daily, arranged the appropriate court dress, and purchased liveries for the household's public retinue.[29] "Your father leaves all these matters to me," she wrote home, "and they have given me no little plague."[30] In the diplomats' world, ceremony and protocol communicated mutual respect and reciprocity to fellow diplomats, and the ability to adapt to the habits of the host country displayed one's place in the world of nations.[31] Women's diplomatic service therefore profoundly shaped United States public diplomacy.

Travelers often relied on the legation to structure their social lives abroad. The diplomatic household performed a variety of social functions for travelling Americans.[32] One of the Bancroft family's regular tasks was to entertain the "cosy little knot of Americans" they met each year in London.[33] These were occasions to socialize, but also for diplomats to vet those deemed worthy of being presented at court. "There is no judgement used by our Minister in these presentations," complained one secretary at the American Legation, "and a privilege evidently extended by the Sovereign for the most distinguished men of our country . . . is, thro' [sic] ignorance, perverted."[34] For travelers, it was an opportunity to secure tickets to watch a session at the Houses of Commons or to fashionable balls. Letters of introduction were a must for travelers seeking access to the social services of American diplomats.[35] These letters attested to the respectability of American citizens, enabling diplomats to carefully select those who would best represent the United States in British society. Constant social vetting and public performance was tiring and tiresome work. The "round of ceremonies, forms, and society," Elizabeth Bancroft wrote home, "is a new study, and invaluable for a short time; but I could not bear it for life."[36] It also drew the ire of some commentators who argued that "too often the Ambassadors of this country abroad, are rather sympathizers with nobles than with the people—with oppressors than with the oppressed."[37]

American society in London centered on Joshua Bates's West End home. Even prior to independence, the West End was home to a notable American colonial presence, as the South Carolinian planter aristocracy moved into the districts north of the New Road (later renamed Regent's Street).[38] Bates's residence transformed the area into an American center once more. The banker's home at 12 Portland Place was a prominent stop for Americans on the "card-and-call" trail of London society. "I find it next to impossible to pay attention to all," complained Bates.[39] "I always feel sorry," he wrote a decade later, "that I cannot devote as much time to my Country men and Country women as they deserve."[40] "It was no small gratification," wrote Joseph Tuckerman to his wife after being entertained by Bates, "at more than 3,000 miles from you to find myself with so many of our own neighbourhood."[41]

In Bates's conception of offshore citizenship, it was the duty of leading migrants to entertain travelers and uphold Atlantic gentility. Travelers were among the key agents interacting with and circulating knowledge about foreign peoples, but they often had deeply ambivalent responses to society and culture in Britain. Among some it stoked national chauvinism. "I know not who can travel with more advantage to himself, or to his country, than a citizen of the United States," wrote William Austin while studying at the Inns of Court, "for, the moment he arrives in Europe, the love of his own country becomes his predominant passion."[42] For others, travel was a struggle between admiration of some aspects of British refinement and strongly held convictions that its aristocracy was "strange and unnatural, if not unreasonable and unjust."[43] For Americans in Britain, travelers were informal embodiments of the United States overseas and possessed the power to shape foreign perception of the young republic. By cultivating genteel manners among American travelers without sacrificing democratic principle, Americans in Britain hoped to raise the international standing of the United States.

Travel was an opportunity for individual and national improvement.[44] Edward Everett, Minister to Great Britain between 1841 and 1845, complained after meeting a party of American travelers that "it grieves me to see how few of our young men who come abroad are sufficiently educated to derive any benefit from foreign travel."[45] Bates, too, complained of "a host of Americans here—some of our wildest schemers, whom I feel very much inclined to kick out of our doors whenever they come in."[46] The Bostonian fastidiously recorded the change in his visitors. "Mr. Ward, the agent of Gracie, Prime & Co.," he wrote to Thomas Wren Ward, "is a sensible man." Nonetheless, he warned, "his manners are objectionable in England, too voluble, but that will wear off. A residence of one year in London would make a perfect gentleman of him."[47] For the expanding American middle classes eager to attain social distinction, travel was an avenue to improvement. "Ropes has been with me this evening," Bates wrote; "he is really a very estimable man and I think you will find him much improved by this trip."[48]

Gentility and manners extended into the diplomatic presentation of the United States overseas by American travelers. London society was cosmopolitan and connections with foreign politicians and notables could be close.[49] In fact, the overseas guests at balls and dinner parties were one of their chief attractions. Just as American diplomats wrestled with the dilemma of both respecting court conventions and representing republican simplicity in their dress, American travelers struggled with the best way to embody the United States overseas.[50] Refined manners promoted the United States' standing in the world of nations, but nationalist outbursts or excessive servility to aristocratic rituals could just as easily reduce it. "Republicans should not cant, nor bluster, nor *slangwhag* any where," advised one journal; "if they condescend to visit monarchical countries, and wish to behold peculiar spectacles, they should conform to established etiquette."[51]

Anxious that the republic be properly represented, Bates played the part of gatekeeper between the would-be American gentry and British elites: those who had mastered Atlantic sociability would be granted access to his connections in British high society. While he found "much good society at command" amongst the American residents of London, "the most vexatious part of one's position here, is that all well bred Americans pass as Englishmen and the *extraordinary* characters . . . pass as exhibiting the true American character."[52] In a letter to Ward, Bates explained his concern that the United States be properly represented overseas:

> I, poor me!, find to what degree I love my country in the mortification I feel at her disgrace, and that it is so all pervading that I cannot say a word in her defence. . . . all efforts are useless and Americans abroad are doomed to that sort of sorrow that I can conceive a brother to feel for a loved sister who had deviated from the paths of virtue. . . . However, I did not mean to bore you with a subject that must be disagreeable to all *true* Americans.[53]

By weeding out those who could not navigate the social rituals of Atlantic gentility, Bates attempted to mediate cultural conflict between Americans and Britons and class tensions among American travelers. "If I bro't [sic] them together without first seeing what sort of people they were, I should offend the higher by mixing them with the lower," he explained to Ward, complaining that "the Americans display none of that equality, or want of aristocratic feeling, which they are famed for."[54] In contrast, Bates found his fellow-migrant George Peabody indiscriminate, since he entertained Americans "whether acquainted with them or not" and consequently "is in no society here."[55] In the transatlantic context of Britain's American community, manners were essential to the conduct of foreign relations: it was politically important that those Americans interacting with elite Britons and foreign diplomats possessed the requisite social standing.

Bates regarded his residence in Britain as a diplomatic mission to improve Anglo-American relations. In 1842, at the height of diplomatic disputes over the location of the Maine-New Brunswick border, he found the prospect of Anglo-American war "suicidal" and wrote four years later that it would be "perfect madness."[56] In 1853, his role as diplomat-financier was cemented after he was appointed umpire of the Anglo-American Joint Claims Convention.[57] Bates was also eager to found an American newspaper in Britain because "some means are wanted of spreading correct knowledge of the United States."[58] These diplomatic gestures were not disconnected from his lifelong fascination with high society in London. In fact, Bates attained a degree of distinction in

British society unmatched by other emigrants. His daughter Elizabeth married Sylvain Van Der Weyer, the Belgian ambassador of King Leopold I and future Prime Minister, which brought close contact with the Court of St James, and in 1842 Queen Victoria and Prince Albert became god-parents to the couple's second child.[59] Perhaps motivated by this social distinction, on April 28, 1842 Bates took the oath of loyalty to the Queen and a motion was passed in the House of Commons to permanently expatriate him from the United States.[60] Bates was careful to disguise his new subjecthood from his American correspondents, but it was a long time coming. "I conclude that you never have made up your mind whether you will return to the United States," Thomas Wren Ward wrote Bates in 1832. "We are driven along from day to day and from year to year by circumstances, and at last," Ward suggested, "find that the thread of life is spun out, or that habit has become fixed." Finally, he revealed, "My opinion has been that you would not leave London."[61]

Bates's preoccupation with regulating diplomatic respectability among American travelers highlights the centrality of American migrants to the formation of ideas about how the United States ought to be represented in the world. Since travelers and migrants were informal embodiments of the nation overseas, these encounters were treated as diplomatic events essential to demonstrating the United States' place in the world of nations. Commentators at home and abroad forewarned travelers not to take on "false pretensions as republicans" but to respect the "essential principles of courtesy, which everyone ambitious of the repute of a gentleman must beware of infringing."[62] These ideas were foundational to the civic nation-alism of American migrants in Britain. But, as will be shown later in this chapter, Young American nationalists rejected such claims, countering that the nation's character and role in the world were the natural outcome of providential republicanism. As this dispute raged in Britain's American community its members continued to shape the scope and nature of the United States' informal foreign relations in the Civil War era.

EXHIBITING THE UNITED STATES

The 1850s began with the defining international event of the Victorian era: the Great Exhibition in London's Hyde Park. The organizers of nineteenth century world's fairs attempted to categorize presumed global differences in national and racial capacity, and project an image of the orderly progress of civilization.[63] One element of that categorization was through encounters with foreign goods, which were thought to embody the underlying principles of their producing nation—powerful evidence that the production of commodity markets was profoundly cultural. Fairs were major transnational productions. Through them the masses of people who could not travel were introduced to the world and they were a platform for nations to present themselves to foreign publics. In London's Crystal Palace seventeen thousand exhibits, representing thirty-two countries, were viewed by six million visitors who gazed with wonder on the cornucopia of agricultural produce, luxury goods, and fine arts brought to London via Britain's empire of free trade. To Protectionist Whigs in the United States, the fair was christened the "Olympiad of British 'Free-trade' and Universal Humbug" and "Exhibition of British Supremacy and Industrious Toadyism of all nations."[64] For bullish Democrats it was an opportunity to prove that "a nest of non-producers in the shape of aristocrats" could not compete "with a young, vigorous, athletic republic like the United States."[65]

The Exhibition's geography itself projected a material and geopolitical map of domination over the world. Britain occupied half the space, while rival nations vied for places at the periphery, and colonial exhibits were reterritorialized around the precepts of imperial administration. For British historians, the Exhibition was a monument to the commodity culture of Victorian England and was at once a world's fair, department store, and shopping mall.[66] But above all the Exhibition blurred the boundary between culture and commodity. The items on display were used as measures of comparative national development and symbols of the progress of global civilization. In specially prepared newspaper supplements, richly illustrated catalogs, and travelogues recounting their voyages through the exhibition space, the British press analyzed the racial, social, and gendered meanings of each object.

Large numbers of Americans crossed the Atlantic to visit the Exhibition. In the estimate of one American commissioner, based on the registry at the American exhibit, as many as 4,000 may have visited by midsummer.[67] "London is full of Americans at present," reported the New York journalist George Wilkes.[68] To abolitionist William Wells Brown's delight, among the visitors were "a goodly sprinkling of my own countrymen, I mean colored men and women, well dressed and moving about with their fairer brethren. This, some of our pro-slavery Americans did not seem to relish."[69] Following a visit to the Crystal Palace, many tourists then traveled to Europe. For these journeys Americans were required to carry a passport, especially if they wanted to enter France.[70] By mid-century, passports were a common—although at twelve by eighteen inches in size not exactly convenient—proof of identity and authority of the issuing state.[71] At the American Legation, the number of passports issued rose dramatically: from 638 in 1845, the number almost doubled just five years later to 1,167, with a further 1,145 issued in the year of the Exhibition itself.[72] In many respects, then, the Exhibition was a major venue of American global connection, exposing American visitors to foreign cultures and broadcasting to the world an image of the United States' place in the community of nations. "It will soon be discovered that republicans in the far west are not so uncivilized as the minions of kingcraft would fain make the world believe," predicted the *New York Herald*.[73]

At the Exhibition's opening, the initial attempt to market the United States to the world was poorly managed—Congress being preoccupied with debating the Compromise of 1850. Having been belatedly appointed as Commissioner and Secretary to the Exhibition, Edward Riddle and Nathaniel S. Dodge arrived in London to find the American section in disarray and its allotted 40,000 square feet almost empty. Since they were unable to authorize any expenditure, the space remained empty on the opening day, leaving the commissioners and public to contemplate the giant cardboard eagle that overhung the display.[74] "The country and its products of art are appropriately typified," observed *Punch* shortly after the Exhibition's opening, "there being plenty of room, which is illustrative of one, and there being a poor supply of the other" (see figure 9).[75] "Why not have some choice specimens of slaves?" the satirical magazine added pointedly.[76]

As objects finally began to arrive, they were subjected to intense scrutiny as emblems of national characteristics. To many British observers, US products symbolized its agrarian simplicity. The United States was described by one official catalog as the "raw material of the whole exhibition," since "it is the demand for food . . . which drives the European to America." "How fitly, then, were the United States represented by ploughs, harrows, drills, wagons, sacks of corn, ears of maize, and barrels of salt meat," concluded its author.[77]

American observers poured scorn on the condescension of British commentators. Visiting the exhibition as jury chair for a technology exhibit, Horace Greeley attacked the "cool contempt" of the British press, who portrayed the United States as "a rude and semi-barbarous community of scattered grain-growers and herdsmen . . . utterly incompatible with a dense population, with general refinement, the upbuilding of Manufactures and the prevalence of the arts of civilized life." "What

THE GREAT DERBY RACE FOR EIGHTEEN HUNDRED AND FIFTY-ONE.

FIGURE 9. In John Leech's imagining of the race of nations, John Bull and Joseph Paxton, the Crystal Palace's designer, lead their foreign rivals. The Yankee Jonathan brings up the rear astride a mechanical contraption made from revolvers and knives, in reference to the mechanical objects displayed in the US section. Brother Jonathan has fallen behind the ranks of civilized nations and even behind a field of colonial participants riding camels, elephants, pigs, zebras and giraffes. In the political economy of "civilization," nations progressed through a process of stadial socio-economic development from hunter-gatherer, to pastoral, agrarian, and finally to an industrialized, commercial modernity (Horsman, *Race and Manifest Destiny*). Image: "The Great Derby Race for Eighteen Hundred and Fifty-One," *Punch*, Jan-June 1851, Punch Cartoon Library / TopFoto.

would you have?" Greeley sneered, since "for years you have been devoting your energies to the task of convincing our people that they should grow Food and Cotton and send them hither in exchange for Wares and Fabrics."[78] Impressed by the wealth and productivity of the British Empire, Greeley nevertheless rejected its message of Free Trade. Instead, the editor fell back on Whig economic orthodoxy to argue that a shield of protective tariffs was the surest guarantor of national development and would create an economically diversified country in which industry would take its place alongside agriculture. Such a program would gradually wean the United States from "its present semi-Colonial dependence on European tastes, European fashions, [and] European fabrication."[79]

For Whigs at home, free trade was synonymous with the "British system." The Whig political economist and "Ajax of Protection" Henry

Carey argued that British free trade "consists in the maintenance of *monopoly,*" was not in keeping with the harmony of interests among nations, and was therefore "repulsive."[80] The British system, Carey wrote in his *Principles of Social Science,* subordinated peripheral, developing economies to the "oppressions" that resulted from "trading centralization."[81] Using the analogy of a wheel, with Britain as its central hub from which emanated "spokes of enormous length," Carey described how "nothing but the most perfect steadiness of movement, would prevent the disruption of its various parts." The peripheral places on each spoke (labelled Kansas, Carolina, Cuba, Mexico, Peru, Chile, India, and Australia) would be ruined under any other circumstances, "the hub alone remaining whole and undisturbed." So it was, Carey surmised, that the world was "dependent on the chances and changes of the British market."[82] Protection, used by Carey in a broad sense that recalled Madison's 1799 warning against "foreign influence" to mean defense against the free movement of British goods and so morals, culture, and ideas into the interior of the United States, was the only answer. Should the United States succumb to the dangerous doctrines of the British System celebrated at the Exhibition, argued one observer in the *American Whig Review,* "the commercial, manufactural, and political ideas of the United States" would be "centralized on London."[83]

In contrast, the emboldened commercial wing of the Democratic Party celebrated free trade's advance. Britain's 1846 abolition of the Corn Laws and its relaxation of the Navigation Acts allowing foreign participation in its intercolonial trade, it was argued, opened the pathway to the economic independence long denied the United States by British mercantilism.[84] Combined with the passage of the Walker Tariff of 1846—the brainchild of a coalition of Southern planters and Western grain producers— Democrats began celebrating the dawn of a decade and a half of freer trade that was arrested only with the Morrill Tariff of 1861. Though free trade had been a Jacksonian article of faith, Young American Democrats viewed it less as the safeguard against monopolistic special interest and more as the precondition for a new era of national economic development and expansion.[85] Nationalistic Democrats thus enjoyed an unlikely partnership with emigrant financiers who successfully negotiated the Mexican War Loan of 1848 and marketed the railroad bonds so central to many Young Democrats' pet infrastructure projects.[86] Yet, as we shall see, even limited cooperation with transatlantic financiers was a bitter pill to swallow for a party so adept at exploiting the rhetorical power of Anglophobia and anti-financier rhetoric in mid-nineteenth-century politics.

Nevertheless, the new Democrats had moved some way toward the views of Americans in Britain who witnessed the limits of US independence firsthand, but also saw the mutual benefits of a thriving Atlantic economy. To promote Atlantic commerce, American emigrants took an active role in shaping the US exhibits at the Crystal Palace. The financier George Peabody advanced the American legation a loan of £3,000 (equivalent to more than £400,000 today) to improve the exhibit and avoid further damage to the republic's international reputation.[87] Keenly aware of the opportunity presented by the exhibition to penetrate European markets and showcase the United States' potential to overseas investors, Peabody had powerful motives for intervening. He was not alone in this assessment. From his desk at the Legation, US minister to London Abbott Lawrence tried to convince James Buchanan in the State Department in the year before the Exhibition that "specimens of the productions of our labour should be sent here' since he was "quite certain that new markets will be opened for their introduction, and our exports increased."[88] When the American exhibits finally arrived British observers were impressed (see figure 10). Altogether American products won more than one hundred and fifty awards at the Exhibition, with McCormick's grain reaper and Colt's repeating pistol singled out by the judges. In contrast to the derision of *Punch*, the *Liverpool Times* declared that "the Yankees are no longer to be ridiculed, much less despised. The new world is bursting into greatness."[89] To many Americans, the Exhibition provided tangible evidence that the United States was internationally competitive, for others that humanity was "becoming more cosmopolite."[90]

To capitalize on the inflated number of Americans in London and the international platform the Exhibition provided, Peabody transformed his usually private Fourth of July dinners into a public fête (figure 11). By mid-century, Peabody's offices in the City were a prominent social center for Americans in Britain. Throughout its operation, Peabody explained, he had "endeavoured in the constitution of its members, and the character of its business, to make it *an American house,* and to give it an *American atmosphere:* to fill it with American journals; to make it a centre for American news and an agreeable place for every American friend in London."[91] At Peabody's office, American visitors could also cash letters of credit, a routine transaction among Anglo-American banks by the 1840s.[92] Peabody set aside large sums of money each year for the entertainment of Americans at sumptuous dinners held at the Star and Garter Hotel, retained an opera box for his American clientele, and dispensed barrels of American apples, Boston crackers, and hominy grits.[93] In one week alone

FIGURE 10. The United States' display at the London Exhibition of 1851 was an esoteric collection that included samples of metal ore, including gold, iron, and a large boulder of zinc ore from New Jersey weighing 16,400 pounds, seen on the right. In the center is a full-sized model of Nathaniel Rider's Suspension Truss Bridge and, behind that, a lump of vulcanized rubber, exhibited by the Goodyear Rubber Company. On the left is a bag of corn, accompanied by bales of cotton from Southern plantations. Somewhat incongruously, the exhibit also included daguerreotypes and a prosthetic limb. The centerpiece of the exhibit, however, was Hiram Powers's white marble sculpture, "The Greek Slave" (seen here with a velvet curtain surrounding it), a female nude sat on a revolving turntable. Image: *Dickinson's Comprehensive Pictures of the Great Exhibition of 1851, from the originals painted for . . . Prince Albert, by Messrs. Nash, Haghe and Roberts* (London, 1854), © British Library Board. All Rights Reserved / Bridgeman Images.

Peabody dined with eighty visiting Americans, and took another thirty-five to the opera.[94] Writing home to his wife in May 1858, the historian John Lothrop Motely explained that he had been "Peabodied."[95] "In bringing the best men of England and America together," argued another traveler, Peabody "cement[ed] a strong national friendly feeling."[96]

For the 1851 dinner, eight hundred American and British guests crowded Willis's Rooms in London's fashionable West End. Such balls were a central feature of political life in the capital and the style and success of society entertainments were key markers of status.[97] Peabody's aim was to show "that all hostile feeling[s] . . . have ceased to have any place

FIGURE 11. George Peabody was an adroit public diplomat whose annual celebrations of Washington's Birthday and the Fourth of July were a central feature of the London Season and brought together Anglo-American elites, "thus uniting the representatives of the two great clans of rival cousins in a magnificent *fete de famille*" ("Fourth of July at London—Mr. Peabody's Festival," *Cleveland Herald,* July 25, 1851). His wealth also enabled successive American Ministers to participate in the Season with none of the expense or sacrifice of republican principles that many commentators feared would result from participation in the social rituals of Great Power diplomacy. Image: "Grand Entertainment to the American Minister," *Illustrated London News,* July 19, 1851, © British Library Board. All Rights Reserved / Bridgeman Images.

in the breasts of the citizens of either of the two great Anglo-Saxon nations."⁹⁸ The spacious ball room was canopied with entwined American and British flags in celebration of the anniversary of American Independence and decorated with busts of Queen Victoria, Prince Albert, George Washington, and Benjamin Franklin. Peabody brought together US consuls from across the UK and Europe, with high-ranking British officials and members of Lord John Russell's Cabinet and the Queen's household, including Sir Edward Cust, the Master of Ceremonies at court responsible for meeting and introducing foreign dignitaries; Charles Wood, Chancellor of the Exchequer; and the government's chief whip, Lord Marcus Hill. Peabody thus exerted his tremendous social and diplomatic power to offer the United States' representatives an opportunity to create contacts and publicly express their respect for one another. The public diplomacy climaxed with the arrival, late in the evening, of the Duke of Wellington, who sat beneath a portrait of George Washington to a "prolonged burst of cheering."[99] Acting on Whig-Yankee ideas of social service, the patrician Peabody used his private fortune to bring a harmony of cultural, social, and economic exchanges to transatlantic relations. Such internationalism drew deeply on the United States' colonial cultural inheritance. "Your idea to bring together the inhabitants of two of the greatest nations upon Earth, united by the ties of blood with a common ancestry," wrote fellow Whig Abbott Lawrence, the American Minister, would "be productive in consummating that harmony of international feeling which should exist between *parent* and *child.*" Lawrence concluded, "I hope and believe that this kind international feeling may strengthen with age."[100]

Peabody also hosted a dinner for one hundred and fifty American and British businessmen and politicians at the London Coffee House, Ludgate Hill. Once again, Peabody cultivated an audience of high-ranking British and American diners. Seated among the American consuls, exhibition commissioners, and traveling entrepreneurs were vice president of the Board of Trade Lord Granville (who would become Secretary of Foreign Affairs in December that year); Thomson Hankey, Governor of the Bank of England; Thomas Baring; and numerous British importers and newspaper editors. With negotiations over a proposed Isthmian Canal high on the diplomatic agenda, it was perhaps unsurprising that the former British *chargé d'affaires* to Bolivia and Minister to Buenos Aires Lieutenant-Colonel J. A. Lloyd; William Gore Ousley; and Sir Henry Bulwer, former minister to Washington and signatory of the Clayton-Bulwer Treaty, were also present.

The business of emigrant foreign relations—establishing trust between diplomatic officials and creating new social and political contacts—was conducted in public dinners of this sort, where elite migrants demonstrated their gentlemanly standing through ceremonial toasts and speechmaking. As the historian Thomas Otte has detailed, members of the British foreign service placed great emphasis on the importance of gentlemanly conduct in international relations and expected foreign diplomats to con-

duct themselves by the same standards.[101] Displays of gentlemanly standing were the primary means of international reciprocity in the Great
Power System. As the senior British diplomat Sir Henry Bulwer told Peabody's guests, public dinners were the most effective means of making "as
public as possible, on all occasions, those great points of union, that must
connect two nations."[102] The dinner was replete with public diplomatic
ceremony aimed at fostering Anglo-American reciprocity. Peabody resur-
rected the ancient custom of circulating a "Loving Cup" to promote
"kind and brotherly feelings between Englishmen and Americans."[103]
While passing the cup each man bowed to his neighbor, who removed the
cover with his "dagger hand" and then drank with the other. "Happily,"
the official proceedings recorded, there was "no longer a 'dagger-hand'
between the United States and England."[104]

The social world of diplomacy was also the venue at which nations
were measured against one another. "I believe it to be a great misfortune
to a nation to be isolated from the world," argued John Chandler Bancroft Davis, secretary at the American Legation, since it was "only by
measuring ourselves with other nations, that we learn our real strength,
and learn, too, our weak points."[105] For Britons and Americans alike, the
harmony of the Atlantic world depended on shared cultural and commercial exchange. Bulwer celebrated a stable transatlantic connection
between nations of "one origin" and "one language," which "also trans-
act their greatest amount of business with each other."[106] As Abbott Lawrence termed it, Britain and the United States shared "the same of *everything* that makes the *man.*"[107] Reflecting on the value of commerce
between the two nations, Thomson Hankey, Governor of the Bank of
England, felt "convinced that we must have a mutual interest in the prosperity of each other." Following from these views the Governor asked, "is
it unnatural that *I* should feel a strong desire to see a sort of 'Zolverein'
[sic] established between the United States and my own country?"[108]

Such a union may have been fantasy (and would continue to be, as
explored in chapter 5), but the frequent expression of this dream was
evidence that transatlantic peace was high on the agenda of Anglo-
American financiers. In Peabody's view the dinners of 1851 promoted a
dialogue "formed on social intercourse and personal friendship" among
the transatlantic business elite that would underpin financial, political,
and diplomatic connections.[109] For the advocates of transatlantic cooperation, this was not the route back to colonial dependence that many
feared but the surest way to secure American economic development and
independence. Yet this stance raised one of the fundamental dynamics of

pre-Civil War American politics. For as long as this model of competitive international interests persisted, the conspiratorial model of colonial dependence would exist as its natural corollary. Similarly, while American migrants continued to be the forefront of transnational contact in the Civil War era, they would be vulnerable to conspiratorial claims that they were the agents of a British plot to recolonize the United States. Ironically, these attacks came from hot-headed Young America, the wing of the Democratic Party most open to a world of free trade.

DENATIONALIZATION

In 1855, John T. Pitman joined Michael Nourse & Co. American & General Patent Agency at 67 Gracechurch Street, at the heart of the City of London. The Rhode Islander quickly adjusted to life overseas, writing to his wife in October 1855 that "I begin to realize though slowly that it may not be all a dream and that I may strangely and mysteriously and for what end I know not, become a citizen of this Great metropolis of the business world."[110] After his family arrived in London, the Pitmans' eldest son John was sent to school in Brunswick, Germany. John Jr.'s residence abroad, however, soon became a source of great anxiety. Early in his stay, John warned his son to "be a little more careful in the spelling or you may possibly forget the orthography of your native tongue."[111] As a visit to England approached, Pitman asked his son whether "it will be difficult to re-acquire your mother-tongue immediately on your return?"[112] A year later, when his studies were coming to an end, Pitman warned that "there is much to like and admire in the German character, yet for a person who is to live and obtain his livelihood in America he must not be too long absent to be *de-Americanized*."[113]

Denationalization was a striking problem for American migrants. As one recent historian of Civil War-era nationalism has argued, national identity was a "variable and multidimensional concept" that people related to in different ways in changing contexts.[114] The complexity of American nationalism was especially evident in Britain's American community, since it witnessed firsthand the shifting intellectual currents of nationhood in the nineteenth-century Atlantic world.[115] New definitions of nationhood and nationalism that originated in Europe emphasized the importance of languages, culture, history, and sometimes race to nationality.[116] Romantic nationalism on both sides of the Atlantic became more particularistic, yet it linked increasing numbers of people to global currents of thought, and nationalists themselves mixed it with cosmopolitan and universal strands that dated back to the Age of Revolution.[117] Living as American citizens in the Atlantic world but beyond the United States' territorial borders, Americans in Britain developed their own ideology of nationalism that embedded the United States deeply in world events.

Despite the frequent claim that nationalism was the supreme form of cultural and political allegiance, antebellum Americans readily accepted its pliability. Unless a ceaseless vigil was maintained, national characteristics could be lost and new ones acquired—especially for those residing overseas and in close proximity to aristocratic institutions.[118] "Republicanism appears to fade more and more out of the characters of a certain class of men, the longer they reside near the glitter and pomp of European courts," claimed one 1849 assessment.[119] Torn between their loyalty to the Union and their lives overseas, many Americans in Britain worried that they might involuntarily lose their nationality. Travelling through Britain to promote the international Bonds of Brotherhood at the center of his peace crusade, Elihu Burritt recorded in his journal after just one year in London that "I am ceasing to be an American, and must return to go through the country."[120] Rejecting the usual analogy of shared Anglo-American kinship, Oliver Wendell Holmes counselled fellow Bostonian John Lothrop Motley not to "stay too long" in England for, "if all the blood gets out of your veins, I am afraid you will transfer your allegiance."[121]

The fear of denationalization, and with it a transfusion of anti-republican values, was felt acutely by Americans resident in non-English speaking parts of the world. Language and nationalism became particularly entwined and a dilemma for many Americans exposed to foreign languages. As one traveler dramatically described it, "the air into which the sounds of foreign speech are for ever rising, is the very atmosphere of exile."[122] Like many of his American contemporaries, J. Pierpont Morgan was enrolled at Göttingen University by his father, Junius Spencer Morgan, who was then the partner of George Peabody.[123] Upon arrival Pierpont found a thriving community of American students in the town, most of whom had enrolled as chemists and engineers.[124] In correspondence to his cousin, James Goodwin, Pierpont described in detail the life of the "American colony." Americans were "pretty well posted upon NY news,"[125] thanks to the circulation of American newspapers; held a regular "blow out" at the Bettman Hotel in the town;[126] and even held their own election in 1856 at which the result was "Buchanan 8, Frémont 5,

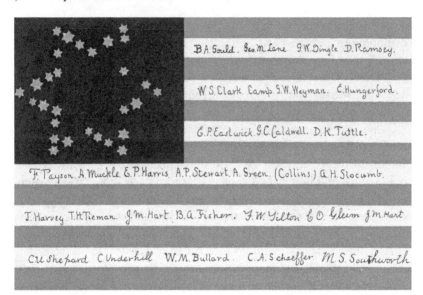

FIGURE 12. In the colony's official history of itself, American students could be found studying at Göttingen since 1812, but it was not until 1855 that the "patriarch" was given the responsibility of officially recording all the activities of the student body. The American students gathered regularly to dine and celebrate American national holidays and in 1861 formed their own baseball team. Image: The American Colony at Göttingen's Flag, Box 1, Folder 37, JP Morgan Papers, The Morgan Library & Museum. ARC 1196.

Fillmore 4."[127] Members of the Göttingen colony recorded their history in a scrapbook and from 1848 handed down a flag to the "patriarch" inscribed with his predecessor's names (figure 12).[128]

American communities in Göttingen, Paris, Rome, and Florence all began using the term "colony" in the 1850s at the precise moment when a generationally conscious Young American movement came to political prominence in the Democratic Party.[129] Historians have most commonly discussed Young America as a romantic nationalist cultural movement that took shape in the pages of John L. O'Sullivan's *Democratic Review* and Evert Duycknick's *New York Literary World*.[130] By the 1840s, Young American authors attempted to jettison the United States' intellectual ancestry by celebrating through literature the nation's unique commitment to the political ideals of liberty and equality, its system of Federalism, and the abundance of its natural environment. But, as Yonatan Eyal has highlighted, "Young America" was a moniker adopted by political operatives, party hacks, and editors within a faction of the Democratic Party. Driven domestically by an agenda of economic and constitutional change, and internationally by the energy of European revolutionaries, Young Americans were deeply engaged with the new demands of an internationally connected age. In many instances American "colonies" in European capitals were the staging grounds for attempts to extend republicanism into the despotic Old World.[131]

Young Americans drew on much wider trends in American culture that excited interest in a new international age. American tourism and travel writing extended the nation's geographic and cultural footprint in the late 1840s and 1850s, as rising incomes in the United States and falling travel costs enabled more Americans to undertake even a modest international trip. *Putnam's, Harper's,* and *Scribner's,* but above all the travel guides published by the London publisher John Murray whetted the public appetite for international engagement with descriptions of foreign ports, peoples, and products. Best-selling travel books by Bayard Taylor, Samuel Sullivan Cox, and Henry Tuckerman popularized European travel even as they reinforced notions of national exceptionalism, Anglophobia, and anti-Catholicism.[132] Travel itineraries were shaped directly by these guides as "commodification transformed travel from a self-created activity to a service purchased from others."[133] In all, Julie Hall estimates that eighteen hundred travel books were published by Americans before 1900.[134] The American reading public therefore made international comparisons habitually and through them placed the United States among the world of nations.

By mid-century, then, American nationalism was inescapably transnational. Just as Young American nationalists felt a patriotic duty to protect the nation from the threat of foreign aristocracy, they felt a duty to spread the benefits of American democracy across the world.[135] Internationally engaged Young American nationalists spread these ideas through American communities overseas as they swelled the ranks of travelers and diplomats. In the American colony at Göttingen, for instance, the historian George Bancroft rubbed shoulders with George Haven Putnam, son of the eponymous London-based publisher and European distributor of the *Democratic Review.* During the Pierce and Buchanan administrations and in the febrile atmosphere of the 1850s, European capitals hosted some of the most incendiary diplomats of the antebellum period. Secretary of State William Marcy stationed John L. O'Sullivan in Lisbon; Louisianan fire-eater Pierre Soulé to the Spanish

court; and August Belmont to the Hague. In Britain, Nathaniel Hawthorne, whose career owed a great debt to the literary circle that orbited
the *Democratic Review,* became the American consul to Liverpool and
Manchester; the *Review*'s former editor, George Sanders, was appointed,
though never confirmed, as Consul General in London; and Daniel
Edgar Sickles was appointed private secretary to James Buchanan at the
American Legation.[136]

Sickles, a hot-tempered New York Democrat who took up his post in
September 1853, soon earned notoriety for his involvement in a diplomatic impasse at Peabody's annual Fourth of July banquet a year later,
his querulous Young American nationalism having been affronted by
the prospect of an American holiday becoming a celebration of transatlantic rapprochement.[137] The clash was larger than the personalities
involved. At stake were competing visions of the United States' engagement with the world in the Civil War era. Sickles no doubt had in mind
a dinner hosted in London earlier in the year by George Sanders. Sanders, a headstrong Kentuckian, hosted a private dinner to celebrate
Washington's Birthday at which he gathered together the luminaries of
the European revolutions, including Giuseppe Mazzini, Garibaldi,
Louis Kossuth, and the hero of the French barricades Alexandre-
Auguste Ledru-Rollin. By endorsing European revolutionaries, Sanders
defined the priorities of Young American internationalism: to spread the
ideas of republican self-government and liberty in the Old World and
abet the overthrow of the *ancien régime.*[138]

Pierce's diplomatic service was imbued with Young American zeal to
transform international affairs and burnish the United States' reputation
as the haven of global republicanism. In this spirit, Sickles demanded
that Peabody restrict participation to Americans only. Peabody refused.[139]
Far from appeased, Sickles was enraged when he found that the portrait
of George Washington was dwarfed by life-sized portraits of Queen Victoria and Prince Albert, while President Pierce had none at all. Lines
uncomplimentary to the British in the "Star Spangled Banner" and "Hail
Columbia" had been removed, which Sickles viewed as a "mutila-
tion."[140] Having endured the passing of the loving cup, the climactic
moment came when Sickles discovered that toasts to Queen Victoria
would be drunk before those to Washington. After Peabody's tribute to
Victoria, Sickles, dressed in the uniform of a Brigadier General of the
New York State Militia, walked from the room instead of drinking.
Hoping to defuse the impasse, which was the talk of fashionable London, Buchanan seized the outbreak of the Spanish Revolution as a pre-

text to send Sickles back to Washington to seek instruction on Cuban policy from the Secretary of State.[141]

Back in the United States, and keen to burnish his Anglophobic credentials, Sickles attacked Peabody's presentation of the United States to the world in the American press. In a letter to the *Boston Post,* Sickles charged that "an unusual amount of 'toadying' was ... done to the Queen and the English." Peabody, Sickles alleged, had delivered "a most servile speech," that offered the President only "lukewarm introductory remarks."[142] Peabody replied through the *Post* and the *Boston Daily Atlas,* defending his actions on the grounds that they were the most diplomatic way to present the United States to British audiences.[143] But that was exactly Sickles's point. From Sickles's vantage, Peabody's "toadying" undermined Young America's faith in the United States as the guardian of international republicanism against the Old World. From Peabody's perspective, a secure United States depended on "a reciprocal dependence" between the two nations.[144] Peabody's view of transatlantic relations flowed seamlessly into his view of the relationship between his attachment to both Britain and the United States: "If I had been born in England I should love it above all other countries, but I happen to be a New Englander and therefore the United States holds the first place in my affections. England ranks next and I am happy to believe that such is the feeling of my countrymen."[145]

Underlying Sickles's nationalist outburst were postcolonial anxieties that American claims to nationhood were being undermined by a transatlantic aristocracy determined to hitch the republic to Britain's economic empire. "These states produce a very considerable number of the worst kind of toadies," opined the Anglophobic newspaper *Young America* shortly after news of the affair broke across the Atlantic, "most of whom flourish by pandering to foreign prejudices and ignoring their own nationality" to become "nabobs and millionaires."[146] These conspiratorial anxieties reflected the ceaseless vigil over individual virtue (and therefore the fate of the nation) that had been central to American nationalism from the beginning, but were also evidence of the growing Romantic notion that an emotional attachment to a particular land or place connected individuals to the nation.[147] As this idea moved to the center of American nationalism, the argument that Americans abroad retained, or even could retain, their voluntary connection to the United States was viewed with increasing hostility. "The right of expatriation is an undeniable one," continued the same editorial in *Young America,* adding that any American should be commended "for publicly proclaiming and exercising his desires in that regard." Peabody had been denationalized, however, and become an "American with an *English heart, English ideas, and English tastes*," whom "true republicans should despise and repudiate." Even though John Bull was "an obnoxious specimen of humanity," even *he* was not guilty of "dodging his nationality, or yielding the preference to any other race or nation."[148] More directly, one outraged correspondent wrote Peabody that he was a "disgrace to the whole Peabody race" and "no longer fit to be called an American citizen."[149]

Peabody and the Young Americans clashed over the intersection of nationality and the duties of international engagement. While Young Americans hoped to change international politics through a radical agenda of intervening in European revolutions (both materially and by example), Peabody hoped to broker a fundamental shift in the Atlantic economy through cooperation. As a guardian of American finances in Britain, he hoped one day to combine Anglo-American rapprochement with making the republic "so developed as to make it independent of the world, and of this Island in particular."[150] Fourth of July celebrations were therefore part of a larger effort at offshore community-building. Standing the argument that residence overseas promoted denationalization on its head, Peabody credited his eighteen-year stint in Britain with having "eradicated the party and sectional feeling which had some influence with me in early life." As a result, he coolly replied to Sickles it "has strengthened my interest in whatever affects the welfare or honor of the whole country."[151] To the Whig editors, significantly endangering transatlantic relations on the flimsy pretext offered by Sickles was a fool's errand. "If there is a true hearted American abroad," reflected one editorial about Peabody, "it is he."[152]

Sickles, meanwhile, mixed concern over the United States' representation overseas with political calculation. "Bent on making capital out of this rare chance," suggested the *New York Herald,* Sickles "anticipated with relish the enthusiastic admiration his conduct would excite." Returning home "an object of patriotic ovation," his path would be "straight to the door of the next presidency."[153] Yet hot-tempered Young Americans in the diplomatic corps and expansionist forays into South America and Cuba stretched American diplomatic credibility in Europe. "Bad enough before," remarked an editorial in *The Examiner,* American diplomacy had now "descended to worse." Sickles's assault, it reflected, did "not illustrate very favourably either the mind or manners of *Young America*."[154] Attacking the nationalism of Young America carried an additional barb in the language of transatlantic diplomacy. Young America and Old England were frequently paired in

British analyses of Anglo-American relations, where "Young America" epitomized the inexperience and juvenility of the republic. At home, *The National Era* called for the immediate recall of "Sickles, Sanders, & Co.," and their replacement with "men who understand the nature of modern civilization," and were "not willing to class the United States with Turkey, Brazil, and Dahomey."[155]

"What higher compliment can an Englishman pay to the United States . . . than to join in celebrating the anniversary of their Declaration of Independence?" the editorial continued, caustically remarking, "we were wrong in the revolutionary war, and now we rejoice in our own misfortune, and we love to acknowledge the inestimable services to liberty of the founders of the Union." It was the worst kind of demagoguery to be "prepared to cultivate ill will with England, at all hazards, and out of all circumstances . . . to gain the most miserable party advantage in America."[156] The fallout from Sickles's outburst further emphasizes that Americans overseas maintained the delicate balance of American foreign relations. Outbreaks of American nationalism overseas were balanced against an account of confidence in the transatlantic connection. As Sickles debited that account, British financiers and politicians looked more askance at American imperialism in the Caribbean and Central America. The United States' ministers to France, Britain, and Spain made a further withdrawal as the editorial went to print, meeting in Ostend for the most public of private discussions regarding the beleaguered island of Cuba. The error-strewn summer of 1854 severely shook confidence in the conduct of American foreign policy and sent the value of American bonds in London tumbling.[157]

Sickles's proscriptions on membership within an overseas national community foreshadowed a hardening of domestic attitudes towards expatriation. "In theory every American is presumed to prefer his own country and her institutions before any other under the sun," began an article titled "The folly of expatriation" in *The Daily National Intelligencer,* "yet what are thousands of them doing, and other tens of thousands trying to do if they can? Abandoning that country, turning their backs upon its Government for the sake of living in Europe." To the *Intelligencer* this was "a libel of the worst kind" since it "affirms by his conduct that the laws, institutions, and Government of his native land have been over-estimated, are not what they have been represented, have no advantage over others." Expatriation was a rejection of the nation, and the expatriate "sells his birthright" in a declaration by act "that the American experiment therefore is a failure."[158]

The controversial character of overseas residence in the 1850s prompted both Buchanan and his Secretary of State Lewis Cass to request legal clarification from their Attorney General Jeremiah S. Black. "There is no *mode* of renunciation prescribed," Black wrote Cass in August 1857. But the Attorney General laid out the accepted practices that constituted legal expatriation, stating that, in his "opinion, if he emigrates, carries his family and effects along with him, manifests a plain intention not to return, takes up his permanent residence abroad, and assumes the obligation of a subject to a foreign government . . . I do not think we could or would afterwards claim from him any of the duties of a citizen."[159] But still, it remained an open question who would make these determinations. Two years later, Black was even more emphatic, declaring that "the general right . . . of expatriation, is incontestable." "Upon that principle this country was populated," he continued, and "we owe to it our existence as a nation."[160] Yet expatriation was not simply a legal state. Because emigrants crossed the categories of traveler, settler, and diplomat, the meanings and purposes of migration were shaped beyond the reach of the statute book in the crucible of American communities around the globe.[161]

Americans in Britain navigated the tensions of creating a new American nationalism in the antebellum era "on the ground" through the variety of social and commercial institutions they created in London and Liverpool. As the 1850s progressed, Americans in Britain continued to lead the debate over the United States' role in world affairs, but the range of voices increased. In Liverpool, Americans used metaphors of commercial empire to depict their residence abroad as the natural outcome of the United States' material Manifest Destiny. For Southerners in the port, that international mission encompassed a global defense of free trade and plantation slavery, which they brought self-confidently to British shores. Meanwhile, in London the trend towards greater proscriptions on offshore nationalism continued. But rather than rely on socially exclusive financiers, overseas community-building was propelled through new institutions that sought to purposefully bring together the disparate elements of Britain's American migrants.

SECTIONAL NATIONALISM IN LIVERPOOL

On June 22, 1857, the USS *Niagara* dropped anchor in the River Mersey. Refitted with complex spooling coils, the sloop was to attempt the laying of the transatlantic telegraph. While preparations for departure continued aboard ship, its officers were courted by city officials hoping to promote the benefits of the joint Anglo-American mission. The city's American community used the occasion to expand its usual annual celebration of American independence. Invitations for a banquet at the Adelphi Hotel were sent to the ship's officers by Stephen Barker Guion, the Black Ball Line's agent in the port and a rising member of Liverpool's emigrant community. Fifty Americans crowded into the Adelphi's dining hall, decorated with engravings of the signing of the Declaration of Independence, President Washington, and the voyage of the *Niagara*. Significantly, this was an Americans-only event designed, in the words of New Yorker Daniel James, resident in Liverpool for three decades, to "let the great nation on the other side of the Atlantic know that her sons have not forgotten her."[162]

Despite the establishment of the American Chamber of Commerce (ACC) at the turn of the nineteenth century, by contrast with events in London American national consciousness in Liverpool developed slowly. The dominance of British merchants in the ACC tempered its nationalist content, and although the Chamber assumed many American civic functions, such as the greeting of American ministers to Great Britain, the language on these occasions was often formally diplomatic and the participants almost entirely British.[163] The mobility of the mercantile community of Liverpool further stalled the development of American civic life in the city. Nonetheless, the port's American residents grappled directly with the tensions of Civil War-era nationalism and internationalism.

The arrival of the *Niagara* appeared to be an opportune moment for the Adelphi dinner's attendees to declare their independence from British institutions. Hoping to extend American exports, Young Americans struck a chord strikingly like that of economic imperialists—echoed by their counterparts in the 1890s (chapter 5).[164] Charles Gano Baylor, the US consul at Manchester, evoked the militant tone of this overseas consciousness, declaring that "our merchants are literally taking possession of the wharves of Europe."[165] The rhetoric of economic nationalism peaked with the oration of George Francis Train. This eccentric tram promoter and world traveler, a Bostonian, fashioned himself as a proponent of "that Young America which pours its energies through all the channels of commerce in all quarters of the globe."[166] Train was equal parts Young American nationalist, Anglophobe, and racial Anglo-Saxonist, a set of lifetime priorities he merged in a brash ideology termed "Spread-Eagleism."

"Train of Boston was instantly upon his legs," editorialized the *New York Tribune*, "and was after that lion in an instant."[167] Responding to the toast of "Our Country," Train set forth a celebration of the United States' commercial ascendancy. "Our eagle stoops to no small flight," he blustered, "as our country is the first of nations." "Stand back, old mother land," he warned, invoking threats of American hegemony over Atlantic commerce, "think of the cotton and the corn—look at our commerce—*remember our history.*" Britain had not to "forget that America is your truest friend, where blood and kindred, laws and religion, bind us by annual contract of one hundred millions sterling to keep the peace." Train's interpretation of Anglo-American friendship was distinctly ambivalent and illustrates one of the central problems of prewar American nationalism: how could Americans strengthen the national community while simultaneously acknowledging the cultural inheritance and material interests that connected them to the British Empire? "Grand as will be the union of the two great Saxon empires," he surmised in a final broadside, "the union of our own fair country is dearer to every American than ought beside."[168]

Train's cocktail of Young American nationalism and Anglo-Saxonism found a receptive audience amongst Liverpool's American community. On the surface, Young Americans' commitment to international free trade and faith in the power of expanding markets also moved them closer to Whig Anglophiles in London. Transatlantic financiers hoped that freer trade between the two nations would reduce the volatility of transatlantic relations, producing a more stable economic environment for the sale of American securities in London and prosperous interdependent trade. Nonetheless, although transatlantic financiers were attracted to Southern advocacy of tariff reductions, most found it hard to cross the Rubicon of slavery. Joshua Bates wished the "the whole country was like New England," since "it would be the happiest country in the world."[169] This divide widened in the 1850s as the belligerence of Southern diplomacy increased. Young American nationalism gained little traction among American financiers in London, not least because of its Anglophobia, but also because many of their connections operated on a London-Wall Street axis—an orientation that took on extreme importance in the Civil War, as will be explored in the next chapter.

By the 1850s, sectional nationalism thrived among Liverpool's American cotton merchants. In the two decades preceding the civil war, cotton imports rose rapidly. Brokering the cotton bales' sale to British clients were prominent Southerners centered around the South Carolinian bank Fraser, Trenholm & Co.[170] Buoyed by ever-strong cotton sales, Southerners in the United States and Britain read with interest about the role of cotton in the industrial pre-eminence of Great Britain, concluding that the staple could be leveraged against British power. Southerners exported their vision of cotton's political economy directly to Great Britain via the *London Cotton Plant a Journal of Tropical Civilisation,* whose first edition appeared in June 1857. The *Cotton Plant* was founded by the Kentuckian Charles Gano Baylor (1826–1907), US Consul to Manchester, and was printed between 1857 and 1859.[171] Baylor was appointed at the same time that the Virginian Beverley Tucker was installed at the Consulate in Liverpool. Tucker's appointment was further proof of Southern Young Americans' desire for the United States to play a more assertive global role—and to confront British anti-slavery. As editor of the Pierce-leaning *Washington Sentinel,* Tucker declared that "Great Britain is, and ever will be, our evil genius." "It abolished black slavery in Jamaica, because it had white slavery at home and Gentoo slavery in Asia; and because black slavery is one of the most essential sources of power on which our government depends," Tucker continued, adding that "if black slavery be abolished, or discredited in the eyes of the world; it would be one of the most fatal blows that could be struck at our national prosperity."[172]

Baylor took up the cause of defending slavery, brazenly lobbying his readers on the benefits of "King Cotton." In its prospectus, advertised in the London press, Baylor described the *Cotton Plant*'s purpose as investigating "the question of negro labor, in its relation to tropical civilisation, and the necessities of European industry." This took the form of a zealous mission "to oppose, upon the broad ground of civilisation and humanity, the free-negro theory of Wilberforce, Brougham, and Clarkson."[173] Baylor intersected with a trajectory of British racism rooted in the decade before the Civil War that viewed the progress of West Indian emancipation with skepticism. In its first issue the *Cotton Plant* announced its "utter detestation of 'slavery' in any form whatever" but claimed that "negro servitude to the white man is not human slavery, but the normal condition of the inferior race, and his natural relation in life." "We hold that the negro is an inferior and specifically different MAN," continued one article, "and can only be christianised and civilised through daily contact with the superior race . . . and is utterly incapable as now constituted of self-government, self-christianity, or self-civilisation."[174]

As Britons weighed the morality of emancipation against its alleged financial cost, Southern confidence in cotton soared.[175] Baylor was also responding to fundamental dynamics of the Atlantic economy. The *London Cotton Plant* is evidence of Southerners' renewed faith in the power of cotton to shape global events after the region escaped the financial crisis that enveloped the North in 1857, in addition to its apparent diplomatic power.[176] As Consul in Manchester, Baylor was ideally placed to see the importance of a stable commercial South to Anglo-American relations. The Consul strategically targeted the British textile districts in Lancashire and Cheshire that depended most on Southern cotton and attempted to challenge British public opinion over the centrality of slave labor to the world economy.[177] Baylor spoke past the American merchants, ship captains, and financiers of Liverpool, Manchester, and London; instead, he had British investors squarely in mind. Forty-three percent of British merchant houses in the United States operated from the ports of Charleston, Savannah, Mobile, and New Orleans, not to mention the disproportionately high levels of investment in bank capital, state bonds, and railroad expansion.[178]

Yet, despite the importance of cotton to British industry, British newspapers drew overwhelmingly on their Northern counterparts for transatlantic news. As Martin Crawford identifies in his study of *The Times*'s place in Anglo-American relations, "the South failed to generate a communicative relationship across the Atlantic comparable to that which undoubtedly flourished between Great Britain and the commercial communities of the Northeast."[179] The *London Cotton Plant* was not so much an attempt to open transatlantic communication channels as it was a bridgehead against British anti-slavery. Like many other Southern internationalists, Baylor viewed economic nationalism and slavery as overlapping concerns since, in the pre-Civil War Atlantic world, the categories of race and nation hardened simultaneously. Embedded in the transatlantic project of classifying peoples, nations, and races, Baylor operated at the vanguard of Southern internationalist thought and anticipated the central intellectual thrust of the Confederacy's public diplomacy in Britain (chapter 4).[180]

NATIONALISM IN LONDON ON THE EVE OF CIVIL WAR

One year after the Liverpool dinner, the London-Americans formed the American Association in London (AAL), through which they aimed to assert control over American civic life in Britain. The AAL attempted to bring practices previously left to socially prominent migrants under the control of a national civic body overseas and to organize philanthropic relief to stranded Americans in Britain. Central to the AAL's formation was Benjamin Moran, Secretary at the American Legation in London.[181]

Moran began his diplomatic career under James Buchanan when he was appointed clerk of the Legation in 1855, before being appointed Assistant Secretary under George Mifflin Dallas two years later. Despite his frosty demeanor, Moran was popular in London literary circles and well-known to officials in Whitehall. He was also a prominent figure among American emigrants, whom he cajoled into supporting his plan to form an American social club in the capital. The Association was formed at a meeting on March 12, 1858 at the residence of Nathaniel S. Dodge, who had moved to London as a commissioner for the American exhibits at the Great Exhibition, with the aim of forming a club "for aiding persons in distress and other purposes."[182] Moran and Dodge were joined by the rare book trader Henry Stevens; Phil Dallas, son of the American Minister; steam engineer Jacob Perkins; and Jesse Weldon Fell, an American cancer specialist working at the Middlesex Hospital.[183] The AAL was the first American association in Britain to be composed of more than a body of professional interests, and cut across the diplomatic, financial, entrepreneurial, and artistic social milieus of Britain's American community (table 2).

The AAL began an incremental movement away from the reliance on individual American residents to organize the social life of Americans in London, not completed until the 1890s. The Association provided a social center at its rooms on Cockspur Street, "where transient visitors might gain information and ask advice, and the deserving of them receive assistance in cases where it was required."[184] The philanthropic aspect of the AAL was its most important innovation. Before the founding of the AAL, destitute Americans relied heavily on the private charity of the consular service and the American community's leading members. "Among other things, all pennyless Americans, or pretenders to Americanism, look upon me as their banker," complained Nathaniel Hawthorne from his post in Liverpool; "I could ruin myself, any week."[185] Edward Everett wrote the Secretary of the Society of Friends of Foreigners in distress that he was unable to contribute funds to the Society since his "private means" were already "heavily drawn on for the relief of distressed countrymen."[186] From Liverpool the American Chamber of Commerce contributed ten pounds each year, beginning in 1822.[187]

The AAL transformed individual philanthropy into a communal act of offshore citizenship. Foreign nationals were particularly at risk in Great Britain when they fell on hard times, since they were ineligible for relief under the Poor Law. Within months of its formation, the AAL attracted a great number of claimants. On September 17, 1858, the

TABLE 2   MEMBERS OF THE AMERICAN ASSOCIATION IN LONDON

Member	Profession	Association Office
John T. Pitman	Patent lawyer	
William M. Ballard	Dentist	
Jonathan C. Wagstaff	Railway investor	
James Buchanan	Minister to the Court of St James	Honorary Member
Frank Campbell	US Despatch Agent	
Benjamin Moran	Sec. of Legation	Managing Committee
George P. Dodge	Businessman	
Nathaniel S. Dodge	Rubber merchant	Treasurer
Phil Dallas	Son of American Minister	Managing Committee
Joseph Rodney Croskey	Consul at Southampton	Managing Committee
Dewey	Preacher	Secretary
Jacob Perkins	Engineer	President, 1858
William R. Ballard	Dentist	
George M. Dallas	American Minister	Vice President
Jesse Weldon Fell	Doctor	Vice President
George Francis Train	Entrepreneur	
Robert Blair Campbell	Consul General	President, 1859
William Henry Hurlbert	*New York Times* correspondent	
Henry Stevens	Rare book dealer	Vice President
James McHenry	Railroad promoter	

Association paid for the burial of Edwin J. Swett, a Bostonian author who had died of consumption; a month later the association paid for the return passage of an American soldier who lost his possessions when the steamship *Hammonia* exploded in Hamburg; and on December 13 it collected money for a Mrs. Smith "to obtain clothes so as to leave for Australia." To Moran, this approach was "honourable to the Society & shews [sic] its usefulness and necessity."[188]

The civic role of the AAL was expanded further when it took control of London's Fourth of July banquet in 1858. For the new generation of American migrants in Britain, remembering the Revolution meant excluding Britons. The 1858 banquet took place at the London Tavern— chosen because it was the venue at which, in 1778, London merchants had refused to subscribe to a loan to carry on the American war.[189] Before dinner the Declaration of Independence was read aloud in front of "none but Americans" and toasts to Independence and the President preceded that to the Queen.[190] The militant tone with which American principles were invoked reflected the insecurity of many Americans overseas about ongoing domestic tumult. "The principles of the American revolution have gone on conquering and to conquer," argued US minister to London George Mifflin Dallas.[191] Nationalist remembrance also required policing both the boundaries of Anglophilia and the acceptable modes of behavior of American migrants. In Moran's view, Peabody had transformed the Fourth into a "great yearly advertising card."[192] After Peabody refused to attend, the Association committee asked him to chair the dinner "as a new proof of your attachment to your country and your countrymen."[193]

The forthright enforcement of American national principles overseas captured a widespread reassessment of Anglo-American relations in Britain's American community. Toasts at the 1858 dinner redrew the United States' place in world affairs by rejecting the prevailing parent-child metaphor used to discuss Anglo-American relations. The American Consul General in London, Robert Blair Campbell, a South Carolinian Democrat and nullifier, declared to the diners that the event signaled that "the day had arrived when they could no longer look at England as the mother, but as the cherished older sister."[194] "England may deal with Europe, Asia, and Africa as she likes—but she must remember that America is a chip off the old block," warned George Francis Train.[195] Still, this reframing retained a familiar ambivalence toward England. Declaring that the United States now stood on equal terms with Great Britain was one thing, but severing the familial connection, symbolically or otherwise, proved quite another. As Train termed it, "Thank God, instinct teaches the lion and the eagle not to prey upon each other!"[196]

On March 5, 1860, the AAL met for what would be the final time. "It was almost determined to dissolve," Moran recorded ruefully in his journal. Lacking the financial support of elite London-based emigrant financiers, Moran asserted that "the fact cannot be denied that we have failed." "I regret to say," Moran added, "that the casual American visitor to London won't join us . . . . They come abroad to see English fops, & won't associate with their own countrymen if it costs them anything."[197] Moran's concluding remarks reveal the extent to which Britain's American community was shot through with tensions arising from social class as well as sectional and partisan identities.

Nonetheless, Americans in London continued to build their overseas community with the launch of the *London American* on May 2, 1860.[198] Although this was not the first American newspaper to be established in Britain, it was the first dedicated to the affairs of the American community in Britain. The *American* sprang directly from the ranks of the professional class of Americans in London who dominated the membership of the short-lived AAL. John Adams Knight and George Haseltine, proprietor and editor respectively, were of a similar class to John C. Pitman, Benjamin Moran, and Jacob Perkins, whose social circles overlapped with those of Peabody and Bates in the forum of national celebrations. Knight, described by Moran as "a quiet sort of soul," was a Philadelphian lawyer who ran the American Law Agency on Chancery Lane and, at one time, specialized in litigating the claims of Americans to British estates.[199] Haseltine, a native of Bradford, Massachusetts, practiced law in St Louis before joining Knight as a barrister at the American Law Agency, where the pair struck up their partnership.

The *American* was anti-slavery, free trade, and radical. The paper promoted the bonds of commerce, finance, and diplomacy, through which it urged "a closer alliance between England and America, believing that the advancement of liberal principles depends in great measure upon their united action." "Commercial and social ties tend strongly to the preservation of peace," the inaugural editorial of the *American* declared to its audience of transatlantic financiers.[200] The twin arms of finance and diplomacy would redress the "partial alienation" between the two nations, and London's American community would be the site of that rapprochement.[201] For the *American* this was a part of a democratic project, rather than an admission of the asymmetry of transatlantic relations. Since America was "strong in her isolation" and England "strong in the energies of her people," stable Anglo-American relations promoted the "interests of commerce, a free press, religious liberty, civilisation, and humanity."[202]

The *American* was one mechanism for creating an American community in London. The publication of American addresses in London, along with the register of American travelers at Morley's Hotel or of those leaving cards at Peabody's offices, became a permanent feature of the *American*. By May 30, 1860, the paper floated the idea of a directory of Americans resident in London.[203] The *American* detailed the components of Anglo-American trade and finance, facilitating the meeting of commercial agents, financiers, merchants, and promoters in the world of London investors. To do so, it listed national locales such as Morley's, the Legation, and Peabody's offices on Old Broad Street in the City. Collated in one place, the outlines of an American community in London were brought into focus. But, through its concentration on transatlantic travel and advocacy of cheap ocean postage, the *American* encapsulates the constant interplay between the desire to forge a distinct national enclave in London and the transnational linkages so integral to the lives of American emigrants.[204]

. . .

The American community in Britain may have been on the frontline of attempts to define American nationality, but it could not unite its citizens. The establishment of the *London Cotton Plant* and the *London American* reflected the assertive sectionalized nationalism emerging in the Union. Baylor's publication brought the coercive language of Southern fire-eaters directly to British audiences. "If she [the South] is denied 'equality' within the Union," the paper warned in August 1858, "she can have 'independence' out of it."[205] The *Cotton Plant*'s threats were made good by secession conventions across the South in the winter of 1860. Confederate statesmen soon expected the triumph of King Cotton abroad, but overestimated British dependence on Southern cotton and underemphasized the interdependence of the economy of the Atlantic world. By contrast, the *London American* stressed the dense tangle of commercial and financial connections between Britain and the United States. The *American* therefore maintained a unionist front throughout the secessionist winter, reflecting the initial hopes of many in Britain's American community that war could be averted.

The transformation of the sectional crisis into the Civil War thrust the wider question of allegiance to the center stage of American life in Britain. With the outbreak of hostilities in April 1861, Americans overseas were forced to choose between Union and Confederate loyalty. As representatives of either, Americans in Britain continued to direct transatlantic diplomacy. Yet they could not make foreign relations exactly as they pleased. The contest to win popular support overseas turned on the decade's long integration of American migrants in British civil society. Although relying on non-state diplomacy carried risks, Henry Adams found that resident volunteer diplomats "can do everything that we cannot do," since "a single blunder on our side would bring the Legation into discredit."[206] The Union may have lacked institutionalized public diplomacy, but what mattered most was the great energy for diplomatic lobbying and depth of social contacts that Americans resident in London, the nation's most critical diplomatic post, could leverage on the Union's behalf—as the Confederacy would find to its cost.

CHAPTER 3

The Emigrants' War

In April 1861, Trafalgar Square was the unlikely center of the Civil War arms trade. From rooms in Morley's Hotel, Union and Confederate agents plotted to sweep British arms stockpiles clean. Henry Stevens, a book dealer resident in London since 1845, oversaw Union procurements.[1] "My first impression was to rush across home and lend a helping hand," he wrote home to Vermont, but admitted, "second thoughts suggest the propriety of following Franklin's example and supporting the good cause in Europe." Stevens wasted little time contacting John C. Frémont and Frederick Billings, who were then passing through London. The trio ran a transatlantic arms ring from Stevens's offices in Morley's, shipping munitions from the ports of Liverpool, Southampton, and Le Havre to Simon Stevens in New York, from whence they were forwarded to the battlefront.[2] Meanwhile, in a nearby room, Caleb Huse, a Yankee Confederate under orders from Jefferson Davis to secure twelve thousand rifles and a battery of field artillery, was busy striking up an exclusive arrangement with the London Armory Company to provide its entire output to the Confederate States.

Stevens's network was remarkably effective for one constructed in such haste. "For the *North*," he wrote jubilantly to the governor of Connecticut, William Buckingham, "a Steel rifled 24 pounder canon [sic], and for the *South*, 50 casks 24 pound solid shot, and 50 24 pound Shells"— the latter to be delivered with lethal force to Confederate soldiers via the former.[3] Further shipments then followed, with 204 cases of artillery shells, and 112 cases containing 2,500 French rifles and 450 French revolvers with 102,000 cartouches and 2 million percussion caps.[4] Stevens, Frémont, and Billings voluntarily filled procurement gaps while the Union coordinated its own purchasing operations. After the Battle of Bull Run, the Union dispatched George Schuyler to London, where he also made Morley's his center of operations and employed Stevens's younger brother, Benjamin Franklin Stevens, as his secretary.[5] Shortly after his arrival, the financier Joshua Bates convinced Barings to finance Schuyler to the tune of $2 million for the purchase of 150,000 small arms from Britain, France, and Austria.[6] In all, an estimated 1,165,000 small arms were sent from Europe to the Union in the first two years of the war.[7]

London was, in the words of Union Minister Charles Francis Adams, "the great theatre of operations."[8] For both Union and Confederacy, Britain was a potential lifeline but also their greatest threat. Diplomats and special agents from both sides hoped to obtain financial and material support for their war effort from Britain's commercial and military arsenals. Southern diplomats hoped that British dependence on slave-grown cotton and its sympathy for struggles of self-determination would lead to the recognition of its diplomats and so its nationhood or, better yet, direct involvement in the conflict. The Union hoped to isolate Southern diplomats in order to prevent recognition, which would grant the Confederacy sovereignty under international law and empower it to negotiate treaties and foreign loans, purchase arms, conduct searches at sea, enter foreign ports, license privateers, and impose blockades.[9] They also hoped to prevent intervention of any sort that would grant the Confederate States a position of equal standing, such as in a negotiated peace settlement or arbitration—a distinct possibility should neutral powers decide that the community of nations as a whole was suffering by the conflict.[10] This battle over recognition and intervention was waged in the theater of British public opinion by specially dispatched agents and emigrant ambassadors whose role as representative Americans took on new impetus in defense of the nation.

Throughout the war, the boundary between diplomat and migrant was blurred more than ever before. Union and Confederate diplomats alike relied, not always with confidence, on a diverse cast of financiers, merchants, activists, and evangelicals to take up the work of foreign relations. Emigrants organized public demonstrations, represented their respective governments in British high society, and maintained transatlantic networks of material aid and political intelligence. From his office near Regent's Park, Charles Francis Adams kept a watchful eye on the diverse activity of informal diplomacy. But the Legation could not risk its diplomatic standing by publicly collaborating with these emigrants. Early in his mission, Adams concluded "it is no time for indulging oddities of any kind."[11] At other times, he cooperated in secret with non-state agents. Adams was the intermediary between Stevens's arms network and Joshua Bates and George Peabody, who supplied the funds required for purchase.[12] "I am not a little uneasy touching the transaction," Adams confided to his diary.[13] With the appointment of Schuyler, Adams "rejoiced" as "it takes off my shoulders the whole of the responsibility which had fallen upon them."[14]

Civil War foreign relations depended on the informal diplomacy of Americans overseas, who shifted their activities from defining the nation to defending it. As a result of decades of integration with British society, loyal Unionists overseas provided connections among British elites through which official diplomats gathered and spread political intelligence and shaped public perception of battlefield events and the war's meaning. Contemporaries recognized this as a unique aspect of the war's diplomatic culture. "The northerners are a unit here as well as at home," wrote one American from London.[15] Throughout the course of Civil War foreign relations, Union and Confederate diplomats and citizens cultivated social and political connections among their British sympathizers.

But they did not do so on equal terms. For the Union, the integration with British elites outlined in the previous chapter provided vital social and political connections that strengthened the nation's foreign relations at its moment of crisis. Confederate agents started on the back foot not simply because of a naïve faith in the diplomacy of "King Cotton" but as a result of the comparative lack of social integration between British and Southern elites.[16] Matthew Karp has convincingly shown that Southern statesmen pursued a proslavery foreign policy abroad through their control and expansion of the military power of the government.[17] Southerners dominated appointments in the Navy and War Departments and, on the eve of the Civil War, also filled a large number of posts in the foreign service. Yet the last Southerner to hold the post of Minister to Great Britain, the Union's most important diplomatic post, was Louis McLane, in his second stint between 1845 and 1846. Of the twenty-three American Ministers to Britain before the Civil War, only six were Southerners.[18] Despite their extensive presence at the Consular level, Confederates in Britain were unknown to influential Britons and were either unacquainted with or not wealthy enough to participate in the elite social world of foreign diplomacy. Few among the Confederate elite sustained transatlantic networks of correspondence that Confederate agents could draw on for letters of introduction granting access to British political circles. Nevertheless, a mobile cast of Confederate agents, naval officers, and propagandists was active in Britain and set about constructing the South's own transatlantic social network.

"The Atlantic" is now a familiar and well-tried way to frame the international history of the Civil War. A number of historians have demonstrated how the "American question" provoked a multiplicity of meanings to embattled radicals and emboldened aristocrats across the Old World.[19] Beyond this international reception, however, transnational historians have less successfully mapped the interleaved social and commercial networks that shaped Union and Confederate foreign relations with Britain.[20] This chapter argues that the social and economic networks created over the antebellum period by American emigrants, as laid out in chapters 1 and 2, significantly enhanced the Union's ability to mobilize the transatlantic material and human resources necessary for conducting effective foreign policy and for engaging with foreign publics. Foreign relations at this time demonstrate emphatically the State Department's reliance on emigrants to achieve its diplomatic objectives.

EMIGRANT DIPLOMACY:
UNION NETWORKS IN BRITAIN

Few Americans in London were surprised when war erupted. "I don't like the looks of things ahead," wrote Junius Spencer Morgan to his partner George Peabody in March 1860, adding that "nobody has confidence in the political future."[21] From his office in Liverpool, Joseph Shipley wrote his partners at Brown Brothers that "on this side all are completely in the dark."[22] Joshua Bates clung to compromise, fearing that "a long and bloody war will be destructive to commerce."[23] Before news of the bombardment of Fort Sumter reached George Peabody, the banker wrote to his hometown newspaper, the *Boston Courier,* that the only hope of restoring the Union was "by concession on the part of the North and a compromise which will secure the best feelings of the border-states."[24] Peabody and Morgan, both New Englanders, were staunch Unionists but privately doubted the North's ability to conquer the South and feared the economic consequences of protracted conflict. Having cut his commercial teeth in the bustling port of Baltimore, Peabody was loyal to his southern friends, but not to their cause. Though some accused him of "carrying water on both shoulders," the banker felt that the cost of preserving the Union was "cheap even at this great sacrifice of blood and treasure."[25] But the prospect of war was, as Daniel James wrote simply, "most appalling to contemplate."[26]

One of the unique features of Union foreign relations was the extent to which it built upon antebellum patterns of informal diplomacy among Americans resident in Britain. During the war, Americans overseas were not only political and cultural embodiments of the republic but were informal diplomatic representatives. The diplomatic life of Charles Francis Adams was populated and shaped by these emigrant diplomats: they were regular guests in his household, shared political intelligence with his staff, and took dramatic steps to improve the image of the United States in British public opinion. This was supplemented by a small but effective group of propaganda and procurement agents, dispatched overseas by the State Department. Secretary of State William Henry Seward sent eleven special agents in two waves to supplement emigrant diplomats at critical times for Union diplomacy.[27] The first was led by Republican Party boss and newspaper editor Thurlow Weed. Weed arrived in 1861 to, as he put it to Lincoln, deliver antivenom to English minds "poisoned" by the "adroit Emissaries of Rebellion."[28] Weed worked "like a giant" penning pro-Union articles for the British press and speaking to large audiences with former Legation secretary Bancroft Davis and the Episcopalian Bishop Charles P. McIllvaine of Ohio.[29] In February 1862, the trio spoke at Exeter Hall, the famed center of British abolition, but were shocked to find that "those from whom we expected cooperation, are the worst enemies of the Union" and "who were so loud against slavery, are now with the South!"[30] Weed also threw himself into London's Season in an attempt to reduce Anglo-American tensions and cultivate sympathetic Liberals in Parliament. The second mission left New York in March 1863, to consolidate the diplomatic glow enjoyed by the Union after the passage of the Emancipation Proclamation.[31]

The Union relied on emigrant diplomats for social connection and political intelligence. The homes, offices, and social life of Britain's American community provided Union agents with an accessible source of information and support. As we have seen, the integration of the London-Americans with the capital's social Season provided access to prominent journalists and politicians from Fleet Street and Whitehall. Throughout the Civil War, the United States' consular service in Britain also underwent significant expansion. In all, the Union boasted twenty-one consulates in the United Kingdom in addition to the Consul General in London and twenty-six Consular agents.[32] Of these posts, eighteen were newly created during the Civil War. In total, then, the Union employed almost fifty diplomats in the British Isles, to which could be added London's group of secretaries.[33] This was an indispensable system of information-gathering for Union diplomacy and espionage, but it was tactically limited by the conventions of Great Power diplomacy and the amount of work that could realistically be conducted by underpaid and inexperienced staff. "The greatest triumph" that could be achieved by Charles Francis Adams, reflected his son Henry, "will be to make no blunders."[34]

Emigrants in London were an essential backchannel of US foreign relations that reduced the exposure of the Legation to "noisy jackasses" like Cassius Clay and Anson Burlingame, ministers to Russia and China respectively, who "have done more harm here than their weak heads were worth a thousand times over."[35] At the heart of this infrastructure were the offices of George Peabody & Co. "During our residence in London, I was everyday at the banking house of Messrs. Peabody & Morgan, where I was accustomed to meet Union friends," remembered Thurlow Weed.[36] Peabody "regarded the ultras of the North and the South as equally mischievous," reflected Weed, who found that the banker's "devotion" to the "Union was so strong that . . . whatever he could do then and there for the Union cause he would do cheerfully."[37] Peabody's was the nucleus of American intelligence in London where, Weed observed, "news from America is hourly expected and tremulously looked for."[38] The bank's telegraph machine received news of the war's turning points before the diplomatic pouch crossed Adams's desk, and Peabody circulated American newspapers among the Union's allies in London and would "voluntarily came out of his way to bring news of an important Union victory" to the legation.[39] It was through Peabody's long relationship with Sir James Emerson Tennent, for instance, that he was able to gather intelligence about the size and strength of the regiments ordered to Canada at the height of the *Trent* Crisis in December 1861.[40]

Peabody's greatest contribution to the Union was his benevolent gift of £150,000 to the London poor in 1862. The New Englander's announcement was perfectly timed, immediately following the conclusion of the *Trent* affair, and shortly preceding the recognition bill presented in Parliament by William Lindsay and John Roebuck in June 1862.[41] Philanthropy and foreign relations were close partners in this respect, as Peabody's dramatic gesture was envisaged as an attempt to "soften" any "asperities of feeling which had unhappily arisen between the two great nations of the Anglo-Saxon family" and would remind "the people of both countries of their common origin and natural sympathy."[42] Even *The Times* was impressed with Peabody's generosity "in a country which is not his own, and in a city which he may any day leave to return to his native land."[43] In response, Peabody was awarded the freedom of the City of London in an elaborate ceremony at the Guildhall and a bronze statue was unveiled in his honor in front of the Stock Exchange.[44] Peabody's donation was a powerful example of the way in which philanthropic diplomacy was central to emigrant foreign relations in the Civil War (chapter 4).[45]

Reflecting on attempts by Americans overseas to direct English public opinion, Adams wrote that it was "wonderful how many of my countrymen consider this to be their mission."[46] But, in the theater of public opinion, voluntary diplomacy was risky. In a letter to Seward after Confederate emissaries had persuaded one Unionist emigrant to hold peace discussions, Adams noted that it "is one of the peculiar circumstances attending the present crisis that many Americans come to this country impressed with a strong conviction that . . . they shall be able to produce a decided effect on public opinion favorable to the United States." Too many "proceed very much in the same way that they would in an election canvass at home" and consequently "do harm rather than good to the cause they advocate."[47]

The risks of breaching diplomatic etiquette were offset by the skillful way that American emigrants in London integrated Union diplomats into the capital's social world. By mid-century Americans featured prominently in the London Season. Bates's partner, the former China trader Russell Sturgis, was a lifelong Adams family friend and proved his loyalty to the Union when he loaned his mansion at 5 Upper Portland Place to the American legation in April 1862. Sturgis also entertained the Adams family regularly at Mount Felix, his suburban villa at Walton-on-Thames, and his wife Lucretia's weekly "at homes" were an established feature of the Season.[48] Similarly, Junius Spencer Morgan's five-story residence at 13 Prince's Gate and his country place in the nearby suburb of Roehampton, and Curtis Miranda Lampson's home at 80 Eaton Square in the heart of aristocratic Belgravia, where the Adams family dined regularly, were prominent London hotspots. These connections placed the Union's diplomatic agents at the center of London's elite social circles and, as pleasant as they may seem today, the constant round of parties, balls, and dinners doubled as key elements of the practice of foreign relations.

Adams and his family found the task of conducting foreign relations in the British social Season arduous. "The ice crust of London society is particularly thick," reflected Adams shortly after arrival, "and my doubt is whether it will ever compensate for the labour of breaking it."[49] Meanwhile, Adams's wife Abigail was given tuition in social and court etiquette by Joshua Bates's wife, Lucretia Augusta Sturgis, and daughter (a close friend of the Queen), and once their diplomatic household was moved to the Sturgis home at Portland Place in May 1862, Abigail began hosting weekly social receptions.[50] Adams, who preferred solitude, complained repeatedly that the effort was "excessively tiresome" and "dreadfully irksome" since it was "the precise point at which the social system of Europe and America most conflict."[51] "The truth is that a life in Europe very generally takes the look of our Institutions out of my countrymen," Adams wrote before the start of the 1864 Season. "They sink into mere Chinese mandarin figures ready to bow on every occasion at the truck of a titled donkey."[52] After visiting Adams the prominent Republican Carl Schurz observed that the Union's chief diplomat was hardly a "shining figure on festive occasions [and] lacked the personal magnetism or sympathetic charm that would draw men to him."[53]

Because of the close interconnection between the political life of Parliament and the wider social life of Victorian London, participation in the Season's dinners and balls, and membership in its salons and clubs, were invaluable for gathering political intelligence. Political gossip flowed freely in London's middle-class and gentlemen's clubs; by mid-century there were more than two hundred, some with sixteen-year waits for admission.[54] In the cosmopolitan social world of Victorian London, Adams could defuse crises and take the pulse of leading opinion-makers. In conjunction, Adams and American emigrants in the city also cemented the Union's support in the closely connected worlds of British radical and anti-slavery politics. Adams' first social invitation came from William E. Forster, the newly elected Liberal Party MP and education reformer. Forster represented the northern mill town of Bradford, where nonconformist anti-slavery was strong, and was himself an outspoken critic of an institution he called "the essence of the south."[55] The mill owner spoke with great moral fervor in support of demands for franchise reform and used his maiden speech to the House of Commons to seek assurances from the government that it had not recognized the legitimacy of secession in South Carolina.[56] Adams and his wife were guests at Forster's home on the banks of the River Wharfe in October 1862, where they went shooting in the Yorkshire Dales and toured Forster's linen mill. Adams left "with regret" and while finding Forster "an unpolished man" observed that he was "in a great degree self-made . . . able and liberal."[57] Alongside John Bright and William Cobden, Forster proved an effective Parliamentarian and a rousing advocate for the Union.[58]

In Palmerston's Cabinet the Union was ably supported by George Campbell, the Lord Privy Seal, who was allied by marriage to the powerful Sutherland family, among the most prominent aristocratic opponents of slavery. The Duke and Duchess's north London home, Argyll Lodge on the King's Road, became a social refuge for Adams and his wife, where they met frequently with Union supporters. The Sutherlands gathered vast amounts of American intelligence from Adams, Motley, and Charles Sumner, head of the Senate Foreign Relations Committee. The connection between Sumner, a lifelong Anglophile who was jokingly referred to as "the duke" by his friends, and the Argyll family was one of the informal diplomatic avenues through which pressure was exerted in both the Lincoln and Palmerston cabinets.[59] At the height of the *Trent* crisis, for instance, Argyll warned Sumner about the effect of Seward's sabre rattling, "which may lead to blood, and perhaps finally to rupture."[60] In turn, in a letter of May 1863 Sumner asked the Duchess to "be my mediator" in passing on information to the Duke.[61] Both Adamses, meanwhile, played an essential role in maintaining wide-ranging social relationships, a fact scarcely acknowledged by the war's previous diplomatic historians. The management of social and political networks was essential to the conduct of foreign relations, which often depended on the Season's round of breakfasts, dinners, and receptions, where they gained useful "scraps of knowledge."[62]

Although Adams claimed to have "little fancy and less aptitude" for the social Season, he and his staff nevertheless spread themselves widely.[63] Peabody dined regularly at the Athenaeum, where Henry Adams was introduced to Richard Monckton Milnes, another Liberal MP from Yorkshire and republican sympathizer.[64] Socially, Milnes was an asset to the Union, promoting its cause at his regular society breakfast parties to which he invited prominent intellectuals and celebrities; in Parliament, where his lofty oratory was ineffective, he was of less use. Together with his father and Benjamin Moran, Henry also frequented the St James Club on the southern corner of Berkeley Square, founded in 1857 for diplomatic secretaries and attachés, speaking with "counts and barons and numberless untitled but high-placed characters."[65] Henry's membership at the St James was backed by Lord Frederick Cavendish, private secretary to Lord Granville and a liberal non-interventionist in the Cabinet.[66] He also dined at the Reform Club with Thurlow Weed (who was armed with letters of introduction from Seward, an honorary member during his 1859 visit), and gathered news about Union victories from Brooks's. All three were Liberal clubs.[67] "I am so little of a club man," reflected Charles Francis Adams, yet he still visited the Reform, Athenaeum, and Travellers' Club (where the Royal Family and Foreign Secretary were members), recognizing the importance of participating in the social world that supported the political life of Parliament.[68]

The Union's agents and supporters depended on outposts in the north of England, too. In Liverpool, the US consulate was the focal point for American activity. It also linked the financial, maritime, and industrial connections of Union support in the region. Thomas Dudley, the US Consul, relied on supporters such as Stewart H. Brown and Joseph Shipley of Brown, Shipley & Co., Samuel Gair of Barings, Daniel James of Phelps, James & Co., Stephen Barker Guion, the manager of the Black Star Line's Liverpool branch, the dry goods merchant Benjamin Franklin Babcock, and Robert Trimble, overseas partner in the New York firm William Watson & Co.[69] James, Guion, and Babcock would become prominent volunteer diplomats. Trimble, an Irishman by birth who migrated to the US in the 1840s before returning to Manchester, lectured tirelessly in Liverpool's anti-slavery circles and exhorted Americans resident in the north of England to demonstrate their anti-slavery credentials.[70] Dudley's consular offices were a social center for Americans passing through the port, but also a hub of Union espionage.[71] As has been well-documented, Dudley built a detailed picture of Confederate activities in Britain through a network of informants, spies, and consular offices in British provincial cities.[72] Meanwhile, Dudley's lifelong interest in free trade led him to cultivate contacts with leading British Liberals.[73]

Such political connections grew throughout the Civil War. Although among American liberal intellectuals the war bred disenchantment with Britain's intransigence over neutral rights, flirtation with Confederate recognition, and hostility to American democracy, the lineaments of a "new self-consciously liberal alliance" also emerged in transatlantic debate.[74] Cobden, Bright, and Sumner engaged in a lively correspondence on the relationship between free trade, peace, and anti-slavery.[75] The information sent to Sumner by Cobden and Bright allowed the powerful Chair of the Senate Foreign Relations Committee to keep his finger on the pulse of Parliamentary opinion. As Leslie Butler has documented, a younger generation of liberal intellectuals also made transatlantic connections during the war, including Irish-born journalist Edwin Godkin, James Russell Lowell, and Charles Eliot Norton in the United States and

Edward Dicey, Goldwin Smith, and John Stuart Mill in England.[76] This emerging liberal alliance highlights the war's transnational impact. The conflict provided the prism needed for Britain's "pro-union intelligentsia" to understand Britain's continuing assault on slavery and a means for navigating the ongoing struggle over Parliamentary reform.[77]

Union diplomacy also spread rapidly through the evangelical networks established in the 1820s and 30s, when the "New-Measures" revivalism of the US traversed the Atlantic along longstanding transatlantic anti-slavery networks (see chapter 1).[78] The Baptist minister and ardent unionist Moncure D. Conway left his Southern slaveholding family for Britain in April 1863, never to return. Conway mixed socially in the reform circles of the English radical Peter Alfred Taylor, elected MP for Leicester in February 1862, who hosted him at his home in London, where the Southerner breakfasted with Richard Cobden, lunched with John Bright, and dined with Robert Browning. Conway lectured vigorously on the immorality of Southern slavery to evangelical audiences throughout the kingdom, and placed numerous articles in the British radical press, chief among which was Bright's *Morning Star*.[79] Conway was joined on the evangelical circuit by Henry Ward Beecher, who arrived in June 1863 and lectured to audiences "foaming" with "madness" over slavery in Manchester, Glasgow, Edinburgh, Liverpool, and London.[80] Beecher was one among many. The Reverend John Sella Martin (an escaped slave), the Episcopalian Bishop Charles Petit McIlvaine of Ohio (who preached at St Paul's Cathedral in February 1862 and counted Prince Albert, Lord Lyons, and Disraeli amongst his contacts),[81] the Congregationalist George B. Cheever, Unitarian W.D. Haley, and army chaplain Crammond Kennedy (also an agent of the National Freedmen's Aid Association) all fit with ease into Britain's denominational reform networks.

Black American activists provided intellectual and organizational muscle to these networks. In the estimation of Richard Blackett as many as forty African American lecturers toured the country agitating on behalf of the Union.[82] "There is no end to the colored here," remarked John Sella Martin upon reaching London in 1861.[83] Some black activists, including the Crafts, Zilpha Elaw, William Powell, Edward Irving, James Watkins, and Henry Highland Garnett had by this time been resident in Britain for some time, and began working for abolition as soon as war broke out. But the war years marked another peak in African-American travel to Britain. These "ministers without portfolio" moved British audiences from soap box and podium and added legitimacy to the abolitionist attack on slavery in the Southern states.[84] Though welcomed on platforms around the country, the work of abolition's ambassadors was laborious. "You are the equal of white people here," Martin wrote one correspondent, but he still found that "you feel quite alone in your equality since all are strangers."[85] Jefferson Davis's former coachman William Andrew Jackson, who lectured to Sunday Schools in the northwest, lamented that he found "quite as much prejudice in England as in America."[86]

These activists worked feverishly alongside British abolitionist societies—despite tensions in the movement over the Union's war aims.[87] Existing groups such as the London Anti-Slavery Society, Aborigines' Protection Society, and British and Foreign Anti-Slavery Society (BFASS) were joined in 1862 by the London Emancipation Society (LES) and the Union and Emancipation Society (UES) of Manchester, and in 1863 by the Ladies' London Emancipation Society (LLES)—not to mention their many allied independent and affiliate local societies. These set the basic template of public meetings, lecturing, fundraising, bazaars, petitioning, and propagandizing at a local and national level. They also disrupted pro-Confederate rallies and produced an onslaught of print in the fight for British public opinion. Toward the end of the war, George Thompson claimed that the combined efforts of the LES and UES had circulated more than 600,000 copies of pamphlets to the British public.[88] Between 1863 and 1864, the LLES circulated as many as 12,000 copies of its own tracts—half written by women—that combatted pro-Confederate propaganda with a powerful critique of the suffering of black and white women under slavery.[89] "Agitation helps us and injures the South," reported Thomas Dudley from Liverpool to William Seward, adding that "these men who have taken hold of this matter are good agitators."[90]

John Sella Martin was the most potent weapon in transatlantic abolition's arsenal. An exceptional orator and organizer, Martin built upon the contacts created by African American abolitionists over the past forty years. His first wartime trip to Britain coincided with the febrile months surrounding the arrival of the Confederate Commissioners James Mason and John Slidell and the *Trent* affair. In September 1861 Martin embarked on a six-month national tour on behalf of the LES with the radical British abolitionist George Thompson.[91] Throughout the tour, Martin insisted that the war was an anti-slavery conflict and attacked William Yancey, the chief Confederate commissioner in Europe, as a "bully" and Confederate free trade proposals as a "bribe."[92] Martin returned to Britain in January 1863, becoming pastor at his patron Harper Twelvetrees's Free Christian Church in Bromley-by-Bow, where he ministered to laborers from Twelvetrees's chemical factory. Martin continued the fight against Confederate recognition, attacking claims that emancipation would lead to servile insurrection by telling audiences that slavery itself "was at all times a chronic state of insurrection against right—against religion, and against mankind."[93] In addition to logging thousands of miles on the lecture circuit, Martin was invited regularly into the drawing rooms of elite Britons to speak with sympathetic MPs (especially the Scottish Peer Arthur Kinnaird, popularly known as "Palmerston's shadow"), nonconformist ministers, peers, and industrialists. All this prodigious activity was reported in detail by the radical, pro-peace *Morning Star,* the BFASS's *Anti-Slavery Reporter,* and the American abolitionist press, renewing and extending longstanding reform connections.

Martin also turned his attention to the war's international significance. Adroitly placing the war in a hemispheric context, the preacher raised the specter of a tropical empire for slavery in Latin America in which an independent Confederacy allied with Spanish Cuba and the Kingdom of Brazil. He detailed the threat this posed to Britain's pursuit of an "anti-slavery" empire in the New World—claims that had been made by Confederate statesmen themselves.[94] Before a crowd of three thousand Londoners in Finsbury, Martin asked:

> What would be the result of the South being independent? The South would join with Spain in conquering central America. Then Brazil would be forced to join a great Southern Confederation. The slave trade would be revived, England in her endeavors to prevent it might be drawn into war, and the result for the black man would be that a system of organized cruelty, even more atrocious than that of American slavery, would be established.[95]

Martin was not content only to rely on the tried-and-tested method of moral suasion, then, but skillfully used the well-oiled machinery of transatlantic anti-slavery to shape the Union's public diplomacy. Martin was far from alone in this endeavor. As we shall see, in the context of the war's international reverberations African American activists' vision of a post-emancipation black Atlantic engaged directly with the ongoing debate over Atlantic political economy and international connection.

The Union drew life-giving diplomatic strength from the capacity of Americans overseas to mobilize these dense circuits of reform, whose members had a long history of transatlantic cooperation. These networks built upon a tradition of lobbying, fundraising, and organizing that was able to exert tremendous pressure on British public opinion and shape the climate of Civil War foreign relations to a remarkable degree. Adams took pains to disassociate himself from their activities since "the smallest suspicion of my agency would do more harm than good," but he was aware of their value to the Union.[96]

CONFEDERATE NETWORKS

The social and cultural foundations of Union diplomacy were laid over several decades. In contrast, the Confederacy could only work with a shallow group of sympathizers in Britain's American community and relied more extensively on Britons who were more than willing to trade with them. Seward quickly removed the Virginian Beverley Tucker and South Carolinian Robert Campbell from their posts in Liverpool and London.[97] "As a general thing," wrote Henry William Lord, US Consul in Manchester, "merchants sympathetic with the rebellion . . . have had no hesitation with regard to selling all the goods they could and have considered it not dishonourable to run the blockade if possible."[98]

Its docks lined with steamers and packets flying the Confederate flag, Liverpool became a rebel hotbed.[99] In the estimation of Benjamin Moran the port was "a nest of pirates."[100] Union officials had difficulty tracking Confederates in Liverpool amidst the mercantile connections between the port, the Caribbean, and the South. In the absence of a strong Southern presence in the port, Confederate agents turned directly to Liverpool's Caribbean traders, who ran the blockade between the Caribbean ports of Nassau and Bermuda and the Southern ports of New Orleans (until its occupation in 1862) and Wilmington, North Carolina.[101] As the Liverpudlian blockade runner Thomas E. Taylor wrote, "firm after firm, with an entirely free conscience, set about endeavoring to recoup itself for the loss of legitimate trade."[102] Revealingly, the Confederacy appointed close to half of its foreign consuls to the Caribbean to coordinate this activity.[103]

Confederate operations in Liverpool, meanwhile, relied on Charles Kuhn Prioleau, the overseas partner of Fraser, Trenholm and Co., the British branch house of John Fraser & Co., based in Charleston. Fraser, Trenholm opened in 1852 under Edward L. Trenholm, before Prioleau and James T. Welsman, a fellow Charlestonian, took it over in 1856. With the outbreak of war Welsman left for New York, leaving Prioleau the sole partner in Britain. Prioleau was a man of social standing in Liverpool, having married Mary Elizabeth Wright, daughter of the wealthy ship-owner Richard Wright. The couple owned a Scottish country estate and lived in some style in a spacious townhouse at 19 Abercromby Square, its foyer decorated with paintings of a palmetto tree and crescent moon—state symbols of South Carolina.

Before any shots were fired, Fraser, Trenholm's steamers shipped arms from New York and Liverpool to Charleston and transported the British-built Blakely cannon used in the bombardment of Fort Sumter.[104] In late 1861 the Confederate Treasury Department designated the bank as its foreign depository—a risky strategy given the firm's narrow escape from insolvency in 1859. Credit was also issued to Confederate agents through the Liverpool branch, though remittances rarely kept pace with expenditure.[105] Confederate agents fanned out across the British Isles on procurement operations from Prioleau's office. As late as 1864, he complained that "armies of contractors and adventurers continue to arrive daily." But, because these agents operated under instructions issued variously from the War, Navy, State, and Treasury departments in Richmond, with limited overall coordination, Prioleau judged that they did little "beyond perhaps precipitating some grand or petty nothing."[106] To Henry Hotze, such men were "leeches" on the Confederate purse.[107]

Besides gathering at Fraser, Trenholm's offices at Rumford Court, Confederates lived at Stoune's boarding house on Gilbert Street and socialized in the offices, dockyards, and warehouses of Liverpool's maritime industries.[108] The Adelphi Hotel, long popular with American travelers, hosted Confederate emissaries and banquets for the Southern Club, founded in the port in 1862. The Southern Club's reading rooms in the Tower Building also provided a haven for Confederates and a platform for visiting speakers to launch pro-Southern campaigns (see figure 13). In October 1862, for instance, Governor Morehead of Kentucky addressed the Club as a "mere wanderer and an exile" and attacked Union supporters for "drenching the entire land in blood in order to produce brotherly affection" before declaring that "the South has shown that she intends under all circumstances and in every contingency to maintain her independence."[109]

Manchester manufacturers made maintaining Confederate independence easier. Southern sympathies ran high among cotton traders, textile manufacturers, and armories in "Cottonopolis" who were eager to do business with Confederate purchasers. Vital supplies of woolens, shoes, trousers, socks, beef, bacon, rifles, cannon, shells, cartridge bags, and other paraphernalia of war made its way from Manchester warehouses to the Confederate front (though not without substantial losses form the

FIGURE 13. In the center of the picture is St Nicholas Church; to its right stands the home of the Liverpool Southern Club, the Tower Building, which enjoyed a prominent view of the steamers and blockade runners entering the port. Image: W. G. Herdman, "Liverpool Landing Stage," 1864, courtesy of Liverpool Record Office, Liverpool Libraries.

blockade).[110] In April 1862, Manchester merchants and industrialists raised a total of £90,000 (roughly £11 million today), which they invested in munitions to supply to the Confederacy.[111] In total, Stephen Wise, the chief historian of Confederate blockade running, has estimated that more than 60 percent of the South's modern arms, three million pounds of lead (one third of the Army's requirements), and 2,250,000 pounds of saltpeter for making gunpowder (two-thirds of its requirements) were imported by its overseas agents.[112] "The amount of funds the rebels must have at their command here is surprising," wrote Adams in his diary.[113]

In London, a range of businesses provided the Confederacy with material support ranging from grapeshot revolvers to buttons. Firms tied to Parliament, such as W. S. Lindsay & Co. and Alexander Collie & Co., were of particular importance, and linked the Confederacy's procurement campaign with the Parliamentary supporters of recognition.[114] The city also provided shelter for Confederate agents. Lindsay's offices at Austin Friars in the City were used frequently by Bulloch and Colin J. McRae. Between September and December 1863, the short-lived London Confederate States Commercial League, which hoped to foster trading connections between Britain and the South, could be visited at St Mildred's Court, the offices of gun manufacturer James Yeomans, who completed a number of contracts on behalf of the Confederacy.[115]

Saville Row housed the Confederate States Commercial Agency, established by Henry Hotze in 1862, which became the London hub of Confederate activity.

Hotze's appointment to the post of Confederate Commercial Agent on November 14, 1861 was a shrewd move. Before his arrival in Britain, Hotze had served a brief diplomatic apprenticeship as Secretary to the American legation in Brussels (1858–59), after which he worked as a journalist for the Mobile, Alabama, *Register*. In Mobile, as is now widely understood, Hotze became acquainted with William L. Yancey, McRae (who would later become the chief Confederate financial agent in Europe), and James D. B. DeBow, editor of *DeBow's Review*.[116] When war broke out, Hotze enlisted as a private in the Mobile Cadets and saw action at the Battle of Bull Run. Robert Bonner has demonstrated that Hotze's early career was shaped by his engagement with international scientific racism. Hotze produced the first translation of Arthur de Gobineau's *Essai sur l'Inégalité des Races Humaines,* which identified race as the motor of human history and stressed the degeneracy of non-white races.[117] This early intellectual engagement and diplomatic experience equipped Hotze perfectly for his post.

Hotze's instructions were to "direct the education" of Britain on Confederate affairs and to convince Europe of the ability of the Southern states "to prosecute the war until their independence shall be no longer assailed."[118] Upon arrival in London, Hotze followed James Mason from social club to social club, aware that these were "the principal foci of public opinion in the metropolis;" in this milieu he took the pulse of English public opinion and even secured a private interview with Chancellor of the Exchequer, William Ewart Gladstone.[119] He established the Confederate Commercial Agency at 17 Saville Row, from where he surveyed the fluctuating fortunes of his cause. British public opinion, Hotze informed Robert Hunter at the Confederate State Department, displayed a "gross, callous, undisguised selfishness and almost brutal indifference" to "our great spectacle on the other hemisphere." After a month's stay in the capital, Hotze was convinced that "most of us have been too rapid in our conclusions and too sanguine in our expectations as regards the policy of Europe and especially England." The English, in Hotze's estimation, had a "cowardly . . . dread of war" and a "repugnance to our institutions which . . . is a part of the national conscience and therefore an honest article of the national creed."[120]

Hotze joined the social whirl of London's Season with panache (satirized by *Harper's* in figure 14), disbursing gifts of American whiskey

FIGURE 14. In this satirical drawing *Harper's* neatly captured the manifold ways Southern agents attempted to sway English opinion by courting senior politicians, the press, and public. But it also captured the essential barrier facing Southern commissioners: they were locked out of British high society and so were forced to sneak into the box besides the Queen's at the Opera and, absent an official invite, to contrive to bump into the Foreign Secretary Lord John Russell on the street. Image: "How the 'Southern Commissioner' tried to mould [sic] public opinion in England," *Harper's Weekly*, July 27, 1861, Library of Congress Prints and Photographs Division.

and Cuban cigars, and spoke in passing of the cultural affinity between the British aristocracy and Southern society, although he, like other Confederate emissaries, had no prewar connections to draw upon. The twenty-six-year-old cultivated British opinion-makers and the press far more effectively than his firebrand counterparts, such as the explosive (and better funded) Edwin DeLeon and the abrasive Mason. Hotze reported in September 1862 that he had employed seven English journalists in the Confederate cause and was himself writing for *The Times*, the London *Standard,* the London *Herald,* and the *Money Market Review,* a small weekly with a big reputation amongst financiers.[121] Although Hotze had a large degree of success penetrating the British press, the Charlestonian soon became convinced of the value of establishing his own sheet "not merely as a means of reading public opinion, but as a channel through which arguments and facts can be conveyed unofficially to the Government itself."[122] Hotze's "little kingdom," *The Index,* came into print on May 1, 1862.[123] *The Index* was Hotze's masterstroke. The paper was much more than a mouthpiece for the Confederate cause and became the physical and symbolic center of the Confederate cause in Europe (see chapter 4).

Confederate agents constructed networks amongst those with substantial commercial ties to the South; many of these men became informal diplomatic and propaganda collaborators. Blockade runners, such as James Spence and Alexander Collie, and shipbuilders sympathetic to the Confederacy found solace in the Liverpool Southern Club and later the Southern Independence Association (SIA).[124] Southern ranks were swelled by textile manufacturers who financed the efforts of Confederate societies and played a prominent role in public debate. Forty-nine of the eighty-three manufacturers and businessmen identified as members of the SIA were directly involved in cotton manufacturing.[125] "Associations of this sort, to do us good," Hotze observed, "must derive their sap from British soil." As such the Confederacy, while it could offer financial and logistical support, could not direct their activity and was, in Hotze's estimation, "therefore like a cork on the waters."[126]

Impressive as these organizations were, they were highly localized. By 1863, all but seven of the SIA's thirty-three chapters were in Lancashire and Cheshire.[127] By contrast, between November 1861 and January 1864, pro-Union forces organized close to one hundred meetings in London and southern England alone.[128] Lancashire was itself by no means a solid pro-Southern bloc, as there were more pro-Union meetings in the county than pro-Confederate—and of the latter, there were none in Liverpool. Pro-Confederate meetings in the county were even turned into spontaneous pro-Union meetings, such as in Stalybridge in September 1862, where workers at a theoretically Southern meeting voted 100 to 1 in favor of a motion that the Southern states were responsible for the cotton famine.[129] Confederate supporters fared especially poorly in the old "petition towns" of the British anti-slavery movement such as Halifax, Bolton, Leeds, Sheffield, Newcastle, Glasgow, and Edinburgh. After the passage of the Emancipation Proclamation in 1863, there were fifty-six working-class demonstrations in support of the Union, the largest of which took place at Exeter Hall where participation was so great that The Strand was crowded with people long before the beginning of proceedings.[130]

Confederate Clubs disseminated propaganda and built connections among local communities. They functioned in the same manner as analogous clubs, such as workingmen's associations or the ACC, with committees, membership fees, and social events, such as lectures, dinners, and public meetings. These were important spaces for Confederate activity. The London Confederate States Aid Association opened an office in late 1862 on Devonshire Street—adjacent to the American Legation at Upper Portland Place—where weekly discussion groups combined propaganda with socialization.[131] Confederate agents followed the progress of these clubs closely, but they could not match the organizational capacity of the pro-Union anti-slavery societies whose protest machinery was in place and could be mobilized with comparative ease.

Over time, Confederate commissioners became effective practitioners of the social dimensions of foreign relations and were welcomed in aristocratic residences, where they were fêted at lavish soirees. Mason and Yancey both lodged at Bedgebury Park, the Kent estate of Tory politician Alexander Beresford Hope. The Reverend Francis W. Tremlett's home in Belsize Park was known affectionately to Commander Mathew Maury and Captain Raphael Semmes as "rebel's roost."[132] The Earl of Wharncliffe's Mayfair mansion was the locale for the founding of the London Branch of the SIA, which drew together the coalition of MPs and Lords organizing on the Confederacy's behalf. The aristocracy provided some, but by no means the only, support for the Confederacy. Of the SIA's approximate 661-strong membership, forty-three names can be identified as either marquises, viscounts, lords, or knights.[133] But membership in the SIA was a far cry from lending financial or material support, and the number of peers who provided substantive assistance can be counted on one hand. Politically, however, they tended to be Tories or old-line Whigs.[134] It was in this respect that Goldwin Smith, the Oxford don and apostle of American democracy in Britain, labelled the SIA "highly aristocratic in its character."[135]

As a number of excellent recent works have made clear, there were no direct patterns of support for North or South based on social class or political party, but it is probable that the Confederacy relied to a much greater degree materially and financially on British aristocratic support. Contemporaries also noted the apparent affinity between the Confederacy and the aristocracy. In Liverpool, Dudley was informed by correspondents that the Confederacy drew its support from "old Tories, stick-in-the-mud Whigs, or paid partisans of Jeff Davis and Co."[136] Aristocratic support was a reflection of long-held views about Parliamentary reform much more than an expression of sympathy for all that the Confederacy stood for. As the Conservative peer Lord Stanley observed, "America is the country of equality, and has succeeded, in the minds of our upper classes, to the place which France filled in the days of the great revolution, when France was regarded as the enemy of aristocracy, monarchy and the church establishment."[137] For others predisposed to view the conflict in ideological terms, the same lesson was drawn. "The real secret of the exultation which manifests . . . over our troubles and disasters," John Lothrop Motley wrote to Bright, "is their hatred not to America so much as democracy in England."[138] Adams surmised the attitude of British peers as turning on "the question of aristocracy and democracy. The former interest wishes us to fail because our success may ultimately be its ruin."[139]

Foreign relations historians should tread carefully through the complexity of British political culture in this period. The Palmerston-Gladstone administration of 1859–65 was a carefully balanced coalition between Peelite conservatives like Gladstone, Whig grandees like Lord John Russell, radicals like John Stuart Mill, and middle-class commercial and industrial men like Forster.[140] The members of that coalition occupied a wide range of positions on the most effective mode of parliamentary reform. Nevertheless, they shared a view with many Conservatives that the maintenance and reform of the nation's institutions (meaning, most often, "the constitution") were two sides of the same coin.[141] Many Liberal politicians positioned themselves as moderates patrolling the ground between the Tories and the radicals, or as Russell put it to his brother in 1849, to stand between "the old fortress of Tory prejudice" and "the high ground of the mountain."[142] The language of British popular liberalism in the 1860s was undoubtedly shaped by the Civil War, as many historians have recognized, but the variety and diversity of British views on electoral reform did not map cleanly onto views of American democracy.[143] While for many the war fit easily into ideological predispositions, as Don Doyle's recent work has so cogently demonstrated, for still others in Parliament and the press it was perfectly possible to view the war (and the Union for that matter) as a cautionary tale of the dangers of democratic excess, remain committed to Parliamentary reform at home, and simultaneously oppose Southern independence.[144] Thus, when Confederate propagandists reached out to Britons as kindred spirits under assault from democratic forces, they often went wide of the mark.

Similar patterns were at work in British anti-slavery opinion. Even anti-abolitionists managed to maintain their anti-slavery credentials by arguing for incremental change over time and an ordered, peaceful transition to freedom rather than "manumission . . . at the point of the sword."[145] Lingering in the minds of many was the British experience of emancipation in the West Indies and the traumatic effects of the Indian "mutiny" of 1857–58, which raised the specter of the precise form of racial uprising that many feared would be the outcome of Lincoln's rash emancipation proclamation, which did not provide for a period of apprenticeship or compensation for slaveowners. The Proclamation was "monstrous, reckless, devilish," according to *Blackwood's Edinburgh Magazine,* which concluded that to defeat the Confederacy the Union "would league itself with Beelzebub, and seek to make a hell of half a continent."[146] For their part, radicals and abolitionists were just as frustrated and could not understand the border states' exemption from the order. "The leaders in the Federal Government are not equal to the occasion," concluded Richard Cobden in a letter to Bright.[147]

Confederate emissaries grasped British attacks as a sign that intervention or mediation were imminent and lobbied hard to convince Britons that slavery would be abolished sooner under an independent Confederacy. Yet they badly misjudged the extent to which Britain had become an "anti-slavery state," to borrow Richard Huzzey's perceptive phrase. As Huzzey argues, the language of anti-slavery was so pervasive that it provided both a model of social change and a versatile language for radicals who compared unfranchised workingmen to slaves, and for moderates, who urged gradualist approaches to emancipation.[148] The latter became a standard line among the South's supporters in Britain. In his pamphlet *The Confederate Secession,* the Tory Peer William Schomberg Robert Kerr argued that "both with regard to the electoral franchise and to slave emancipation, it may be possible to advance too hurriedly; and in that case, our philanthropy does more harm than good."[149] Such gradualism lay behind perhaps the most widely-read defense of Southern secession, James Spence's *American Union,* which ran through four editions in English and was translated into several languages before the war's end. According to Benjamin, Spence was "the most energetic and resourceful friend the Confederacy had in England."[150] Yet the book declared slavery "a gross anachronism, a thing of two thousand years ago—the brute force of dark ages obtruding into the minds of the nineteenth century." "Remove from slavery, as it is well to do, all romance and exaggeration," he continued, "it remains a foul blot, from which all must desire to purge the annals of the age."[151]

Confederate diplomats struggled against the variety of anti-slavery opinion. Even Hotze found his "own voice too feeble to pierce through the callous selfishness which, like animal fat, coats the hearts of these Old World nations."[152] Enthusiastic public support for the Union among the British middle and working classes following the Emancipation Proclamation terminally damaged Confederate diplomacy. Early in 1863, Confederate statesmen and commentators reassessed the rebel nation's place in the world. The *Richmond Examiner* complained bitterly that rebel commissioners were "now waiting in servants' halls and on the back stairs" at the Foreign Office and in society.[153] Locked out of British social and political circles, Confederate emissaries gathered gossip where they could, but struggled to sift fact from fiction. "The Confederate States are doomed to disappointment and chagrin" in their foreign relations, reflected the *Examiner* at the close of the year.[154] "We have no friends in the world," thundered Confederate Congressman W. G. Swan of Tennessee, adding that it was about time that his peers "discard the maudlin balderdash about our 'anglo-Saxon [sic] kindred,' and understand that once and for all that, next to New England, our worst enemy in the world is old England."[155]

Yet, through the Anglo-Saxonism Swan invoked only to deplore, surprising affinities between Union and Confederate public diplomacy emerged and portended the future contours of Anglo-American imperial collaboration. The informal diplomacy of the Southerners Hotze and George McHenry and pro-Union ideologue George Francis Train intersected in the forum of transatlantic interchanges regarding race. In the process they aided the dissemination of the fundamental principles governing late-nineteenth century conceptions of the Anglo-Saxon's mission to civilize inferior races. Their pseudo-scientific racial theory may have drawn heavily from popular mid-century currents of Anglo-Saxonism and anti-black racism, but looked beyond the context of slavery to the pursuit of common transimperial goals. These ideas rode emergent racial and imperial knowledge circuits, but Union diplomacy continued to be most effective in longstanding transatlantic evangelical, abolitionist, and humanitarian networks—made clear, as we shall soon see, by the United States Sanitary Commission's London Branch, which successfully leveraged these connections in defense of the Union.

CHAPTER 4

Empire, Philanthropy, Public Diplomacy

The "American question" provoked a staggering variety of meanings for embattled radicals and emboldened aristocrats across the Old World.[1] As Don Doyle has recently described it, contemporary Europeans viewed the conflict as "a decisive showdown between the forces of *popular* versus *hereditary* sovereignty, *democracy* versus *aristocracy*, *free* versus *slave* labor, all rolled into one grand epic battle taking place in the distant American arena."[2] In the British case, the idea of a "grand epic battle" between the forces of progress and reaction has proven especially appealing because it reflects the furious domestic battles over parliamentary reform that animated the nation throughout the 1860s. "You are fighting the battle of liberalism in Europe as well as the battle of freedom in America," the English liberal Richard Cobden assured the radical Republican Charles Sumner in January 1865.[3] Union and Confederate propagandists appealed to a global audience through the conceptual currents of liberalism, nationalism, and race that crisscrossed the Atlantic in the mid-nineteenth century. In the process of defining nationhood and nationality and of mobilizing domestic economies to fulfill the demands of industrial warfare, Northerners and Southerners not only turned to analogous global events but attempted to illustrate how effectively interwoven their respective sections were within the global economy.[4]

An unintended consequence of historians' focus on the ideological conflict between democracy and aristocracy has been the neglect of one of the central optics through which British commentators and Americans overseas framed the war's meaning: empire.[5] British political historians have recently shifted focus from the class-defined meanings of the Victorian nation that have preoccupied historians of Civil War foreign relations to the intersections of nation, empire, race, and anti-slavery.[6] For outward-looking Northerners and Southerners alike, situating the Civil War within the context of the expanding power and scope of British imperialism and domestic debates over imperial policy came naturally. Although divided over how best to harness British imperial power to their own ends, Confederates and Unionists overseas were forthcoming about the supposed convergence of interests between their respective governments and British imperial self-interest. Emigrant diplomats engaged closely with the post-emancipation dilemmas of Britain's supposedly anti-slavery empire and embraced the racial hierarchies that buttressed British imperialism. This chapter places Union and Confederate public diplomacy into this imperial framework.

Pro-Union Americans in Britain relied on the *London American* for their diplomatic voice. The *American*'s editors, John Adams Knight and A. W. Bostwick, quickly rallied behind the Union cause, blamed the war on Southern intransigence, and reported the lecture campaign of its owner, George Francis Train. Train's propaganda mixed radical Young American republicanism with appeals to shared Anglo-Saxon superiority over the world's "uncivilized" inhabitants. Through appeals to imperial identity, Union and Confederate diplomacy forged unexpected affinities. Confederate agitation was coordinated by Henry Hotze through his now well-known propaganda journal *The Index,* whose offices on Fleet Street were just two doors down from the *American*'s.[7] Hotze and his fellow propagandists portrayed Southern slavery as the economic engine of the global economy and simultaneously attempted to spread American racial "science" amongst European race theorists. The ideas of Train and Hotze intersected in these intellectual circles that anticipated transimperial race-making in the late nineteenth century.

In the war's final year, transnational currents of humanitarianism shaped Union diplomacy. Managed by the energetic Edmund Crisp Fisher, the United States Sanitary Commission's London Branch brought new verve to Union diplomatic strategy. Fisher distributed Sanitary Commission literature through American networks in Britain and channeled financial and material support for the Union from Americans overseas. The London Branch's mission is emblematic of the emergence of new transnational networks whose lineage can be directly linked to the global impact of the US Civil War. Fisher's London Branch had roots in Britain's

American community and subsequently forged new intellectual connections between humanitarian movements on both sides of the Atlantic. For their own part, Fisher and his allies found that the longstanding associational and civic life of the London-Americans and Britain's network of charitable and reform organizations were the ideal vehicle for mobilizing British moral suasion behind the Union cause. The Sanitary Commission's humanitarian impulse therefore looked forward to the emergence of international society in the early twentieth century, but despite its progressive orientation was equally entwined with the Anglo-Saxon mythologizing increasingly central to Anglo-American relations.

EMPIRE AND RACE IN CIVIL WAR FOREIGN RELATIONS

In the war's early months, George Francis Train was the most vocal Union propagandist in Great Britain. Train first arrived in Britain in the fall of 1850 to undertake his commercial apprenticeship with the White Diamond Line of Enoch Train & Co. (owned by his father's cousin), a Boston-Liverpool packet line shipping Staffordshire crockery, iron and steel, and various other dry goods.[8] The Bostonian then had a varied and impulsive career touring the globe as a partner in Caldwell, Train & Co. He returned to Britain once more in 1858 as a promoter of street railways in Liverpool, Birkenhead, and London. With the outbreak of the Civil War, Train reinvented himself again as the Union's chief booster. The self-proclaimed prophet of "Spread-Eagle" American nationalism entertained tenaciously throughout London, hosting dinners and banquets marked by spontaneous renditions of "De Camptown Races" with improvised verses.[9]

Train brought persistence and urgency to the Union's public diplomacy in Britain. Between January 1861 and March 1862, Train made twenty-three major public addresses in addition to hosting countless breakfasts and lunches, often on days of US national celebration, and writing numerous articles for the *London American*.[10] Under Train's influence, the *American* exhorted emigrants into activity. "If there ever was a time when Americans residing abroad should express their patriotism, that time is now," the *American* implored.[11] Disdaining the moral treachery of neutrality, Train chided his audience, "sojourn abroad does not destroy patriotism."[12] Through the *American* he scolded prominent emigrant bankers for "waiting for victories before hoisting the Secession or Union Flags."[13] Train's speeches praised the United States' revolutionary past and commitment to political liberty, but he was more interested in shocking his audiences than persuading them and could barely disguise his habitual Anglophobia. In June 1861, Train hosted a pro-Union banquet at the Westminster Palace Hotel in commemoration of the Battle of Bunker Hill. Like Peabody's Fourth of July celebrations, Train's guest list was designed to maximize the public diplomacy of the occasion. More than a dozen prominent British newspaper editors were present alongside the authors George Augustus Sala and Thomas Colley Grattan; the publisher George Routledge; and Paul Julius Reuter, founder of Reuter's Telegram Company. The dinner, Train told the assembled company, was convened "in the hope of counteracting the evil effects of those *secession* journalists and statesmen who cheer so loudly whenever the 'bursting of the republican bubble' is alluded to."[14]

Train appealed directly to Britain's self-conception as an anti-slavery empire. Britain, he claimed, "must acknowledge that the republic is a success, or keep on as she has done, siding with the rebels." "We must hang some new pictures on the wall," he taunted, of "abolitionist England sitting affectionately in the lap of negro slavery." Train repeatedly linked the Civil War to America's ongoing struggle to consolidate the legacy of the American Revolution, arguing that sectional strife was the culmination of the revolutionary process. "Our revolution is a war of ideas—a war of freedom—a war for oppressed mankind," he told an audience in May 1862, contrasting it with the policy of Britain whose "idea of liberty is freedom for England and slavery for all mankind."[15] "Thank God, America is emancipated from England," he told an audience in June, "and intends now to turn the tables and patronize England as England has formerly patronized America."[16]

By strategically manipulating the Irish Question, Train's English tour became a platform to prove his credentials as a pro-Union Democrat committed to the revolutions of 1848. Speaking at a meeting of the Irish Brotherhood of St Patrick in London in August 1862, Train distilled his Anglophobia into a prediction of England's impending downfall. According to Train, in the ideological battle between empire and self-determination *the American rebellion is the world's rebellion,* and the life of America is the death of England."[17] Outlining a fanciful system to decolonize Britain's white settler colonies of Canada and Australia, Train told the assembled Irishmen that *"The downfall of England is rapid . . . when its extremities decay."*[18] Should Irishmen overcome sectarian prejudices and clashes, he predicted, a united Ireland would result under the benign influence of American republicanism. "Cry Union in America and Liberty in Ireland," Train bellowed.[19]

Neutrality and belligerent rights raised questions over empire and foreign relations in unexpected ways throughout the war. Like many Union supporters, Train's Anglophobia was born from frustration with Britain's failure to maintain a strict neutrality. By blessing the Confederacy with the rights of a belligerent power through the Neutrality Proclamation of May 13, 1861, the Palmerston administration brought these issues to the center of debates over Anglo-American relations. Before his audience at the Bunker Hill commemoration, Train challenged the assembled Britons:

> Change positions for a moment. Did America hasten to acknowledge the Irish Rebellionists as belligerents, and send a hostile fleet off the Irish shore to encourage the Irish? Suppose the United States had dispatched a squadron to the mouth of the Thames with instructions to await the issue of the rising of the Chartists? Did America assist Papineau in Canada? Do we sympathise with the New Zealanders? . . . Did not America share the deepest interest in the success of the British arms in India? Did not our people put the flags at half-mast throughout the land when the death of Havelock fell like a knell upon the nations?[20]

The reciprocal duty of neutrality in Anglo-American relations was perhaps Train's strongest argument and placed him in the mainstream of Union opinion. But, by the end of the war, and once back on American soil, Train used the issue to stoke Irish-American nationalism further. "All that I ask now," he told the Fenian Congress in Philadelphia, "is that America shall acknowledge Ireland as a belligerent."[21] "It is our duty, as England has done so much for our blacks to do something for her whites," Train continued. According to Train, living conditions in Ireland were "below the level of our lately enslaved negroes."[22] Like many Young Americans overseas, Train made little distinction between nationalist aspirations and the United States' global interests.

However limited Train's ideas appear, his emphasis on national self-determination, the strict application of international legal norms, and racial proscriptions placed him in dialogue with many of the leading intellectual currents of the mid-nineteenth century. Before the war, Train drew from popular currents of mid-century Anglo-Saxonism and predicted that "the two great branches of the Anglo-Saxon race" would cooperate "under the flag of our own happy land and the strong arm of England."[23] In another summary of the war's meaning, Train argued that it was "working out a new destiny for our western civilization," and that "humanity" had "gone to America to pass its manhoood."[24] The Bostonian therefore exported a vision of the United States in which

The G. F. TRAIN:

Going it like Thunder, with Bull on track.

FIGURE 15. Train's dramatic personality and speaking style were the source of much curiosity and amusement to contemporary observers. The Bostonian was parodied as George Augustus Strain, "the self-elected representative of Yankeedoodledom," in one pamphlet circulating London in June 1861 that attacked Train as "as the bould [sic] advocate of secession and negro bondage" (Anon., *Bunkum Hill Festival* [1861], 2). The pamphlet is anonymously written but is in the collection of emigrant book dealer Henry Stevens (Folder 29, Henry Stevens Family Correspondence, VHS). Though it was at times impossible to balance his contradictory motives, Train's persistent lecturing lent some urgency to the Union's cause in the war's early months and placed the question of neutrality before the British public in dramatic fashion. Image: "The G. F. Train: Going it like thunder, with bull on track," *Vanity Fair,* July 26, 1862, Lin 2906.5, Houghton Library, Harvard University.

its racial origins, liberalism, and contribution to the ongoing processes of civilization would confer international legitimacy on its democratic-republican nationhood. But his emphasis on cooperative empire antici-pated the Anglo-American racialism of the late nineteenth century. Seen in this light, Train's hope "to cement forever the union of England and America" appears prescient.[25] Thirty-five years after the US Civil War, elements of his vision of a reciprocal Anglo-American empire would flourish in the American "colony" in London (see chapter 5).

Train cut an eccentric figure in London (captured in figure 15). In some circles, Train was known as the "Yankee Bull in an English China Shop." Train's eccentricities frustrated most Americans in Britain, however. According to Benjamin Moran, Train was "a complete charlatan" and a "mad dog."[26] "Mr. Train speaks, or rather raves, once a week in some public room," wrote the *Saturday Review,* "and one of the functions of the *London American* is to report the violent absurdities of which he thus delivers himself."[27]

Nevertheless, Secretary of State William Henry Seward viewed the *American* as a worthwhile enterprise and contributed $100 to the publication in 1862 to help it become a "permanent thing in England."[28] Train left England in early 1863, shortly after his arrest for inciting Irish revolutionaries. The *American* was left in the hands of his secretary George P. Bemis, but soon folded. Train and the *American*'s successes were mixed. While the *American* became the focal point for Union agitation in the opening years of the war, agents of public diplomacy were most effective when they exploited the intersection of Britain's American emigrant community with British high society—as the case of the London Branch of the United States Sanitary Commission highlights. More revealing is Train's intersection with the discourse of race in Confederate diplomacy. When contrasting the imperial-monarchical rule of Britain over Ireland, Train stoked Fenian grievances and played on popular racial prejudices by declaring that in the United States "five negroes are allowed three votes by the Constitution, which makes a negro three-fifths of a man; but in England he is not counted so high as the cattle of the field or the trees in the forest."[29] This was no mere rhetoric: Train cultivated intellectual connections with European and American racial theorists and viewed civilization and white republican rule as synonymous. In so doing, Train implicated himself in the crosscurrents of the Confederacy's voice in Europe, *The Index.*

Henry Hotze's propaganda paper was the centerpiece of a major Confederate publishing arm in Britain that commissioned and financed the publication and circulation of pro-Southern publications and intelligence.[30] Once established the paper secured correspondents in Dublin, Frankfurt, Berlin, Versailles, Paris, Turin, and even Australia, in addition to New Orleans, Norfolk, New York, and Hartford (CT), eventually achieving a modest estimated circulation of 2,500.[31] Its editorial pages, all penned by Hotze, lobbied for the recognition of Southern independence and hoped to "delve deeply" into "the rich mines of British thought" and bring the South "back to a closer intellectual communion with the parent source of their language and literature."[32] *The Index* set forth the intellectual case for recognition based on the Confederacy's right to self-determination and commitment to free trade. Hotze invoked the ethnicity of Southern nationhood, emphasizing the heroism of Confederate soldiers and their leaders in contrast to the tyrannous rule of the North over the South. "It is impossible to enslave eight millions of people who prefer ruin and death to national dishonour," Hotze wrote in a typical editorial, adding that "the independence of the South will break down a monopoly that impoverishes the world. Posterity will wonder at the apathy with which nations conscious of the advantage of free trade beheld the contest."[33]

The power of Hotze's argument was not solely in its appeal to the framework of romantic nationalism but in its blending of King Cotton's political economy with an expansive vision of the South's place at the heart of the nineteenth century global economy. In Hotze's vision, free trade, cotton, and vast agrarian resources would bring stability and prosperity to the Anglo-Southern dominance of the global marketplace.[34] Hotze invoked British economic self-interest in terms that would appeal to an incipient imperial economy. "The independence of the South, opening to unrestricted free trade a market of fabulous capacity for production and consumption," he argued in June 1862, "would be equal to the discovery of another India."[35] Hotze tenuously claimed that "the Southerners were the first people in modern times to advocate the principle of Free Trade" but had "been kept from putting their favourite theory into practice for years by the legislative aggression of the North."[36] Hotze made the argument most succinctly, and ill-advisedly, when he wrote of the Southern economy: "they produce all that England consumes, they consume all that England produces."[37] Other Confederate propagandists echoed Hotze's view of the interdependence of the British and Confederate economies. In *The South Vindicated,* Hotze's collaborator James Williams pointedly argued that Southern planters were "the overseer[s] for Great Britain, while Great Britain is but the factor of the planter."[38]

Founded as the effects of the cotton famine took hold in British textile districts, *The Index*'s core argument was that the partnership between transatlantic free trade and Southern cotton would cement African slavery's centrality to the world's economic system.[39] Hotze dismissed the attempts of the Manchester-based Cotton Supply Association and its supporters, such as the industrialist Thomas Clegg, to gain supplies of cotton from India and the Empire as "chimerical," goaded Britons over the economic failure of West Indian emancipation, and taunted that the Union viewed "the Union Jack as a paltry rag."[40] Such a strategy was almost rewarded in the summer of 1862, when Robert E. Lee pushed George McClellan's Army of the Potomac out of Virginia and staked the Confederacy's military claim for independence. As news of McClellan's retreat from the Peninsula filtered across the Atlantic, Hotze took advantage of a growing British sense that the North was incapable of overcoming Southern armies and argued that Britain's "listless scepticism" over Southern recognition had brought "the wolf" to Lancashire's door as the supply of cotton dwindled. Not to recognize the South threw it open to the "success of England's most dangerous rival and bitterest foe," and the new master of American cotton would be the Morrill Tariff.[41]

Hotze's faith in cotton's power continued throughout the war. In a December 1863 editorial, the propagandist warned that "jubilations" over the end of Lancashire's cotton famine were "altogether premature." The famine, Hotze wrote, had exposed the vulnerabilities of Britain's textile industry such that spinners were "as willing to depend on charity as to accept the scantily remunerated work which is all that can now be offered them."[42] Similarly, Hotze collaborated in the publication of George McHenry's *The Cotton Trade* (1863), which he praised as a volume that "does not beat about the bush."[43] In McHenry's analysis, even if Britain succeeded in developing India's cotton industries, the Colonial Office would only reinforce the importance of the Southern states' commercial dynamo. "As the vast sums of money now flowing back to India develops the resources of that country under the careful management of the British race," McHenry postulated, "the demand for English manufactured goods will greatly augment, and furnish occupation for the increased slave-labour of the South."[44]

Confederate propagandists framed Southern economics in world-historical terms. "What is the genius of modern civilization?" *The Index*'s editor asked subscribers in June 1862, before answering that "commerce is the chosen apostle of Christianity and civilization." The South was the economic engine of civilization, wrote Hotze, and supplied the world with slave-produced cotton, sugar, tea, coffee, and tobacco. "Do away with them," he wrote, "and the world must return to the *status* of the sixteenth century."[45] The North's campaign against the South, he later warned, "aims at converting into a barren waste one of the most fertile and productive regions of the inhabited globe."[46] In the slaveholder's view of the mid-nineteenth-century global economy, to borrow Matthew Karp's phrasing, "slavery and progress had proved impressively congruent."[47]

With British intervention still a slim possibility in May 1862, Hotze placed the South in a transatlantic racial context that celebrated its "closer affinity of blood to the British parent stock, than the North, with its mongrel compound of all the surplus population of the world." Maintaining a revealing silence about Anglo-American imperial rivalry in Central and South America, Hotze argued that Britain and the Confederate states were "natural allies and best friends" bound by "mutual interests" of descent, manners, and commerce. While the South was Britain's "natural offspring," according to *The Index,* the North was "if not as a bastard, at least a relative of doubtful legitimacy."[48]

Southern elites invoked transatlantic cultural connections in a bid to redefine the South's relationship to the wider world in the face of challenges from the unfolding process of global emancipation and nation-building. Far from being isolated and parochial, planter-politicians conceived of themselves as members of a cosmopolitan, hemispheric planter class that, united with slaveholders in the Caribbean and Latin America, possessed an acute awareness of global affairs. Alert to the counter-currents in British thought over the success of emancipation in the West Indies, Hotze promoted this vision vigorously, and in one typical passage warned that the South risked becoming "a Jamaica on a larger scale."[49] In the aftermath of British emancipation new forms of colonial labor management emerged around the Empire that encouraged slave-holding elites in the belief that they could protect slavery in the Americas. Yet, like Southern planters, Hotze could not demonstrate the centrality of the Southern economy to global affairs with enough power to overcome skepticism that the fate of the British economy was entwined with the fate of slavery in the South.

Confederate commissioners found early in the war that the South's appeal would be limited in a nation exposed to a wealth of knowledge on Southern slavery.[50] Early vexation with British abolitionism found expression through the flexible framework of American Anglophobia, as some Southern apologists in Britain, frustrated by the failure of recognition, harangued the hypocrisy of the British anti-slavery state. "For *nearly every drop of blood* which flows through the veins of the slaves of the United States," charged James Williams of Kentucky, "our mother *England has received the price in gold!*"[51] Southern writers had a point when they highlighted the many degrees of "unfreedom" that existed in the British Empire. In histories of slavery and abolition from a north Atlantic perspective, the 1833 Emancipation Act is rightly viewed as a watershed moment. But as one historian has recently pointed out, the chronology of emancipation across the Empire was far from uniform.[52] The Indian Empire, for instance, was exempt from the 1833 Act, and slave trading was not abolished in the region until 1843—slave owning not until 1862. Around the Empire, various forms of apprenticeship, transportation, and penal servitude both predated and outlasted Atlantic slavery and proved enduring means of satisfying colonial labor needs across the globe. In fact, this was made entirely possible because British foreign policy prioritized the battle to end the international slave *trade* rather than promoting foreign emancipation as the most effective method of achieving its objective of ending slavery.[53]

African American activists engaged directly in this debate. But they looked forward instead to an Atlantic world in which free cotton and free labor were the guiding principles of political economy, arguing that both could be advanced by harnessing the Colonial Office's use of abolition to advance its imperial objectives. The search for a solution to this problem led them toward advocating an alliance between abolition, emigration, and the exact "cotton lobby" Hotze hoped to entice with promises of free trade. Before the war, John Sella Martin had declared that emigration and cotton cultivation overseas was "one of the best means to break a link that binds England to this country with such subserviency that she cringes before the great 'Cotton King.'"[54] At a celebration of West Indian emancipation organized by the Leeds Young Men's Anti-Slavery Society in August 1861, William Howard Day encouraged fugitive slaves to avail themselves of the opportunity to migrate to West Africa where they might "produce a supply of cotton to set off against the American slave-grown cotton," which would collapse cotton prices and "strike a fatal blow at the existence of slavery."[55] At another meeting in Birmingham, Day combatively argued that the cotton famine was the "direct consequence of disregard by the Anglo-Saxon races of the rights of the African" but, "with God's truth in one hand, and political economy in the other," African American emigrants could elevate "their brother black men."[56] In July 1860 Day, Martin Delany, Robert Campbell, Henry Highland Garnett, and William Craft (also active in the free produce movement) founded the African Aid Society and throughout the war, promoted free black settlement and cotton cultivation of the Niger Valley.[57] Though highly contentious, these projects were not simplistic counterparts to white imperialism, but a continuation of debates among the free black community over emigration's ambivalent relationship to black Atlantic political identity and anticolonialism and how cotton colonization schemes might further bolster Britain's support for black liberation.

By 1863 there could no longer be any doubt that the British public was hostile toward Southern slavery. "The longer I remain in Europe," Hotze reflected from Saville Row, "the more I become impressed how extremely difficult and delicate the treatment of the subject of slavery is."[58] After the release of the Emancipation Proclamation on January 1, 1863, *The Index*'s editorials descended into full-blooded scientific racialism. In spite of some hostility to Lincoln's message in the British press, notably in the pages of *Punch* and the *Times,* Hotze proceeded with caution, stoking white self-interest with appeals to the benevolence of Southern slavery.[59] "Who would disregard divine and human laws in the blindness of fanaticism which does evil that good may come of it," asked Hotze shortly after the Emancipation Proclamation; "who would set the interest of four million blacks above those of eight million whites, of humanity at large, and of civilization?" He repeated the credo of Southern pro-slave ideologues who contended that slavery was racial philanthropy, arguing that "the hand can not [sic] surely have been an unfriendly one which has thus raised the negro from the turpitudes of the African savage."[60]

The Index placed slavery within an allegedly impartial scientific framework of social hierarchy throughout the world. Slavery was another genus of such English patterns as class hierarchy or the historical subordination of women. Both instances, said Hotze, proved that "intellectual inferiority, and consequently physical, political, and social subordination, are not incompatible with happiness, which does not consist in equality, but in each one performing the part adapted to his or her capacity."[61] Nonetheless, as the Confederate cause drew criticism for its support of slavery, Hotze intensified his paternal rhetoric. "The danger, if danger there is," he wrote, "is the negro's not the white man." "Vilified" and "slandered" by "both honest and dishonest fanaticism," slavery as an institution was undermined, and with it, the security of the enslaved: "The white man everywhere can prosper without it; it is as yet an unsolved problem whether the black man can." Assailed by this fit of fanaticism, the South would be excused from, "the African blood already shed and to be shed in this war."[62]

Hotze, like Baylor before him, moved in currents of international scientific racialism. As Robert Bonner has argued, Hotze forged Anglo-American intellectual connections that anticipated the racial consensus of late nineteenth century empire-building.[63] He cooperated in the establishment of the Anthropological Society in London, an association devoted to the discussion of empire, slavery, and missionary work in Africa and Asia.[64] The Society's work was advertised through the pages of *The Index,* lending the sanction of the Confederacy by inference. Well-known Confederates George McHenry and Albert Taylor Bledsoe sat on the Society's committee. The former, son of the emigrant Confederate George McHenry, resident in London, was funded by Hotze to the tune of £300 in 1864, far more than was supplied to any other individual.[65] (McHenry's uncle James also resided in London, sided with the Union, and was a close friend of Benjamin Moran.)

McHenry launched scathing attacks on the abolitionist movement as a "blood-thirsty party" and made an impassioned defense of white supremacy over Southern slaves, who were, he fancifully claimed, "the happiest race on the face of the globe."[66] "History proves that the natural condition of the black race is one of servitude in its very worst form," he wrote in his most successful Civil War work, *The African Race in America* (1862).[67] In *The African Race* and *The Cotton Trade in America* (1863), McHenry's views on race and slavery were shaped by transatlantic scientific racism. Like Hotze, McHenry drew strongly from the American school of ethnology, and particularly upon the celebrated work of American ethnographer Samuel George Morton and the long lineage of European racial theorists connected to him that included Franz Joseph Gall, Georges Cuvier, John-Joseph Virey, and Johann Caspar Spurzheim.[68]

Together, McHenry and Hotze intervened in a British imperial debate over the capacities of non-white laborers within the Empire. Hungry for cheap labor, successive British governments were apparently satisfied with various forms of "free" bonded labor regimes and were confident that they did not compromise popular understandings of anti-slavery.[69] Within that discussion, some Britons looked to the Southern states as a laboratory for testing whether African-American racial characteristics were fixed, or if slavery had conditioned so-called racial traits.[70] McHenry and Hotze assured their British readers it was the former. "The Negro's unfitness for civilization," wrote Hotze in November 1863, had been predetermined, and it was "only by observation and experiment that we can determine the exact place in nature which the Negro race should hold."[71] Hotze and like-minded Confederate polemicists therefore linked the Confederate cause to the new race sciences gaining momentum in Victorian Britain in an attempt to direct attention "away from bondage to the shared Anglo-American commitment to white supremacy."[72]

Popular phrenological circuits also connected Hotze and McHenry to George Francis Train. Train deplored the "negromania" of Exeter Hall and its "negropolists."[73] Hotze, the overseas apostle of "American School" racial theory, similarly hoped to correct "the heresies that have gained currency in science and politics—of the equality of the races of man."[74] In a speech redolent of these themes, Train told one British audience in March 1862 that "American slavery is a stepping-stone *to the negro* from African barbarism to Christian Civilization."[75] "In America," he continued, "the Caucasian race has elevated his [the negro's] intellect, as it has improved his physique." But, Train conceded, the "civilized man" could improve them "only as far as he can," for to go further, "*you must first put inside his thick skull nine cubic inches more of brain!*"[76] Train arrived at his crude phrenology by way of the religious sanction of slavery in Leviticus 25 and Exodus 21 and the phrenologist Samuel Roberts Wells, editor of the popular *American Phrenological Journal,* who attended his first pro-Union rally in London on 19 June 1861.[77] The second major influence on Train was James McHenry, who introduced him to the phrenologists Frederick Bridges; Cornelius Donovan, founder of the London Phrenological Society; and Orson Squire Fowler of New York.

Hotze and Train alike sustained the connection between international politics and scientific racialism. Hotze failed to link this successfully to Confederate recognition, and later complained to Judah P. Benjamin that Confederate failure was grounded in the inability of Europeans to appreciate the "unsolved and unprecedented problems involved in the management and education of the African race."[78] It was through the avenue of informal diplomacy that transnational intellectual connections were forged between western racial theorists, who in turn cemented the international legitimacy of racial hierarchy in the post-Civil War decades.[79] The decline of slavery coincided with the expansion of empire and new dilemmas for sustaining white rule. The racial consensus emphasized by these ideologues was encoded over the next half century in new Anglo-American imperial formations. Informal diplomats and overseas agents offer an opportunity for historians of American foreign relations not simply to "thicken" the Civil War's global context, but, through their discussions of racial capacity, connect the war to the century-long challenge of governing and maintaining multiracial imperial projects in Britain and the United States.[80]

THE DIPLOMACY OF HUMANITARIANISM

The Civil War reinvigorated Anglo-American humanitarian movements, as thousands of American men and women volunteered to contribute to wartime relief efforts—fertile ground into which new movements advanced their cause.[81] Patriotic and Christian impulses were institutionalized in June 1861 in the form of the United States Sanitary Commission (USSC), which worked alongside the War Department to organize field hospitals, train nurses, and treat the sick and wounded.[82] The transnational circulation of humanitarian activists and the emergence of new networks of sanitary reform between scientific elites in American and European cities were equally important to the activities of the USSC—as were the philanthropic and diplomatic energies of American emigrants in Britain.[83]

The transatlantic celebrity of Florence Nightingale and the popularity of her 1863 volume *Notes on Hospitals* fueled the interest of American philanthropists in battlefield sanitation, while the British Sanitary Commission of the Crimean War provided the model for the organization of USSC hospitals.[84] The USSC drew heavily from the work of English sanitarians who recommended the disposal of waste, the necessity of ventilated wards, and rapid transportation from battlefield to hospital bed.[85] Such transformations also depended upon the transnational dissemination of information regarding health and disease to train nurses, educate army surgeons, and efficiently organize relief infrastructure. The USSC's scientific philanthropy, then, drew from an international context in which issues of public health, sanitation, and humanitarianism were being examined by new, non-state associations that emphasized the collection and study of data and collaboration with the state.[86]

These transnational currents of scientific philanthropy also increased the international footprint of the USSC itself, with the founding of two overseas branches in 1864. The origins of this international mission were in Paris. Prompted by a "wave of patriotic devotion" that had "rolled across the Atlantic," a coalition of Americans in the City of Love were corralled by Charles S. P. Bowles and his brother William B. Bowles, senior partners of the international financiers Bowles Brothers, into forming a European branch of the Sanitary Commission.[87] Bowles collected $13,372.72 in donations, shipped large amounts of high-grade brandy for medical purposes to Sanitary Commission field hospitals, and forwarded tons of gifts for sale at the New York Sanitary Fair. Bowles was appointed the official USSC Foreign Agent in Europe in the summer of 1864 and was active in the emerging forums of international aid. This mixed approach to relief and agitation would also be adopted by the USSC's London Branch.

This group was founded in a meeting held at the London offices of sewing machine manufacturers Wheeler and Wilson's on February 20,

1864, attended by US Consul General Freeman Harlow Morse, Cyrus M. Field, Judge John G. Winter of Georgia, R. Hunting, and Henry Starr of the firm Wheatley, Starr & Co.[88] Field provided impetus for the new movement in March with a gift of 1,000 tons of coal to be sold at the New York Sanitary Fair. The US Consul in Liverpool, Thomas Haines Dudley, arranged for the American-owned Guion & Co. (managed by Henry Guion of New York) to ship the coal free of charge.[89] In March, a second meeting at the London Tavern, this one chaired by William M. Evarts, in London as legal counsel for the *Alabama* claims, finalized the details of the London Branch's organization, at which the gathered American residents and visitors pledged to "make a combined effort to swell the contributions in aid" of the USSC's efforts.[90] Under guidance from the Commission's President Henry Bellows, the London Branch was conceived as a mission "to convince Englishmen of the strength of democratic or popular institutions" undergoing a "terrible trial" and to "prove" that the "republican bubble had *not* burst."[91]

As with Union foreign relations more broadly, the London Branch mobilized the financial, philanthropic, and social networks laid by the previous decade of organization among American society in London. Peabody and Co., Barings, and Brown, Shipley were nominated as its banks of deposit. Goods would be shipped from London by Wheatley, Starr & Co. and Liverpool by Guion & Co. free of charge.[92] Diplomatic and consular agents were mobilized in support of the Branch. Benjamin Moran, Benjamin Nunn, Charles Lush Wilson, and Freeman Harlow Morse in London, and Thomas Dudley in Liverpool, distributed pamphlets on behalf of the USSC and coordinated the transport of gifts. Its executive and subscription committees were drawn from the diverse character of London-America, but its most high-profile members were those with the greatest social standing. These migrants were integral to the London Branch's success, as they granted access to elite social circles as well as the knowledge they possessed of Union supporters in Britain. At the second meeting, these transatlantic figureheads were appointed to senior positions in the Branch's organizing committee.

If prominent Americans in Britain provided social capital, Edmund Crisp Fisher, an otherwise obscure Illinoisan, provided the momentum. Described by Moran as "a reliable man," Fisher's tenure as secretary was both energetic and entrepreneurial.[93] Through his efforts, the London Branch become both a conduit for donations and gifts from Britain and a far-reaching propaganda arm. From his base in London, Fisher moved quickly and appointed English journalist Frederick Milnes Edge as agent in Manchester. Soon after he penned a circular to "All Americans known to be resident in Britain," in which he exhorted them to contribute to the commission's work. Before Britain's American community lay "a duty which we owe to our country in her hour of danger, battle and death;—a duty forced upon us by every consideration of humanity;—a duty to whose imperative calls no reflecting man can turn a deaf ear."[94]

Fisher opened reading rooms at 21 Cockspur Street near Trafalgar Square, opposite the headquarters of the pro-Confederate Southern Association. More importantly, it was a short walk from Morley's Hotel on the Square's eastern side and the Union Hotel on the western side, both popular with American visitors. Described in the press as "a kind of Union and Emancipation Club, where all who believe in civil and religious liberty may meet to read, chat, write, and rest," the rooms acted as the hub of Union philanthropy.[95] Inside, visitors browsed copies of USSC publications such as the *Bulletin* and *Reporter*, examined maps of US battlefields, and consulted a register of Americans resident in London. Moran then persuaded Fisher and Ezekiel Elliott (head of the USSC's Bureau of Vital Statistics, then touring Britain to promote the science of sanitary reform) that it was "of *national interest* that there is in London [a] headquarters for loyal Americans" to influence "public sentiment in Europe."[96] Although it was thought inadvisable to actively seek financial contributions from Englishmen, Elliot hoped to "quietly strengthen the hands and voices of our earnest English friends," such as the sanitary reformer Edwin Chadwick and the public health statistician Edwin Lankester.[97]

The USSC London Branch successfully coordinated all the elements of London-American society, in addition to the interwoven philanthropic, anti-slavery, and religious networks in Britain outlined in chapter 3. Fisher's second appeal chided Americans in Britain for their "ungenerous apathy," but addressed a wider audience of sympathetic Britons and "especially churches." Fisher exhorted the members of these diverse networks to support "a work which has placed America in the foremost rank of charity, religion and humanity."[98] It was in Britain's churches that Fisher could utilize a shared culture of transatlantic evangelicalism and cultivate a fertile audience for the USSC's interdenominational Christian philanthropy that reached into local communities around Britain. Religious emissaries had cultivated this audience before him, and Fisher attempted to utilize the shared Protestant culture that underlay these diplomatic missions by forwarding pamphlets to British churchmen.

Transatlantic evangelicalism was just one vein of the vast arterial network of philanthropy, reform, and activism drawn upon by the USSC. Fisher cultivated links with Elihu Burritt, then lecturing in England after the shattering of domestic support for his international peace movement.[99] Burritt, the self-styled "Learned Blacksmith," was a protégé of the recently deceased English abolitionist Joseph Sturge, whose patronage in the 1840s gave him the ear of Quaker abolitionists in the Midlands in addition to more than 50,000 men and women who had pledged to support his League of Universal Brotherhood during his 1846 tour across the country. The effervescent John Sella Martin, who sat on the subscriptions committee, provided connections with the African American anti-slavery lecture circuit and grassroots pro-union and abolitionist organizations. Thomas Bailey Potter, President of the Union and Emancipation Society, spread sanitary commission materials among the organization's members.[100] Through this constituency Fisher prepared the ground for the Sanitary Commission's message of Christian philanthropy at a politically sensitive moment.

Sensing that the public mood was shifting towards war-weariness by the fall of 1864, Fisher flooded Britain with USSC pamphlets to emphasize the compassion of the Union war effort. "I am pegging away at English ignorance and prejudice," Fisher wrote to Bellows in December 1864.[101] Between October 1864 and April 1865, Fisher circulated USSC publications to high-profile members of British society including the Prince of Wales, Lord Granville, and George Grey; local and university libraries; and civil society organizations including the Society of Manufactures and Commerce, and the Athenaeum. Fisher also cultivated British military establishments including the Admiralty, the Royal Artillery Library, the Army Medical Library, and the Colonial Office. Nonetheless, he found the English "slow to move, and hard to convince." Writing to Jenkins in New York, he argued that "they have for so long a period been educated to believe that no good could come out of an 'American Nazareth.'" But he remained optimistic that through the Branch's auspices "a vast amount of ignorance and prejudice have been removed, and the American character is its best and noblest aspect."[102]

Judging the success of such advocacy missions is almost impossible, but Fisher certainly increased the profile of the Sanitary Commission among the British public. Some sense of the scale of this effort can be gauged from the frequent delivery of new materials to Fisher from New York. Jonathan Woods, a clerk in the New York office's Document Bureau, forwarded large packages of Sanitary Commission pamphlets to

London and Paris. In September 1864 Woods sent Fisher two hundred copies of the Commission's fortnightly *Bulletin* and maps of Andersonville Prison.[103] As new pamphlets emerged, Fisher capitalized on their propaganda potential. In early 1865 he obtained hundreds of copies of Robert McKenzie's *America and her Armies* and forwarded them to newspaper editors, bankers, cabinet members, and bishops. Soon the flow became a flood. In February 1865, Dudley received thirty thousand copies of the Sanitary Commission *Reporter.*[104] One month later, Woods sent Fisher copies of the *Narrative of Suffering,* medical and surgical monographs, complete sets of the *Reporter* and *Bulletin,* financial reports, Katharine Prescott Wormeley's *Sketch,* the Commission's *Narrative of its Works and Purposes,* and the *Memorial* of the Philadelphia Fair.[105] Using US consuls as local distributors, Fisher engaged grassroots Union organizations, philanthropic associations, and interested local elites.

The English Branch also helped to organize events for Sanitary Commission agents. When Ezekiel B. Elliott visited London to attend a meeting of the Society for the Promotion of Social Science in 1864, Fisher arranged a speaking tour to specialists interested in the physiognomy and mortality of the Union Army.[106] Fisher himself also lectured to select groups of scientists and military officers. In late 1864, he delivered his lecture "Military Discipline and Volunteer Philanthropy" to the first Social Science Congress in the northern city of York. He was next invited to speak before the Royal United Service Institute, a defense academy dedicated to the study of naval and military science. Following the tour he distributed a pamphlet version of the lecture to "leading Englishmen" at British universities and scientific and military institutions.[107] Fisher portrayed the Commission to the British public as a volunteer regiment of the Federal Army and described its work as "absolutely Samaritan," while simultaneously being the "power maneuvering the lever" of the Federal Army.[108]

The timing of the London Branch's public campaign was prescient. "*I eschew carefully all political discussion,*" Fisher somewhat disingenuously informed Jenkins in New York, when in fact he was the mastermind of a well-organized counterattack on Confederate propaganda.[109] In hopes of reigniting the recognition debate, Hotze's *Index* began reprinting articles from the *Richmond Examiner* detailing the "barbarous treatment" of prisoners of war and placing the blame for the end of prisoner exchanges at the door of Union officials.[110] After an outburst of pro-Union support following the Emancipation Proclamation, Britons were becoming increasingly frustrated by the war's cost in human life (see figure 16). Confederate

THE AMERICAN JUGGERNAUT.

FIGURE 16. Here the *Punch* artist John Tenniel portrays the horrors of mechanized warfare. The war's terrible cost in human life, the apparent inability of either side to inflict a knockout blow, and the news of starvation among the civilian population and the mistreatment of prisoners by both sides prompted humanitarian concerns in the British press. This reality was brought home most shockingly in the illustrations of Tenniel and the *Illustrated London News* artist Frank Vizetelly. Image: "The American Juggernaut," *Punch*, September 3, 1864, The Cartoon Collector / Heritage-Images / TopFoto.

propagandists in Britain attempted to channel this frustration towards a new petition campaign among pro-Confederates that now centered on the inhumane length of the war rather than direct recognition after the failure of Roebuck's motion in 1863.[111] The route to recognition, many pro-Southern ideologues now believed, lay in appealing to British humanitarian sentiment to force an armistice.[112]

To fan the flames further, James Spence, recently relieved of his position as the Confederate States' financial agent in Europe, organized a four-day "Southern Bazaar" for Liverpool's pro-Confederates in October. Ironically, Spence hoped to capitalize on the same humanitarian impulses as the USSC, by exciting "sympathy for the great sorrows and suffering that now afflict a people of our own race" to force a negotiated peace.[113] "Public opinion has quite come round to the belief that the North is staggering under its last efforts," Spence wrote Mason.[114] More than ten thousand British sympathizers visited the Bazaar at Liverpool's St George's Hall, decorated with Confederate flags and portraits of Stonewall Jackson, to see such attractions as Robert E. Lee's pipe and crosses made from the wreckage of Fort Sumter.[115] A roaring success, the event was extended to a fifth day, and Spence's final profits totaled more than £17,000 (more than £2 million today) in aid of the Southern Prisoner's Relief Fund.[116]

The Bazaar was, however, the last stand of the retreating Southern cause in Britain. Spence, Hotze, and their supporters had failed to create a viable pro-Southern coalition and were forced onto rapidly shrinking ground by the success of British abolitionist societies in winning support for the North. Writing under pseudonyms in the British press, Fisher countered Confederate claims of Union mistreatment and emphasized the Christian rather than sectional character of the Sanitary Commission. Fisher dismissed the Bazaar's organizers as "sundry aristocrats and fashionables" and appealed to British patriotism by depicting the USSC as "borrowing much from the saint-like labors" of Florence Nightingale and laboring "on purely philanthropic grounds—helping alike both friend and foe, rebel and loyalist, and looking only to suffering humanity." Finally he called on Unionists in Britain to "eclipse this Southern and sectional bazaar" and "to repel the insidious efforts" of Spence to substitute the republic for a "slave empire in the nineteenth century of the Christian era."[117]

Fisher did not have to press this point very hard. The Confederate Bazaar raised impressive amounts of money, but paled in comparison to the work of Fisher and allied campaigns such as the Freedmen's Aid movement. Following the Emancipation Proclamation approximately fifty societies were founded in Britain, many at the initiative of women, to provide material and financial aid to freed slaves.[118] These local groups, coordinated through the National Committee of British Freed-Men's Aid Societies, shipped clothing, tools, and cash to refugee camps in the South.[119] They were joined by the agents of American societies, including Quaker abolitionist Levi Coffin and D.A.M. Storrs on behalf of the Freedmen's Aid Society, Robert J. Parvin for the American Freedmen's and Union Commission, Charles C. Leigh for the National Freedmen's Relief Association of America, Dudley Haynes, who lectured on behalf of the London-based Freedmen's Aid Society, and once again John Sella Martin, who acted as agent for the American Missionary Association, having been sent to "use my old connections here."[120] Martin lectured British audiences with a "holy indignation" and appealed to British ideals of self-help to request aid for preparing the newly-emancipated slaves for freedom. "The negroes distrusted their own powers," he told an audience of Glaswegians in August 1865, "because they had never been called on to exercise them as independent men." Slaveholders would not "yield their grasp upon the neck of their victims without a great struggle," but the now-former slaves could be prepared for the struggle if "the people of this country could make the negro believe that all their avowed interest and oft-repeated protests against the evils of slavery, and oppression were earnest and real."[121] Between 1863 and 1868 an estimated £120,000 in financial aid and £20,000 of goods were donated by the British societies to this end (more than £13.5 million and almost £2.3 million today respectively).[122] Coffin alone raised a further $100,000 in money and gifts in Britain.[123]

British humanitarians thus provided Fisher with a broad movement, knowledgeable about the American crisis and its consequences, through which to advance the USSC's cause. Fisher pressed Confederate inhumanity on the British public by circulating the Sanitary Commission's *Narrative of Privations and Sufferings* (1864) to members of the Palmerton cabinet, philanthropists, and British elites.[124] Dudley and Fisher collaborated to distribute tens of thousands of copies. According to the Liverpool consul it was "beyond question the best book to circulate in this country that has been sent to us."[125] "You can't reach the English mind with argument," Dudley wrote Fisher, "they can only be moved by acts like these of cruelty, surpassing anything that has been practiced in this age and only finding counterparts in the dark ages of the world."[126] "The distribution of the *Narrative of Suffering* [sic] has come at a very good time," Fisher wrote to the USSC General Secretary, J. Foster Jenkins, "for the public mind has of late been especially drawn to the *so called* sufferings of Rebel Prisoners."[127]

In February 1865 alone, Dudley was sent and distributed fifty-five thousand copies of the *Narrative* around Britain.[128] Fisher forwarded copies to every member of the Houses of Lords and Commons, the Cabinet, and to all members of the UES.[129] Driven by the increasing momentum of the Commission's cause, Fisher drew on his contacts in evangelical and philanthropic networks.[130] Fisher's campaign consolidated the PR effect of Sherman's occupation of Savannah in December 1864 and the fall of Fort Fisher in January 1865, which, combined with the *Narrative*'s report of Confederate cruelty, helped to bolster the perception of the Union's moral purpose to British observers.[131]

USSC pamphlets joined a flood of works about the war from grassroots union organizations, middle class intellectuals, and upper class reactionaries—not to mention the constant coverage in British national and local newspapers. Fisher's efforts were not simply another voice in the chorus, however. USSC literature universalized the conflict's meaning and emphasized the humanity inherent in the Union military campaign despite its tremendous human cost. Fisher exploited the war's international audience and never doubted that the USSC's Christian and philanthropic mission could act as a transnational pressure point on British public opinion. Reflecting on the Branch's purpose after the war, Fisher concluded that it had been "a missionary" and a "schoolmaster" that had instilled "into the minds of Englishmen the lessons of our struggle."[132] How far it shaped or transformed English opinions on the war is, of course, impossible to say, but in raising the profile of the Sanitary Commission Fisher agitated issues that were easily allied with the philanthropic and Christian impulses that fueled much British support for the Union. "The mask has been raised," wrote one of Fisher's correspondents from the British Army, "and the people of all countries where copies of your Treatment of Prisoners are read can see the Southern pall bearers of starvation chuckle their shoulders and curse the moment your association peered into their death like recesses."[133]

The London Branch's greatest strength was its ability to build on longstanding networks of Americans in Britain. These networks also provided a steady flow of financial donations to the London Branch's activities. As knowledge of the USSC grew in Britain the London Branch received increasing numbers of donations in cash and kind for sanitary work. "We accept foreign assistance only in the name of a cosmopolitan sympathy," wrote Bellows in his advice to Fisher, adding that it would promote "a common bond among Christians and men, the world over."[134] Rather than rely exclusively on such philanthropy, Fisher was more active in his solicitation of funds from the London-Americans. In his first circular to Americans in Britain, Fisher wrote that although the "tangible monetary aid that we in England can render may be a mere drop in the mighty stream of benevolence," the "God-speed you from a foreign shore" would nonetheless "soothe many an aching brow."[135]

Emigrant financiers on the London committee gave generously. The largest donation to the London Branch came at the end of May 1864, when George Peabody gave £8,000. That was in addition to the £500 he had given to fairs in Boston, New York, Philadelphia, and Baltimore, bringing the total to £10,000. Although it did not quite match the donation of £150,000 (roughly more than £18 million today) he made to the London poor in 1862 (and his subsequent addition of $2,500,000 to that fund) the 1864 donation was a ringing endorsement of Fisher's enterprise and the Commission's efforts.[136] In this instance, the ageing Peabody wanted to express his endorsement of "a real Christian charity" and to help "alleviate the pains and give comfort to the sick and wounded of both the northern and southern armies."[137] Peabody's gifts to the London poor and Sanitary Commission in the war years were part of more than $10 million given away between 1856 and his death in 1869 to projects on both side of the Atlantic that he hoped would tie the English-speaking peoples closer together.[138]

Despite rumors circulating from the Paris Branch that the "Copperhead element" existed "to no small extent among the prominent Americans of London," they in fact gave generously.[139] Joshua Bates (£1,000), James McHenry (£1,000), Alexander Brown (£300), Russell Sturgis (£100), and Stewart H. Brown (£100) provided donations from the financial elites of Britain's American community. Meanwhile, American merchants in Britain added further funds. From Liverpool, the shipping magnate Henry Gair provided not only free transportation for gifts in kind to Sanitary Fairs but donated £1,000, followed by gifts from Henry Starr (£391), Curtis Miranda Lampson (£250), and Stephen Guion and Benjamin F. Babcock (£100 each). Donations from Charles Francis Adams (£100), Charles Lush Wilson (£50), Freeman Harlow Morse (£20), and Benjamin Moran (£10) highlight the synergy of the US diplomatic elite in Britain with the Sanitary Commission's mission in Britain.[140] The London Branch also benefited from the generosity of native Britons, such as the citizens of Cardiff, who gave more than £850 in April 1863. "I feel I am addressing a fellow countryman," wrote one Glaswegian as he sent a small gift through Thomas Dudley.[141]

Overall, gifts through the London Branch totaled $36,790.42 and accounted for more than half of the total donations from Europe, which stood at $65,976.44 (more than $500 million and $1 billion respectively today).[142] Financial donations were supported by gifts in kind to Fairs in New York and Chicago. In Britain, Fisher depended on Thomas Dudley to organize the shipment of huge numbers of gifts received in Britain.[143] Long-standing philanthropic practices in Britain of sending gifts to American anti-slavery bazaars were a good fit for Fisher's model of philanthropy.[144] Donations came from Britons and Americans alike and included practical items such as tin plates, cutlery, needlework, wool, rifle parts, and iron wire.[145] But the cases forwarded by Dudley also included luxury items to be sold at fairs in the US, such as perfumery sent by the railroad promoter James McHenry and oil paintings from former Treasury Secretary Robert J. Walker, in Britain as a special envoy charged with discrediting the Erlanger Loan, an attempt by the Confederacy to raise $15 million of cotton-backed bond sales through the French financial house Emile Erlanger & Co.[146]

In London, donations to Fisher's branch were not only an expression of support for the Union but an extension of the longstanding civic life of the London-Americans. Americans in the capital demonstrated their connection to the United States through the assumption of extradiplomatic duties such as the disbursement of funds for stranded sailors and travelers, through the founding of newspapers that sought to promote knowledge of the United States, and by taking up the reins of informal lobbying and propagandizing where ministers and consuls could not tread. Fisher's London Branch was so successful because he drew on the interleaved social worlds of commerce, diplomacy, and philanthropy of Britain's American emigrant community.

As evidence of the widening progressive connections between Britain and the United States in the Civil War era, concerned citizens in the United States reached across the Atlantic in aid of Britons suffering through the cotton famine that began in 1862. Leaders of the New York Chamber of Commerce quickly mobilized support for working-class Britons. At a specially called general meeting in November, $26,000 was raised within minutes. William Earle Dodge, the "Merchant Prince" of New York, donated $5,000; John Taylor Johnson, a railroad executive and art collector, subscribed $2,500, as did the Babcock brothers. Alexander T. Stewart, a wealthy New York department store owner, donated $10,000 for the operatives, while another firm offered to transport 1,800 tons of supplies to Lancashire sufferers. Donations of provisions flooded in from Northern and Western states, including one thousand barrels of flour from the social reformer and abolitionist Gerrit Smith.[147] In Liverpool, the goods were received by prominent American residents Daniel James, Stephen B. Guion, and Benjamin Franklin Babcock, who distributed them around the affected region in the winter of 1862–63 through local relief committees.[148] "It is making a good impression all over the country," James reported to the committee.[149]

The International Relief Committee collected more than $120,000 in donations and shipped almost 16,000 barrels of flour, 500 bushels of corn, 375 boxes of bread, 50 cases of pork, and other foodstuffs.[150] This dramatic diplomatic gesture inspired many activists in the British Freedmen's Aid movement and reinforced the transatlantic community of sympathy that underlay emerging connections among international humanitarians. The voluntary, humanitarian diplomacy seen here was reinforced by the international language of Anglo-Saxonism increasingly central to transatlantic relations. The "piteous cry of the starving operatives of the mother country" resonated so strongly amongst New York's merchants, according to the Chamber's official history of the event, since they were "'bone of our bone,' and all endeared to us by a common language, a common literature, and a common origin."[151] As the *Freedmen's-Aid Reporter* expressed it after the war, the "wise and generous co-operation" among "transatlantic Christians and philanthropists" was of "incalculable value" in drawing "into closer friendship the spiritual and moral conservatism of the two great branches of the Anglo-Saxon race."[152]

Ironically, both Union and Confederate diplomatic strategies reified the perception of this shared transatlantic racial identity. The emphasis on race in Confederate diplomacy intersected with a trajectory of racial science that sits uncomfortably alongside the humanitarian impulses emanating from the Union's propagandizing in Britain. Nonetheless, as the concept of Anglo-Saxonism evolved over the coming decades in the context of rapid British imperial expansion across Africa and in conversation with new scientific racisms, evolutionary biology, and eugenics, those differences were easily reconciled. Anglo-Saxon civilization, as it would be subscribed to in Britain's American community by the close of the nineteenth century, was an identity of whiteness based on the assumption that Anglo-Americans were best suited to manage subject, "uncivilized" races in a humane and "scientific" manner. Humanitarianism, colonial governance, and racial science became mutually reinforcing in this imperial context.[153] Although renewed diplomatic crises would be stoked by the Civil War's immediate aftermath, this ideology was refined in the cockpit of Britain's American community and pressed into the service of a series of American "invasions" of British social and economic life.

CHAPTER 5

American Invasions

After the Civil War, wrote London's *Saturday Review,* "the tide of inter-course between the Continents" of Europe and North American had become a second "Gulf Stream."[1] Copper and iron, coal and steam figuratively shrank the ocean and ushered in a new age of Atlantic travel and exchange. "Like shuttles in a loom," reflected the journalist Hiram Fuller, "these gigantic steamers flying to and fro between Europe and America are weaving nations closer and closer together." Through "increasing international intercourse," Fuller continued, "trade is ben-efited, opinions are modified, manners are improved, and minds are expanded and cosmopolitanised."[2]

What impact did these expanding, interwoven connections have upon American migration, the Atlantic world, and the United States' relationship to a global economy in the making? American migrants remained key protagonists in interpreting the material changes of the "shrinking" world in the final third of the nineteenth century. But it was still not an age of frictionless globalizing: the exchange of foreign goods, ideas, and capital remained contentious. "Before time had been annihi-lated by the telegraph, and distance abolished by steam, nations were comparatively isolated; and the American most of all," complained one critic of the "un-American tendencies" of international travellers in 1891, by which time the Atlantic Ocean had been "bridged by steamers and flashed out of existence by electric cable." Through such connec-tions, this jeremiad continued, the United States remained vulnerable to foreign influences, for "the consequence is that while Europe borrows many of our ideas, America borrows more of hers."[3] In light of this, how are we to understand the ongoing tension between independence and interdependence in the post-Civil War Atlantic world?

This chapter begins with the revolution in transport, communications, and travel that transformed the Atlantic in the final third of the century, and which underpinned the variety of American "invasions" of British social and economic life. Although the diplomatic antagonisms of the Civil War lingered in the popular political imagination, American travel to Britain boomed alongside the increasing affordability, comfort, and speed of the Atlantic crossing. American travel had a dramatic impact on Britain. Distinct American spaces, media, and social clubs emerged that catered to tourists and migrants alike. "Americans reappear in numbers in English society," observed the *Anglo-American Times* just eighteen months after Appomattox; "great hotels are laid out expressly to secure their custom, and the fashionable shops begin to feel the weight of their patronage. . . . American inventions, American notions, American drinks, are again coming prominently forward."[4]

Beginning in the 1870s, travel was increasingly depicted as "invasion," and migration as a colonization that reversed earlier patterns of Atlantic settlement. "Our fathers went west to make their fortunes," wrote one British journalist at the turn of the century, but "their sons are coming east to do the same."[5] The men and women who made up the invading forces now belonged to an American "Colony" in Britain. By 1895, the revived *London American* reflected on the "complete little pocket edition of the USA [that] has been dropped into the midst of the Queen's capital":

> We have fashionable Americans entertaining princes, literary Americans running papers and magazines, bohemian Americans living in lodgings, convivial Americans congregating in clubs, mercantile Americans engaged in business, good Americans pointing the way to Kingdom-come, bad Americans getting into jail, and legal Americans trying to get them out. In fact, John Bull has no longer an excuse to plead unfamiliarity with us; he has a sample of every case at his very door.[6]

But were these American migrants the best representatives the United States could send? Precisely because, as one commentator wrote in 1868, migrants were "vital links between far-away lands and our own, whereby our character and career as a nation . . . are manifest," the questions of who, and what traits, should represent the United States overseas continued to be hotly contested by American nationalists who feared the "abandonment of the principles of the political and social creeds of republicanism" among Americans abroad.[7] "We have principles to represent, migratory colonies to protect, mutual interests to cherish, and a national life to vindicate and honor all over the world," argued the *Atlantic Monthly* in 1868.[8] Ten years later in E. L. Godkin's *Nation*, American diplomats were described as "social representatives," men "whose principal business is to give foreigners a fair idea of what we consider our best society."[9]

The problem was, Americans could no more agree on who represented the "best" of American society in the final third of the century than they had in the two that preceded it. This was especially so in the case of travelling American women. As Kristin Hoganson has demonstrated, the Civil War intensified the emphasis on manhood in, and fraternal character of, US politics. While participation in party politics helped to define the nature of male identity in this period, women's public politics, by contrast, often took the form of representing abstract principles of the common good, including justice, liberty, the nation, or womanhood itself.[10] As women's travel increased, many commentators argued that American women overseas should embody the common good to foreign audiences, moving them to center stage in the ongoing discussion of US independence. For some, women's mobility was of itself problematic because female travelers seemed to be "following a way so much opposed to that which nature seems to have traced for them" by travelling overseas.[11] For others, it was proof of the United States' continued colonial dependence. Elite intermarriage was especially problematic, especially for the many women who married into the British nobility and thereby became denationalized Americans. "Alone and in exile, often despised, she has simply won a gilded misery," surmised *Harper's Bazaar.*[12]

London was the central hub of both a global imperial system and the web of credit that dominated world commerce. Fortunes were made in Britain's capital from the colossal growth of world trade, whose value rose tenfold between 1850 and 1913.[13] A huge proportion of the world's trade depended on London for the financial instruments that commerce required: sterling was the currency of international trade, the "bill on London" the usual form of payment, and the gold standard the pillar of commercial stability. American banks, including Morton, Rose & Co.; Seligman Brothers; Cooke, McCulloch & Co.; and Clews, Habicht & Co., all gravitated toward London's dynamic City, where they generated new investment flows and merchandized directly to British investors. From London these banks created vast, long-distance distribution networks for marketing American railway securities in Europe, oversaw the Treasury Department's refunding operations (in 1871, Cooke, McCulloch was made the United States' agent in Europe), and made fortunes from the foreign exchange business. Union victory created a surge in demand for US government securities in foreign markets that pushed the value of government bonds held abroad to more than one billion dollars by 1869, accompanied by $243 million in railroad securities.[14] Affirming Britain's continued dominance of American finance, in 1890 there were more American stocks listed on the London Stock Exchange than on Wall Street.[15] While the United States' domestic capital markets were developing quickly in this period, more than £836 million of British investment had poured into the United States by 1914—one fifth of Britain's total capital exports.[16]

For these reasons, economic nationalists revived antebellum anxieties about the United States' colonial dependency.[17] Henry Carey began the post-Civil War era hoping to expose British free trade as "the precise system that was advocated in England before the Revolution as the one required for retaining the Colonies in a state of vassalage."[18] Carey urged the United States' political leaders to "free the country from foreign dictation" and "become really independent" or rather "become *Americanized.*"[19] In fact, the United States' foreign linkages proved central to its achievement of economic independence. Britain remained the nation's key trading partner, but American migration and exports powered a significant shift in Anglo-American relations. Britain's share of US imports fell dramatically, from 42 percent in 1849–58 to 21 percent in 1889–98. Britain's imports from the United States, meanwhile, accounted for about 50 percent of all Europe's imports from the United States between 1879 and 1898.[20] The rapid expansion of US trade, which raised fears of the "Americanization" of Britain, was closely linked to American emigration. The American migrant community anchored US commercial and cultural expansion in Britain in the century's final three decades. American "invaders" came to manage overseas branches and establish relationships with local wholesalers and producers, to coordinate sales and overcome logistical hurdles, to manufacture, and to invent new markets—in the process managing the transnational conduits of personnel, knowledge, and goods central to the expansion overseas of American corporate power. As one British commenter observed, "where the goods come, the drummers follow, and in their wake come men of their own account."[21]

By the end of the century, Britain's American "colony" was the agent of US economic and cultural expansion. According to *Harper's*,

American nationality left an "unmistakable stamp" on the "features, costume, and manners" of Americans abroad, who "roll through Europe like so many erratic globules of mercury, refusing to blend with foreign substances, but with an irresistible natural affinity for each other."[22] But, although the relationship between migration and national power had been well-established, it was never the case that American migrants refused to interact with their British hosts. As one migrant observed at a Fourth of July celebration in 1895, emigrants "were not keeping Independence Day in the heart of the British Empire because England was weak, but rather because England was strong."[23] At national events organized by the American Society in London and "at homes" by the Society of American Women in London, American migrants cultivated close social, political, and business connections with elite Britons, including the administrators and ministers who manned the Colonial Office and Board of Trade—just as they had done in the antebellum period. At these events too, Americans in London continued to act as emigrant ambassadors, using public civic events to extol the transatlantic community of blood, language, culture, and race and to urge the peaceful arbitration of Anglo-American disputes. By the final third of the century, then, American migrants engaged in a transatlantic debate over the imperial collaboration of the Anglo-Saxon peoples and encouraged deeper political and economic cooperation between two "kindred" empires.

"THE GRAND AMERICAN ARMY OF INVASION"

Just as after the Revolution, Americans crossed the Atlantic in great numbers soon after the end of the Civil War. As early as June 1866, the *Anglo-American Times* reported on the "tide of travel from America," noting that the year's tourist numbers had already beaten previous records—an indication that "the height of the American immigration has not been reached."[24] On arrival, Liverpool's docks continued to "puzzle, confound, and awe."[25] Those arriving against the backdrop of the ongoing *Alabama* Claims dispute looked across the Mersey to the Lairds shipyard, whose sympathy for the South had given "enormously to the cause of our enemies," as "a matter of business as well as of sentiment."[26] While antebellum travelers often expressed disappointment at the city's resemblance to port cities at home, many now expressed pride over the United States' influence on the city. "American commerce has been a great stay of this city, and the intercourse has left its trace," wrote the young Kansan Noble Prentis, delighted that in his "rambles about town [he] met with Washington Street, Maryland and Baltimore streets, and other traces of American influence. The American population must be considerable, and American goods are everywhere advertised."[27] By 1886, British commentators had reversed the postcolonial anxieties reflected in Harriet Beecher Stowe's assessment that Liverpool was a "real New York-ish place," and celebrated the port as "the New York of Europe, a world-city rather than merely British provincial."[28]

The Atlantic crossing itself had changed dramatically in the postwar period. By the final third of the nineteenth century, the transatlantic passenger trade had completed the shift from sail to steam. Beginning in the 1870s, ten-thousand-ton coal-guzzling liners were launched that halved the cost and, in some cases, reduced the time of the Atlantic crossing by a week.[29] Port infrastructure raced to keep up with the new technology; by the twentieth century some liners were almost 800 feet long.[30] By 1875, transatlantic travelers could choose between twelve steamship lines making the crossing to Liverpool for as little as $100 (still a considerable sum, given that between 1870 and 1900 the average annual salary of a non-farm worker never exceeded $500, estimated as the minimum a family needed to survive).[31] Following the rise of steam, between 1851 and 1900 more than £100 million was invested in English ports and harbors.[32] In 1855, only seven of Liverpool's docks handled steamers, by 1870 this figure had risen to twenty.[33] In 1882, tram routes were extended to the pierhead to cater to the swelling volume of people spilling out of the liners, and in 1886 the Mersey Railway transported travelers directly to the shore in Cheshire. Finally, in 1893 the Liverpool Overhead Railway ran along the dock road, which serviced local commuters and transatlantic travelers alike.

Where the forests of masts had delighted the antebellum traveler, the postbellum tourist gazed in awe at the "huge crafts stretched in a long line in the middle of the Mersey in front of the city."[34] According to *Frank Leslie's,* because of the steamer "the vastness of the waters no longer awes," and the Atlantic crossing had passed "out of association with tears and misgivings; it is almost commonplace, and the achievement of it confers no distinction upon a man even among his intimates and admirers."[35] For those of a more delicate disposition the new technology hardly delighted. "The motion of riding a screw-steamer is like riding a gigantic camel that has the heart disease," wrote Ella Thompson, warning that the three-thousand-mile trip was "at the best . . . a sort of intermediate state between death and life."[36] As the "tea kettles" of the 1840s gave way to the "steam palaces" of Cunard, the White Star

Line, and the Inman Line, however, American tourism boomed. In 1870, transatlantic travelers numbered approximately 35,000, but fifteen years later this figure surpassed 100,000 per year. By the end of the 1914 season, an estimated 250,000 American tourists had travelled through Europe.[37] As one travel writer noted, American tourists were as "plentiful . . . as flies at a sugar barrel."[38]

The steam revolution transformed trade too. Transatlantic freight rates fell 75 percent between 1860 and 1900.[39] In 1825, Liverpool's inward traffic had been 1.2 million tons. By 1865 it had risen to 4.7 million tons, and by 1900 to 12.4 million.[40] Whole streets close to dockside areas were now taken over with warehousing, cold storage, and coal bunkering. "To stand in the Liverpool docks is to stand in the shipping centre of the world," reflected one visitor, "to see the flags that pass the Bell Buoy at Liverpool Bar, is to seen the ensign covering and guarding more wealth than any other city has ever had flowing through its commercial veins and arteries."[41] Flowing through these commercial arteries were merchants, migrants, and sailors from around the world, contributing to the port's cosmopolitan character.[42] "All of us in Liverpool, are to a great extent citizens of the world," wrote the *Liverpool Critic* in 1877, "for everything around us tells us of far-off countries and foreign ways, and in our midst are constantly natives of so many distant lands that we insensibly imbibe and learn to practice peculiarities not British."[43]

Yet, as one traveler noted on arrival, Liverpool's docks may have been "crammed with the ships of all nations, carrying every commercial flag" but among them the Stars and Stripes was a "scarce article."[44] As a result of the Civil War, the United States' lead in Atlantic shipping was wiped out and British bottoms now dominated in both freight and passengers.[45] The spread of new capitalist infrastructure, including transatlantic cables after 1866, increased market integration and lowered the cost of trade and time spent in port waiting for cargo, all of which helped anxious traders to manage risk. "The products of the earth will tend more quickly to the points where they are required," enthused one Anglo-American paper, adding that the "violent fluctuations which disturb trade and turn sober merchants into gamblers will be lessened."[46] The cable also fostered the creation of new commercial intelligence intermediaries such as Reuter's, Havas, Wolff's, and the Associated Press.[47] Transatlantic traders adjusted quickly to prices on key stock and commodity exchanges, and to new opportunities brought by near-instantaneous (although, at £2 for a minimum of ten words between Britain and New York from 1869, costly) news received remotely through the cable.[48] Thanks in part

FOR BETTER OR WORSE.

Neptune *(The Heavy Father).* " BLESS YE, MY CHILDREN ! "

FIGURE 17. Here, Uncle Sam and an indifferent Britannia are married by Neptune in an ambivalent celebration of the successful laying of the Atlantic cable. The coiled wires wrapped around Neptune's waist capture the Victorian joy at taming nature. "Literally it annihilates distance, and brings the empires within talking range," celebrated the *Anglo-American Times* ("The Anglo-American Telegraph," August 4, 1866). Marriage was often used as a metaphor for understanding the collapse of time and space brought about by the cable between Britain and the United States. On the laying of the first, though ultimately failed, cable in 1858, *Punch* had declared "the splice under the ocean may be deemed a nuptial knot . . . May no divorce act ever separate those who're now united by the Sub-Atlantic splice!" ("The Subatlantic Splice," August 21, 1858). But transatlantic nuptials provoked controversy in both societies. Image: Charles Keene, "For Better or Worse," *Punch,* August 11, 1866, Oxford Science Archive / Heritage-Images.

to the cable's reporting of precise information at great speed, by 1876 US cotton exports to Liverpool had exceeded those of 1860—though the bales arrived mostly on British ships.[49]

Although the telegraph increased the trading and financial interdependence of the Liverpool-US connection, its central role in changing Atlantic business practices undermined the communal life of American emigrants in the port (see figure 17).[50] American ship captains and merchants who happened to be caught in the city continued to celebrate the Fourth of July, as Americans did around the world, but without the organized associations of the antebellum period.[51] For Americans after the Civil War, in the words of one travelogue, Liverpool was simply "the doorstep of England."[52]

London, on the other hand, was, in the declaration of one American tourist, "not a city but an empire, a nation in itself, a province of brick and mortar, a maze of streets and houses and pleasure parks, a metropolis not of one land, but of the entire globe."[53] "London is in fact fast becoming a country," wrote one traveller, "the biggest Babel in the world."[54] London proved as bewildering in the second half of the century as it had in the first, taxing the imaginations of American travel writers who struggled to capture the capital's mobility, growth, and rapid transformations. "Its present magnitude awes you," wrote Edward Thwing in 1888.[55] The London-based *Anglo-American Times* "computed" that London encompassed 10,500 squares, streets, and terraces, 370,000 houses, and covered some 121 square miles.[56] According to *the American Traveller's Guide* printed in 1873, London's population increased at the rate of "a birth every twelve minutes."[57] It was a "huge monster," wrote Noble Prentis, while for the journalist William Croffut, it was "circuitous, somber, and vast—a fog-ridden, far-reaching prison of stone."[58] London was not only a monster, it was expanding. By 1871, the population of Britain's imperial capital was a little less than 3.3 million, an increase from 2.8 million just a decade earlier.[59] Perhaps the best way to capture its sprawling growth and flowing mobility was not to capture it all. "London is beyond me, and will ever be," wrote one traveler in the mid-1890s. "New York, Chicago, and Philadelphia I can comprehend, can carry them geographically in my mind, but London, no. We seem to be in the middle of a world that is all city."[60]

"Swallowed up and lost in the throngs" of London was a "perfect army of American travelers."[61] At his desk in the American Legation, Benjamin Moran was buffeted by the "oppressive force" of a "torrent of Americans."[62] For the remainder of his time as First Secretary, Moran complained of the "great mass of American seaweed" and "curiosity loving wafers" that washed up in London (see figure 18).[63] "It is a pity for England that she has so many historic spots dear to Yankees," he wryly noted.[64] "We know him only too well," wrote London's *Saturday Review* of the American tourist, "revolving round romantic Europe in the eccentric orbit of a flying boomerang . . . an unsatisfied hunger of

LONDON

PARIS

THE AMERICANS TAKING LONDON

PARIS

EXCHANGE

PARIS.

COLUMN OF JULY

BOURSE

PISA

LEANING TOWER

RUSH UPON A FIRST CLASS HOTEL

IN A THOUSAND HANSOM CABS

VIENNA

DELIGHT OF THE HOTEL KEEPERS

NAPLES

VESUVIUS

ANTWERP CATHEDRAL

SPAIN.

GIBRALTAR.

THE AMERICAN PURSE

THE DINING ROOM

FIGHT FOR A SMALL BED

ROME

ST PETERS

SWITZERLAND

TELL'S CHAPEL

BRITANNIA BRIDGE

expectation in his wistful eyes."[65] Thanks to new steamship services and the city's mania for improvement, London had become a modern tourist city. The newly-fashionable Strand with its luxurious hotels, running between Trafalgar Square and Fleet Street, was the "promenade *par excellence* of American visitors in London."[66] Still, the affordability of the Atlantic crossing allowed the less well-to-do to "mingle the pleasures of sight-seeing with the horrors of a Bloomsbury boarding-house."[67]

The new travel infrastructure further integrated transatlantic reform networks and cemented London's place as a key hub for this activity. A steady stream of urban reformers, social workers, muckrakers, and teachers—both white and black—crossed the Atlantic to assess British reform experiments (especially in London's East End) and consider the possibility of their transferal to the United States.[68] International organizations grew rapidly in number and gathered experts and activists at international congresses whose proceedings were published and reported on widely in transatlantic journals such as the *North American Review, Forum,* and *World's Work.*[69] One British journalist observed an "unconscious influence that the trans-Atlantic branch of the English-speaking race exercises on the cis-Atlantic branch, and . . . any great social or political movement on the one side finds its counterpart on the other."[70] Though the final third of the century has been deemed "the Atlantic era in social politics," this is not broad enough.[71] Thanks to the globe-spanning communications and technological infrastructure of the Empire, the aspirations of Atlantic reformers became more global in their dimensions, building

FIGURE 18. With increasing frequency, American travel overseas was depicted as "invasion". By the 1870s, writes Maureen Montgomery, travel to Europe had become "an integral part of a broader pattern of America bourgeois consumption" ("Natural Distinction," 27). London was often just one stop on a wider itinerary. Boat and rail services to Europe could be taken from Charing Cross Station and luxurious hotels lined Northumberland Avenue, connecting the Strand to the north bank of the Thames. Rome was now just sixty hours from London, Paris only eleven. As the *New York Times* described it, the American middle classes travelled overseas "not from any spontaneous inclination, [but] only because so many others have gone; because it is held to be desirable; because it seems to add to their consequence" ("Two Kinds of Travelers," May 5, 1879). "Many patriotic persons shake their heads and sigh over the enormous amount of money thus taken out of the country, and over the folly of going to London, Paris, Berlin, St Petersburg, Switzerland, the Nile, or Palestine, while the magnificent attractions of their own country a comparatively neglected," claimed the article accompanying Arthur Lumley's illustration, adding that there was "some reason for complaint." Image: Arthur Lumley, "Summer Invasion of Europe by Americans," *Harper's Weekly,* August 8, 1873, 694, P 207.6 F, Houghton Library, Harvard University.

from older patterns of transatlantic exchange to abolish the shared moral problems of white Anglo-Saxondom. But networks of counterimperial solidarity also built on London's tentacular reach. "Nowhere can one get such a good idea of what is transpiring in all parts of the world as in London," wrote Booker T. Washington during one visit. "London has her 'feelers' in every part of the globe," he continued, and the "colonial system brings each year hundreds of representatives of all races and colors from every part of the world."[72] Such representatives would provide the basis for a "transnational expression of counter solidarity," a space to create non-white reform cultures, and one "answer to the emergence of a global politics of whiteness."[73]

Some American travelers fancied that "by their continual pushing about" they had transformed the city itself. American travelers, wrote Curtis Guild in 1888, "have done much to improve [the] means of travel, to introduce conveniences, comforts, and facilities of their invention, often temporarily used by foreigners to please their visitors, but finally permanently adopted themselves."[74] Although Guild overstated the case, the American tourist market did lead to the creation of distinct "American" spaces in the capital. Not far from Charing Cross station stood Charles Alvin Gillig's United States Exchange, according to one newspaper the "headquarters of Americans in London," where Americans could meet fellow countrymen and, for a small fee, "loaf" over US newspapers.[75] Another short walk away was Low's Exchange on the western side of Trafalgar square that offered a Post Office, banking facilities, and reading rooms, and McArmor's American news Reading Room near the Haymarket Theatre. Close nearby at No. 2, Cockspur Street was the American Rendezvous, opened by the Great Eastern Railway Company, which provided telephones, messenger service, and a baggage drop that shuttled visitors' luggage between Liverpool and the grand hotels lining Trafalgar Square.[76] At the east end of Pall Mall was the office of the Pennsylvania Railroad Company decorated with views of the Alleghenies. In these spaces, Americans could browse the pages of the *Anglo-American Times,* the *American Traveller, America,* or the *Anglo-American Register* for information on the arrival and departure of American travelers, look up hotels and restaurants, or consider its discussion of transatlantic relations.[77] Tourists continued to rely on American banks in the city for the advance of credit—and they in turn remained social centers. The American Express Co. in Pall Mall, Cooke, McCulloch & Co. (until 1873), and smaller houses such as Mellville, Fickus, Seligman Bros., and Morton, Rose & Co., extended lines of credit to American travelers and residents alike. Cooke, like Peabody before him with a shrewd eye for the lucrative sums to be made from Americans abroad, offered a sitting room for American travelers on the second floor of his bank.[78] Americans sometimes sought long lines of credit to take advantage of London's luxury emporiums or to make the hop across the Channel. Exhausted after the day's shopping or sightseeing, they found a host of restaurants, bars and hotels offering "American" comforts aimed at both travelers and British consumers. Travelers refreshed themselves at the Horse Shoe Hotel, where the bar offered "American drinks for American Visitors," tidied their appearance at Henry Rosenberg's American Barbershop, outfitted themselves at the American tailor Westoby's, and cured homesickness at Robert Jackson's "American Fancy Groceries." American soda fountains' advertising declared they offered England's new favorite beverage, while Fuller's offered American confectionary in ten branches across the city.[79] Sports fans might even take a trip to Brixton Hill to watch the colony's Baseball League.[80] "America is all here!" exclaimed Henry Adams on a return visit to London in 1880.[81]

In American London, emigrant life continued to build on the civic foundations laid in the antebellum period. George W. Smalley, the *New York Tribune*'s London correspondent, was American London's social leader. Smalley arrived in 1866 and used his home in Hyde Park Square to entertain prominent London-Americans including Moncure Conway, the artist George Henry Boughton, Cyrus Field, and the bankers Hugh McCulloch and Isaac Seligman. As ever, longtime members of the diplomatic corps joined these private citizens in emigrant life, including American Despatch Agent Benjamin Franklin Stevens, Benjamin Moran, and his successors at the legation Ehrman Syme Nadal (a self-described "professional exile") and William J. Hoppin, who referred to this group alternately as London's "American Circle" and its "American Colony."[82] Emigrants continued to celebrate Washington's Birthday and the Fourth of July and to provide relief for the "flood of people in distress" who washed up in the capital through the Society for the Relief of Americans in Distress, founded in 1866.[83]

American travelers and migrants took center stage in the ongoing interplay between the ultimate aim of achieving social, cultural, and economic independence from the Old World and the necessity of close international connection while independence remained a work in progress. As in the antebellum period, cosmopolitan nationalists argued that transatlantic travel would have "a strong effect in moulding the opinions of these nations, speaking the same language, in assimilating institutions, and in correcting erroneous ideas which mostly proceed from ignorance of each other."[84] To a degree, faith in travel's uplifting effects signaled a growing confidence in the United States' participation as an equal among "civilized" nations. "Europe to-day is a great inspirer to America and a great teacher," commented *Scribner's*, noting that the traveler "usually comes back a better American than he goes away."[85] Yet antebellum anxieties about the pernicious impact of transatlantic gentility continued with the increasing globalization of cultural and social exchanges. "The greater number of Americans who are abroad labor under the idea that they are studying and improving themselves," argued one observer, but "they are not. They are simply undergoing a process of denationalization."[86] This familiar specter indicated that the romance of reunion had not produced a strong sense of shared national identity. "A national character can hardly exist without a strong love of country," responded one writer to the question of "What is an American?" "Nobody can claim that for us at present," the writer continued, since "thousands of our people expatriate themselves because life is easier, pleasanter, or cheaper elsewhere," and as a result, "they carry their wealth and what weight they command (and *that* they forfeit in so doing) to other countries."[87]

For the *Anglo-American Times,* these travelers were just the "advance scouts" of a "Grand American Army of Invasion." The invaders would not be "content with robbing England of all her elegant articles of art and manufacture," the paper continued, but would proceed to "make prisoners of her fair daughters and carry them in triumph to the New World."[88] Yet, as American women moved to the center stage of discussions of "representative Americans" overseas, other commentators were driven to wonder if the benefits of foreign travel were not "counterbalanced by all they lose in the way of the Spartan virtues; in the love of humanity, of simplicity, of republicanism; and of their country—in short, by their denationalization."[89] "When Americans sell their daughters to European profligates for a title, and pay millions to boot; when republicans in profession become tuft-hunters in practice, and haunt the back stairs of palaces," asked Carlos Martyn in *Arena,* "is it not time to cry a halt?"[90]

"DENATIONALIZED DAMSELS"

Eased transatlantic travel fueled a dramatic growth in the number of American women in London. "As the world grows smaller the number of women travelers grows great," reflected the American reporter Margherita Arlina Hamm in 1899, adding that the "greater security, economy and rapidity of travel have opened new opportunities for ambitious women."[91] Singers, artists, authors, and journalists all made the crossing to build their careers in London's bustling cultural scene.[92] Tourists, however, predominated. Travel was an opportunity not only to see the world, but for *parvenus* to demonstrate social standing, shop, and create new contacts among elite society both at home and abroad. Many elite American women made repeat crossings, demonstrated in public through the lists of departures and arrivals printed in newspapers such as the *Anglo-American Times* and the *London American,* each time reinforcing their elite status. Magazines and journals offered regular columns on the "art" of travel, ranging from budgeting, seasickness, and arranging accommodation and itineraries, to European fashion and social customs, tipping, and interpreting Old World encounters.[93] Women's travel was a significant element of popular and material culture in the late nineteenth century, as Kristin Hoganson has demonstrated so evocatively. Overseas travelers provided the middle-class public in the United States with access to fashionable goods and knowledge of foreign taste and style.[94]

As with antebellum migrants, these women were understood by audiences in the United States to be representative Americans overseas. In this role, an image of the "American Girl" developed on both sides of the Atlantic. Typical depictions focused on her beauty and style, but never failed to point out the narrow line between virtue and vice.[95] Even those defending American women overseas admitted they were prone to "sin" against the morality and public taste of fashionable society.[96] Done properly, travel was enlightening and an opportunity to learn from fellow Anglo-Saxons, but it could also lead to the acquisition of "a bundle of vices, wrapped in a tissue of nobility."[97] American women in Britain had only one object in mind, according to *Lippincott's:* "to obtain an *entrée* into . . . society," and indeed many women continued to request presentation at court.[98] Worse still, travel was an admission of the United States' ongoing cultural deficiency, stimulating a "tendency to ape everything European and decry everything American."[99] The result, wrote *Harper's Bazaar,* was a class of "denationalized damsels."[100] This was scarcely an "invasion" then, but rather seemed to epitomize Henry Cabot Lodge's 1883 insistence that "colonialism in the United States" remained a "deep-seated" and persistent "malady."[101]

For transatlantic activists, close Anglo-American connections were less evidence of subservience than they were of a carefully cultivated interdependence. The radical breadth of the American women's movement was reflected in diverse Atlantic connections. Suffragists, temperance advocates, missionaries, anti-vice campaigners, health experts, spiritualists, and sanitary reformers developed dense networks from Atlantic crossings, through which they shared political tactics and ideas.[102] Atlantic reform ties were rarely single-issue and typically cross-fertilized.[103] The famed Blackwell family, for instance, may have grown out of the anti-slavery and women's movements, but a brief survey of just one family member's reform CV emphasizes the diversity of interests motivating transatlantic reform. In 1869, Elizabeth Blackwell, the first woman to obtain a medical degree in the United States, settled in London.[104] Elizabeth lived a self-described "progressive life" in Britain and agitated on causes as diverse as vivisection, temperance, the opium trade, women's education, universal suffrage, sexual health, civil liberties, and public morals. Alongside English progressives, in 1871 Blackwell co-founded the National Health Society, which aimed to spread public health information and promote formal health training for women. Three years later she co-founded the London School of Medicine for Women, and between 1878 and her death in 1910 published a dozen volumes and many other articles in progressive journals such as William T. Stead's *Pall Mall Gazette* on assorted reform topics.[105] Elizabeth shared news of English developments with her brother Henry, editor of the New England Woman Suffrage Association's weekly *Woman's Journal*. Travel overseas was a fixed part of the Blackwells' activism. "I should have been very glad had you been able now to continue your education by the larger method of travel instead of the smaller method of books," Elizabeth wrote her twenty-year-old niece Alice Stone Blackwell in 1877, "for I think you would now gain from European travel."[106] The Atlantic crossing remained a rite of passage for any self-respecting activist.

Postwar reform movements built especially on the connections between British evangelicals and humanitarians that had sustained transatlantic anti-slavery, but which now exposed new coercive labor practices and racial discrimination worldwide. Nowhere is this more apparent than in the 1893 and 1894 British anti-lynching campaigns of the black activist Ida B. Wells.[107] Wells's invitation overseas came from Catherine Impey, a Quaker activist with strong connections among Friends in Britain and the United States, whose other correspondents included Frederick Douglass and Albion Tourgée. From 1888, Impey began editing the monthly anti-racist newsletter *Anti-Caste*, which enjoyed a circulation of 3,500, and in 1893 co-founded the Society for the Recognition of the Brotherhood of Man, which stood at the center of a growing network of radical anti-racist activists and early anti-colonial nationalists.[108] In its methods, this network did not break radically from abolitionism. Wells's tours of Britain aimed to build up popular support just as African-American fugitives had done before the war; all of her activities were dutifully reported in *Anti-Caste* and its successor *Fraternity,* which reprinted reports of lynchings and biographies of early civil rights campaigners in the United States, as Caroline Bressey has shown.[109] Wells joined other "African American feminist transnationalists" circulating through the black Atlantic who believed the road to racial progress ran through Britain.[110] Among them were the educators Fanny Jackson Coppin and Georgiana R. Simpson, who visited Britain in 1888 and 1897 respectively, and Hallie Quinn Brown, who lectured on topics including "Racial Distinctions in America" and "The Progress of Negro Education" during one visit in 1895. In 1899 Brown spoke at the London conference of the International Council of Women, where she was joined by Margaret Murray Washington, principal of the Tuskegee Normal Institute, as official representatives of the National Association of Colored Women. Others would later attend the first Pan-African Conference in 1900. At key moments, Wells brought the anti-racist, philanthropic, and feminist networks in which she operated together to exert moral pressure against the United States—often appealing directly to their historic lineage to encourage them to "step into the arena again, so as to see if they could not yet accomplish something for the good old cause."[111] After reports from Arkansas of the lynching of James Perry for allegedly introducing smallpox to the town of Knoxville in June 1894, Wells spoke before the Protestant Alliance, Women's Protestant Union, and Congregational chapels in London, and all passed resolutions condemning lynching that were then forwarded to Thomas Bayard, the US Ambassador to London, alongside similar resolutions from the Aborigines' Protection Society and other temperance unions.[112]

Wells's mobilization of British moral pressure against American racism followed a well-established model of black transnational activism—a continuity that added legitimacy to her message. As she told one congregation in Liverpool, lynching "was simply a continuation of the disabilities of the slaves before their freedom was gained."[113] Wells praised "the moral agencies at work in Great Britain" that "did much for the final overthrow of chattel slavery," adding that "they can in like manner pray and write and preach and talk and act against civil and industrial slavery; against the hanging, shooting, and burning alive of a powerless race."[114] Wells pressed this message with urgency, as Sarah Silkey has brilliantly investigated. On her 1894 trip, Wells lectured to ten gatherings in Liverpool that "averaged a thousand persons each," and in London alone lectured before thirty-five different public gatherings under the title "What can England do for us?,", in addition to numerous engagements at the homes and clubs of her allies.[115] Wells's tours took place against the backdrop of a celebratory embrace of Anglo-Saxon kinship among transatlantic liberals, but aimed to exploit the moral and geopolitical divisions within that emerging transnational racial formation.[116] "It was a fearful thing to know," Wells reflected to British audiences, "that atrocities were being committed by civilized Anglo-Saxons."[117] By directing her "searchlight" onto the "criminal assaults" of white America, Wells hoped to isolate the United States from the international community of Anglo-Saxons.[118] "America cannot and will not ignore the voice of a nation that is her superior in civilization," Wells told readers of the *Birmingham Daily Post*—by this point a familiar appeal to Britain's superior moral sentiment.[119]

In the hands of diverse women reformers Anglo-Saxonism was used to pursue radically different ends. Wells's anti-racist mission sat uncomfortably alongside the World Woman's Christian Temperance Union's (WWCTU) embrace of Anglo-Saxon global moral leadership. Convinced that the British Empire's global infrastructure provided the key to halting the moral contagions of alcohol's spread among colonized peoples, the WWCTU networked extensively through Britain after its founding in 1884. Ideas of self-improvement appealed to middle-class women, and by 1910 the WWCTU's British branch, 157,000 strong, was the largest outside of the United States.[120] One of the appeals of the WWCTU was its embrace of the language of Anglo-Saxon motherhood. At the Union's 1886 convention an emotional crowd gave rapturous applause as its leader Frances Willard proclaimed, "for the first time in history the imperial mother and the dauntless daughter of the Anglo-Saxon race clasp hands in a union never to be broken."[121] British reformers responded in kind. Stead's *Review of Reviews* described the Union's special 1892 meeting in Britain as a "marvellous uprising of the serious, intelligent, and religious women of the English-speaking world for the protection and sanctity of home-life" and "the moral elevation of women everywhere."[122] Through the fusion of the "cult of true womanhood" and Anglo-Saxon exceptionalism, then, the WWCTU embarked on a mission to strengthen English-speaking hegemony and preserve the integrity of the Anglo-Saxon family.

Rhetorical claims of familial reconciliation were underpinned by elite intermarriage. In the age of the transatlantic marriage, heiresses stood out to British observers as one of the most distinctive American presences in the capital. Marriage became one of the dominant themes of Anglo-

American relations in this period, dissected by journalists and novelists alike.[123] British dailies noted that transatlantic matches occurred "so often of late years that one might sometimes be inclined to regard it as a design of Providence that England should become half American and America half English."[124] Although decried in equal measures as a sign of American Anglomania and the Americanization of Britain, transatlantic marriages were important signifiers of Anglo-American rapprochement.[125] Socially aspirant American families arrived in London from the 1870s onwards at a time when the pathways for entry into the British aristocracy were relaxing. Despite old prejudices against upper-middle-class professions, businessmen and especially financiers found their passage into the upper classes relatively easy, smoothed by the willingness of Britain's hereditary elite to align itself with new sources of power.[126] The aristocracy had little choice. In the words of David Cannadine, "the new super-rich stormed the citadels of social exclusiveness."[127] Western land speculators and mining entrepreneurs, robber barons, and the titans of Wall Street were all part of this new moneyed elite that, according to an anxious press, wanted to "market their daughters among the nobility of Europe" to demonstrate their prestige to the "snobbish, monarchist . . . upper circles" of American society.[128] For equally anxious Britons, they were pushing at an open door: "The latch-string of English society hangs outside the door for an American," concluded London's *Daily News.*[129]

Between 1870 and 1914 sixty marriages were contracted between British peers and Americans, and forty between younger sons and Americans—10 percent of all aristocratic marriages in Britain.[130] In Europe as a whole, the total was closer to 450.[131] International marriages, such as that between Consuelo Vanderbilt and Charles Spencer-Churchill, the 9th Duke of Marlborough in 1895, deepened antebellum links between wealthy Americans and aristocratic British banking families. Gravitating to the mansions of the fashionable West End, these women contributed to the vibrant social life of London in significant ways, crossing paths with one another at dinners, balls, or the fashionable parties of the Prince of Wales's "Marlborough House Set." Americans bought or rented fashionable London addresses in the social sanctuaries of Grosvenor Square, Park Lane, and Piccadilly and increasingly set the social tone—at an estimated cost of between £4,000 and £5,000 per Season.[132] Society reciprocated by "worshipping the almighty Dollar unabashed."[133]

Perceptions of American brides were wildly exaggerated, as some members of the aristocracy fought a rearguard action against their encroachment. "The American woman was looked upon as a strange

FIGURE 19. Young women were said to be especially vulnerable to the Old World baubles of rank and aristocracy—epitomized by the so-called "dollar princess" ("Another noble man among us," *Life*, November 8, 1888, 280). The European Svengali was a popular trope in the literature on Anglo-American marriages. According to the *Chicago Daily Tribune* in 1878, "an Englishman of rank seldom seeks the hand of an American girl in marriage unless his prudent eye has measured the proportion of her dowry" ("Anglo-American Marriages," August 4, 1878). Image: Samuel Ehrhart, "The European Svengali and the trillbys of the 'four hundred'—he hypnotizes 'em every time!," *Puck*, October 2, 1895. Library of Congress Prints and Photographs Division.

and abnormal creature," reflected Jennie Jerome Churchill, perhaps the most famous of these brides, "with habits and manners something between a Red Indian and a Gaiety Girl. Anything of an outlandish nature might be expected of her."[134] Unrefined, unscrupulous, and possibly tainted with "uncivilized blood," this American influence signified "Mammon worship," was "feminine, frivolous, and fleeting," and "helped to make [society] shallower, more extravagant, and more vulgar than it ever was before," in the reflection of one commentator.[135] A great deal of British invective stemmed from a conflation of the changing composition of aristocratic society—a process already taking place—with the arrival of these foreign brides. As social barriers lowered, the conquered English aristocrats, it was argued, were forced "to bend the knee . . . and pass under the transatlantic yoke"—a striking mirror image of American concerns over the presentation of Americans at Court.[136] From the American side of the Atlantic, the American brides of English peers were the victims, at best, of "sentimental sensibilities and alluring foreign scenes," and at worst "toadyism" and "the common exchange of money on one side and title on the other."[137] To the British journalist and social reformer William T. Stead, "when there is no love in the matter, it is only gilded prostitution."[138]

The "invasion" of the American woman, as with other tourists and emigrants, was entwined with new, bellicose perceptions of the United States' world power.[139] "She comes, is seen, and conquers," declared the *London American* in October 1895.[140] To an anonymous "Anglo-American" in *Harper's Weekly,* each marriage represented a "fresh American victory, another ancestral domain seized and occupied, another prize snapped up."[141] Others lauded these American women as the "the exponent of emancipation" for their European counterparts.[142] Some British commentators reached similar conclusions. "Through the breaches thus made in the ramparts," continued Stead in his anatomy of the Americanizing influence of transatlantic marriages, "a whole flood of American ideas are pouring into Europe."[143] Yet intermarriage was also an effective route into the world of Anglo-Saxondom and began to feature prominently in analyses of world affairs.[144] Far from "invasion," this was configured as interdependence. "In the making of nations," wrote the intellectual Charles Waldstein, "intermarriage is the most important factor welding the diversity of race into the unity of nationality."[145] Turning to the marriage of Mary Leiter, a Chicagoan heiress, to George Nathaniel Curzon, the future Viceroy of India, Stead saw "a foreshadowing of things to come, when Britain and America, happily united in the permanent ties of a race alliance, may pool their resources and devote their united energies to the work of ameliorating the lot of the impoverished myriads." To Stead, Anglo-American intermarriage was "the touch of nature which makes the whole world kin."[146]

"LITTLE AMERICA": EMIGRATION, INTERDEPENDENCE, EMPIRE

Transatlantic marriage and migration deepened the points of contact between British and American elites—contacts multiplied by the emergence of the American Colony in the mid-1890s. American social clubs for both men and women, journals, directories, and patriotic celebrations in London shaped the disparate American spaces of the British capital into a coherent world. "We have no politics," claimed the *Lon-*

don American's editor, "except 'America for Americans,' 'Europe for the Americans,' and 'everything else under the sun for the Americans.'"[147] By depicting migration as colonization, migrants continued to shape the representation of US power overseas. As was the case in the antebellum era, emigrant foreign relations centered on the "intricately interwoven" social and political duties of foreign representatives.[148] By 1895, however, Americans no longer understood the months of February to August as the "London Season" but the "American Season."[149] For some commentators, the "colonizing" of the "absentee" American with "an eye to court and fashionable society" was "a mode of life conducive to denationalization."[150] To leading migrants, the United States' participation in the cosmopolitan world of "civilized" empires depended on "fraternal demonstrations of goodwill" toward their British hosts and the celebration of the common ties of kinship, culture, and race among Anglo-Saxon elites.[151] Through the American Colony, the assertion of world power through migration and demonstration of shared leadership of the Anglo-Saxon imperial world were advanced.

By 1895, the number of Americans in the capital for the "American Season" was close to twenty-five thousand, and the year proved a turning point for American London.[152] In April, the *London American* was revived as "a chronicle of the American colony in Europe." American goods and services were listed in its pages; celebrations advertised and reported; passenger arrivals announced; and leading emigrants profiled. In short, the *American* provided a compendium of American London that enabled American in Britain to "imagine" the contours of an American Colony and American residents and travelers to familiarize themselves with American financial and business elites in London. The *American* shifted the focus of American activity in London onto permanent offshore clubs, societies, and businesses and away from the "shifting social element" of travelers.[153] In the words of the *American,* these locations were "American in inception, American in practical utility, American in thoroughness, American in trustworthiness, and American in comfort and convenience."[154] Permanency implied power and legitimized claims that migration was a colonizing activity.

In the same year that the *London American* was reborn the American Society in London (ASL) was formed. In March, Humphrey Baker Chamberlain, a real estate magnate from Denver; Patrick A. Collins, US Consul General; and Benjamin Franklin Stevens (described as the Colony's "patriarch") met and founded the Society for "the promotion of patriotic and social life amongst Americans residing in London."[155] The ASL fostered a shared sense of American identity by bringing together the disparate elements of American London described above into a self-described Colony. "The elements of such a society have been here for years," observed the *London American* but were "scattered" and "dispersed silently" across the "Babylon of the Old World." Chamberlin was the "magnetic individual" who consolidated "all these scattered elements" and united them "in allegiance to our common homeland."[156]

Migrant associations like the ASL were key agents in the transmission of US commerce and culture. Businessmen dominated the Society: between 1895 and 1914, thirteen of its chairman were businessmen or financiers. The ASL was a place where the business community socialized and shared information about British and European commercial practices, explored more fully below. Like emigrant clubs and Chambers of Commerce of all nationalities around the world, its members celebrated their patriotism at lavish banquets and opened their doors to American travelers and diplomats. It was, US Ambassador Thomas Bayard asserted at its inaugural dinner, "the nucleus . . . of patriotic association" among Americans in London and "a perpetual and recognised centre and rendezvous for Americans."[157] Bayard and its other members embraced the entanglement of commercial and cultural expansion encapsulated by these migrants. The ASL, Bayard argued, was "nothing but an organisation for the advancement of everything American" and a place where "American traditions, American sentiments, and American expressions should have their day in court and place of hearing." Interdependence among nations brought new opportunities for national expansion, the Ambassador observed: "the world was being brought closer together, and the principles and meanings and moral force of [the US] Government must have its own measure and its own weight."[158]

American women remained prominent among the United States' emigrant ambassadors. In March 1899, the Society of American Women in London (SAW) was founded at a meeting of seventy-six American women, including the author and suffragist Elizabeth Robins and Jane Croly, founder in 1868 of the Sorosis Club for women in New York and of the General Federation of Women's Clubs in 1898. SAW, its constitution stated, was dedicated to "the promotion of social intercourse" and aimed "to bring together women who are engaged in literary, artistic, scientific, and philanthropic pursuits, with the view of rendering them helpful to each other and useful to Society."[159] Headquartered at Prince's, a restaurant in Piccadilly, SAW was a social hub for resident American women and sponsored concerts, lectures, and debates alongside its weekly "at homes" where travelers and residents could mingle informally over tea.[160] The Society counted journalists, actresses, singers, philanthropists, social-ites, and some of the heiresses discussed previously among its members, all drawn from the social world of the American colony and many were also members of other clubs in London and New York.[161] SAW was there-fore a place where the well-connected could help other American women to establish themselves as independent professionals in the chaotic metropolis. Its members referred to SAW as "Little America," continuing the tendency of late nineteenth-century Americans in Britain to identify their institutions with the extension of US national space.[162]

Nevertheless, although the Society hoped "to keep up the spirit of Americanism" its members embraced the opportunities offered by trans-atlantic connections.[163] Chiefly, SAW was enmeshed within the expand-ing world of London's women's clubs. The number of women's clubs expanded and diversified, from just a handful in the 1870s to twenty-four by 1899, and forty-seven by 1906.[164] By the time of SAW's founding, women in the capital could choose from a multitude of new social clubs, including the Alexandra Club, the Ladies' Athenaeum (founded by Jennie Churchill), the Ladies' Imperial (for women members of the Conservative and Liberal Unionist Parties), and the Empress, among many others. These clubs tended to cluster north of Piccadilly (the center of London's men's clubs), closer to Oxford and Regent streets, and provided spaces for relaxation and socializing as well as a center for participating in polit-ical debate. In prewar England, urban women's clubs spread from "the butterfly of fashion" to the "working bee" and became symbols of wom-en's independence and emancipation.[165] If, as the author George Augustus Sala quipped, men's clubs were "a weapon used by savages to keep white women at a distance," women's clubland provided access to public space and was one of the building blocks of prewar feminist culture.[166]

SAW was another transnational institution among a "flurry of institu-tionalization" that characterized the women's movements of the 1890s, further deepening transatlantic exchanges among Anglo-American reformers.[167] The Society celebrated its creation "without any masculine collaboration" and worked alongside feminist London.[168] On July 3, 1899, the Society entertained the delegates to the second International Congress of Women (ICW), which represented the diverse interests of all women, and across the ten days, more than sixty sessions discussed wom-en's work in philanthropy, education, and social reform. The guests included the ICW's president May Wright Sewall, Emmeline Wells, Susan B. Anthony, Anna Howard Shaw, Sarah Hackett Stevenson, Mira Lloyd

Dock, and Charlotte Perkins Stetson, among others from international women's reform movements.[169] Socialization was a central element of the ICW program. As Leila Rupp has written, the conferences, committee meetings, and social functions of transnational activists were an "international ground" in which activist alliances were knit together and women's commitment to internationalism was affirmed.[170] According to one of SAW's members, the contacts forged at the dinner "proved a source of inspiration and encouragement of incalculable value to the society."[171] To some, SAW's involvement proved that "the Stars and Stripes have always been leaders in nearly all the liberating and upward movements of their sex."[172] In the words of Mrs. Hugh Reid Griffin, by contrast, it was just "one more link in the chain that bound the Anglo-Saxon race together."[173] As with other transnational groups in the 1890s, then, SAW was a place in which both national loyalties and internationalism co-existed.

Like the SAW, the American Society in London encapsulates the centrality of migration to the entanglement between domestic and foreign affairs. As in the 1850s, American migrants continued to act as informal ambassadors. This was dramatically revealed by the eruption of the Venezuela Crisis in the summer of 1895. As rumors of war circulated, the *London American* proclaimed loudly that American migrants were "the true representatives of the country" and that "in the hands of members of our American colony in London . . . all American interests are reposed."[174] American migrants threw themselves into the social world of diplomacy. Only two years before the Venezuela Crisis, the American Minister had been upgraded to an Ambassador, making Thomas Bayard the first American to hold the highest diplomatic rank and London the site of the first American Embassy in the world. His Congressional salary did not match the estimated $35,000–$50,000 annual expenditure of the London mission, however.[175] "A diplomat out of society is at a great disadvantage, for the simple reason he does not learn the secrets of his craft," wrote *Harper's Weekly*. "An impecunious ambassador would be ridiculous," the journal continued; "the country will be better represented by a self-respecting minister than by an ambassador who is the object of universal commiseration."[176] As one commentator surmised: "Shabby gentility and diplomacy do not go together."[177] Leading migrants again had both capital and social standing to act as overseas representatives where diplomats might have neither. Contemporaries continued to note that "comparatively small consequence is attached to the American Embassy in comparison with the position assumed by the embassies of other nations" since there were "so many Americans" in Britain who "monopolise public esteem and carry out, as individuals, the representation of their country."[178]

As the Venezuelan Crisis rocked transatlantic relations throughout 1895 and 1896, emigrant representatives proved their worth by promoting Anglo-American cultural, commercial, and racial reciprocity. At the ASL's Fourth of July celebration in 1896, James Bryce, author of the three-volume *American Commonwealth* (1888), was special guest speaker. After dinner, Bryce waxed lyrical about Anglo-American friendship, mixing metaphors of blood, kinship, and race and arguing that "in the Union Jack and the Stars and Stripes we have got the same colors, although the pattern is different."[179] The chairman of the society, pharmacist Henry S. Wellcome, re-oriented the ASL around these themes by downplaying its national exceptionalism. "The object of this Society was not to set up a little corner of America in England," he claimed, but to "promote that friendly feeling amongst all who speak our common tongue."[180]

Loud calls for arbitration of transatlantic crises came from pacifists on both sides of the ocean—and were especially loud among London's American emigrants.[181] Arbitration had been a concern of Britain's American community since the 1850s, when Joshua Bates was appointed an umpire on the Anglo-American Joint Claims Convention. This made for brisk Atlantic business but was also grounded in commitment to Anglo-American partnership. Peace became the byword for racial and imperial unity. "The achievements of the Victorian era surpass anything in the world's history," noted Wellcome at an ASL Thanksgiving Banquet in 1896, "above all, in the arts of peace."[183] At the beginning of 1897, migrants seemed to get their way in the proposed Olney-Pauncefote Treaty, which committed the United States and Great Britain to arbitrate all their disputes for the next five years—before the US Senate rejected it. The ASL's commitment to international arbitration was given full expression in a testimonial to the outgoing American Ambassador, Thomas Bayard, in May 1897 who was presented with a twenty-inch-tall gold loving cup at a cost of £2,000. An inscription around the base praised Bayard for his "zealous work in strengthening the sentiments of mutual respect and affection which bind together the peoples of the two great English-speaking nations."[182]

Essential to the conception of late nineteenth century Anglo-American relations was a "friendly" competition for titular leadership of the Anglo-Saxon race, a competition that would be the guarantor of peaceful international relations. The moral superiority of the "English-speaking peoples" was invoked repeatedly by the evening's speakers. Sir Richard

Webster QC, the Conservative Attorney General for England, lauded the English-speaking world as a "community of feeling, a community of rivalry, a community of enthusiasm, and a community of endeavour for good work." 1896, he argued, marked the year when "progress" had "been made towards a rivalry in the arts of peace, in which both nations should do their utmost to be first."[184] Webster and his fellow speakers echoed the sentiments of a wide element of the peace movement that lauded the idea of an Anglo-Saxon imperial alliance. "We want no foreigners to come between us, interfering in our family differences," argued longtime pacifist William T. Stead. Peace would be founded, he contended, in an "Anglo-American union by way of arbitration."[185]

The ASL was known affectionately as the "exile club," and its quarterly meetings on Washington's Birthday, the Fourth of July, Decoration Day, and Thanksgiving followed the same pattern.[186] Here the mutability of Anglo-Saxonism shows its face once more. Peace was the latest addition to the common principles thought to unite Britain and the United States. Increasing use of the term "English-speaking peoples" in the 1890s intersected with the emotive and aspirational appeal of metaphors of Anglo-American kinship.[187] The English language was understood as the vessel of customs, culture, and law—all of which were transmitted through Anglo-Saxon blood.[188] Anglo-Saxonism's apostles imagined a reunion, or at least an informal alliance, based on these dense Anglo-American connections.[189] Anglo-Saxonist ideology has long been understood as underpinning turn-of-the-century transatlantic diplomatic cooperation.[190] But in such accounts, Anglo-Saxonism is itself a static, even monolithic set of ideas. Its dynamic construction as a self-conscious bond connecting Britons and Americans is best viewed from the social world of the American colony where Britons and Americans engaged in Anglo-Saxon race-making.

The mixed metaphors of blood, kinship, and race bisected the discussion of Empire on both sides of the Atlantic.[191] This was especially evident in the wake of the short Spanish-American war of 1898. The English journalist Edward Dicey was representative of many in his jubilation that the United States shared British "imperial instincts" and was now "prepared to carry out that manifold destiny which is the birth right of the Anglo-Saxon race."[192] Many more Americans welcomed the Anglo-Saxon tributes flooding across the Atlantic and invoked the British Empire as a model for the emerging American sibling; for their part, British Imperial Federationists hoped to inaugurate "Greater Britain," a geopolitical union of the United Kingdom with its settler colonies, buttressed by an Anglo-American alliance built of a shared racial heritage.[193] The celebrations and institutions of the American "colony" gave form to this complex set of common solidarities as a venue through which Britons and Americans could affirm cultural and racial affinities.

The London-Americans basked in the imperial glow of 1898, too. As an "advance picket of Americans" overseas they continued to function as representatives of the new US Empire.[194] When news crossed the Atlantic of the sinking of the USS *Maine* in Havana Harbor in March 1898, the London-Americans gathered at the Hotel Cecil and pledged to send remittances to memorials for the fallen sailors.[195] Thereafter they followed developments closely. When war broke out a month later, American emigrants responded enthusiastically and joined in British celebrations of the United States' latest imperial acquisitions at a joint Anglo-American banquet in June. The Banquet was the brainchild of Lord Coleridge, a British liberal peer and judge; the American Robert Newton Crane, attorney of the US Embassy and outgoing president of the ASL; Robert Chester Maxwell, an American advertising agent; and the MP Alexander Claude Forster Boulton. The dinner was attended by a cross-section of Englishmen in the capital, including authors, MPs, lawyers, businessmen, financiers, and preachers, and, significantly, twelve former or current colonial administrators, including Governors-General, members of the colonial office, and a former Secretary of State for the Colonies. Alongside Crane was the incoming ASL President, the railway investor James L. Taylor, and the US Military Attaché General Harris. Speakers praised the moral character of the Anglo-Saxon race and the new unity of the Old and New World—"joint ministers of the same mission of liberty and progress," as Taylor termed it. The progress of civilization and the future of peace was refracted through an alliance of the British and US polities. "United the Anglo-Saxon race will march on towards the parliament of man and the federation of the world," declared the Baptist Reverend Dr. John Clifford, advocate of the social gospel and future President of the Baptist World Alliance.[196]

The joint banquet gave a social context to the cognitive shift taking place among Americans and Britons, in which they increasingly envisaged their empires as a joint, Anglo-Saxon project. As the London-Americans' Fourth of July celebrations began in 1898, the wires crackled with news of Admiral Dewey's victory at Manila Bay, signaling the beginning of the United States' Pacific empire. Under entwined American and British flags more than three hundred Americans in London and their British guests celebrated American independence. After singing the

FIGURE 20. In popular images, the United States and Britain were depicted as sharing in the extension of civilization worldwide through the new amicability of national symbols (although here the reunion of Britannia and Columbia was set against the backdrop of gathering war clouds) (Tuffnell, "Iconography of Anglo-American Inter-Imperialism"). It was, wrote Albert Shaw in the July 1898 American edition of the *American Monthly Review of Reviews,* the "era of Anglo-American good feelings" (22.) Image: Louis Dalrymple, "After Many Years," *Puck,* June 15, 1898, Library of Congress Prints and Photographs Division.

national anthems, the Secretary of State for the Colonies, George Robinson, the Marquis of Ripon, toasted President McKinley and told the celebrants that it was "to the highest interest of our two nations that we should walk together both hand in hand" (see figure 20). US Ambassador John Hay echoed his sentiments and embraced rivalry as the central facet of the processes of Anglo-Saxon "civilization." "We shall still compete with each other and the rest of the world," Hay suggested, "but the competition will be in the arts and the works of civilisation, and all the lovers of goodwill on the face of the earth will profit by it."[197]

"Civilization" functioned, in this instance, as a transnational analogy. For Britons, as for American proponents of Anglo-Saxon empire, 1898 was a watershed for the United States because it was perceived to have learned British (and therefore Anglo-Saxon) standards of behavior in the civilizing process. "America stands at the parting of the ways," opined James Bryce. "Shall it become a great conquering and foreign ruling people?" he asked, "or shall it pursue its great claim to advance mankind, because it was the first to try the great experiment of popular government and to try it upon the grandest scale?" To do the latter would be to share with Britain "the task of spreading knowledge, liberty, and enlightenment."[198] Late nineteenth-century proponents of Empire viewed nations along a comparative scale of stadial development, progression along which was a pedagogical process. British commentators, such as William T. Stead, referenced the learned behaviors of civilized nations in his observation that the US was now "treading the same steps which we have trod . . . shouldering responsibilities which have weighed down our shoulders for many generations past."[199]

Some in the United States looked with pride on Britain's settler colonies as a progressive force for global civilization, and it was taken for granted by statesmen and commentators that the "English-speaking race" would play the dominant role in its worldwide spread.[200] Many Americans were members of the newly-formed Anglo-American League. Founded in July 1898, the League boasted as many as five hundred members drawn from the House of Commons and committed Anglo-Saxonists such as Lord Brassey and James Bryce.[201] The League launched the *Anglo-American Magazine,* published in both London and New York, and hoped that it would facilitate co-operation between the two nations. Prominent citizens in New York launched a companion committee to reciprocate the Anglo-Saxon platitudes of the London branch.[202] Two hundred and sixty Americans were members of the Atlantic Union, a club established in 1901 by Sir Walter Besant and dedicated to the promotion of a formal union between the two English-speaking nations.[203] These were joined in 1902 by the Pilgrims of Great Britain, founded "to promote good-will, good-fellowship, abiding friendship, and everlasting peace between the United States and Great Britain."[204]

Increasingly, US citizens were recognized as imperial fellow travelers in British colonial institutions. Several Americans, for instance, were either members or speakers at the Royal Geographic Society (RGS). The RGS held considerable appeal to merchants and financiers in the late nineteenth century because of the greater interest it expressed in developing commercial geography from the 1870s.[205] The Pennsylvanian explorer May French Sheldon was among the first fifteen female members of the society, admitted in November 1892 after her trip through East Africa the previous year. The American Arthur Donaldson Smith won its Gold Medal in 1901 for his exploration of Lake Rudolph (now Lake Turkana) in the rift valley of Kenya and Southern Ethiopia; previous American recipients included John C. Frémont in 1850. In return for the publicity, Burroughs Wellcome & Co. provided free medical equipment for Sheldon's 1890–91 expedition, as it had for Henry Morton Stanley's 1887–89 expedition to rescue Emin Pasha.[206] As for Stanley, the naturalized American explorer, he was eventually knighted for his now highly contentious exploration of Africa. These Americans resemble the scientific and exploratory "sub-imperialists" identified by Robert A. Stafford, "who transformed the physiology of the Imperial state in the manner of symbiotic parasites that create niches for themselves in return for services to their host."[207]

The imperial reciprocity of Americans also took the form of dramatic acts of public diplomacy. In 1899, Jennie Blow, the American wife of A. A. Blow, the manager of the Slieba Gold Mining syndicate in South Africa, approached Jennie Jerome Churchill with the idea of equipping a hospital ship to support British actions in the Boer War. Churchill quickly formed the American Ladies' Hospital Ship Society to raise funds. Re-purposing the slogan "Remember the Maine," the Hospital Ship Society raised £41,957 through the private subscriptions of American women in London in just two months.[208] With the funds the Society purchased the *Maine* from the Atlantic Transport Company while the Tilbury Docks Company paid for its refurbishment into a 187-bed hospital.[209] In December, a party of three American doctors, twenty-nine male attendants, and a similar number of nurses arrived in the UK to take possession of the ship. After being entertained by the Queen at Windsor Castle, the group were guests of honour at a large "at home" hosted by SAW at the Hotel Cecil and attended by the American Ambassador, the Prince of Wales, and Rudyard Kipling.[210]

British and American firms also provided gifts in kind, among which was an ambulance donated by Elisabeth Ogden, wife of the American Ambassador Whitelaw Reid.[211] Medical equipment and drugs for the *Maine* were provided by Burroughs Wellcome in an elaborate medical chest tooled with allegorical designs representing the unity of Britain and the United States. The City of London Volunteers similarly left for South Africa equipped with Burroughs Wellcome supplies.[212] The company's owner, Henry S. Wellcome, adroitly navigated the interface of American expansion with British imperialism. Wellcome was instrumental in founding the ASL and fostered a diverse social life in London through which he assiduously courted financial and colonial elites in the city. Moreover, he rarely missed an opportunity to promote Anglo-American rapprochement (and the Wellcome brand) through diplomatic gift-giving. The

Bayard Testimonial Cup, for instance, was a Wellcome creation, and the same instinct for diplomatic stage management lay behind his decision to donate a portrait of Pocahontas to the US Senate in February 1899.[213] Such imperial collaborations could only have been imagined by the propagandists of the 1860s.

Networks of transnational racial solidarity were not reserved to white imperialists alone. Black Atlantic activists organized across colonial boundaries against racism and empire. Though small, black London was the meeting point for diasporas of African descent, where they shared ideas, pursued education, and created new spaces in which to articulate transnational anti-colonial solidarities.[214] Mobile African Americans continued to shape these new spaces and identities. Among the most influential black radical networks were those that radiated from the African Association (AA), which aimed to reform the Empire's systemic practices of segregation and exclusion—practices that one of its founders later dubbed a product of the "vicious virus of Americanism."[215] Founded in 1897, the AA was built by a group of London-based activists whose networks stretched to black peoples around the Atlantic world. It was the brainchild of the South African Alice Kinloch, who lectured on race relations for the Aborigines' Protection Society (then the foremost voice for the rights of peoples of color in Britain and the empire), Sierra Leonean lawyer Thomas J. Thompson, the Antiguan minister Henry Mason Joseph, and above all the AA's energetic secretary Henry Sylvester Williams, who had left Trinidad in 1891 for the United States and who arrived in London in 1896 to study law at Gray's Inn.[216] Membership in the AA was limited to peoples of African descent only, though honorary membership was reserved for white sympathizers from the philanthropic and anti-racist networks discussed above. Williams quickly arranged national and transatlantic lecture tours, published early works of black radical anti-imperialism and the short-lived *Pan-African* newspaper, and began lobbying Parliament and government ministers on race questions in the Empire.[217]

The Association's most significant success was the Pan-African Conference of 1900, which met between July 23 and 25 in Westminster Town Hall.[218] Williams's ambition was that the Conference would be the "precentor to the 20th Century"—and though dwarfed in scale by the 1911 Universal Races Congress in the city, its advent was an important early attempt to take on the formidable political and intellectual challenge of confronting the new global politics of whiteness.[219] Among the forty attendees were more than a dozen men and women from the United

States, South Africa, the West Indies, Abyssinia, Sierra Leone, Liberia, and Haiti. Among the African American transatlantic activists were W.E.B. Du Bois, Thomas Calloway, and the sisters Fannie Barrier Williams and Ella D. Barrier, who were visiting Europe as curators of the American Negro Exhibit at the Paris Exposition; former US consul to Luanda (1887–88) Henry Francis Downing, who had settled in London in 1895; AME Bishop and President of the National Afro-American Council Alexander Walters, who was appointed the Congress's President; Ada Harris, a reporter with both the *Indianapolis World* and *Indianapolis Freeman;* Annie H. Jones, who addressed the conference on "The Preservation of Race Individuality"; and the feminist sociologist Anna Julia Cooper. Cooper's address on "The Negro Problem in America" "flailed her country for its Christian shortcomings" and praised black peoples as the "most stable element in trans-Atlantic energy."[220] "For the first time in the history of the world," Walters declared in his opening remarks, "black men had gathered together from all parts of the globe with the object of discussing and improving the condition of the black race."[221]

The conference rested on the bedrock of transatlantic anti-slavery, evident in the conferees' lobbying of Queen Victoria to act more humanely toward black South Africans and resolutions acknowledging the past achievements of British anti-slavery.[222] Du Bois appealed to the historical consciousness of this legacy in his famous "To the Nations of the World" address, but the conference began the incremental distancing of black activism from its old alliance with liberals and radicals in the anti-slavery movement. Supporters of Wells's anti-lynching campaign at the Society for the Brotherhood of Man, and representatives from the Aborigines' Protection Society, British and Foreign Anti-Slavery Society, Native Races and Liquor Traffic Commission, and Quakers were permitted to attend as observers only.[223] However incremental such action seems, the political vision of the meeting was expansive. Du Bois recognized racial segregation as elemental to the global imperial and capitalist processes shaping the modern world. "Let not the cloak of Christian missionary enterprise be allowed in the future, as so often in the past, to hide the ruthless economic exploitation and political downfall of less developed nations," Du Bois exhorted, resisting prevailing discourses that naturalized the colonial project of uplifting subject races. "In any case," he had warned, "the modern world must remember that in this age when the ends of the world are being brought so near together the millions of black men in Africa, America and the Islands of the Sea, not to speak of the brown and yellow myriads elsewhere, are bound to have a great influence upon the world in the future."[224] Though the plans made for permanent committees and further conferences quickly withered, the emerging internationalist politics and evocative recasting of subjugated black peoples from a global minority to a "black world" of millions did not fail to inspire future activists.[225] Pan-Africanist congresses met again five more times by 1945, as black internationalists did at other transnational conferences, to challenge colonial rule and establish the diasporic political and intellectual bonds necessary for dismantling the global color line.[226]

In the American Colony, then, were the hallmarks of emigrant foreign relations: a set of offshore clubs, civic events, and media that organized American society in the capital; the cultivation of close contacts with Britons through socialization that sped the integration of offshore Americans with London's political elites; and the ongoing role of emigrant ambassadors in shaping the United States' public diplomacy. The Atlantic social, political, and commercial networks created by American emigrants drove Anglo-American interdependence in the late nineteenth century. "As between the people of Great Britain and the United States," observed the progressive American investigative journalist and social reformer Albert Shaw, "the bonds are so numerous and are interwoven so closely that the worst blunders of their governments could not now alienate two nations so closely akin."[227] The American Colony also played a key role in representing these networks as the product of shared Anglo-Saxon traits. Historians of the British Empire have highlighted the importance of co-ethnic social networks in London for the development of trade around the British settler dominions. "Trade can often develop more readily, and effectively," write Gary Magee and Andrew Thompson, "among people sharing a common identity, whether that identity is ethnic, religious or political."[228] American migrants did their best to reaffirm such common racial and linguistic identity. As the *Anglo-American Times* put it in October 1865, "commerce is the ring with which these two foremost nations of the earth are wed."[229] This is the overlooked imperial context of the American Colony, whose social connections with British elites proved central to the invasion of American manufactures that provoked fears of Americanization among British observers.

COMMERCIAL AND INDUSTRIAL INVADERS

By 1902, Britons and Americans were engaged in a "fight for the Atlantic."[230] Britain was besieged, according to Frederick MacKenzie, by an

FIGURE 21. Parodying Washington Irving's tale of Rip Van Winkle, the American colonist who falls asleep only to find he has slept through the American Revolution, an aged John Bull awakes to find an army of Uncle Sams invading Britain with raw materials and manufactured goods. "We slept while our rivals went ahead," complained MacKenzie's *American Invaders* (x). The American invasion featured strongly in William T. Stead's *Review of Reviews,* which began publishing an illustrated supplement, entitled "Wake Up! John Bull," in July 1901. Stead celebrated the American invasion as a sign of the vitality of the English-speaking race, however, claiming in December 1901 that "the time has come for . . . a national Trust of all English-speaking peoples," noting that it would be an element of "patriotic pride" if the firm were called "John Bull and Sons." He conceded nevertheless that "Uncle Sam and partners" would better reflect the United States' "leading position in the combination" ("The Americanisation of the World," *Review of Reviews,* December 1901, 653). Image: William H. Walker, "John Bull as Rip Van Winkle," *Life,* October 17, 1901, P267.2, Houghton Library, Harvard University.

"industrial army" attacking "five hundred industries at once" (see figure 21).[231] While allowing that Britain gained a great deal "by the interchange of ideas, and by the adoption of American notions," MacKenzie told his readers they must "decide whether we are going to be a subordinate people, allowing the Americans to take the supreme rule of our industries, or whether we are going to retain our old chieftainship."[232] It was a striking reversal of Henry Carey's fears from only three decades earlier that British trade and capital was "paving the way for a return to a state of colonial dependence greater than has existed at any period since the peace of 1783."[233] Instead, British commentators asked repeatedly, "Are we doomed to a subordinate commercial position?"[234] Leading the "invasion" were American migrants, responsible for managing the establishment of American firms in Britain, advertising new goods to British consumers, and cultivating social connections with British financial institutions and elites. "The old country will become the new home of the American colonists," observed Britain's foremost analysts of the political economy of the American invasion, William T. Stead.[235]

Indeed it had. American firms spread rapidly across Britain in the final third of the nineteenth century, exercising the newfound ability of the United States to diversify its trading links.[236] "There are two kinds of American commercial invaders," wrote Frank Fayant, London correspondent of the *New York Herald,* in a 1902 analysis of the connection between migration and commercial expansion: "those who bring to England goods made in America, and those who come here to reorganize English industry."[237] American goods flooded British markets. In addition to the United States' long history of supplying raw materials and foodstuffs to British manufacturers, the "menace" of American commercial invaders in the late nineteenth century came armed with mass-manufactured goods.[238] Key to understanding the power of the language of "invasion" through which this capitalist expansion was interpreted was the growing sense that goods embodied the racial and cultural essence of the nation that produced them.[239] Skill, ingenuity, and strenuous manhood were the *leitmotifs* of British commentators who found the key to American success in the national history of "a young and vigorous race let loose among the incalculable treasures of a virgin continent."[240]

Mobile American manufacturers exploited the way Britons learned of the races, peoples, and nations of the world through goods. In 1887, Queen Victoria's golden jubilee year, a group of Americans intent on breaking into British markets hosted an American Exhibition at Earl's Court. Its objects were threefold: to display US products to buyers in Britain and the Empire, to attract future investment in the United States, and to increase US foreign trade.[241] On entering the exhibition space, visitors encountered a vast painting depicting the view of New York harbor from the deck of a Hudson steamer, after which they passed through each of the fifty states, organized across 100,000 square feet of space from east to west. The halls were crowded with American goods: large-scale industrial manufactures such as locomotives, rolling stock, boilers, windmills, and watermills; mass-manufactured items with interchangeable parts such as typewriters, firearms, sewing machines, watches, toys, and electric motors; chemical goods including explosives, soaps, oils, and cosmetics; and mass-produced clothing, confectionary, liquor, and preserved foods. In the rear of the official guide, groaning with lavish ads for American goods, the visitor could find details about where to order the articles on display.[242] A bigger attraction was the Buffalo Bill's Wild West Show's first appearance in London for the duration of the event, a pairing that tied the vigorous expansion of American goods to the story of American's strenuous racial conquest of the frontier.[243] If the Great Exhibition of 1851 had been a statement of the Empire of Free Trade's economic vitality, 1887 was the evidence of American manufacturers' blossoming independence.

Exhibiting was just one of the labor-intensive ways for American migrants to create new markets in Britain. Another was to be the first mover in new industries.[244] According to Frederick MacKenzie, the American "incomers . . . acquired control of almost every new industry created during the past fifteen years."[245] American firms were attracted to Britain because it was often cheaper to manufacture in plants closer to key markets, rather than transport them across the Atlantic. Singer Sewing Machine had pioneered this strategy after opening its Glasgow factory in 1867.[246] But soon the migration of enterprise became a regular transatlantic flow. The English and American Boot and Shoe and General Machine Company arrived in 1882, followed by the Remington Typewriter Company in 1886; and the Gatling Gun Works and American International Goodyear Machinery Company in 1889. A year later the American Special Machine Company, the Campbell American Machine Company, and Rockingham Machine Company all opened depots through which to compete with British industry.[247] American chemicals and pharmaceuticals similarly boomed in Britain. Burroughs Wellcome was formed by the American pharmacists William S. Burroughs and Henry S. Wellcome in September 1880 and introduced American-style gelatin coated pills into Britain from its plant and research laboratories on the banks of the Thames; in 1889 Eastman Photographic began manufacturing film for its popular Kodak cameras from its factory in Harrow.[248] More dramatic was the arrival of Westinghouse Electric and Manufacturing Company in 1901, which erected an enormous industrial complex, including several thousand workers' homes, at Trafford Park, Manchester, to make parts for Britain's electric railways along standardized American designs.[249] As first movers in these industries, American firms soon achieved a market power that was difficult for British competitors to dislodge.[250]

American businesses also expanded into the provision of public utilities in Britain. Building on domestic innovations in the delivery of electricity and telephone systems, American businesses turned to Europe as the next field of investment, establishing English subsidiaries to market products under American patents. American firms introduced the telephone into Britain in 1879 when Colonel George R. Gourard managed the Edison Telephone Company in London and Colonel William H. Reynolds was head of the Bell Telephone Company. The two firms merged in May 1880 to form the United Telephone Company, which completed the installation of American-made telephone systems in London under license from the British Government.[251] The General Electric Company built new works in Birmingham in 1900, where it joined Brush Electric, which moved to nearby Loughborough the year before.[252] In some respects, this was British capital come full circle—British financiers had invested heavily in General Electric and Edison, as well as Eastman Kodak, US Steel, and Pullman's—and so the "invasion" came partly at the behest of British pocketbooks.[253]

Migration anchored commercial expansion. The importation of specialized skills and knowledge followed the employment of American engineers and foremen in industrial works. Electrical apparatus makers; erectors, fitters, and turners; and boot and shoe makers followed the wave of American entrepreneurs invading Britain in these industries. The Anglo-American Brush Electric Light Corporation enticed American engineers to its plant in Lambeth, London, which opened in 1880 and, in the case of William Bruce Fuller's sweet factory, which opened on Wardour Street in 1895, it was reported that "wherever it has been possible to employ an American in the business he has done so."[254] As American industries exported products and new manufacturing technologies into the British economy, managers brought their own skilled foremen and technicians with them. American firms required resident overseas representatives, advertising agents, middle managers, clerks, and commercial travelers to administer British-based branches—but also to remain close to the United States' chief creditor. White collar service industries were also on the rise. By the 1880s, the "Big Three" of the American insurance industry—Mutual Life, New York Life, and Equitable Life—had expanded into Britain. To get American goods to the market, J. Walter Thompson's advertising agency established a London office on the Strand in 1899 to "annex the entire British domain to the advertising realm of the ambitious American manufacturer who sighs for more worlds to conquer."[255]

US historians should tread carefully around the agitation of Britons over the growth of US trade in Britain. The "American invasion" was interdependent with Britain's construction of global transportation, communication and financial infrastructure.[256] Long-distance trade was challenging in this period, and the creation of a successful trading network required American migrants in London to take advantage of the global commercial reach of the British Empire and its supremacy over freight and services.[257] Residence in London brought proximity what the historian John Darwin has called the "information milieu" of lobbies, colonial agents, international shipping companies, and financiers of the Victorian Empire.[258] It was also the center of global commercial intelligence, or "the listening post for commercial opportunities in every continent."[259] This listening post had global reach thanks to the cabling of the planet with telegraph wires connecting distant stock and commodity exchanges, cities, ports, nations, and continents.[260]

Social clubs formed in this dynamic imperial city were also the basis of successful trading networks. The wide array of voluntary clubs and associations in London provided opportunities for personal advancement, mutual support, and for developing relationships between businesses, and official and professional groups.[261] Contact with members of British imperial officialdom offered firsthand knowledge of the Empire's markets and investment potential. American entrepreneurs joined the diverse world of social clubs-cum-commercial lobbies. These included the Imperial and American Club, founded in 1885 as a "rendezvous and headquarters for leading colonials, Americans, and Anglo-Indians visiting London, where they may meet gentlemen of position residing in England in social intercourse" and "unite the English-speaking peoples of all parts of the world."[262] The Imperial and American was followed two years later by the American Club, which boasted a membership of more than one thousand Britons and Americans, founded "with the primary object of promoting social intercourse between those who have been, or are still, connected with the Western Hemisphere."[263] The American Club was a crossroads of British and American imperial enterprise in these markets, where commercial intelligence could be shared in an informal setting. Among the Club's American members were the pharmacists Wellcome and Burroughs, bankers John Pierpont Morgan and Anthony Joseph Drexel, railroad magnate William Kissam Vanderbilt, real estate investor John Jacob Astor, and publishing giant Joseph Pulitzer. Through the Club these American entrepreneurs could meet with a host of Crown Colony Agents, MPs, cabinet members, and British entrepreneurs.

The American Society in London ought to be viewed in the context of this thriving world of British imperial clubs. The direct commercial impact of the ASL is hard to document, but it is clear that it was a commercial intermediary that enabled Americans to draw on the "empire-minded or imperial oriented interests in the metropolis" for their information on colonial markets, just as did British investors in Canada, Australia, and South Africa.[264] At the ASL's 1898 Fourth of July Banquet, for example, the British guests featured the former Secretary of State for the colonies and Viceroy of India George Robinson; former Governor-General of Canada and India Frederick Hamilton-Temple-Blackwood; William Des Voeux, former Governor-General of Fiji and Hong Kong; Donald Stewart, a member of the council of the Secretary of State for India; and Sir Charles Evans Smith, the Consul-General of Zanzibar, among a host of peers, MPs, bankers, and businessmen. Through these social webs, Anglo-American elites could cultivate connections, exchange commercial intelligence on overseas markets, and generate interest in American goods and services.[265]

The American Colony had an "information milieu" of its own too. American newspapers in Britain were key intermediaries in the transfer of knowledge. The *London American,* which merged with the *Anglo-American Times* in 1901 to form the *Anglo-American Press,* whose masthead read "one kin, one people, one purpose," featured regular biographies of leading businessmen and pointed to the "invasion" of particular American products.[266] The colony's newspapers were joined by the *Directory of Americans in London.*[267] The *Directory* was published by the San Franciscan William B. Bancroft, who arrived in London in 1896 as manager of the American Trading Company. The *Directory*'s "main purpose" was to "keep track" of "the bonds of amity between the people of the United States and Great Britain . . . an association which is founded on a kinship of trading interests as well as a kinship of blood."[268] The *Directory* provided a compendium of London's American residents, businesses, and social centers.[269] Similar in content was the *American Blue Book,* established in 1905 by Bancroft's brother Basil and his wife Genevieve, which built on the "steady growth of unity and friendly and business interests" between the American colony and its hosts.[270] The *Blue Book*'s directory of American businesses in London ran to ninety-four pages, and was joined by lists of titled Americans and the city's American residents. These "many Anglo-American alliances, the unity of business and family interests, and steady growth of the Colony," wrote one contributor, were signs of a "conciliation and happy intercourse between the two peoples."[271]

Powerful currents of interdependence lay behind the American "invasion." The "true American in London has no spirit of the invader," counselled the *Blue Book,* but rather a "duty to become even in miniature an integral part of the Empire."[272] At the close of the century, the ability to project power through, and to bind other nations into, mutually beneficial patterns of interdependence was the new measure of the United States' ability to act as in independent power in world affairs. Joseph Hodges Choate, the American ambassador between 1899 and 1905, depicted the "invading forces" of Americans as "spinning fast cords of connexion between the two countries . . . proving their mutual dependence." The metaphor is apt for the American colony, whose diverse cords—institutional, social, and cultural—intersected with British politics and London society at various points. Each of these scattered points blended to form a distinct sense of American nationality and national space in Britain. Choate phrased this sense of consolidation differently, capturing the nascent power of the United States in this process, noting that "each [cord] by itself may be of trifling strength, but are together like the strands of the Lilliputians."[273]

Were British concerns over the "invasion" of American commerce warranted? American emigrants in Britain were the visible agents of the dramatic growth of US trade in this period—from a value of $513 million in 1875 to $2.4 billion by 1914.[274] Between 1877 and 1900 US exports doubled in value and by the latter date constituted 15 percent of world exports.[275] Mostly, Britons viewed this dramatic growth through the relative decline of Britain as an exporter of manufactures to the United States and continued anxieties that Britain's open domestic markets were vulnerable against US protectionism.[276] A foretaste of future competition came in 1900, when the British Exchequer placed a loan of £15 million to finance the Boer War in New York through J.P. Morgan to great success—another four followed between 1900 and 1902, all oversubscribed.[277] Striking as this moment was, however, the United States became "the greatest debtor nation in history" in this period, and Britain remained the republic's principal source of foreign investment (three-quarters of the total by the end of the century), its lender of last resort, and its shipper—all of which the "invasion" depended on.[278] Like their counterparts in the American Colony, many Britons viewed rising American competition as part of a healthy competitive interdependence. "We require competition, opposition and adversity to grasp . . . that we are neither omnipotent nor omniscient,"

COLONEL JONATHAN J. BULL;

Or, What John B. may come to.

FIGURE 22. The new hybridity of Anglo-American icons enabled the British and American public to navigate the shared cultural and economic entanglements of the late-nineteenth and early-twentieth century Atlantic. Like the artist Victor Gillam, who depicted John Bull and Uncle Sam as having ingested the globe into a single stomach ("It ought to be a Happy New Year," *Judge*, January 7, 1899), *Punch*'s Bernard Partridge merged John Bull and Brother Jonathan into a single figure, completing the reunification of the two nations. Image: Bernard Partridge, "Colonel Jonathan J. Bull: Or, what JB may come to," *Punch*, November 27, 1901, Punch Cartoon Library / TopFoto.

wrote the shipping line owner and Liberal Party MP Christopher Furness in 1902, concluding that "as our fathers have struggled to obtain supremacy, so we their sons must struggle to maintain it."[279] In itself, that was a significant shift. Only fifty years before, the "fight for the Atlantic," as MacKenzie would have it, was the United States' struggle to achieve independence from the British Empire. It was now recognized as a global imperial partner, curiously celebrated in a new symbol of Anglo-American relations, Colonel Jonathan J. Bull (figure 22).

Epilogue

Emigrants, Americanizers, Colonizers

Edwardian Londoners found themselves in the grip of an "American phase."[1] At the climax of Edward VII's coronation year, American emigrants in London staged a self-proclaimed "lesson in American expansion" to Edwardian Britons. The lesson took the form of the "America in London" exhibition at the Crystal Palace.[2] On May 31, 1902, the exhibition opened to crowds of well-heeled day-trippers who thronged to the "People's Palace" and marveled at displays of US manufacturing and art work, watched bicycle races, and rode a looping centrifugal railway. To its committee of emigrant organizers the array of goods and attractions had demonstrated "the magnitude and importance of . . . the 'American invasion.'"[3] But the organizers also envisaged it as an exhibition "of international moment" that would bring "the two Anglo-Saxon races into more intimate association."[4]

The "America in London" exhibition captured the ongoing dualism of independence and interdependence: it was a display of "American" products, the majority of which had been manufactured on British soil by businesses managed by American migrants; it delivered dual, and seemingly irreconcilable, messages of nationalist commercial "invasion" and transatlantic partnership; and finally, in the absence of initiatives from the State Department, American migrants took it upon themselves to act as representative Americans. By the Edwardian period, Americans overseas were viewed as dynamic, energetic national representatives—

a far cry from the colonial dependents depicted in earlier analyses. Older fears of the nation's overseas representatives bending the knee to foreign sovereigns and succumbing to the "tinsel" of aristocracy receded. Instead, Americans took pride in the centrality of their fellow citizens to the economic and social life of their former colonial master, viewing each "social triumph" overseas as a sign of the United States' growing international standing.[5] In fact, keeping up to speed with the whirl of the London Season and demonstrating transatlantic connection was essential to display social standing in the elite circles of New York, Boston, and Newport.[6] "Not so long ago," reflected Wisconsin-born Ralph Blumenfeld from London in March 1905, it was not believed "consistent with Jacksonian simplicity and democracy to rub shoulders with monarchical aristocracy in its country houses. But that is all past and gone, and a man, even though he be American, may with perfect impunity accept invitations when and wherever he likes, even in a monarchy!"[7] In July the same year, *Harper's Bazaar* boasted that "the storm center of London society is unquestionably the American Colony."[8]

The key to navigating Atlantic entanglements, then, was not isolation, but to Americanize transatlantic connections and to demonstrate power through the nation's ability to ensnare others in webs of interdependence. "Britons are becoming more exercised over a manifestation among themselves which might be designated Yankomania," wrote Earl Mayo in 1902, the same year that a trust led by J. P. Morgan had bought out the Leyland, White Star, and Dominion lines and planned to do the same to Cunard, reversing British dominance of Atlantic shipping. "The Yankees, as our British cousins like to call us, have turned the tables completely," he told readers of *The Forum*, "and are to-day exerting a greater influence on English life than ever the English did on American ideals and habits."[9] Mayo highlighted the "all pervasiveness" of American influence over social customs, culture, and commercial life with an imagined open-top bus tour from Piccadilly Circus through the Strand to Pall Mall. From the top deck of the bus, Mayo's tourer viewed

'American' tailor shops, 'American' tobacconists, 'American' shoe stores, 'American' bars and restaurants by the score, and even 'American' patent medicines and soda-fountains. In many places he will find a more specific welcome extended to him in the signs before the shops, such as 'Outfitters to American tourists' and 'American patronage solicited.' If he looks through a newspaper he will not only observe the effect American typesetting and stereotyping machinery have extended on its appearance, but he will also find a great deal of American news in addition to accounts of lynchings, swindles, and atrocious crimes—formerly the only trans-Atlantic [sic] events chronicled by the London prints—is being published. In the restaurants he will find American dishes; on the book-stalls he will see American books: and everywhere he will hear characteristic American expressions.[10]

Mayo's "Yankomania" echoed, but reversed, anxieties over the Anglomania of American elites.[11] Almost fifty years before Mayo wrote, William Henry Seward had declared the War of Independence "the first act in the great drama of decolonization on this continent."[12] To many American commentators, the drama of decolonization was entering its final act: an American invasion that would tip the balance between interdependence and dependence in favor of the United States. What "began as a trade invasion," Mayo told his American readers, "rapidly grew into a trade conquest."[13] "The American invasion has turned into an army of occupation," echoed *Harper's Weekly* in 1904.[14] That occupation, commercial and social, was chronicled ceaselessly by American journals. As Americans shed many of their anxieties over the role of migrants in expanding the nation's Atlantic connections, they transformed the drama of decolonization into one of colonial conquest, a heady vision of a transition from the Anglicization of America to the Americanization of Britain. "London is one of America's most important colonial possessions," concluded one survey of emigrant life in the capital.[15]

Even the city's subterranean spaces were not safe from "colonization." Nothing captures the American "invasion" of the British capital quite so well as the London Underground. By 1900, London was home to more than six million souls and expanding rapidly—since 1871 it had added two and a half million inhabitants, equivalent to adding two Berlins, a Paris, or a New York City.[16] Much of this growth could be found in its outer ring of suburbs. On a typical workday, more than 1,250,000 people travelled into and out of the city. "Every year," wrote one Briton, London became, "more of an *entrepôt*, or receiving-place, of hundreds of thousands of men and women who pour in during the day, and spread themselves over a thousand square miles of territory before night."[17] While the horse remained the backbone of the capital's transit network, London's underground railway was expanding to meet these new demands. The metropolis was becoming, in one memorable phrase, a "two-decked city."[18] While American visitors to the capital in the 1870s marveled at the engineering feats of Victorian Britons, Edwardian commuters plunged into the blue clay beneath the Thames and the bustling streets above through tunnels built "by American energy . . . on American plans and with American material."[19]

While British investors lumbered uneasily to create a transport system worthy of an imperial capital, Charles Tyson Yerkes, a robber baron fresh from transforming mass transit in Chicago, founded the Underground Electric Railways Company of London (UERC) in August 1900. With the help of backers in the United States to the tune of $17 million, Yerkes had established a stranglehold on the London underground system in a matter of months.[20] Through the UERC, Yerkes negotiated a buyout of the Metropolitan District Railway; the partially completed Baker Street and Waterloo Railway; the Charing Cross, Euston, and Hampstead Railway; and the Great Northern, Piccadilly, and Brompton Railway. Over the next five years, Yerkes expanded and modernized the Underground with the help of his American engineer-in-chief James Russell Chapman, who brought with him an army of skilled American foremen to oversee the tunneling process and electrification of the tube system.[21]

Yerkes's capture of London's famous transport system highlighted how US technological innovation, technical expertise, and growing investment capital were in high demand in Britain. According to one writer, Yerkes launched his "onslaught on London in the van of the American invaders," and scoffed at Britain's "adherence to tradition" and enslavement in the "fetters of an obsolete past."[22] To the satirical magazine *Punch,* Yerkes was Jonathan M. Yankes, head of the "Great American Pioneer and British Isles Development Trust," boasting that he would "start in under the pond with our Pan-Anglo-Saxon Submarine Toob."[23] Yerkes's chief innovation was to introduce the new Price Rotary Excavator, which allowed his engineers to tunnel up to seventy-three feet per week, forcing its way, in the words of one contemporary observer, "like a giant scientific mole, through the bowels of the earth."[24] To power the newly electrified system, Yerkes constructed the Lots Road Power Station on the Chelsea Tidal Creek between 1902 and December 1904. The station burned seven hundred tons of coal a day in its 5,500 kilowatt generators, built by British Westinghouse—subsidiary of the Pittsburgh-based Westinghouse Electric and Manufacturing Company.[25] Rolling stock was purchased from the American Car and Foundry Company.

The completion of Yerkes's Central Line in 1900 dramatically opened up the West End's shopping and entertainment centers, especially along Bayswater and Oxford Street, to London's suburbanites.[26] The West End was marked all over by the new consumer culture: posters, enamel signs, electric lights, ads splashed over vast billboards, and enlarged store windows vied to entice middle-class shoppers.[27] Carriages, cabs, omnibuses, and motor cars (many manufactured by Ford, which had captured one quarter of the English market by 1913) bowled past shoppers, plastered in further ads for soaps, teas, whiskeys, hotels, restaurants, and cigarettes.[28] American businesses' products joined the riot of commodities imported from the Empire and continent. "No matter what quarter of the world he comes from," wrote the author P. F. William Ryan, "his countrymen have a colony here, and the colony has its shopkeepers."[29] Piccadilly, Pall Mall, and the Strand were favored spots for a variety of American businesses; St Ermins Hotel in St James Park was favored by tourists as "America's Home in England."[30] According to the American journalist Elizabeth Banks, these locales created "such a volume of American accent, American vivacity, and American dressing as would be apt to convince a foreigner dropping suddenly into the scene that London was the chief city of America."[31] By 1909, shoppers could take in the latest of the capital's "Americanisms"—Gordon Selfridge's new department store, which opened on Oxford Street in March.

Commerce and migration fueled one another and propelled the "invasion." "Thousands of Americans, representing hundreds of lines of commercial production, are doing a thriving business in London and the other principal cities of John Bull's domain," Mayo observed.[32] "London has become a sort of clearing house for Americans," another London correspondent noted in 1906.[33] The acceleration and visibility of this new American invasion startled many Edwardian Britons, who began to view consumer culture as a dangerous foreign import.[34] Late Victorian and Edwardian commentators associated Americanization with the "hustle and haste" of its businessmen and the "anarchical," "degenerate" young women who travelled overseas.[35] Yet the "Americanization" of London's commercial culture was simply another iteration of the ongoing dualism between dependence and interdependence in the Atlantic. While at times highly contested, US products and social customs were welcomed by many British consumers. British businesses adopted the moniker "American" as an enticement precisely because the characteristics that its detractors fretted over—cheapness, convenience, efficiency, novelty—appealed to shoppers. "Having tasted the fruit that he had been warned was evil," Mayo remarked dryly, "the English consumer . . . is eager for more."[36] Where some saw competitive advantage, others saw an economics of interdependence. "Close trade relations foster friendship, and there has been no part of English life that has not been affected by American enterprise," wrote one author in the progressive journal *World's Work*.[37] As a Briton wrote in response to Mayo's account, the detractors of the "American Invasion" had "considerably underestimate[d] the receptivity that England habitually shows to ideas coming from outside."[38]

Historians have also underestimated the receptivity of the American invaders to Britain's imperial state. It is tempting to view the late-Victorian and Edwardian "American Invasion" as the first stirrings of the Anglo-American imperial transition and the germ of the "American Century."[39] But such reasoning is faulty. Yes, American goods took British consumers by storm and added to domestic fears over "national efficiency" and "race deterioration" exposed so publicly by the South African War.[40] The political economy of the Edwardian Empire was shifting and, by some measures, losing ground to its rivals: its share of world trade was declining steadily; manufactures made up an increasing share of British imports; and some even began to doubt the political economy of free trade, which had been so central to democratic culture and national identity in Britain.[41] In industrial production, the United States overcame Britain to become the largest global steel producer in 1887, the largest extractor of iron ores (1889), and the largest producer of pig iron (1890).[42] There were also signs of a shift in the geo-politics of Anglo-American relations. In 1901 the Hay-Pauncefote Treaty recognized the United States' ascendancy in the Caribbean, as Britain gave up on its longstanding interest in controlling a future Isthmian Canal.[43] "The United States should hold the iron gate of the two oceans," reflected an essayist in London's *Fortnightly Review,* adding that "we ought not to be found in America's way where our interests are secondary and hers are supreme."[44] The growth of American commercial competition was seen to be part of this pattern.[45] "We need to be inoculated with some of the nervous energy of the Americans," concluded former Prime Minister Lord Archibald Rosebery in 1901, attacking "national self-complacency."[46]

It must be kept in mind, however, that the political economy of Atlantic interdependence continued to underpin the "American Invasion" of world markets. Britain's Edwardian Empire retained, arguably even enhanced, the dominance it enjoyed in the spheres of finance and banking. As John Darwin has convincingly argued, the Edwardian Empire thrived as an "agency state," that is, a provider of commercial services such as foreign exchange, credit, and insurance.[47] London remained the world's money market, and it dominated both global communications (by 1910 the Empire controlled 260,000 miles of international cable mileage, one half of the global total), and international shipping (where its mercantile fleet stood at 10 million tons, four times as much as its closest rival, Germany).[48] Although Britain's share of world trade fell amidst the surge of worldwide traffic, it still imported and exported more than any other nation—and 60 percent more than the United States.[49] As striking as British fears of the American "invasion" may appear, then, they are best understood amidst a range of intersecting arguments over the future relationship between the British Empire and the United States.[50] This discussion dated back to the early 1890s and generated a flowering of proposals, differing in ambition and rationale, for Anglo-American collaboration under the banner of "Greater Britain."[51] And even those, like Stead, who recognized a gradual intra-racial shift taking place, noted that Britons had "no reason to resent the part the Americans are playing in fashioning the world in their image, which, after all, is substantially the image of ourselves."[52]

While the language of "invasion" seems prescient, then, it was a telling instance of how deeply nation-building and transnational connection were interwoven by the end of the nineteenth century. The American invaders were not merely an outward projection, or part of a nation of outposts, isolated from foreign cultures and people. Rather, they engaged closely with the world beyond the United States. "Americans have learned that Europe is not so very far away, after all," surmised one American analyst in 1907. "If this country of ours is ever to be as great intellectually and artistically as it is physically and financially, the impetus must come from Europe. This does not mean that we should blindly follow," he continued, "but it does mean that the more nearly we get in touch with the best there is in the fields of art, music, and architecture, the better equipped we shall be to do good work at home."[53] In short, it took the world to produce the nation. This is much less the history of invasive emigrant occupiers and frictionless projection into the world than it is a history of integration, interdependence, and the constant and careful maintenance of transnational connection: the hallmarks of emigrant foreign relations.

American emigrants in Britain anchored the United States in the world. Emigrants worked hard to integrate with, and represent the United States to, British political and social elites, embedding American foreign relations in the London Season and the culture of Great Power diplomacy. It was emigrants who created the associational clubs at which to entertain British business elites, the chambers of commerce necessary for managing long-distance trade and who kept a watchful eye for germane opportunities to reap the lucrative rewards offered by the British agency state. And, finally, emigrants were central to the transnational production of American nationalism, mediating foreign influences on the United States and acting as critical foils against which to define the nation. Viewed from this perspective, emigrant foreign relations are integral to United States history. Historical actors recognized this too. In 1857, *Harper's Weekly* depicted the emergence of American communities overseas as the inevitable product of "Yankee enterprise" that "like Nature, abhors a vacuum, and consequently pervades all space." "After sweeping the wide continent of America in its restless movement," the journal opined, "it is away in a whirl encircling the rest of the world." American entrepreneurs were busy "emptying foreign gold into American pockets" and "driving such a thriving business in those centers of civilization, Paris and London."[54] The world, of course, was not a vacuum, but *Harper's* had precisely located the human activity that collapsed the boundaries between the United States and the rest of the globe.

American migrant communities are important not because they expand the cast of Americans "in the world" or because they might "thicken" the historical context of key moments of US national development, but for the profound questions they pose for the ongoing historical project of situating the United States in the world. How were transnational connections created and maintained, by whom, and what was their relationship to other global or imperial networks? How were these activities received "at home" and by the "colonies"' host societies? What institutions and technologies sustained transnational entanglements, and what asymmetries did they embed in international relations? In short, beyond the frictionless language of "flows," "currents," and "waves" of connection, how does transnational connectivity work? The answer to these questions are important to all historians interested in examining how global connections and interactions shaped nation-building, economic development, and foreign relations in the nineteenth century. By reflecting on how the migrants in this book navigated the tensions between independence and interdependence, the ways they pushed beyond the horizon of the nation and encountered the challenges of a connecting world head on, we can also reflect on the central dynamic in the history of the United States' engagement with the world (and, for that matter, of many societies' engagement with the world). This is the ongoing tug-of-war between the nation's deep, necessary, and diverse entanglement with the world and the equally insistent effort to draw clear lines between the inside and the out, to bound currents of transnational exchange in an effort to control and define the nation against them. Migrant communities offer one vantage point from which to view the this ever-shifting dynamic, revealing not only their centrality to the history of the United States but to shaping the world in which we live.

Notes

LIST OF ABBREVIATIONS

ACC   American Chamber of Commerce Minute Books, Liverpool Public Record Office, Liverpool, UK

BMJ   Benjamin Moran Journals, Library of Congress, Washington, DC

CFAD   Charles Francis Adams Diary, Massachusetts Historical Society, Boston, MA

EBA   English Branch Archives, United States Sanitary Commission Papers, New York Public Library, New York, NY

FRUS   *Foreign Relations of the United States* (Washington, DC: Government Printing Office, 1879–1880)

HL   Houghton Library, Harvard University, Cambridge, MA

HuL   Huntington Library, San Marino, CA

LoC   Library of Congress, Washington, DC

LPRO   Liverpool Public Record Office, Liverpool, UK

MHS   Massachusetts Historical Society, Boston, MA

ML   The Morgan Library, New York, NY

NYHS   New York Historical Society, New York, NY

NYPL   New York Public Library, New York, NY

PL   Phillips Library, Salem, MA

RIHS   Rhode Island Historical Society, Providence, RI

VHS   Vermont Historical Society, Barre, VT

USSC   United States Sanitary Commission Papers, New York Public Library, New York, NY

WL   Wellcome Library, London, UK

INTRODUCTION

1. Frederick MacKenzie, *The American Invaders* (London: Grant Richards, 1902), 142–43. See also "Lord Rosebery on National Culture," *The Times*, October 16, 1901; Christopher Furness, "The Old World and the American 'Invasion': A Review of the Industrial Situation," *Nash's Pall Mall Magazine*, March 1902, 362–63; Benjamin H. Thwaite, *The American Invasion* (London: Simpkin, Marshall, Hamilton, Kent & Co., 1902). In the United States Frank A. Vanderlip's *The American Commercial Invasion of Europe* (New York: Scribner's, 1902) appeared in the same year.

2. MacKenzie, *American Invaders*, 4.

3. William T. Stead, *The Americanisation of the World, or, the Trend of the Twentieth Century* (London: Review of Reviews, 1902), 358.

4. Ibid., 349. John Hobson, "The Approaching Abandonment of Free Trade," *Fortnightly Review,* March 1902, 435.

5. This distinction is made forcefully by Kristin Hoganson in *Consumer's Imperium: The Global Production of American Domesticity* (Chapel Hill: University of North Carolina Press, 2007).

6. Brandon Dupont, Alka Ghandi, and Thomas Weiss, "The Long-term Rise in Overseas Travel by Americans, 1820–2000," *Economic History Review* 65, no. 1 (2012): 144–67.

7. Sheila Croucher, "Americans Abroad: A Global Diaspora?," *Journal of Transnational American Studies* 4, no. 2 (2012): 1–33.

8. Douglas Bradburn, *The Citizenship Revolution: Politics and the Creation of the American Union, 1774–1804* (Charlottesville: University of Virginia Press, 2009), 101–38. For an overview of the transformation of the concept of expatriation from one including foreigners to excluding Americans, see Nancy Green, "Expatriation, Expatriates, and Expats: The American Transformation of a Concept," *American Historical Review* 114, no. 2 (2009): 307–28. For a broad historical synthesis of the legal evolution of expatriation law in the US, see I-mien Tsiang, *The Question of Expatriation in America Prior to 1907* (Baltimore: Johns Hopkins Press, 1942). As used today "expatriate" is of relatively recent coinage—as late as the 1930s it was still used primarily as a verb meaning "to banish". For an excellent discussion of these issues in relation to the British Empire, see John Darwin, "Orphans of Empire," in *Settlers and Expatriates: Britons over the Seas,* ed. Robert Bickers (Oxford: Oxford University Press, 2010).

9. *Emigration and Expatriation are the Citizen's Practical Declarations of Independence, Speech of John W. Chanler of New York, February 6, 1868* (Washington, DC: F. &. J. Rives & G.A. Bailey, 1868), 5.

10. Aristide R. Zolberg, "The Exit Revolution," in Nancy L. Green and François Weil, eds., *Citizenship and Those Who Leave: The Politics of Emigration and Expatriation* (Urbana: University of Illinois Press, 2007), 33–63. See

also Ben Herzog, *Revoking Citizenship: Expatriation in America from the Colonial Era to the War on Terror* (New York: New York University Press, 2015).

11. In the first hundred years since census taking began in the United States in 1790, there were only two attempts to count the American population overseas. In 1840, when citizens on US Naval vessels were counted, and in 1900 when counts of the overseas population was reported, see Karen M. Mills, "Americans Overseas in U.S. Consulates," U.S. Department of Commerce, Bureau of the Census Technical Paper 62 (Washington, DC: Government Printing Office, 1993).

12. Charles A. Logan (US Legation, Guatemala City), to William E. Evarts, August 20, 1879, *FRUS*, 143–45.

13. For extradition see Katherine Unterman, *Uncle Sam's Policemen: The Pursuit of Fugitives Across Borders* (Cambridge, MA: Harvard University Press, 2015); Eileen P. Scully, *Bargaining with the State from Afar: American Citizenship in Treaty Port China, 1844–1942* (New York, Columbia University Press, 2001) on extraterritoriality; and Mae M. Ngai, *Impossible Subjects: Illegal Aliens and the Making of Modern America* (Princeton, NJ: Princeton University Press, 2004) on exclusion. For an international history of the intensification of treaty-making in the nineteenth century, see Edward Keene, "The Treaty-Making Revolution of the Nineteenth Century," *International History Review* 34, no. 3 (2012): 475–500.

14. Bickers, ed., *Settler and Expatriates;* Gary Magee and Andrew S. Thompson, *Empire and Globalisation: Networks of People, Goods, and Capital in the British World* (Cambridge, UK: Cambridge University Press, 2010), 137–43; Kent Fedorowich and Andrew S. Thompson, *Empire, Migration and Identity in the British World* (Manchester, UK: Manchester University Press, 2013).

15. Lars Maischak, *German Merchants in the Nineteenth-Century Atlantic* (Cambridge, UK: Cambridge University Press, 2013); Robert Lee, ed., *Commerce and Culture: Nineteenth-Century Business Elites* (Farnham: Ashgate, 2011); Sam A. Mustafa, *Merchants and Migrations: Germans and Americans in Connection, 1776–1835* (Aldershot, UK: Ashgate, 2001); Charles A. Jones, *International Business in the Nineteenth Century* (New York: New York University Press, 1987). Scott Marler's work on New Orleans contrasts the port's merchants with their British counterparts, see Marler, *The Merchants' Capital: New Orleans and the Political Economy of the Nineteenth Century South* (Cambridge, UK: Cambridge University Press, 2013). British merchants could be found in ports around the world; in addition to the works cited above, see Louise H. Guenther, *British Merchants in Nineteenth-Century Brazil: Business, Culture, and Identity in Bahia, 1808–1850* (Oxford: Centre for Brazilian Studies, University of Oxford, 2004); Vera Blinn Reber, *British Mercantile Houses in Buenos Aires, 1810–1880* (Cambridge, MA: Harvard University Press, 1979).

16. Kevin C. Murphy, *The American Merchant Experience in Nineteenth-Century Japan* (London: Routledge Curzon, 2002); Jacques M. Downs, *The Golden Ghetto: The American Commercial Community at Canton and the Shaping of American China Policy, 1784–1844* (Hong Kong: Hong Kong University Press, 2015).

17. Ernest P. Earnest, *Expatriates and Patriots: American Artists, Scholars, and Writers in Europe* (Durham, NC: Duke University Press, 1968), 38–70;

Daniel Kilbride, *Being American in Europe, 1750–1860* (Baltimore: Johns Hopkins University Press, 2013); Brooke Blower, *Becoming American in Paris: Transatlantic Politics and Culture Between the World Wars* (New York: Oxford University Press, 2010), 24; Emily Burns, "Puritan Parisians: American Art Students in Late Nineteenth-Century Paris," in *A Seamless Web: Transatlantic Art in the Nineteenth Century*, ed. Cheryll May and Marian Wardle (Newcastle upon Tyne: Cambridge Scholars, 2014), 123–47; Harvey A. Levenstein, *Seductive Journey: American Tourists in France from Jefferson to the Jazz Age* (Chicago: Chicago University Press, 1998); Nancy Green, *The Other Americans in Paris: Businessmen, Countesses, and Wayward Youth, 1880–1941* (Chicago: University of Chicago Press, 2014); Philipp Ziesche, *Cosmopolitan Patriots: Americans in Paris in the Age of Revolution* (Charlottesville: University of Virginia Press, 2010); Annamaria Elsden, *Roman Fever: Domesticity and Nationalism in Nineteenth-Century American Women's Writing* (Columbus: Ohio State University Press, 2004); Theodore E. Stebbins, *The Lure of Italy: American Artists and the Italian Experience, 1760–1914* (New York: N.H. Abrams, 1992); Leonardo Buonomo, *Backward Glances: Exploring Italy, Reinterpreting America* (Madison, NJ: Fairleigh Dickinson University Press, 1996); William L. Vance, "The Sidelong Glance: Victorian Americans and Baroque Rome," *New England Quarterly* 58, no. 4 (1985): 501–30.

18. Daniel B. Shumway, "The American Students of Gottingen," *German American Studies Annals* 8 (1910): 171–254; Carl Diehl, *Americans and German Scholarship, 1770–1870* (New Haven, CT: Yale University Press, 1978).

19. William Schell, *Integral Outsiders: The American Colony in Mexico City, 1876–1911* (Wilmington, DE: SR Books, 2001); John M. Hart, *Empire and Revolution: The Americans in Mexico Since the Civil War* (Berkeley: University of California Press, 2002); Jason Colby, *Business of Empire: United Fruit, Race, and U.S. Expansion in Central America* (Ithaca, NY: Cornell University Press, 2011); Donna Gabaccia, *Foreign Relations: American Immigration in Global Perspective* (Princeton, NJ: Princeton University Press, 2012), 77–92; Paul A. Kramer, "Empires, Exceptions, and Anglo-Saxons: Race and Rule between the British and United States Empires, 1880–1910," *Journal of American History* 88, no. 4 (2002): 1315–53.

20. Ian Tyrrell, *Reforming the World: The Creation of America's Moral Empire* (Princeton, NJ: Princeton University Press, 2010); Heather Sharkey, *American Evangelicals in Egypt: Missionary Encounters in the Age of Empire* (Princeton, NJ: Princeton University Press, 2008).

21. Eric Schlereth, "Privileges of Locomotion: Expatriation and the Politics of Southwestern Border Crossing," *Journal of American History* 100, no. 4 (2014): 995–1020.

22. Brooke L. Blower, "Nation of Outposts: Forts, Factories, Bases, and the Making of American Power," *Diplomatic History* 41, no. 3 (2017): 439.

23. Ian Tyrrell, *Transnational Nation: United States History in Global Perspective since 1789* (Basingstoke, UK: Palgrave Macmillan, 2007); Steven Hahn, *A Nation Without Borders: The United States and its World in the Age of Civil Wars, 1830–1910* (New York: Viking, 2016); Thomas Bender, *A Nation Among Nations: America's Place in World History* (New York: Hill and Wang, 2006);

Sam Haynes, *Unfinished Revolution: The Early American Republic in a British World* (Charlottesville: University of Virginia Press, 2010). On the British side, see John Darwin, *Unfinished Empire: The Global Expansion of Britain* (London: Allen Lane, 2012); Magee and Thompson, *Empire and Globalisation;* James Belich, *Replenishing the Earth: The Settler Revolution and the Rise of the Anglo-World, 1783–1939* (Oxford: Oxford University Press, 2009). For an international approach, see Christopher A. Bayly, *The Birth of the Modern World, 1780–1914: Global Connections and Comparisons* (Oxford: Blackwell, 2004).

24. One of the best analyses of "transnational connectors" can be found in Pierre-Yves Saunier, *Transnational History: Theory and History* (Basingstoke, UK: Palgrave Macmillan, 2013), 33–46.

25. Eliga H. Gould, *Among the Powers of the Earth: The American Revolution and the Making of a New World Empire* (Cambridge, MA: Harvard University Press, 2012).

26. Quoted in George C. Rogers, *Evolution of a Federalist: William Loughton Smith of Charleston (1758–1812)* (Columbia: University of South Carolina Press, 1962), 101.

27. James F. Shepherd and Gary M. Walton, "Economic Change after the American Revolution: Pre- and Post-War Comparisons of Maritime Shipping and Trade," *Explorations in Economic History* 13, no. 1 (1976), 419; Kenneth Morgan, "Business Networks," in *The Early Modern Atlantic Economy,* ed. John McCusker and Kenneth Morgan (Cambridge, UK: Cambridge University Press, 2000), 61.

28. Peter J. Marshall, "Britain Without America: A Second Empire?," in *The Oxford History of the British Empire. Volume 2, The Eighteenth Century,* ed. Peter J. Marshall (Oxford: Oxford University Press, 1998), 581.

29. Edmund Morford, *An Inquiry into the Present State of the Foreign Relations of the Union: As Affected by the Late Measures of Administration* (Philadelphia: Samuel F. Bradford, 1806), 7–8.

30. Darwin, *Empire Project,* 36–37.

31. Brian Schoen, *The Fragile Fabric of Union: Cotton, Federal Politics, and the Global Origins of the Civil War* (Baltimore: Johns Hopkins University Press, 2009), 2.

32. Sven Beckert, "Emancipation and Empire: Reconstructing the Worldwide Web of Cotton in the Age of the American Civil War," *American Historical Review* 190, no. 5 (2004): 1408.

33. Jim Potter, "Atlantic Economy, 1815–1860: The USA and the Industrial Revolution in Britain," in *Studies in the Industrial Revolution: Presented to T. S. Ashton,* ed. L. S. Pressnell (London: Athlone Press, 1960), 279.

34. Census of England and Wales, 1861–1911. Table XXVII. England and Wales number and country of birth of all foreigners, in registration divisions, Population tables. England and Wales. Vol. II. Part 1, 1861, lxxv-lxxvi. Accessed via: http://www.histpop.org/ohpr/servlet.

35. *The Stranger in Liverpool; or, An Historical and Descriptive View,* 12th edition (Liverpool: Thomas Kaye, 1841), 131.

36. Graeme J. Milne, *Trade and Traders in Mid-Victorian Liverpool: Mercantile Business and the Making of a World Port* (Liverpool. UK: Liverpool University Press, 2000), 32.

37. Sven Beckert, *Empire of Cotton: A New History of Global Capitalism* (London: Allen Lane, 2014), 219.

38. Matthew Carey, *A View of the Ruinous Consequences of a Dependence on Foreign Markets* (Philadelphia: M. Carey & Son, 1820), 4.

39. George R. Taylor, *The Transportation Revolution, 1815–1860* (New York: Reinhart, 1951), 106.

40. Henry Carey, *How to Outdo England Without Fighting Her* (Philadelphia: H. C. Baird, 1865), 77.

41. Kathryn Boodry, "August Belmont and the World the Slaves Made," in *Slavery's Capitalism: A New History of American Economic Development,* ed. Sven Beckert and Seth Rockman (Philadelphia: University of Pennsylvania Press, 2016), 163–79.

42. Tyrrell, *Transnational Nation,* 96.

43. Beckert, "Emancipation and Empire," 1405–38.

44. Julian Roche, *The International Cotton Trade* (Cambridge, UK: Woodhead Publishing, 1994), 10.

45. Darwin, *Empire Project,* 117.

46. Ibid., 116.

47. Simone M. Müller, *Wiring the World: The Social and Cultural Creation of Global Telegraph Networks* (New York: Columbia University Press, 2016), 49.

48. Ranald Michie, *The City of London: Continuity and Change Since 1850* (London: MacMillan, 1992), 134.

49. Census of England and Wales, 1891, Table CVIII. Number of foreigners of various nationalities, and proportion to total foreigners, 1891, 1901, and 1911, General report, England and Wales, 1911, xviii, http://www.histpop.org/ohpr/servlet.

50. "The American Colony in London," *Harper's Weekly,* July 30, 1904.

51. "Episodes of the Month," *National Review,* June 1902, 517.

52. *Congressional Record,* February 27, 1902, 57th Cong., 1st Sess., 2201.

53. George B. Waldron, "Europe's Peril from Yankeeism," *The Chautauquan: A Weekly Newsmagazine* (October 1901), 38.

54. Konstantin Dierks, "Americans Overseas in the Early Republic," *Diplomatic History* 42, no. 1 (2018): 1–16. My thoughts here have also been shaped by two seminal articles by British imperial historians: Simon Potter and Jonathan Saha, "Global History, Connected History and Connected Histories of Empire," *Journal of Colonialism and Colonial History* 16, no. 1 (2015), and Tamson Pietsch, "Rethinking the British World," *Journal of British Studies* 52, no. 2 (2013): 441–63.

55. Seth Rockman, "What Makes the History of Capitalism Newsworthy?," *Journal of the Early Republic* 34, no. 3 (2014): 439–66.

56. Michael Zakim, *Accounting for Capitalism: The World the Clerk Made* (Chicago: University of Chicago Press, 2018).

57. John J. McCusker, "The Demise of Distance: The Business Press and the Origins of the Information Revolution in the Early Modern Atlantic World," *American Historical Review* 110, no. 2 (2005): 295–321; Richard John, "Recasting the Information Infrastructure for the Industrial Age," in *A Nation Transformed by Information: How Information Has Shaped the United States*

from Colonial Times to the Present, ed. Alfred D. Chandler Jr. and James W. Cortada (New York: Oxford University Press, 2000), 68–86.

58. Brian Rouleau, *With Sails Whitening Every Sea: Mariners and the Making of an American Maritime Empire* (Ithaca, NY: Cornell University Press, 2014), 5.

59. John Overton Choules, *The Cruise of the Yacht* North Star: *A Narrative of Mr. Vanderbilt's Party to England, Russia, Denmark, France, Spain, Italy, Malta, Turkey, Madeira, Etc.* (New York: Evans and Dickerson, 1854), 53.

60. Edwin J. Perkins, "Tourists and Bankers: Travelers' Credits and the Rise of American Tourism, 1840–1900," *Business and Economic History,* 2nd ser., 8 (1979): 16–28.

61. *London American,* August 9, 1895.

62. A notable exception is Nicole Phelps's *U.S.-Habsburg Relations from 1815 to the Paris Peace Conference: Sovereignty Transformed* (Cambridge, UK: Cambridge University Press, 2015).

63. Ron Robin, *Enclaves of America: The Rhetoric of American Political Architecture Abroad, 1900–1965* (Princeton, NJ: Princeton University Press, 1992); Jane C. Loeffler, *Architecture of Diplomacy: Building America's Embassies* (New York: Princeton Architectural Press, 1998); Blower, "Nation of Outposts," 439.

64. "American Diplomats in London," n.d., *San Francisco Argonaut,* in Vol. 11, William Jones Hoppin Papers, HL.

65. August 31, 1857, *The Journal of Benjamin Moran, 1857–1865,* ed. Sarah Agnes Wallace and Frances Elma Gillespie (Chicago: University of Chicago Press, 1947), I:123.

66. Joshua Bates to Thomas Wren Ward, July 14, 1831, Folder 3, Box 10, Thomas Wren Ward Papers, MHS.

67. "American Diplomacy," *Morning Post,* October 30, 1854.

68. Daniel Kilbride, "Travel, Ritual, and National Identity: Planters on the European Tour, 1820–1860," *Journal of Southern History* 69, no. 3 (2003): 549–84; Michael O'Brien, "European Attachments," in *Conjectures of Order: Intellectual Life and the American South, 1810–1860* (Chapel Hill: University of North Carolina Press, 2004), I:90–161.

69. Huw David, *Trade, Politics, and Revolution: South Carolina and Britain's Atlantic Commerce, 1730–1790* (Columbia: University of South Carolina Press, 2018), see especially Chapter 6; T.H. Breen, *Tobacco Culture: The Mentality of the Great Tidewater Planters on the Eve of the Revolution* (Princeton: Princeton University Press, 2001), epilogue.

70. O'Brien, *Conjectures of Order,* 111–25.

71. Quoted in Ibid., 109.

72. Nicholas J. Cull, "Public Diplomacy: Taxonomies and Histories," *Annals of the American Academy of Political and Social Science* 616 (2008): 31–54.

73. "Good Advice to our Diplomatic Agents Abroad," *New York Daily Times,* August 18, 1853. Emphasis added.

74. James Buchanan to William L. Marcy, October 28, 1853, in *The Works of James Buchanan Comprising his Speeches, State Papers, and Private Correspondence,* ed. John Bassett Moore (New York: Antiquarian Press, 1908–11), IX:75–77.

75. Nancy Shoemaker, "The Extraterritorial United States to 1860," *Diplomatic History* 42, no. 1 (2018): 36–55.

76. Paul Quigley, *Shifting Grounds: Nationalism and the American South, 1848–1865* (New York: Oxford University Press, 2012); Eric Hobsbawm, *Nations and Nationalism since 1780: Programme, Myth Reality* (Cambridge, UK: Cambridge University Press, 1991); Nicholas Guyatt, *Providence and the Invention of the United States, 1607–1876* (Cambridge, UK: Cambridge University Press, 2007).

77. Wilbur Zelinsky, *Nation into State: The Shifting Symbolic Foundations of American Nationalism* (Chapel Hill: University of North Carolina Press, 1988); Paul C. Nagel, *One Nation Indivisible: The Union in American Thought, 1776–1861* (New York: Oxford University Press, 1964).

78. Amy Kaplan, *The Anarchy of Empire in the Making of U.S. Culture* (Cambridge, MA: Harvard University Press, 2002); Joane Nagel, "Masculinity and Nationalism: Gender and Sexuality in the Making of Nations," *Ethnic and Racial Studies* 21, no. 2 (2010): 247; Catherine Hall, *Civilising Subjects: Metropole and Colony in the English Imagination, 1830–1867* (Chicago: University of Chicago Press, 2002); Linda Colley, *Britons: Forging the Nation, 1707–1837* (New Haven: Yale University Press, 1992).

79. Abbott Lawrence to John M. Clayton, July 5, 1850, Vol. 9, Abbott Lawrence Papers, HL.

80. Mary Piesse to Andrew Stevenson, May 23, 1837, Vol. 5, Stevenson Family Papers, LoC. Emphasis in original.

81. Reginald Horsman, *Race and Manifest Destiny: The Origins of American Racial Anglo-Saxonism* (Cambridge, MA: Harvard University Press, 1981); Anders Stephanson, *Manifest Destiny: American Expansion and the Empire of the Right* (New York: Hill & Wang, 1996); Kramer, "Empires, Exceptions, and Anglo-Saxons," 1315–53; Gary Gerstle, "Theodore Roosevelt and the Divided Character of American Nationalism," *Journal of American History* 86, no. 3 (1999): 1280–1307.

82. Marilyn Lake and Henry Reynolds, *Drawing the Global Colour Line: White Men's Countries and the International Challenge of Racial Equality* (Cambridge, UK: Cambridge University Press, 2008), 3.

83. Richard Olney, "International Isolationism of the United States," *Atlantic Monthly*, May 1898, 588.

84. Bluford Adams, "World Conquerors or a Dying People? Racial Theory, Regional Anxiety, and the Brahmin Anglo-Saxonists," *Journal of the Gilded Age and Progressive Era* 8, no. 2 (2009): 189–215; Gail Bederman, *Manliness & Civilization: A Cultural History of Gender and Race in the United States, 1880–1917* (Chicago: University of Chicago Press, 1995), 185–87; Kristin Hoganson, *Fighting for American Manhood: How Gender Politics Provoked the Spanish-American and Philippine-American Wars* (New Haven, CT: Yale University Press, 1998).

85. Stuart Anderson, *Race and Rapprochement: Anglo-Saxonism and Anglo-American Relations, 1895–1904* (London: Associated University Presses, 1981); Charles S. Campbell, Jr., *Anglo-American Understanding, 1898–1903* (Baltimore: Johns Hopkins University Press, 1957); Kramer, "Empires, Exceptions, and Anglo-Saxons," 1320–35.

86. Elizabeth Stordeur Pryor, *Colored Travelers: Mobility and the Fight for Citizenship before the Civil War* (Chapel Hill: University of North Carolina Press, 2016), 2.

87. Ibid., chapter 4; Michael A. Schoeppner, *Moral Contagion: Black Atlantic Sailors, Citizenship, and Diplomacy in Antebellum America* (Cambridge, UK: Cambridge University Press, 2019); Edlie L. Wong, *Neither Fugitive nor Free: Atlantic Slavery, Freedom Suits, and the Legal Culture of Travel* (New York: New York University Press, 2009).

88. *Charleston Mercury,* September 6, 1823.

89. Frederick Douglass, "What to the Slave is the Fourth of July?", *The Frederick Douglass Papers. Series One: Speeches, Debates, and Interviews,* eds. John W. Blassingame and John R. McKivigan (New Haven, CT: Yale University Press, 1979–92), II:387.

90. "Americans in Europe," *New York Times,* October 29, 1855.

91. Carlos Martyn, "Un-American Tendencies," *Arena,* September 1891, 432.

92. Gerstle, "Theodore Roosevelt"; Stephen Tuffnell, "'Uncle Sam is to be Sacrificed": Anglophobia in Late Nineteenth-Century Politics and Culture," *American Nineteenth Century History* 12, no. 1 (2011): 77–99.

93. *Washington Post,* December 16, 1883.

94. *Life,* February 9, 1911; "Americans Abroad," *Home Journal,* February 2, 1850.

95. April 15, 1869, Vol. 22, BMJ.

96. "Denationalized Americans," *Harper's Bazaar,* August 1, 1885, 490; "Americans Abroad," *Harper's Bazaar,* May 16, 1868, 458.

97. Kaplan, *Anarchy of Empire in the Making of U.S. Culture.*

98. "Types of Americans Travelling in Europe," *The Independent,* September 25, 1884. Emphasis in original.

CHAPTER ONE. INDEPENDENCE AND INTERDEPENDENCE

1. James Fenimore Cooper, *Gleanings from Europe: England* (Philadelphia: Carey, Lea and Blanchard, 1837), II:16.

2. Ibid., 2:46.

3. Ibid., 2:134.

4. James Fenimore Cooper, "Sam Slick in England," *North American Review* 58 (January 1844), 214.

5. [James Madison], "Foreign Influence," *Aurora* [Philadelphia], January 23, 1799.

6. Jay Sexton, "Epilogue," in *British North America in the Seventeenth and Eighteenth Centuries,* ed. Stephen Foster (Oxford: Oxford University Press, 2013). This chapter draws on the recent revival of interest in US political economy; see Dael A. Norwood, "What Counts? Political Economy, or Ways to Make Early America Add Up," *Journal of the Early Republic* 36, no. 4 (2016): 753–81.

7. Sam W. Haynes, *Unfinished Revolution: The Early American Republic in a British World* (Charlottesville: University of Virginia Press, 2010), 18.

8. Calvin Colton, *The Life, Correspondence, and Speeches of Henry Clay* (New York: A. S. Barnes & Co., 1857), V:221.

9. Kariann Anemi Yokota, *Unbecoming British: How Revolutionary American Became a Postcolonial Nation* (New York: Oxford University Press, 2011), 18, 11; A. G. Hopkins, *American Empire: A Global History* (Princeton, NJ: Princeton University Press, 2018), 142–91; Sexton, "Epilogue."

10. Jose C. Moya, "Modernization, Modernity, and the Trans/formation of the Atlantic World in the Nineteenth Century," in *The Atlantic in Global History, 1500–2000*, ed. Jorge Calizares-Esguerra and Erik R. Seeman (London: Routledge, 2016), 181; John Darwin, *Unfinished Empire: The Global Expansion of Britain* (London: Penguin, 2012), 167–78; C. A. Bayly, *The Birth of the Modern World, 1780–1914: Global Connections and Comparisons* (Oxford: Blackwell, 2004), 136–37; A. G. Hopkins, "The United States, 1783–1861: Britain's Honorary Dominion?' *Britain and the World* 4, no. 1 (2011): 244.

11. Jay Sexton, *The Monroe Doctrine: Empire and Nation in Nineteenth-Century America* (New York: Hill & Wang, 2011), 5–8.

12. Eliga Gould, "Independence and Interdependence: The American Revolution and the Problem of Postcolonial Nationhood, circa 1802," *William and Mary Quarterly* 74, no. 4 (2017): 731–32.

13. Alison Games, "Migration," in *The British Atlantic World, 1500–1800*, ed. David Armitage and Michael J. Braddick (Basingstoke, UK: Palgrave Macmillan, 2009), 33–52. See also Bernard Bailyn, *The Peopling of British North America: An Introduction* (New York: Knopf, 1988), 36. Between 1760 and 1820, Africans outnumbered Europeans by 4.9 to 1; see James Horn and Philip D. Morgan, "Settlers and Slaves: European and African Migrations to Early Modern British America," in *The Creation of the British Atlantic World*, ed. Carole Shammas and Elizabeth Mancke (Baltimore: Johns Hopkins University Press, 2005), 20.

14. Julie Flavell, *When London Was Capital of America* (New Haven, CT: Yale University Press, 2010).

15. Nancy L. Rhoden, "The American Revolution: The Paradox of Atlantic Integration," in Foster, ed., *British North America*, 256–88.

16. Maya Jasanoff, "Revolutionary Exiles: The American Loyalist and French Émigré Diasporas," in *The Age of Revolutions in Global Context, c. 1760–1840*, ed. David Armitage and Sanjay Subrahmanyam (Basingstoke, UK: Palgrave Macmillan, 2010), 47; Alan Kulikoff, "Uprooted Peoples: Black Migrants in the Age of the American Revolution," in *Slavery and Freedom in the Age of the American Revolution*, ed. Ira Berlin and Ronald Hoffman (Charlottesville: University Press of Virginia, 1983), 144; Alfred N. Hunt, *Haiti's Influence on Antebellum America: Slumbering Volcano in the Caribbean* (Baton Rouge: Louisiana State University Press, 1988), chapter 2; Jennifer K. Snyder, "Revolutionary Refugees: Black Flight in the Age of Revolution," in *The American South and the Atlantic World*, ed. Brian Ward, Martyn Bone, and William A. Link (Gainesville: University Press of Florida, 2013).

17. Games, "Migration," 50; Peter J. Marshall, *The Making and Unmaking of Empires: Britain, India, and America c. 1750–1783* (Oxford: Oxford University Press, 2007), 50. On the transformation of immigration from servitude to

free passengers see Aaron S. Fogelman, "From Slaves, Convicts and Servants to Free Passengers: The Transformation of Immigration in the Era of the American Revolution," *Journal of American History* 85, no. 1 (1998): 43–76.

18. "Going Abroad," *Dollar Magazine,* July 1851, 19.

19. Peter J. Marshall, "Britain and the World in the Eighteenth Century: II, Britons and Americans," *Transactions of the Royal Historical Society* 9 (December 1999): 14.

20. Brandon Dupont, Alka Ghandi, and Thomas Weiss, "The Long-Term Rise in Overseas Travel by Americans, 1820–2000," *Economic History Review* 65, no. 1 (2012): 148. The authors calculate that 27,000 US citizens travelled overseas in 1860.

21. For more on the migrant character of the city see Colin G. Pooley, "Living in Liverpool: The Modern City," in *Liverpool 800: Culture, Character & History,* ed. John Belchem (Liverpool, UK: Liverpool University Press, 2008), 174–95.

22. Thomas Baines, *Liverpool in 1859: The Port & Town of Liverpool, and the Harbour, Docks, and Commerce of the Mersey in 1859* (London: Longman, 1859), 9.

23. John J. McCusker, "The Demise of Distance: The Business Press and the Origins of the Information Revolution in the Early Modern Atlantic World," *American Historical Review* 110, no. 2 (2005): 295–321.

24. Jacob M. Price, "What Did Merchants Do? Reflections on British Overseas Trade, 1660–1790," *Journal of Economic History* 49, no. 2 (1989): 267–84; David Hancock, *Citizens of the World: London Merchants and the Integration of the British Atlantic Community, 1735–1785* (Cambridge, UK: Cambridge University Press, 1995).

25. Edmund Burke, "Letter II. On the Genius and Character of the French Revolution as it Regards Other Nations," in *The Works of the Right Honourable Edmund Burke* (London: J. C. Nimmo, 1887), V:380.

26. "A Looking Glass for London," *Monthly Supplement of the Penny Magazine,* January 31, 1837.

27. *The Times,* June 4, 1851.

28. Haynes, *Unfinished Revolution,* 16.

29. Surveys of Americans in Britain invariably focus on the cultural pilgrimage of American travelers and authors to their "ancestral" home. See Robert Balmain Mowat, *Americans in England* (London: George G. Harrao & Co., 1935); Richard Kenin, *Return to Albion: Americans in England, 1760–1940* (New York: Holt, Rinehart and Winston, 1979); Henry Steele Commager, *Britain Through American Eyes* (New York: McGraw & Hill, 1974).

30. July 7, 1840, Vol. 1, Folder 5, Box 1, March Family Papers, PL.

31. Benjamin Silliman, *A Journal of Travels in England, Holland, and Scotland, and of the two Passages over the Atlantic* (Boston: T. B. Wait & Co., 1810), 1:75.

32. Nathaniel S. Wheaton, *A Journal of a Residence during Several Months in London* (Hartford, CT: H. & F. J. Huntington, 1830), 31.

33. "European Letters," *New York Observer and Chronicle,* October 21, 1843.

34. Harriett Beecher Stowe, *Sunny Memories of Foreign Lands* (Boston: Phillips, Sampson & Company, 1854), I:17. See also John Jay Smith, *A Summer's Jaunt Across the Water* (Philadelphia: J.W. Moore, 1846), 75. Not all travellers agreed; see Charles S. Stewart, *Sketches of Society in Great Britain and Ireland* (Philadelphia: Carey, Lea, & Blanchard, 1834), 20.

35. See especially Rhoden, "Paradox of Atlantic Integration."

36. Foster Rhea Dulles, *Americans Abroad: Two Centuries of European Travel* (Ann Arbor: University of Michigan Press, 1964), 27.

37. Joshua Bates to Thomas Wren Ward, June 2, 1833, Folder 8, Box 10, Ward Papers, MHS.

38. Donna Brown, "Travel Books," in *A History of the Book in America, Vol. 2, An Extensive Republic: Print, Culture, and Society in the New Nation, 1790–1840*, ed. Robert A. Gross and Mary Kelley (Chapel Hill: University of North Carolina Press, 2010), 449–58. According to the literary historian Larzer Ziff, during the first half of the nineteenth century only religious writings exceeded in quantity the number of travel books reviewed and travel narratives published in American journals (*Return Passages: Great American Travel Writing, 1780–1910* [New Haven, CT: Yale University Press, 2000], 59).

39. Mordecai Noah, *Travels in England, France, Spain, and the Barbary States in the Years 1813–14 and 15* (New York: Kirk and Mercein, 1819), 36. For the English origins of the Grand Tour, see Jeremy Black, *The British Abroad: The Grand Tour in the Eighteenth Century* (New York: St Martin's, 1992). For its prevalence among planters see Michael O'Brien, *Conjectures of Order: Intellectual Life and the American South, 1810–1860* (Chapel Hill: University of North Carolina Press, 2004), I:100–61; Daniel Kilbride, "Travel, Ritual, and National Identity: Planters on the European Tour, 1820–1860," *Journal of Southern History* 69, no. 3 (2003): 549–84.

40. Yokota, *Unbecoming British*, 203; Flavell, *Capital of America*, 67.

41. Flavell, *Capital of America*, 67, 91–93; Samuel Lewis, "List of the American Graduates in Medicine in the University of Edinburgh," *New England Historical and Genealogical Review* 42 (1988): 159–65; C. E. A. Bedwell, "American Middle Templars," *The American Historical Review* 25, no.4 (1920): 680–89; J. G. de Roulhac Hamilton, "Southern Members of the Inns of Court," *North Carolina Historical Review* 10 (1933): 273–80; *The Inner Temple Admissions Database:* http://www.innertemple.org.uk/archive/itad/index .asp. By the end of the eighteenth century, an average of twelve medical students per year enrolled at Edinburgh; see Helen Dingwall, "The Importance of Being Edinburgh," in *Centres of Medical Excellence? Medical Travel and Education in Europe, 1500–1789*, ed. Ole Peter Grell, Andrew Cunningham, and Jon Arrizabalaga (Farnham: Ashgate, 2010), 312. On the influence of Edinburgh graduates on the development of the American medical profession see Lisa Rosner, "Thistle on the Delaware: Edinburgh Medical Education and Philadelphia Practice, 1800–1825," *Social History of Medicine* 5, no. 1 (1992): 19–42.

42. Haynes, *Unfinished Revolution*, 51–77.

43. Passenger fares are notoriously difficult to calculate with accuracy; some clarity has been brought by Brandon Dupont, Drew Keeling, and Thomas Weiss, "First Cabin Fares from New York to the British isles, 1826–1914,"

NBER Working Paper 22426, https://www.nber.org/papers/w22426.pdf, and John Killick, "An Early Nineteenth-Century Shipping Line: The Cope Line of Philadelphia and Liverpool Packets, 1822–1872," *International Journal of Maritime History* 22, no. 1 (2000): 74. For more on transatlantic passenger lines see William M. Fowler, Jr., *Steam Titans: Cunard, Collins, and the Epic Battle for Commerce on the North Atlantic* (New York: Bloomsbury, 2017); Robert Greenhalgh Albion, *Square-Riggers On Schedule: The New York Packets to England, France, and the Cotton Ports* (Princeton, NJ: Princeton University Press, 1983), 233–35.

44. Daniel Kilbride, *Being American in Europe, 1750–1860* (Baltimore: Johns Hopkins University Press, 2013), 83–84. For a broad overview of women's travel writing see Susan L. Roberson, "American Women and Travel Writing," in *The Cambridge Companion to American Travel Writing,* ed. Alfred Bendixen and Judith Hamera (Cambridge, UK: Cambridge University Press, 2008), 214–27.

45. "Americans in London," *Literary Souvenir,* September 7, 1839, 107.

46. "Going Abroad," *Dollar Magazine,* July 1851, 21.

47. "International Copyright," *Southern Literary Messenger,* June 1844, 340. See also "Going Abroad," *Ballou's Pictorial Drawing-Room Companion,* November 21, 1857.

48. Thomas Haskell, "Capitalism and the Origins of the Humanitarian Sensibility, Part 1," in *The Antislavery Debate: Capitalism and Abolitionism as a Problem of Historical Interpretation,* ed. Thomas Bender (Berkeley: University of California Press, 1992), 153.

49. On colonial religious links see: Susan O'Brien, "A Transatlantic Community of Saints: The Great Awakening and the First Evangelical Network, 1735–1755," *American Historical Review* 91, no. 4 (1986): 811–32.

50. Richard Carwardine, *Transatlantic Revivalism: Popular Evangelicalism in Britain and America, 1790–1865* (Westport, CT: Greenwood Press, 1978).

51. Frank Thistlethwaite, *Anglo-American Connection in the Early Nineteenth Century* (Philadelphia: University of Pennsylvania Press, 1959), 76–102.

52. Merle Curti, *American Philanthropy Abroad* (New Brunswick, NJ: Transaction Books, 1988); Margaret McFadden, *Golden Cables of Sympathy: The Transatlantic Sources of Nineteenth-Century Feminism* (Lexington: University Press of Kentucky, 2009).

53. Caleb McDaniel, *The Problem of Democracy in the Age of Slavery: Garrisonian Abolitionists & Transatlantic Reform* (Baton Rouge: Louisiana State University Press, 2013), 77–79.

54. J. F. Maclear, "The Evangelical Alliance and the Antislavery Crusade," *Huntington Library Quarterly* 42, no. 2 (1979): 143.

55. Leslie Butler, *Critical Americans: Victorian Americans and Transatlantic Liberal Reform* (Chapel Hill: University of North Carolina Press, 2007); Daniel T. Rodgers, *Atlantic Crossings: Social Politics in a Progressive Age* (Cambridge, MA: Harvard University Press, 1998).

56. McDaniel, *The Problem of Democracy in the Age of Slavery,* 53–56.

57. Key works framing this field are Betty Fladeland, *Men and Brothers: Anglo-American Antislavery Cooperation* (Urbana: University of Illionis Press,

1972) and Richard J.M. Blackett, *Building an Antislavery Wall: Black Americans in the Atlantic Abolitionist Movement, 1830–1860* (Baton Rouge: Louisiana State University Press, 1983).

58. Paul Gilroy, *The Black Atlantic: Modernity and Double Consciousness* (London: Verso, 1993).

59. Van Gosse, "'As a nation, the English are our friends': The Emergence of African American Politics in the British Atlantic World, 1772–1861," *American Historical Review* 113, no. 4 (2008): 1005.

60. Frederick Douglass, *My Bondage and My Freedom* (New York: Miller, Orton & Mulligan, 1855), 417.

61. Vanessa D. Dickerson, *Dark Victorians* (Urbana: University of Illinois Press, 2008), 61; Elizabeth Stordeur Pryor, *Colored Travelers: Mobility and the Fight for Citizenship Before the Civil War* (Chapel Hill: University of North Carolina Press, 2016), chapter 5. The moment of setting foot on British soil is often one of the most dramatic elements of black travellers' accounts and inspired moving literary passages; for the importance of travel more broadly, both metaphorically and literally for African American literature, see John Gruesser, "Travel Writing," in *The Oxford Companion to African American Literature,* ed. William L. Andrews, Frances Smith Foster, and Trudier Harris (New York: Oxford University Press, 1997), 735–36.

62. C.L. Remond to M.H. Usher, April 29, 1840, Folder 7, Box 1, Remond Family Papers, PL.

63. Hannah-Rose Murray, "'With almost electric speed': Mapping African American Abolitionists in Britain and Ireland, 1838–1847," *Slavery & Abolition* 40, no. 3 (2019): 522–42.

64. Sarah Meer, *Uncle Tom Mania: Slavery, Minstrelsy, and Transatlantic Culture in the 1850s* (Athens: University of Georgia Press, 2005), 4. For new approaches to abolitionist campaigning see "African Americans and Transatlantic Abolition, 1845–1865," *Slavery & Abolition* 33, no. 2 (2012): 181–336.

65. Blackett, *Building an Antislavery Wall,* 4.

66. "People's Convention at Worcester," *National Anti-Slavery Standard,* July 13, 1848.

67. Paul A. Gilje, *Liberty on the Waterfront: American Maritime Culture in the Age of Revolution* (Philadelphia: University of Pennsylvania Press, 2004); Nathan Perl-Rosenthal, *Citizen Sailors: Becoming American in the Age of Revolution* (Cambridge, MA: Harvard University Press, 2015).

68. Brian Rouleau, *With Sails Whitening Every Sea: Mariners and the Making of an American Maritime Empire* (Ithaca, NY: Cornell University Press, 2014), 6–7, 9; W. Jeffrey Bolster, *Black Jacks: African American Seamen in the Age of Sail* (Cambridge, MA: Harvard University Press, 1997), 2; Gilje, *Liberty on the Waterfront,* 26.

69. *Charleston Mercury,* September 3, 1823.

70. Michael A. Schoeppner, *Moral Contagion: Black Atlantic Sailors, Citizenship, and Diplomacy in Antebellum America* (Cambridge, UK: Cambridge University Press, 2019). Local laws against free black sailors were not the only ones aimed at policing the boundaries of citizenship by controlling ingress; see also Hidetaka Hirota, *Expelling the Poor: Atlantic Seaboard States and the*

Nineteenth Century Origins of American Immigration Policy (New York: Oxford University Press, 2017).

71. Edlie L. Wong, *Neither Fugitive nor Free: Atlantic Slavery, Freedom Suits, and the Legal Culture of Travel* (New York: New York University Press, 2009), 16.

72. Edward Rugemer, *The Problem of Emancipation: the Caribbean Origins of the American Civil War* (Baton Rouge: Louisiana State University Press, 2008), 259.

73. Irvin D. S. Winsboro and Joe Knetsch, "Florida Slaves, the 'Saltwater Railroad' to the Bahamas, and Anglo-American Diplomacy," *Journal of Southern History* 79, no. 1 (2013): 51–78; Ikuko Asaka, "'Our Brethren in the West Indies': Self-Emancipated People in Canada and the Antebellum Politics of Diaspora and Empire," *Journal of African American History* 97, no. 3 (2012): 219–39.

74. Edward B. Rugemer, "Slave Rebels and Abolitionists: The Black Atlantic and the Coming of the Civil War," *Journal of the Civil War Era* 2, no. 2 (2012): 179–202. In Britain, black subjects were legally entitled to unimpeded entry and right to abode; see David Kilingray, "'A Good West Indian, a Good African, and in Short, a Good Britisher': Black and British in a Colour-Conscious Empire, 1760–1950," *Journal of Imperial and Commonwealth History* 36, no. 3 (2008): 365.

75. Herman Melville, *Redburn* (London: Penguin, 1976 [1849]), 277.

76. Ray Costello, *Black Salt: Seafarers of African Descent on British Ships* (Liverpool, UK: Liverpool University Press, 2012), 73–94. Britain's black community has been sketched in broad outline by a number of writers, including Anthony Barker, *The African Link: British Attitudes to the Negro in the Era of the Atlantic Slave Trade, 1550–1807* (London: Cass, 1978); James Walvin, *Black and White: The Negro and English Society, 1555–1945* (London: Penguin, 1973), and Douglas A. Lorimer, *Colour, Class, and the Victorians: English Attitudes to the Negro in the Mid-Nineteenth Century* (Leicester, UK: Leicester University Press, 1978), 40.

77. Bolster, *Black Jacks,* 19.

78. Stephen J. Braidwood, *Black Poor and White Philanthropists: London's Blacks and the Foundation of the Sierra Leone Settlement, 1786–1791* (Liverpool, UK: Liverpool University Press, 1994), 22–27.

79. Winston James, "The Black Experience in Twentieth-Century Britain," in *Black Experience and the Empire,* ed. Philip D. Morgan and Sean Hawkins (Oxford: Oxford University Press, 2004), 347.

80. In 1858 the *Aborigine's Friend and Colonial Intelligencer* suggested that there were enough African merchants in the city to form their own trade association; see Barker, *African Link,* 56. Also see Shompa Lahiri, "Contested Relations: The East India Company and Lascars in London," in *The Worlds of the East India Company,* ed. Huw V. Bowen, Margarette Lincoln, and Nigel Rigby (Woodbridge, UK: Boydell Press, 2002), 170.

81. Barker, *African Link,* 35.

82. Ibid., 29. On the evidence of black servants and seamen in London see Norma Myers, *Reconstructing the Black Past: Blacks in Britain, 1780–1830* (London: Frank Cass, 1996), 64–78.

83. Michael Banton, The Coloured Quarter: Negro Immigrants in an English City (London: Jonathan Cope, 1955), 26.

84. Walvin, Black and White, 198; Banton, The Coloured Quarter, 27.

85. Bolster, Black Jacks, 158.

86. Louis Simond, Journal of a Tour and Residence in Great Britain During the Years 1810 and 1811 (Edinburgh: George Ramsay and Company, 1815), 242.

87. For a superb discussion of the role of violence among American sailors see Rouleau, With Sails, 102–33. On the importance of national symbols to sailors see Matthew Rafferty, The Republic Afloat: Law, Honor, and Citizenship in Maritime America (Chicago: University of Chicago Press, 2013), 205–7.

88. "Outrages by American Sailors in Liverpool," Hampshire Advertiser, April 3, 1858.

89. "Aristocracy of the Skin," Liverpool Mercury, August 21, 1846. Seamen were paid, on average, 45 shillings per month (at 20 shillings to the pound); see Arthur L. Bowley, Wages in the Nineteenth Century United Kingdom (Cambridge, UK: Cambridge University Press, 1900), 78.

90. W.G. Allen to G. Smith, 14 May 1859, ProQuest Black Abolitionist Papers Online, https://www.proquest.com/products-services/blk_abol_pap.html.

91. Fladeland, Men and Brothers, 347.

92. Edward Scobie, Black Britannia: A History of Blacks in Britain (Chicago: Johnson Publishing Company, 1972), 119.

93. Walvin, Black and White, 190.

94. The Liberator, July 25, 1851.

95. "Reciprocal Trade Between the United States and the British Provinces," The Merchants' Magazine and Commercial Review, June 1, 1849, 584.

96. Abigail Adams to John Quincy Adams, 6 September 1785, Founding Families: Digital Editions of the Papers of the Winthrops and the Adamses, ed. C. James Taylor (Boston, 2016), http://www.masshist.org/apde2.

97. Yokota, Unbecoming British, 62–115.

98. Quoted in Joanna Cohen, Luxurious Citizens: The Politics of Consumption in Nineteenth-Century America (Philadelphia: University of Pennsylvania Press, 2017), 29.

99. J. Leander Bishop, A History of American Manufactures from 1608 to 1860 (Philadelphia: Edward Young & Co., 1866), I:8.

100. Drew R. McCoy, The Elusive Republic: Political Economy in Jeffersonian America (Chapel Hill: University of North Carolina Press, 1980), 76.

101. Peter J. Marshall, Remaking the British Atlantic: The United States and the British Empire after American Independence (Oxford: Oxford University Press, 2012, 280.

102. Brian Phillips Murphy, Building the Empire State: Political Economy in the Early Republic (Philadelphia: University of Pennsylvania Press, 2015), 5, 39–43; Brian Balogh, A Government Out of Sight: The Mystery of National Authority in Nineteenth Century America (Cambridge, UK: Cambridge University Press, 2009), 26.

103. Quoted in Cathy D. Matson and Peter S. Onuf, A Union of Interests: Political and Economic Thought in Revolutionary America (Lawrence: University Press of Kansas, 1990), 69.

104. Brian R. Mitchell, *British Historical Statistics* (Cambridge, UK: Cambridge University Press, 1988), 494.

105. Andrew Oliver, ed., *The Journal of Samuel Curwen Loyalist* (Cambridge, MA: Harvard University Press, 1972), I:990.

106. Quoted in Marshall, *Remaking the British Atlantic,* 237.

107. Quoted in Stanley S. Chapman, *Merchant Enterprise in Britain: From the Industrial Revolution to World War One* (Cambridge, UK: Cambridge University Press, 1992), 150.

108. Alison Olson, *Making the Empire Work: London and American Interest Groups, 1690–1790* (Cambridge, MA: Harvard University Press, 1992), 178–184.

109. The brothers Alexander and Henry Baring, for instance, married Anne Louisa and Maria Matilda Bingham in 1798 and 1802, respectively. The match consolidated Barings' investment in Maine and afforded Alexander, then Barings's American agent, access to the wealthy elite of Philadelphia; see Philip Ziegler, *The Sixth Great Power: Barings, 1762–1929* (London: Collins, 1988), 61–78.

110. Jack M. Sosin, *Agents and Merchants: British Colonial Policy and the Origins of the American Revolution, 1763–1775* (Lincoln: University of Nebraska Press, 1965), 3.

111. James F. Shepherd and Gary M. Walton, "Economic Change after the American Revolution: Pre- and Post-War Comparisons of Maritime Shipping and Trade," *Explorations in Economic History* 13, no. 4 (1976), 420.

112. Charles R. Ritcheson, *Aftermath of Revolution: British Policy Toward the United States, 1783–1795* (Dallas, TX: Southern Methodist University Press, 1969), 188.

113. *Annals of Congress,* 1st Cong., 1st sess., 238.

114. The extensive historiography on this topic need not be recounted here; for the best treatments see McCoy, *The Elusive Republic,* 136–65; Max Edling, *A Hercules in the Cradle: War, Money, and the American State, 1783–1867* (Chicago: University of Chicago Press, 2014), chapter 3.

115. Ibid., 77.

116. J. Wattenberg, *Statistical History of the United States: From Colonial Times to the Present* (New York: Basic Books, 1976), 886.

117. On the Panic of 1819, see Murray Newton Rothbard, *Panic of 1819: Reactions and Policies* (New York: Columbia University Press, 1962).

118. James Madison to Richard Rush, November 13, 1823, James Madison Papers, LoC, http://hdl.loc.gov/loc.mss/mjm.20_0630_0632.

119. Chapman, *Merchant Enterprise,* 82.

120. Moya, "Modernization, Modernity," 183.

121. Joseph Hopkinson, *Lecture upon the Principles of Commercial Integrity, and the Duties Subsisting between a Debtor and His Creditors* (Philadelphia: Carey and Lea, 1832), 6–7.

122. "Overtrading," *Southern Cultivator,* April 26, 1843.

123. Sven Beckert, *Monied Metropolis: New York City and the Consolidation of the American Bourgeoisie, 1850–1896* (New York: Cambridge University Press, 2001), 31.

124. "Deed of Partnership," May 24, 1810, Folder 20, Box 2, Appleton Family Papers, MHS.

125. Nathan Appleton to Eben Appleton, July 21, 1811, Folder 22, Box 2, Appleton Family Papers, MHS.

126. *Minutes of Evidence, upon taking into consideration several petitions, presented to the House of Commons, respecting the orders in council*, 1808, 16–23, ProQuest House of Commons Parliamentary Papers Online, https://parlipapers.proquest.com/parlipapers/docview/t70.d75.1808-001761/usgLog RstClick!!?accountid=13042.

127. Sheryllynne Haggerty, *The British Atlantic Trading Community, 1760–1810: Men, Women, and the Distribution of Goods* (Leiden: Brill, 2006); Chapman, *Merchant Enterprise*, 93–98.

128. For this more broadly see Beckert, *Monied Metropolis*.

129. Daniel James to William E. Dodge, March 31, 1836, Box 2, Phelps, Dodge & Co. Records, NYPL.

130. James to Dodge, December 7, 1837, Box 2, Phelps, Dodge & Co. Records, NYPL. Emphasis in original.

131. For contemporary understandings of "confidence," see Jessica M. Lepler, *The Many Panics of 1837: People, Politics, and the Creation of a Transatlantic Financial Crisis* (New York: Cambridge University Press, 2013), 9. On the problems of trust in Atlantic trade more broadly see Robert Greenhalgh Albion, *The Rise of New York Port, 1815–1860* (New York: Charles Scribner's Sons, 1939), 236–37; Olson, *Making the Empire Work*, 182; Haggerty, *British Atlantic Trading Community*, 110–13; and Norman Stanley Buck, *The Development of the Organisation of Anglo-American Trade, 1800–1850* (New Haven, CT: Yale University Press, 1925), 108.

132. Quotations from Daniel James to William E. Dodge, July 7, 1836, April 7, 1838 Box 2, Phelps, Dodge & Co. Records, NYPL. Emphasis in original.

133. On credit reporting see Rowena Olegario, *Culture of Credit: Embedding Trust and Transparency in American Business* (Cambridge, MA: Harvard University Press, 2006), 36–79.

134. William Brown to Joseph Shipley, April 14, 1838, Folder 8, Box 3, Brown Brothers-Harriman Papers, NYHS.

135. William E. Bowen to Shipley, July 13, 1843, Folder 1, Box 4, Brown Brothers-Harriman Papers, NYHS.

136. A.H. Arkle, "The Early Coffee Houses of Liverpool," *Transactions of the Historical Society of Lancashire and Cheshire* 64 (1912): 1–16.

137. Ronaldo Munck, *Reinventing the City? Liverpool in Comparative Perspective* (Liverpool, UK: Liverpool University Press, 2003), 40.

138. Baines, *Liverpool in 1859*, 122.

139. Henry Smithers, *Liverpool, Its Commerce, Statistics, and Institutions with a History of the Cotton Trade* (Liverpool, UK: T. Kaye, 1825), 187.

140. Baines, *Liverpool in 1859*, 119.

141. July 1801, ACC, Vol. I. The Chamber existed until 1908. W.O. Henderson's "The American Chamber of Commerce for the Port of Liverpool," *Transactions of the Historic Society of Lancashire and Cheshire* 85 (1933): 1–61, is the only study of the institution. To reinforce the importance of charac-

ter and trust for antebellum traders, Maury was described by one traveller as "highly esteemed by all for the benevolence of his character"; see Wheaton, *Journal of a Residence During Several Months in London,* 26.

142. *Illustrated London News,* March 30, 1867, 318.

143. September 22, 1815, ACC, Vol. I. Backhouse was a former merchant and future under-secretary of state. For his activities as a go-between for John Gladstone and George Canning during the war of 1812, see Sydney George Checkland, *The Gladstones: A Family Biography, 1764–1851* (Cambridge, UK: Cambridge University Press, 1971), 73; R.A. Jones, "Backhouse, John (1784–1845)," *Oxford Dictionary of National Biography* (Oxford University Press, 2004), http://www.oxforddnb.com/view/article/50517. For the ACC's lobbying during debate over the Repeal of the Corn Laws in 1846, see petitions sent to Robert Peel, October 23, 1841 and February 14, 1842, ACC, Vols. I & II. Prior to this, the ACC worked with Philip Sansom of the Committee of American Merchants in London; see August 1, 1807 & January 7, 1808, ACC, Vol. I.

144. These were James Maury (1801), Samuel S. Gair (1832), William Maury (1836), Joseph Shipley (1839), William Brown (1843), Washington Jackson (1855), and Stephen Barker Guion (1862). Alex McGregor also served as vice president in 1813, but was not president.

145. Mary Beth Norton, *The British-Americans: The Loyalist Exiles in England, 1774–1789* (London: Constable, 1974), 67–68; Maya Jasanoff, *Liberty's Exiles: The Loss of America and the Remaking of the British Empire* (London: Harper Press, 2011), 115.

146. 17 May 1842, July 9, 1845, 20 October 1846, November 10, 1851, ACC, Vol. II.

147. April 7, 1842, ACC, Vol. II.

148. Sven Beckert, *Empire of Cotton: A New History of Global Capitalism* (London: Allen Lane, 2014), 234–35.

149. Albion, *Rise of New York Port,* 236–37, 261–62.

150. On Britons in the United States see Albion, *Rise of New York Port,* 235–51; Thistlethwaite, *America and the Atlantic Community,* 17–18; Andrea Mehrlander, *The Germans of Charleston, Richmond, and New Orleans During the Civil War Period, 1850–1870: A Study and Research Compendium* (Berlin: De Gruyter, 2011).

151. Ralph W. Hidy, "The Organization and Function of Anglo-American Merchant Bankers, 1815–1860," *The Journal of Economic History* 1, no. 1 (1941): 53–66.

152. Edward Everett, *Speech at the Dinner Given in Honor of George Peabody, Esq., of London* (Boston: Henry W. Dutton & Son, 1857), 7.

153. "Mr. Biddle and His British Brethren," *The Globe* [Washington], June 7, 1837. Emphasis in original.

154. See, for instance, "The Times," *The Globe* [Washington], April 12, 1837; "New York Accusers," *The Globe* [Washington], April 29, 1837; "Speculation and Overtrading," *Daily Herald and Gazette* [Cleveland, OH], May 2, 1837; "The Cause and the Remedy," *New York Spectator,* May 15, 1837; Citizen of Massachusetts, *The Times: Or, The Pressure and its Causes Examined; An Address to the People* (Boston: privately printed, 1837), 59.

155. "The Public Spirit of the Whigs," *The Globe,* May 23, 1837.

156. Tom Newlin to Joseph Shipley, June 14, 1837, Folder 21, Box 2, Brown Brothers-Harriman Papers, NYHS.

157. William E. Brown to Joseph Shipley, June 29, 1843, Folder 1, Box 4, Brown Brothers-Harriman Papers, NYHS.

158. William E. Brown to Joseph Shipley, September 15, 1847, Folder 16, Box 4, Brown Brothers-Harriman Papers, NYHS. Emphasis in original.

159. Tamara Plakins Thornton, "Capitalist Aesthetics: Americans Look at the London and Liverpool Docks," in *Capitalism Takes Command: the Social Transformation of Nineteenth-Century America,* ed. Michael Zakim and Gary J. Kornblith (Chicago: University of Chicago Press, 2012), 172.

160. Henry B. McClellan, *Journal of a Residence in Scotland, and Tour Through England, France, Germany, Switzerland and Italy* (Boston: Allen and Ticknor, 1834), 93.

161. McClellan, *Journal of a Residence in Scotland,* 94; "London and Liverpool Contrasted," *New England Galaxy,* January 9, 1829; Orville Dewey, *The Old World, and the New: Or, a Journal of Reflections and Observations Made on a Tour in Europe* (New York: Harper & Brothers, 1836), I:22; "Mrs. Edmond's Letters from Europe," *Christian Reflector,* July 11, 1844. On Liverpool's warehouses see Giles Colum and Bob Hawkins, *Storehouses of Empire: Liverpool's Historic Warehouses* (Liverpool, UK: English Heritage, 2004) and G. A. Bremner, "The Metropolis: Imperial Buildings and Landscapes in Britain," in G. A. Bremner, ed., *Architecture and Urbanism in the British Empire* (Oxford: Oxford University Press, 2016), 133.

162. Zachariah Allen, *The Practical Tourist, or, Sketches of the State of the Useful Art, and of Society, Scenery, &c. &c. in Great Britain, France, and Holland* (Providence, RI: A. S. Beckwith, 1832), 20–21.

163. "Mrs. Edmond's Letters from Europe," *Christian Reflector,* July 11, 1844; Stewart, *Sketches of Society,* 14; Joshua White, *Letters on England* (Philadelphia: M. Carey, 1816), 9; "Docks and Commerce of Liverpool," *Mechanics' Magazine,* January 1833, 37.

164. Francis Edwin Hyde, *Liverpool and the Mersey: An Economic History of a Port, 1700–1970* (Newton Abbott, UK: David and Charles), 77.

165. Dewey, *Old World, and the New,* I.22; "European Letters," *New York Observer and Chronicle,* October 21, 1843.

166. McClellan, *Journal of a Residence in Scotland,* 94.

167. Silliman, *Journal of Travels in England,* I:57.

168. Aytoun Ellis, *Heir of Adventure: The Story of Brown, Shipley & Co. Merchant Bankers, 1810–1960* (London: Brown, Shipley, 1960), 22.

169. George Francis Train, *My Life in Many States and Foreign Lands* (Boston: D. Appleton and Company, 1902), 121.

170. McClellan, *Journal of a Residence in Scotland,* 102.

171. Beckert, *Empire of Cotton,* 85; Chapman, *Merchant Enterprise,* 83.

172. Brian Schoen, *The Fragile Fabric of Union: Cotton, Federal Politics, and the Global Origins of the Civil War* (Baltimore: Johns Hopkins University Press, 2009), 122–23.

173. Thomas Kettell, "The Future of the South," *De Bow's Review,* September 1856, 308–23. For more on Kettell, see Matthew Karp, *This Vast Southern Empire: Slaveholders at the Helm of American Foreign Policy* (Cambridge, MA: Harvard University Press, 2016), 130, 132–33.

174. Giorgio Riello, *Cotton: The Fabric that Made the Modern World* (Cambridge, UK: Cambridge University Press, 2013); Walter Johnson, *River of Dark Dreams: Slavery and Empire in the Cotton Kingdom* (Cambridge, MA: Harvard University Press, 2013), 280–303; Beckert, *Empire of Cotton;* Frank Trentmann, *Empire of Things: How We became a World of Consumers, From the Fifteenth Century to the Twenty-first* (London: Allen Lane, 2016), 64–71.

175. Schoen, *The Fragile Fabric of Union;* Beckert, *Empire of Cotton,* 199–241. See also Calvin Schermerhorn, *The Business of Slavery and the Rise of American Capitalism, 1815–1860* (New Haven, CT: Yale University Press, 2015).

176. Trentmann, *Empire of Things,* 64–71.

177. Kenneth Morgan, "Liverpool's Dominance in the Transatlantic Slave Trade, 1740–1807," in *Liverpool and Transatlantic Slavery,* ed. D. Richardson, S. Schwarz, and A. Tibbles (Liverpool, UK: Liverpool University Press, 2007), 22–23.

178. D. M. Williams, "Liverpool Merchants and the Cotton Trade, 1820–1850," in *Liverpool and Merseyside: Essays in the Economic and Social History of the Port and its Hinterland,* ed. John R. Harris (London: Cass, 1969), 182–211.

179. Schoen, *Fragile Fabric of Union,* 49; Hopkins, "The United States, 1783–1861," 239.

180. Schoen, *Fragile Fabric,* 122.

181. Albion, *Rise of New York Port,* 95–121, 267.

182. Schoen, *Fragile Fabric of Union,* 48.

183. William Austin, *Letters from London, Written During the Years 1802 & 1803* (Boston: W. Pelham, 1804), 18.

184. Brian Howman, "Abolitionism in Liverpool," in *Liverpool and Transatlantic Slavery,* ed. Richardson, Schwartz, and Tibbles (Liverpool, UK: Liverpool University Press, 2007), 277–78; Blackett, *Building an Anti-Slavery Wall,* 53, 55, 66–67.

185. Lance E. Davis and Robert J. Cull, "International Capital Movements, Domestic Capital Markets, and American Economic Growth, 1820–1914," in *The Cambridge Economic History of the United States: The Long Nineteenth Century,* ed. Stanley Engerman and Robert Gallman (Cambridge, UK: Cambridge University Press, 2000), 745.

186. For an in-depth study of the structures of the Browns' mercantile practice see John Killick, "The Cotton Operations of Alexander Brown and Sons in the Deep South, 1820–1860," *Journal of Southern History* 43, no. 2 (1977): 169–94. A fuller narrative account, although less analytical, is Edwin J. Perkins, *Financing Anglo-American Trade: The House of Brown, 1800–1880* (Cambridge, MA: Harvard University Press, 1975).

187. Perkins, *Financing Anglo-American Trade,* 34–36.

188. Quoted in Ibid., 41.

189. Gair was elected president of the ACC in 1834. The Rathbones' representative in the United States was Henry Gair, Samuel's son. Samuel's daughter, Lucretia, was married to William Rathbone in 1847. Rathbone himself had served an apprenticeship with Barings in London.

190. Peter E. Austin, *Baring Brothers and the Birth of Modern Finance* (London: Pickering & Chatto, 2015), 40.

191. Ralph W. Hidy, *The House of Baring in American Trade and Finance: English Merchant Bankers at Work, 1763–1861* (Cambridge, MA: Harvard University Press, 1949), 82–83. The connection to Sturgis was reinforced through marriage, as Bates's wife was Lucretia Augustus Sturgis, a cousin of William Sturgis.

192. Stanley S. Chapman, *The Rise of Merchant Banking* (London: Allen & Unwin, 1984), 26.

193. Quoted in Ibid., 27.

194. Ron Chernow, *The House of Morgan* (London: Simon & Schuster, 1990), 4.

195. Ibid., 7.

196. Jay Sexton, *Debtor Diplomacy: Finance and Foreign Relations in the Civil War Era* (Oxford: Oxford University Press, 2005); Hopkins, *American Empire*, 142–90.

197. Mira Wilkins, *The History of Foreign Investment in the United States to 1914* (Cambridge, MA: Harvard University Press, 1898), 61–6.

198. Hopkins, *American Empire*, 165.

199. Davis and Cull, "International Capital Movements," 746–47.

200. Chernow, *House of Morgan*, 4.

201. Haynes, *Unfinished Revolution*.

202. David Morier Evans, *The City; Or, The Physiology of London Business; with Sketches on 'Change and at the London Coffee Houses* (London: Baily Brothers, 1845), 122; *The Morning Post*, September 16, 1825.

203. Everett, *Speech at the Dinner*, 7.

204. See Jim Potter, "Atlantic Economy, 1815–1860: The USA and the Industrial Revolution in Britain," in *Studies in the Industrial Revolution: Presented to T.S. Ashton*, ed. L.S. Pressnell (London: Athlone Press, 1960), 236–81.

205. For financiers' links with New England see Sexton, "The Baring Years," *Debtor Diplomacy*, chapter 1.

CHAPTER TWO. REPRESENTATIVE AMERICANS

1. February 1, 1859, *The Journal of Benjamin Moran, 1857–1865*, ed. Sarah Agnes Wallace & Frances Elma Gillespie (Chicago: University of Chicago Press, 1947), I:123.

2. Leonore Davidoff, *The Best Circles: Society, Etiquette and the Season* (London: Cresset Library, 1973), 26.

3. H. Cunningham, "Leisure and Culture," in *The Cambridge Social History of Britain, 1750–1950. Volume 2: People and their Environment*, ed. F.M.L Thompson (Cambridge, UK: Cambridge University Press, 1990), 291; K.D.

Reynolds, *Aristocratic Women and Political Society in Victorian Britain* (Oxford: Clarendon, 1998), 169, 185.

4. "An American Lesson to European Diplomacy," *Littell's Living Age,* October 1, 1859, 12; Nicole Phelps, *U.S.-Habsburg Relations from 1815 to the Paris Peace Conference: Sovereignty Transformed* (Cambridge, UK: Cambridge University Press, 2013); Jeremy Black, *British Diplomats and Diplomacy, 1688–1800* (Exeter, UK: University of Exeter Press, 2001); Thomas Otte, *The Foreign Office Mind: The Making of British Foreign Policy, 1865–1914* (Cambridge, UK: Cambridge University Press, 2011); Catherine Allgor, "'A Republican in a Monarchy': Louisa Catherine Adams in Russia," *Diplomatic History* 21, no. 1 (1997): 15–43. For a useful illustration of the art of turning gentlemanly advantages to diplomatic advantage see Robert Schulzinger's perceptive analysis of the careers of Henry White, William H. Buckler, and Lloyd Carpenter Griscom in Robert D. Schulzinger, *The Making of the Diplomatic Mind: the Training, Outlook, and Style of United States Foreign Service Officers, 1908–1931* (Middletown, CT: Wesleyan University Press, 1975), 16–22.

5. On the cost of diplomatic life see Allgor, "'Republican in a Monarchy,'" 29.

6. George Wilkes, *Europe in a Hurry* (New York: H. Long & Brother, 1853), 107.

7. Beckles Willson, *America's Ambassadors to England (1785–1928): A Narrative of Anglo-American Diplomatic Relations* (London: John Murray, 1928), 263–66.

8. Reynolds, *Aristocratic Women,* 154; David Cannadine and Simon Price, ed., *Rituals of Royalty: Power and Ceremonial in Traditional Societies* (Cambridge, UK: Cambridge University Press, 1987), 1–2.

9. Pliny Miles to GP, October 29, 1851, Folder 1, Box 193, Papers of George Augustus Peabody, PL.

10. Daniel Kilbride, *Being American in Europe, 1750–1860* (Baltimore: Johns Hopkins University Press, 2013), 77.

11. Nathaniel Hazeltine Carter, *Letters from Europe, comprising the Journal of a Tour through Ireland, England, Scotland, France, Italy and Switzerland in the Years 1825, '26, and '27* (New York: G. & C. Carvill, 1827), I:58.

12. Speech given in honour of George Peabody, Esq., of London by the citizens of the old town of Danvers, October 9, 1856, Reel 54, Edward Everett Papers, MHS.

13. Carter, *Letters from Europe,* I:374.

14. Ibid., I:420. For more on Young Americans overseas, and their activities in the 1848 Revolutions, see Timothy Mason Roberts, *Distant Revolutions: 1848 and the Challenge to American Exceptionalism* (Charlottesville, VA: University of Virginia Press, 2009); Yonatan Eyal, *The Young America Movement and the Transformation of the Democratic Party, 1821–61* (Cambridge, UK: Cambridge University Press, 2007), 116–41.

15. "Our Ministers Abroad," *Saturday Evening Post,* March 23, 1850.

16. Samuel Fiske, *Mr. Dunn Browne's Experiences in Foreign Parts* (Boston: Jewett, 1857), 19–20.

17. Liza Picard, *Victorian London: The Life of a City, 1840–1870* (London: Weidenfeld & Nicolson, 2005), 60.

18. Theodore Witmer, *Wild Oats, Sown Abroad. Or, On and Off Soundings; Being Leaves from a Private Journal by a Gentleman of Leisure* (Philadelphia: T.B. Peterson, 1853), 44.

19. John W. Corson, *Loiterings in Europe: or, Sketches of Travel in France, Belgium, Switzerland, Italy, Austria, Prussia, Great Britain, and Ireland* (New York: Harper & Brothers, 1848), 268.

20. Nathaniel S. Wheaton, *A Journal of a Residence during Several Months in London* (Hartford, CT: H. and F.J. Huntington, 1830), 40, 56. For more American views on the London fog, see Christine Corton, *London Fog: The Biography* (Cambridge, MA: Harvard University Press, 2015), 157–64.

21. Wilkes, *Europe in a Hurry*, 31.

22. Henry B. McLellan, *Journal of a Residence in Scotland, and Tour through England, France, Germany, Switzerland and Italy* (Boston: Allen and Ticknor, 1834), 228.

23. Richard Metz Kenin, *Return to Albion: Americans in England, 1760–1940* (New York: Holt, Rinehart and Winston, 1979), 87–88; Arthur Bailey Thompson, *The Visitor's Universal New Pocket Guide to London* (London: Ward and Lock, 1861), 6.

24. James F. Clarke, *Eleven Weeks in Europe; and What May be Seen in that Time* (Boston: Ticknor, Reid & Fields, 1852), 59.

25. Allgor, "'A Republican in a monarchy,'" 15–43.

26. Elizabeth Bancroft to children, November 8, 1846, Folder 2, Box 16, Bancroft-Bliss Family Papers, LoC.

27. Elizabeth Bancroft to children, November 1, 1846, Folder 2, Box 16, Bancroft-Bliss Family Papers, LoC.

28. Elizabeth Bancroft to William and Alexander Bliss, April 12, 1847, in Elizabeth Davis Bancroft, *Letters from England, 1846–1849* (New York: Scribner's and Sons, 1904), 23–24; Mark Antony DeWolfe Howe, *The Life and Letters of George Bancroft* (New York: C. Scribner's Sons, 1908), 53–98.

29. Elizabeth Bancroft to Isaac Davis, February 7, 1847, in Davis, *Letters from England*, 17.

30. Elizabeth Bancroft to William and Alexander Bliss, January 19, 1847, in Ibid., 15.

31. Markus Mössland and Torsten Riotte, "Introduction: the Diplomats' World," in *The Diplomats' World: A Cultural History of Diplomacy, 1815–1914*, ed. Mössland and Riotte (New York: Oxford University Press, 2008), 15–16; Robert Ralph Davis, Jr., "Diplomatic Plumage: American Court Dress in the Early National Period," *American Quarterly* 20, no. 2 (1968): 164–79.

32. Aaron Smith Willington, *A Summer's Tour in Europe, in 1851: In a Series of Letters Addressed to the Editors of the Charleston Courier* (Charleston, SC: Walker & James, 1852), 16.

33. Elizabeth Bancroft to children, November 3, 1846; January 1, 1847, Folder 2, Box 16, Bancroft-Bliss Family Papers, LoC. See also June 4, 1843, Diary, Reel 37, Vol. 160, Edward Everett Papers, MHS, as well as entries for May 27, 1842; June 16, 1842; July 2, 1843; August 20, 1843; June 14, 1844.

34. March 2, 1859, *Journal of Benjamin Moran*, I:512.

35. David Renshaw to Andrew Stevenson, August 25, 1836; Martin Van Buren to Stevenson, August 28, 1836; and S. Beardsley to Stevenson, August 11, 1837, Vols. 3 & 6, Stevenson Family Papers, LoC.

36. Elizabeth Bancroft to Isaac Davis, January 27, 1847, in Davis, *Letters from England,* 12.

37. David W. Bartlett, *What I Saw in London: Or, Men and Things in the Great Metropolis* (Auburn, NY: Derby and Miller, 1852), 17.

38. Julie Flavell, *When London was Capital of America* (New Haven, CT: Yale University Press, 2010), 18–20.

39. Joshua Bates to Thomas Wren Ward, June 2, 1833, Folder 8, Box 10, Ward Papers, MHS.

40. Bates to Ward, November 3, 1847, Folder 22, Box 11, Ward Papers, MHS.

41. August 15, 1833, Vol. 11, Box 3, Joseph Tuckerman Papers, MHS.

42. William Austin, *Letters from London Written During the Years 1802 & 1803* (Boston: W. Pelham, 1804), 2–3. For more examples see John Overton Choules, *The Cruise of the Yacht* North Star; *A Narrative of Mr. Vanderbilt's Party to England, Russia, Denmark, France, Spain, Italy, Malta, Turkey, Madeira, Etc.* (Boston: Gould and Lincoln, 1854), 103; Matthew Flournoy Ward, *Letters from Three Continents, By M., The Arkansas Correspondent of the Louisville Journal* (New York: D. Appleton, 1851), 17, 341.

43. Dewey, *The Old World and the New,* II:248.

44. Kilbride, *Being American in Europe,* 85.

45. May 29, 1842, Diary, Reel 37, Volume 158, Everett Papers, MHS.

46. Bates to Ward, June 16, 1843, Folder 1, Box 11, Ward Papers, MHS.

47. Bates to Ward, December 21, 1831, Folder 3, Box 10, Ward Papers, MHS.

48. Ibid.

49. See Reynolds, *Aristocratic Women,* 184–85.

50. Davis, Jr., "Diplomatic Plumage," 164–79; Kilbride, *Being American in Europe,* 69.

51. "Letters from Europe," *American Quarterly Review,* December 1, 1827, 560.

52. Bates to Ward, October 3, 1833, Folder 9, Box 10, Ward Papers, MHS. Emphasis in original.

53. Bates to Ward, April 26, 1843, Folder 2, Box 11, Ward Papers, MHS. Emphasis added.

54. Bates to Ward, October 3, 1833, Folder 9, Box 10, Ward Papers, MHS.

55. Bates to Ward, July 26, 1850, Folder 11, Box 12, Ward Papers, MHS.

56. Bates to Ward, January 31, 1842 & January 1, 1846, Folder 16, Box 10 & Folder14, Box 11, Ward Papers, MHS.

57. Jay Sexton, *Debtor Diplomacy: Finance and Foreign Relations in the Civil War Era* (Oxford: Oxford University Press, 2005), 61–69.

58. Bates to Ward, October 4, 1841, Folder 14, Box 10, Ward Papers, MHS. See also Bates to Ward, November 18, 1841 & Ward to Bates, December 14, 1841, Folder 15, Box 10, Ward Papers, MHS.

59. Bates to Ward, July 4, 1842 & August 1, 1842, Folder 19, Box 10, Ward Papers, MHS.

60. April 29, 1842, Diary of Joshua Bates, Box 1, Vol. 3, The Baring Archive, London.

61. Ward to Bates, June 27, 1832, Folder 5, Box 10, Ward Papers, MHS.

62. "Letters from Europe," *American Quarterly Review,* December 1, 1827, 560.

63. The literature on world's fairs is vast; see in particular Paul Greenhalgh, *Ephemeral Vistas: The Expositions Universelles, Great Exhibition, and World's Fairs, 1851–1939* (Rochester, NY: University of Rochester Press, 2005). On American fairs see Robert W. Rydell, *All the World's a Fair: Visions of Empire at American International Expositions, 1876–1916* (Chicago: University of Chicago Press, 1984).

64. "The World's Fair," *American Whig Review,* February 1851, 102.

65. *New York Herald,* November 26, 1850.

66. Thomas Richards, *The Commodity Culture of Victorian England: Advertising and Spectacle, 1851–1914* (Stanford, CA: Stanford University Press, 1990); Jeffrey A. Auerbach, ed., *Britain, the Empire, and the World at the Great Exhibition of 1851* (Abingdon, UK: Routledge, 2008).

67. William A. Drew, *Glimpses and Gatherings During a Voyage and Visit to London and the Great Exhibition in the Summer of 1851* (Augusta, ME: Homan & Manley, 1851), 322.

68. George Wilkes, *Europe in a Hurry* (New York: Long, 1853), 40.

69. William Wells Brown, *The American Fugitive in Europe: Sketches of Places and People Abroad* (Boston: Jewett, 1855), 195–96.

70. Craig Robertson, *The Passport in America: The History of a Document* (New York: Oxford University Press, 2010), 15.

71. Ibid., 26–40; John Torpey, *The Invention of the Passport: Surveillance, Citizenship, and the State* (Cambridge, UK: Cambridge University Press, 2000).

72. Willson, *America's Ambassadors to England,* 263.

73. *New York Herald,* February 13, 1851.

74. Robert Van Riper, *A Life Divided: George Peabody, Pivotal Figure in Anglo-American Finance, Philanthropy and Diplomacy* (London: Lightning Source, 2000), 72; Robert F. Dalzell, *American Participation in the Great Exhibition of 1851* (Amherst, MA: Amherst College Press, 1960), 40.

75. "A hint for the American non-exhibitors," *Punch,* June 14, 1851, 246.

76. "America in Crystal," *Punch* 20, Jan-June 1851, 209; "American contributions to the Great Exhibition," *Punch* 20, Jan-June 1851, 218. In Richard Doyle's centerfold illustration "May, Day Eighteen Hundred and Fifty-One," products from California are similarly unloaded by a pair of black slaves as Brother Jonathan watches on (*Punch* 20, Jan-June 1851, 181–82).

77. John Tallis, *History and Description of the Crystal Palace and the Exhibition of the World's Industry in 1851* (London: John Tallis & Co., 1852), II:83.

78. Horace Greeley, *Glances at Europe: in a series of letters from Great Britain, France, Switzerland, etc., during the summer of 1851; including notices of the Great Exhibition, or World's Fair* (New York: Dewitt & Davenport, 1851), 91.

79. Ibid., 94.

80. Henry Carey, *The Harmony of Interests, Agricultural, Manufacturing, and Commercial* (Philadelphia: J. S. Skinner, 1851), 223, emphasis in original. For more on Carey see Daniel Walker Howe, *The Political Culture of the American Whigs* (Chicago: University of Chicago Press, 1979), 109–22.

81. Henry Carey, *Principles of Social Science* (Philadelphia: J. B. Lippincott, 1853–59), III:220.

82. Ibid., III.221–22. Some scholars have noted that this was precisely the aim of many free traders; see Scott D. James and David A. Lake, "The Second Face of Hegemony: Britain's Repeal of the Corn Laws and the American Walker Tariff of 1846," *International Organization* 43, no. 1 (1989): 1–29.

83. "The World's Fair," *American Whig Review*, February 1851, 107.

84. Eyal, *Young America Movement*, 42; "A Few Free Thoughts on Free Trade," *The United States Magazine and Democratic Review*, April 1840, 341–47.

85. Eyal, *Young America Movement*, 40–44.

86. Sexton, *Debtor Diplomacy*, 53–60.

87. Nathaniel S. Dodge to Peabody, May 6 & November 9, 1851; Edward Riddle to Peabody, May 13, 1851, Folder 6, Box 192, Papers of George Augustus Peabody, PL; Riper, *Life Divided*, 73.

88. Abbott Lawrence to James Buchanan, August 23, 1850, Abbott Lawrence Papers, HL.

89. Dalzell, *American Participation in the Great Exhibition of 1851*, 51–52.

90. "America at the Great Exhibition," May 31, 1851.

91. Draft speech for a dinner at Danvers MA, 1856, Folder 4, Box 197, Papers of George Augustus Peabody, PL. Emphasis in original.

92. Edwin J. Perkins, "Tourists and Bankers: Travelers' Credits and the Rise of American Tourism, 1840–1900," *Business and Economic History*, 2nd ser., 8 (1979): 16–28.

93. "History: London Firms," undated MS, pp. 5–6, Folder 25, Box 1, Papers of Junius Spencer Morgan, ML.

94. Ron Chernow, *The House of Morgan* (London: Simon & Schuster, 1990), 7.

95. John Lothrop Motely to M. Motley, 30 May 1858, in *The Correspondence of John Lothrop Motley*, ed. G. W. Curtis (New York: Harper and Brothers, 1889), I:243.

96. Choules, *The Cruise of the Yacht North Star*, 47.

97. The most fashionable balls could attract as many as double the number at Peabody's. In spite of the protestations of some American Democrats to the contrary, Washington politics ran to many of the same social rituals; see Catherine Allgor, *Parlor Politics: In Which the Ladies of Washington Help Build a City and a Government* (Charlottesville: University Press of Virginia, 2000).

98. "Grand Entertainment to the American Minister," *Illustrated London News*, July 19, 1851. A detailed description can also be found in "The Fourth of July in London," *The Weekly Herald* [New York], July 26, 1851.

99. Ibid.

100. Abbott Lawrence to Peabody, July 5, 1861, Folder 1, Box 193, Papers of George Augustus Peabody, PL. Emphasis added.

101. Otte, *The Foreign Office Mind*, 12.

102. *An Account of the Proceedings of the Dinner Given by Mr. George Peabody to the Americans Connected with the Great Exhibition at the London Coffee House, Ludgate Hill, on the 27th October 1851* (London: William Pickering, 1851), 42.

103. Ibid., 62.

104. Ibid., 15.

105. Ibid., 49.

106. Ibid., 36–37, 42.

107. Ibid., 25. Emphasis in original.

108. Ibid., 59. Emphasis in original. The 1833 Zollverein Treaties created a customs union between a coalition of German states to manage tariffs and economic policies. The treaties took effect on January 1, 1834, and paved the way for the unification of the German Territories, excluding Austria, later in the century.

109. After-dinner speech, estimated 1850–54, Folder 4, Box 197, Papers of George Augustus Peabody, PL.

110. John T. Pitman (JTP) to Caroline Pitman, October 3, 1855, Folder 19, Box 3, John Talbot Pitman Papers, RIHS.

111. JTP to John Pitman Jr. (JP Jr.), February 12, 1858, Folder 1, Box 3, Pitman Papers, RIHS.

112. JTP to JP Jr., January 29, 1859, Folder 1, Box 3, Pitman Papers, RIHS.

113. JTP to JP Jr., July 12, 1860, Folder 1, Box 3. See also: CP to JTP, July 25, 1860, Folder 4, Box 1, Pitman Papers, RIHS. Emphasis added.

114. Paul Quigley, *Shifting Grounds: Nationalism and the American South, 1848–1865* (New York: Oxford University Press, 2012), 5.

115. Quigley, *Shifting Grounds,* 6; Roberts, *Distant Revolutions;* Eyal, *Young America Movement,* 93–116.

116. Reginald Horsman, *Race and Manifest Destiny: The Origins of American Racial Anglo-Saxonism* (Cambridge, MA: Harvard University Press, 1991), 27–32.

117. Anthony Smith, *The Nation in History: Historiographical Debates about Ethnicity and Nationalism* (Hanover, NH: University Press of New England, 2000).

118. Kilbride, *Being American in Europe,* 98–100.

119. "Our representatives abroad," *Saturday Evening Post,* September 8, 1849. See also "Going Abroad," *Ballou's Pictorial Drawing-Room Companion,* November 21, 1857.

120. November 21, 1848, Vol. 12, Journal of Elihu Burritt, Elihu Burritt Collection, New Britain Public Library, New Britain, CT.

121. Oliver Wendell Holmes to Motley, April 29, 1860, in Curtis, *Correspondence of John Lothrop Motley,* I:342.

122. Dewey, *Old World and the New,* II:237.

123. For a broad view of Americans in Göttingen see Paul G. Buchloh and Walter T. Rix, *The American Colony in Göttingen: Historical and Other Data Collected Between the Years 1855 and 1888* (Göttingen, Germany: Vandenhoeck & Ruprecht, 1976).

124. J. Pierpont Morgan (JPM) to James Goodwin, April 29, 1856, Folder 3, Box 4, JP Morgan Papers, ML.

125. JPM to James Goodwin, May 21, 1856, Folder 3, Box 4, JP Morgan Papers, ML.

126. JPM to James Goodwin, June 17, July 1 & August 22, 1856, Folder 3, Box 4, JP Morgan Papers, ML.

127. JPM to James Goodwin, November 4 & November 18, 1856, Folder 4, Box 4, JP Morgan Papers, ML.

128. Göttingen notes, 1855–1857, Folder 33, Box 1, JP Morgan Papers, ML.

129. Individual expatriates very occasionally did so, but the instances are exceptionally rare; see Caroline Pitman to JP Jr., October 11, 1857, Folder 3, Box 3, Pitman Papers, RIHS.

130. Edward L. Widmer, *Young America: The Flowering of Democracy in New York City* (New York: Oxford University Press, 1999); W. T. Kerrigan, "'Young America!': Romantic Nationalism in Literature and Politics, 1843–1861," (Ph.D. diss, University of Michigan, 1997).

131. Roberts, *Distant Revolutions,* 21–41.

132. Bayard Taylor, *Views A-Foot: or, Europe Seen with Knapsack and Staff* (New York: Wiley & Putnam, 1846); Samuel Sullivan Cox, *A Buckeye Abroad; or, Wanderings in Europe, and in the Orient* (New York: G. P. Putnam, 1852). Henry Tuckerman produced numerous books about travel in Europe, including *The Italian Sketch Book* (New York: J. C. Riker, 1848), *Rambles and Reveries* (New York: James P. Giffing, 1841), and *A Month in England* (New York: Redfield, 1853). For an overview of American travel literature before the Civil War see Alfred Bendixen, "Travel Books about Europe before the Civil War," in *The Cambridge Companion to American Travel Writing,* ed. Alfred Bendixen and Judith Hamera (Cambridge, UK: Cambridge University Press, 2009), 103–27.

133. Kilbride, *Being American in Europe,* 83–84.

134. Julie E. Hall, "'Coming to Europe,' Coming to Authorship: Sophia Hawthorne and Her *Notes in England and Italy*," *Legacy* 19, no. 2 (2002): 137.

135. Quigley, *Shifting Grounds,* 23.

136. Eyal, *Young America Movement,* 110.

137. Riper, *A Life Divided,* 103.

138. Eyal, *Young America Movement,* 94; Yonatan Eyal, "A Romantic Realist: George Nicholas Sanders and the Dilemmas of Southern International Engagement," *Journal of Southern History* 78, no. 1 (2012): 107–30.

139. Ibid., 102; William A. Swanberg, *Sickles the Incredible* (New York: C. Scribner's Sons, 1956), 95.

140. *New York Times,* November 6, 1854.

141. Philip Shriver Klein, *President James Buchanan: A Biography* (University Park: Pennsylvania State University Press, 1962), 237. See also Buchanan to Sickles, December 22, 1854, *The Works of James Buchanan,* ed. John Bassett Moore (New York: Antiquarian Press, 1960), IX:290–91.

142. *Boston Post,* July 21, 1854.

143. *Boston Daily Atlas,* September 7, 1854. Peabody received a flood of letters in support of his actions; see W. B. Rose to Peabody, August 7, 1854;

G. P. A. Healy to Peabody, August 27, 1854; T. A. Adams to Peabody, September 21, 1854; Fitzroy to Peabody, November 4, 1854; Unknown to Peabody, November 5, 1854; J. B. Maclinson to Peabody, December 28, 1854, Folder 2, Box 193, Papers of George Augustus Peabody, PL.

144. Undated Speech, estimated 1852, Folder 4, Box 197, Papers of George Augustus Peabody, PL.

145. Ibid.

146. *Young America*, August 3, 1854, Vol. 160, Papers of George Augustus Peabody, PL.

147. For more on place-based nationalism see Quigley, *Shifting Grounds*, 33–34.

148. *Young America*, August 3, 1854, Vol. 160, Papers of George Augustus Peabody, PL. Emphasis added. For similar arguments see "Americans in Europe," *New York Times*, October 29, 1855.

149. "Young America" to Peabody, August 3, 1854, Folder 7, Box 193, Papers of George Augustus Peabody, PL.

150. Peabody to Unknown, n.d. (c. 1840–45), Folder 1, Box 197, Papers of George Augustus Peabody, PL.

151. *Boston Daily Atlas*, September 7, 1854.

152. "Our representatives abroad," *The National Era*, October 26, 1854.

153. *New York Herald*, November 8, 1854.

154. *The Examiner*, October 18, 1854.

155. "Our representatives abroad," *The National Era*, October 26, 1854. Dahomey is present-day Benin.

156. Ibid.

157. Sexton, *Debtor Diplomacy*, 59.

158. *Daily National Intelligencer*, January 12, 1856.

159. J. S. Black to Lewis Cass, August 17, 1857, in *Official Opinions of the Attorneys General of the United States* (Washington, DC: Government Printing Office, 1866), IX:62, http://www.heinonline.org/HOL/Index?index=agopinions /oag&collection=agopinions.

160. J. S. Black to James Buchanan, July 4, 1859, in Ibid., IX:358–59.

161. See also Eileen P. Scully, *Bargaining with the State from Afar: American Citizenship in Treaty Port China, 1844–1942* (New York: Columbia University Press, 2001); Brooke L. Blower, *Becoming Americans in Paris: Transatlantic Politics and Culture Between the World Wars* (New York: Oxford University Press, 2011).

162. *New York Herald*, July 26, 1857.

163. "Address to Mr. M'Clane, The American Minister," *Liverpool Mercury*, July 24, 1846; "Entertainment to the American Minister," *Liverpool Mercury*, December 17, 1850; "Banquet to the Hon. R. J. Walker, of the United States," *Liverpool Mercury*, November 25, 1851.

164. Widmer, *Young America*, 202–23. For the 1890s, see chapter 6.

165. *New York Herald*, July 26, 1857.

166. George Francis Train, *Young America Abroad* (London: Seth Low, 1857), vi.

167. George Francis Train, *Spread-Eagleism* (New York: Derby & Jackson, 1860), 74.

168. Ibid., 69–71. Emphasis added.

169. Bates to Ward, October 17, 1841, Folder 14, Box 10, Ward Papers, MHS.

170. Liverpool's most prominent Southerners were William Trenholm, Rutson Maury, Charles Kuhn Prioleau, and his subordinate Alan Stewart Hanckel.

171. The paper was a reincarnation of Baylor's *American Cotton Plant,* sometimes appearing as the *Cotton Plant and Southern Advertiser,* published in Washington DC and Baltimore between April 1852 and June 1857. Baylor was also the owner-editor of the *Daily American Times,* a paper supporting direct free trade between the Southern states and Europe.

172. "Our Foreign Policy," *Washington Sentinel,* September 24, 1853.

173. "The London Cotton Plant. Prospectus," *Daily News,* June 11, 1858.

174. *London Cotton Plant,* June 12, 1858, quoted in "The Slave Trade in 1858," *Edinburgh Review* 220 (October 1858).

175. Brian Schoen, *Fragile Fabric of Union: Cotton, Federal Politics, and the Global Origins of the Civil War* (Baltimore, MA: Johns Hopkins University Press, 2009), 220–21; Gerald Horne, *The Deepest South: The United States, Brazil, and the African Slave Trade* (New York: New York University Press, 2007); Edward B. Rugemer, *The Problem of Emancipation: The Caribbean Roots of the American Civil War* (Baton Rouge: Louisiana State University Press, 2008).

176. Sexton, *Debtor Diplomacy,* 135.

177. Matthew Mason, "'A World Safe for Modernity': Antebellum Southern Proslavery Intellectuals Confront Great Britain," in *The Old South's Modern Worlds: Slavery, Region, and Nation in the Age of Progress,* ed. L. Diane Barnes, Brian Schoen, and Frank Towers (New York: Oxford University Press, 2011), 48.

178. Mira Wilkins, *The History of Foreign Investment in the United States to 1914* (Cambridge, MA: Harvard University Press, 1989), 74; P. L. Cottrell, *British Overseas Investment in the Nineteenth Century* (London: Macmillan, 1975), 19–29; Schoen, *Fragile Fabric of Union,* 204–5.

179. Martin Crawford, *The Anglo-American Crisis of the Mid-Nineteenth Century: The Times and America, 1850–1862* (Athens: University of Georgia Press, 1987), 13.

180. Michael O'Brien, *Conjectures of Order: Intellectual Life and the American South, 1810–1860* (Chapel Hill: University of North Carolina Press, 2004), I:215–52.

181. March 6, 1858, *Journal of Benjamin Moran,* I:259.

182. March 6, 1858, Ibid, I:259.

183. March 12, 1858, Ibid, I:265; for a contemporary portrait of Fell see *Harper's Weekly,* June 27, 1857.

184. *The Morning Chronicle,* July 6, 1858.

185. Nathaniel Hawthorne, *The English Notebooks, 1853–1856,* ed. Thomas Woodson and Bill Ellis (Columbus: Ohio State University Press, 1997), 49.

186. Edward Everett to J. Labouchere, April 11, 1844, Reel 22, Volume 47, Everett Papers, MHS.

187. July 1801, ACC Minute Books, I, LPRO.

188. September 17, 1858, *Journal of Benjamin Moran,* I:429.

189. July 6, 1858, Ibid., I:364.

190. Ibid.

191. "The American Association of London," *Standard,* July 6, 1858.

192. June 17, 1858, *Journal of Benjamin Moran,* I:348.

193. July 10, 1858, Ibid., I:368.

194. "The American Association of London," *Standard,* July 6, 1858.

195. Train, *Spread-Eagleism,* 108.

196. Ibid., 112.

197. March 6, 1860, *Journal of Benjamin Moran,* I:643–44.

198. April 16, 1860, Ibid., I:657.

199. January 18, 1860, Ibid., I:631.

200. *London American,* May 2, 1860.

201. Ibid.

202. Ibid.

203. *London American,* May 30, 1860.

204. "Americans in Europe," *London American,* August 8, 1860; "Washington Friend's Musical," May 30 1860; "Emigrant Life in the United States and Canada," October 17, 1860; "Michigan to intending migrants," November 21, 1860; "Who is in fault?', February 20, 1861.

205. *London Cotton Plant,* August 21, 1858, quoted in *The Atlantic Monthly,* November 1858, 760.

206. Henry Adams to Charles Francis Adams Jr., January 31, 1862, in *A Cycle of Adams Letters, 1861–1865,* ed. Worthington Chauncey Ford (London: Constable, 1921), I:108.

CHAPTER THREE. THE EMIGRANTS' WAR

1. Henry Stevens, *Henry Stevens—His Autobiography & Noviomagus Club* (Larchmont, NY: Sons & Stiles, 1978), 20–21.

2. Henry Stevens to Gov. Fairbanks, May 11, 1861, Misc #1324, Henry Stevens Family Correspondence, VHS.

3. Wyman W. Parker, *Henry Stevens of Vermont, American Rare Book Dealer in London, 1845–1886* (Amsterdam: N. Israel, 1963), 241. Emphasis in original. See also Simon Stevens to Parents, n.d. (c. early November 1861), Folder 31, Stevens Correspondence, VHS.

4. Parker, *Henry Stevens,* 242.

5. Ibid.

6. Jay Sexton, *Debtor Diplomacy: Finance and Foreign Relations in the Civil War Era* (Oxford: Oxford University Press, 2005), 104; William H. Seward to Abraham Lincoln, n.d. (1861), Abraham Lincoln Papers, LoC.

7. Carl L. Davis, *Arming the Union: Small Arms in the Civil War* (Port Washington, NY: Kennikat Press, 1973), 53–54, 64; James Bulloch to Stephen Mallory, August 13, 1861, *Official Records of the Union and Confederate*

Navies in the War of the Rebellion, Series II (Washington, DC: Government Printing Office, 1894–1922), III.83–87.

8. September 28, 1861, CFAD (online edition: http://www.masshist.org /publications/cfa-civil-war).

9. Norman Ferris, *Desperate Diplomacy: William H. Seward's Foreign Policy, 1861* (Knoxville: University of Tennessee Press, 1976), 21–23.

10. Howard Jones, *Blue and Gray Diplomacy: A History of Union and Confederate Foreign Relations* (Chapel Hill: University of North Carolina Press, 2010), 253–84.

11. May 15, 1861, CFAD.

12. May, 22, June 4 & 28, August 9, 1861, CFAD; Parker, *Henry Stevens,* 240.

13. June 7, 1861, CFAD.

14. August 16, 1861, CFAD.

15. "The feeling abroad," *New York Times,* June 15, 1861.

16. David Paul Crook, *The North, The South, and the Powers, 1861–1865* (New York: Wiley, 1974); Jones, *Blue and Gray Diplomacy;* Charles Hubbard, *The Burden of Confederate Diplomacy* (Knoxville: University of Tennessee Press, 1998).

17. Matthew Karp, *This Vast Southern Empire: Slaveholders at the Helm of American Foreign Policy* (Cambridge, MA: Harvard University Press, 2016). For further work focusing on the outward-facing nature of Southern statesmen see Brian Schoen, *The Fragile Fabric of Union: Cotton, Federal Politics, and the Global Origins of the Civil War* (Baltimore: Johns Hopkins University Press, 2009); Matthew Pratt Guterl, *American Mediterranean: Southern Slaveholders in the Age of Emancipation* (Cambridge, MA: Harvard University Press, 2008); Robert Bonner, *Mastering America: Southern Slaveholders and the Crisis of American Nationhood* (Cambridge, UK: Cambridge University Press, 2009); Robert E. May, *The Southern Dream of a Caribbean Empire, 1854–1861* (Baton Rouge: Louisiana State University Press, 1973); Edward B. Rugemer, *The Problem of Emancipation: the Caribbean Roots of the American Civil War* (Baton Rouge: Louisiana State University Press, 2008).

18. These were Thomas Pinckney, James Monroe, William Pinckney, James Barbour, Andrew Stevenson, and Louis McLane.

19. Don H. Doyle, *The Cause of All Nations: An International History of the American Civil War* (New York: Basic Books, 2015). This literature is especially well developed in the case of Britain; see Richard J. M. Blackett, *Divided Hearts: Britain and the American Civil War* (Baton Rouge: Louisiana State University Press, 2001); Alfred Grant, *The American Civil War and the British Press* (London: McFarland & Co., 2000); Martin Crawford, *The Anglo-American Crisis of the Mid-Nineteenth Century: The Times and America, 1850–1862* (Athens: University of Georgia Press, 1987); Duncan Andrew Campbell, *English Public Opinion and the American Civil War* (London: Boydell Press, 2003).

20. A notable exception is Sexton, *Debtor Diplomacy,* which examines transatlantic financiers. On some of the problems and challenges of transnational and global approaches to the Civil War, see "Interchange: Nationalism and Internationalism in the Era of the Civil War," *Journal of American History* 98, no. 2 (2011): 455–89.

21. Junius Spencer Morgan to George Peabody, March 30, 1860, Papers of Junius Spencer Morgan, ML.

22. Joseph Shipley to James Brown, May 17, 1861, Folder 8, Box 9, Brown Brothers-Harriman Papers, NYHS.

23. April 28, 1861 (see also, 5 May 1861), Diary of Joshua Bates, Vol. 8, Bates Papers, ING Baring Archive, London.

24. George Peabody to Sherman, March 9, 1861, Peabody Papers, PL.

25. December 30, 1861, *The Journal of Benjamin Moran, 1857–1865*, ed. Sarah Agnes Wallace and Frances Elma Gillespie (Chicago: Chicago University Press 1947), II:933. Peabody is quoted in Franklin Parker, *George Peabody: A Biography* (Nashville: Vanderbilt University Press, 1971), 115.

26. Daniel James to William E. Dodge, May 8, 1861, Phelps Dodge & Co. Papers, Box 16, NYPL.

27. These were: John Pendleton Kennedy, Charles P. McIlvaine, Bancroft Davis, Archbishop John Hughes, Henry S. Sanford, William M. Walker, Thurlow Weed, Robert C. Winthrop, Edward Everett, William Whiting, and William M. Evarts.

28. Thurlow Weed to Abraham Lincoln, December 27, 1861, Lincoln Papers, LoC.

29. Henry Adams to Frederick William Seward, January 30, 1862, Charles Petit McIlvaine Letters, Book 61, Kenyon College, OH.

30. Thurlow Weed to William H. Seward, 4 February 1862, Lincoln Papers, LoC.

31. Douglas H. Maynard, "The Forbes Aspinwall Mission," *Mississippi Valley Historical Review* 45, no. 1 (1958): 67–89.

32. These figures were compiled with the help of Walter B. Smith, *America's Diplomats and Consuls of 1776–1865* (Arlington, VA: Foreign Service Institute, US Department of State, 1986), 56–61. For Consuls the figures are: England 11 (inc. Consul General); Wales 1; Scotland 3; Ireland 7. For Consular Agents: England 16; Wales 6; Ireland 4.

33. At the Legation, Charles Francis Adams employed his son Henry as his private secretary, Charles Lush Wilson as Secretary of the Legation, and Benjamin Moran as Assistant Secretary. The Consul General in London and the Falmouth Consulate also had both a vice and deputy consul; Liverpool and Leeds had a Vice Consul.

34. Henry Adams to Frederick William Seward, January 30, 1862, in *The Letters of Henry Adams, Volume 1: 1858–1868*, ed. Jacob C. Levenson (Cambridge, MA: Harvard University Press, 1982), 274.

35. Henry Adams to Charles Francis Adams, Jr., June 10, 1861, in Ibid., 238; "Volunteer Diplomacy," *New York Times*, July 2, 1861.

36. *New York Times*, December 23, 1869.

37. Ibid.

38. Thurlow Weed, *Letters from Europe and the West Indies, 1843–1862* (Albany, NY: Weed, Parsons and Company, 1866), 691.

39. Parker, *Peabody*, 123; see also August 14, 1863, CFAD.

40. Thurlow Weed to William H. Seward, December 4, 1861, Lincoln Papers, LoC.

41. January 16, 1862, CFAD.

42. *Times,* July 11, 1862.

43. *Times,* March 26, 1862.

44. "Presentation of the Freedom of the City to Mr. Peabody," *Lloyd's Weekly Newspaper,* July 13, 1862.

45. Merle Curti, *American Philanthropy Abroad: a History* (New Brunswick, NJ: Rutgers University Press, 1963).

46. April 15, 1862, CFAD.

47. Charles Francis Adams to William Henry Seward, June 25, 1863, *FRUS,* I:278–79.

48. Henry Adams to Charles Francis Adams Jr., April 11, 1862, in Ibid., I:292.

49. 14 June 1861, CFAD.

50. Henry Adams to Charles Francis Adams Jr., May 16, 1861 & September 14, 1861, in Levenson, *Letters of Henry Adams, Volume 1,* 236, 252; Charles Francis Adams, Sr., May 5, 1862, CFAD.

51. May 24, 1862, July 1, 1863, 22 June 1861, CFAD.

52. March 3, 1864, CFAD.

53. Carl Schurz, *The Reminiscences of Carl Schurz* (New York: The McLure Company, 1907), II:246. See also June 9, 1863, CFAD; "American Representatives Abroad," *New York Times,* January 26, 1862.

54. Amy Milne-Smith, *London Clubland: A Cultural History of Gender and Class in Late Victorian Britain* (Basingstoke: Palgrave Macmillan, 2011), 28.

55. *The Times,* October 3, 1861.

56. Patrick Jackson, *Education Act Forster: A Political Biography of W. E. Forster* (Madison, NJ: Fairleigh Dickinson University Press, 1997), 83.

57. October 15, 1862, CFAD.

58. Jackson, *Education Act Forster,* 80–93.

59. David Herbert Donald, *Charles Sumner and the Coming of Civil War* (Chicago: University of Chicago Press, 1981 [1960]), 51.

60. Argyll to Sumner, June 4, 1861, in *Memoirs and Letters of Charles Sumner,* ed. Edward L. Pierce (Boston: Roberts Brothers, 1894), IV:31.

61. Charles Sumner to the Duchess of Argyll, c. May 1863, Papers of Charles Sumner, HuL.

62. February 14, 1865, CFAD.

63. May 24, 1862, CFAD.

64. Henry Adams to Charles Francis Adams, Jr., February 20, 1863, in Levenson, *Letters of Henry Adams, Volume 1,* 331–32.

65. Henry Adams to Charles Francis Adams, April 11, 1862, Ibid., 292.

66. Henry Adams to Charles Francis Adams, June 18, 1853, Ibid., 363.

67. Henry Adams to Charles Francis Adams, May 16, 1862, Ibid., 297–98.

68. May 18, 1862, CFAD.

69. Sir William Brown to Thomas Haines Dudley, December 10, 1863, Box 16, Thomas Haines Dudley Papers, HuL.

70. Robert Trimble to Dudley, March 4, 1864, Box 18, Thomas Haines Dudley Papers, HuL; Robert Trimble, *Slavery in the United States of North*

America (London: Henry Young, 1863); *The Negro North and South: The Status of the Coloured Population in the Northern and Southern States Compared* (London: Whittaker & Co., 1863); *Popular Fallacies Relating to the American Question* (London: Whittaker & Co., 1863).

71. David Hepburn Milton, *Lincoln's Spymaster: Thomas Haines Dudley and the Liverpool Network* (Mechanicsburg, PA: Stackpole Books, 2003).

72. Brainerd Dyer, "Thomas H. Dudley," *Civil War History* 1, no. 4 (1955): 401–13. For more on Union surveillance see H.C. Owsley, "Henry Shelton Sanford and Federal Surveillance Abroad, 1861–1865," *Mississippi Valley Historical Review* 48, no. 2 (1961): 211–28.

73. Charles B. Wilson to Dudley, June 27, 1864, Box 20, Cobden to Dudley, September 13, 1864, Box 21, John Stuart Mill to Dudley, February 9, 1865, Box 24, Thomas Haines Dudley Papers, HuL. Dudley was also present at Bright's famous Rochdale speech in support of the Union; see Thomas Haines Dudley, "Three Critical Periods in Our Diplomatic Relations with Great Britain during the Late War," *Pennsylvania Magazine of History and Biography* 17, no. 1 (1893): 40–43.

74. Leslie Butler, *Critical Americans: Victorian Intellectuals and Transatlantic Liberal Reform* (Chapel Hill: University of North Carolina Press, 2007), 78.

75. Stephen Meardon, "Richard Cobden's American Quandary: Negotiating Peace, Free Trade, and Anti-Slavery," in *Rethinking Nineteenth Century Liberalism: Richard Cobden Bicentenary Essays,* ed. Anthony Howe and Simon Morgan (Aldershot, UK: Ashgate, 2006), 208–29; Marc-William Palen, "The Civil War's Forgotten Transatlantic Tariff Debate and the Confederacy's Free Trade Diplomacy," *Journal of the Civil War Era* 3, no. 1 (2013): 35–61; James Ford Rhodes, "Letters of John Bright to Charles Sumner, 1861–1872," *Proceedings of the Massachusetts Historical Society* 45 (1911), 148–59.

76. Butler, *Critical Americans*, 79.

77. Ibid., 81; Brent E. Kinser, *The American Civil War in the Shaping of British Democracy* (London: Routledge, 2016).

78. See Richard Carwardine, *Transatlantic Revivalism: Popular Evangelicalism in Britain and America, 1790–1865* (Westport, CT: Greenwood Press, 1978); Richard J.M. Blackett, *Building an Antislavery Wall: Black Americans in the Atlantic Abolitionist Movement, 1830–1860* (Baton Rouge: Louisiana State University Press, 1983).

79. John D'Entrement, *Southern Emancipator: Moncure Conway, The American Years, 1832–1865* (New York: Oxford University Press, 1987), 185; *Times,* June 17, 1863.

80. Henry Ward Beecher, *Patriotic Addresses in England and America, 1850–1885: On Slavery, the Civil War, and the Development of Civil Liberty in the United States* (New York: Fords, Howard & Hulbert, 1888), 640.

81. Weed, *Letters from Europe,* 758.

82. Blackett, *Divided Hearts,* 188; Richard Blackett, "African Americans, British Public Opinion, and Civil War Diplomacy," in *The Union, The Confederacy, and the Atlantic Rim,* ed. Robert E. May (West Lafayette, ID: Purdue University Press, 1995), 69–101; Richard Blackett, "African Americans, the

British Working Class, and the American Civil War," *Slavery and Abolition* 17, no. 2 (1996): 51–67.

83. Quoted in Benjamin Quarles, "Ministers without Portfolio," *Journal of Negro History* 39, no. 1 (1954), 39.

84. Quarles, "Ministers without Portfolio."

85. Richard J. M. Blackett, *Beating Against the Barriers: Biographical Essays in Nineteenth-Century Afro-History* (Baton Rouge: Louisiana State University Press, 1986), 207.

86. Quoted in Blackett, *Divided Hearts,* 40.

87. Caleb McDaniel, *The Problem of Democracy in the Age of Slavery* (Baton Rouge: Louisiana State University Press, 2013), 226–31.

88. Blackett, *Divided Hearts,* 155.

89. Clare Midgley, *Women Against Slavery: The British Campaigns, 1700–1870* (London: Routledge, 1992), 180.

90. Dudley to Seward, February 20, 1863, Despatches from U.S. Consuls in Liverpool, 1790–1906, RG 59, National Archives, Washington, DC.

91. "Rev. J. Sella Martin in London," *Douglass' Monthly,* February 1862.

92. "Rev. J. Sella Martin's Farewell to England," *Liberator,* February 28, 1862.

93. London *Morning Star,* March 26, 1863.

94. See Patrick J. Kelly, "The Cat's Paw: Confederate Ambitions in Latin America," in *American Civil Wars: The United States, Latin America, Europe, and the Crisis of the 1860s,* ed. Don Doyle (Chapel Hill: University of North Carolina Press, 2017), 58–81.

95. "Great Emancipation Meeting in Finsbury," *Liberator,* May 29, 1863.

96. Charles Francis Adams to William Henry Seward, February 19, 1863, in *FRUS,* 1:136.

97. Southerners also occupied consular positions in the following key posts: Alexander Derbes (Louisiana), Marseille; Edwin DeLeon (South Carolina), Alexandria; John T. Pickett (Kentucky), Vera Cruz; Richard Kidder Meade Jr. (Virginia), Rio de Janeiro.

98. Henry William Lord to Henry Wilding, July 3, 1862, Box 6, Thomas Haines Dudley Papers, HuL.

99. *London American,* May 29, 1861; *Liverpool Mercury,* November 28, 1861.

100. Benjamin Moran to Dudley, September 25, 1863, Box 6, Thomas Haines Dudley Papers, HuL. See also *Liverpool Mercury,* July 23, 1861, December 21, 1861, June 28, 1862, May 30, 1863.

101. Liverpool's Caribbean trade was strong throughout the nineteenth century; see Graeme J. Milne, *Trade and Traders in Mid-Victorian Liverpool: Mercantile Business and the Making of a World Port* (Liverpool: Liverpool University Press, 2000), 55–8.

102. Thomas E. Taylor, *Running the Blockade: A Personal Narrative of the Adventures, Risks and Escapes During the American Civil War* (London: John Murray, 1897), 10. For a detailed account of the West Indies role in the Civil War see Kenneth Blume, "The Mid-Atlantic Arena: The United States, the

Confederacy, and the British West Indies, 1861–1865," (Ph.D. diss., State University of New York at Binghamton, 1984).

103. Thomas Schoonover, "Napoleon is Coming! Maximilian is Coming? The International History of the Civil War in the Caribbean Basin," in May, *Union, Confederacy and the Atlantic Rim,* 112.

104. Francis Hughes, "Liverpool and the Confederate States: Fraser Trenholm and Company Operations During the American Civil War," (Ph.D. thesis, Keele University, 1996), 59–60; Stephen R. Wise, *Lifeline of the Confederacy: Blockade Running During the Civil War* (Columbia: University of South Carolina Press, 1991), 47.

105. Douglas B. Ball, *Financial Failure and Confederate Defeat* (Urbana: University of Illinois Press, 1991), 70–71; Wise, *Lifeline of the Confederacy,* 47.

106. Charles Kuhn Prioleau to Caleb Huse, January 12, 1864, Reel 3, Fraser Trenholm Papers, Liverpool Maritime Museum, Liverpool, UK; Hubbard, *Burden of Confederate Diplomacy,* 91.

107. Henry Hotze to Judah P. Benjamin, August 6, 1864, *Official Records of the Union and Confederate Navies,* III:1185.

108. Prioleau hosted Confederate shipmen whenever they arrived in Liverpool, and gave letters of introduction and gifts of cash; see James Morris Morgan, *Recollections of a Rebel Reefer* (Boston, MA: Houghton Mifflin Company, 1917), 108–10; Joshua Nunn to Thomas Dudley, April 20, 1865, Thomas Haines Dudley Papers, HuL.

109. *Liverpool Mercury,* October 13, 1862.

110. Harold S. Wilson, *Confederate Industry: Manufacturers and Quartermasters in the Civil War* (Jackson: University Press of Mississippi, 2002), 122–38.

111. Thomas Dudley to William Henry Seward, April, 11 & 16, May 2, 1862, Thomas Haines Dudley Papers, Microfilm, David Bruce Centre Library, Keele University, Keele, UK. Many thanks to Martin Crawford for the loan of this material.

112. Wise, *Lifeline of the Confederacy,* 226.

113. May 10, 1862, CFAD.

114. A comprehensive list can be found in John D. Bennett, *London Confederates: The Officials, Clergy, Businessmen, and Journalists who Backed the American South During the Civil War* (London: McFarland, 2007), 161–63.

115. *The Index,* October 1, 1863.

116. Hubbard, *Burden of Confederate Diplomacy,* 99.

117. Robert Bonner, "Slavery, Confederate Diplomacy, and the Racialist Mission of Henry Hotze," *Civil War History* 51, no. 3 (2005):291–95. A useful selection of Hotze's writings are collected together in Lonnie A. Bennett, ed., *Henry Hotze, Confederate Propagandist: Selected Writings on Revolution, Recognition, and Race* (Tuscaloosa: University of Alabama Press, 2008).

118. Robert M. T. Hunter to Henry Hotze, November 11, 1861, *Official Records of the Union and Confederate Navies,* III:315.

119. Henry Hotze to Robert M. T. Hunter, February 1, 1862, Letter Book of C. S. A. Commercial Agency London, Papers of Henry Hotze, LoC; Henry Hotze to Judah P. Benjamin, August 4, 1862, *Official Records of the Union and Confederate Navies,* III:506.

120. Ibid.

121. Hotze to Benjamin, September 26, 1862, Hotze Papers, LoC.

122. Hotze to Benjamin, November 14, 1862, Hotze Papers, LoC.

123. Hotze to George Witt, September 10, 1864, Hotze Papers, LoC.

124. Wise, *Lifeline of the Confederacy,* contains an exhaustive appendix that details the ships involved in blockade running, and their success (231–328); Hughes, "Liverpool and the Confederate States," performs a similar breakdown on the firms involved in blockade running from Liverpool (305–6).

125. Blackett, *Divided Hearts,* 102.

126. Hotze to Benjamin, March 12, 1864, Hotze Papers, LoC.

127. Blackett, *Divided Hearts,* 99.

128. Ibid., 196.

129. "Meeting at Stalybridge on Intervention in America," *Bee-Hive,* October 4, 1862.

130. "Negro Emancipation—Great Meeting at Exeter Hall," *Bee-Hive,* January 31, 1863.

131. Charles Francis Adams to William Henry Seward, December 18, 1862, *FRUS,* I:18.

132. Raphael Semmes, *Memoirs of Service Afloat: During the War Between the States* (Baltimore: Kelly, Piet & Co., 1869), 348.

133. Blackett, *Divided Hearts,* 100.

134. Ibid., 68.

135. Goldwin Smith, *Letter to a Whig Member of the Southern Independence Association* (Boston: Ticknor and Fields, 1864), 35.

136. Blackett, *Divided Hearts,* 93.

137. Quoted in John Vincent, ed., *Disraeli, Derby and the Conservative Party: Journals and Memoirs of Edward Henry, Lord Stanley, 1848–69* (Hassocks, UK: Harvester Press, 1978), 179.

138. George M. Trevelyan, *The Life of John Bright* (London: Constable, 1913), 314.

139. February 19, 1862, CFAD.

140. John Vincent, *The Formation of the Liberal Party, 1857–1868* (London: Constable, 1966).

141. Peter Ghosh, "Gladstone and Peel," in *Politics and Culture in Victorian Britain: Essays in Memory of Colin Matthew,* ed. Peter Ghosh and Lawrence Goldman (Oxford: Oxford University Press, 2006), 46–73; Angus Hawkins, *Victorian Political Culture: "Habits of Heart and Mind"* (Oxford: Oxford University Press, 2015), 235; Robert Saunders, "Lord John Russell and Parliamentary Reform, 1848–67," *English Historical Review* 120, no. 489 (2005): 1289–1315.

142. Quoted in Saunders, "Lord John Russell," 1293. The "mountain" was the name given to a group of extreme Jacobins during the French revolution.

143. Eugenio F. Biagini, *Liberty, Retrenchment, and Reform: Popular Liberalism in the Age of Gladstone* (Cambridge, UK: Cambridge University Press, 1992), 67–84.

144. Margot Finn, *After Chartism: Class and Nation in English Reform Politics, 1848–1874* (Cambridge, UK: Cambridge University Press, 1993);

Doyle, *Cause of All Nations;* Campbell, *English Public Opinion,* 134–62; "Sovereignty and Secession," *Saturday Review,* December 27, 1862, 765–66.

145. *Household Words,* August 1856, 133.

146. "The Crisis of the American War," *Blackwood's Edinburgh Magazine,* November 1862, 636.

147. Richard Cobden to John Bright, October 9, 1862, in *The Letters of Richard Cobden, 1860-1865,* ed. Anthony Howe and Simon Morgan (Oxford: Oxford University Press, 2015), IV:331.

148. Richard Huzzey, *Freedom Burning: Anti-Slavery and Empire in Victorian Britain* (Ithaca, NY: Cornell University Press, 2016), 77–93.

149. William Schomberg Robert Kerr, *The Confederate Secession* (London: W. Blackwood and Sons, 1864), 101.

150. Judah P. Benjamin to James M. Mason, October 28, 1862, *Official Records of the Union and Confederate Navies,* III:581–82.

151. James Spence, *The American Union* (London: Richard Bentley, 1861), 131–32.

152. Hotze to Benjamin, August 27, 1863, *Official Records of the Union and Confederate Navies,* III:877.

153. *Richmond Examiner,* January 15, 1863.

154. "The foreign policy of the government," *Richmond Examiner,* December 5, 1863.

155. William Graham Swan, *Foreign Relations: Speech of Hon. W. G. Swan, of Tennessee, Delivered in the House of Representatives of the Confederate States, February 5, 1863* (Richmond, VA: Smith, Bailey & Co., 1863), 5.

CHAPTER FOUR. EMPIRE, PHILANTHROPY,
PUBLIC DIPLOMACY

1. Don H. Doyle, *The Cause of All Nations: An International History of the American Civil War* (New York: Basic Books, 2015); Richard J. M. Blackett, *Divided Hearts: Britain and the American Civil War* (Baton Rouge: Louisiana State University Press, 2001); Alfred Grant, *The American Civil War and the British Press* (Jefferson, NC: McFarland & Co., 2000); Martin Crawford, *The Anglo-American Crisis of the Mid-Nineteenth Century:* The Times *and America, 1850-1862* (Athens: University of Georgia Press, 1987); Duncan Andrew Campbell, *English Public Opinion and the American Civil War* (London: Boydell Press, 2003).

2. Doyle, *Cause of All Nations,* 7, emphases in original; Thomas Bender, *A Nation Among Nations: America's Place in World History* (New York: Hill & Wang, 2006), 116–81; "Interchange: Nationalism and Internationalism in the Era of the Civil War," *Journal of American History* 98, no. 2 (2011): 455–89.

3. Quoted in Harry C. Allen, "Civil War, Reconstruction, and Great Britain," in Harold M. Hyam, ed., *Heard Round the World: The Impact Abroad of the Civil War* (New York: Knopf, 1969), 65.

4. Don Doyle, *Nations Divided: America, Italy, and the Southern Question* (Athens: University of Georgia Press, 2002).

5. Richard Huzzey, "The British Empire and the Crises of the Americas in the 1860s," in *American Civil Wars: The United States, Latin America, Europe, and the Crisis of the 1860s*, ed, Don Doyle (Chapel Hill: University of North Carolina Press, 2017), 82–100.

6. For the development of this historiography see Antoinette Burton, ed., *After the Imperial Turn: Thinking with and Through the Nation* (Durham, NC: Duke University Press, 2003). See also Catherine Hall, *Civilising Subjects: Colony and Metropole in the English Imagination, 1830–1867* (Chicago: University of Chicago Press, 2002); Catherine Hall, Keith McClelland, and Jane Rendall, eds., *Defining the Victorian Nation: Class, Race, Gender, and the British Reform Act of 1867* (Cambridge, UK: Cambridge University Press, 2000). For the emergence of the British anti-slavery empire see Richard Huzzey, *Freedom Burning: Anti-Slavery and Empire in Victorian Britain* (Ithaca, NY: Cornell University Press, 2012).

7. "The American War in London," *Saturday Review,* August 2, 1862.

8. George Francis Train, *My Life in Many States and Foreign Lands* (New York: D. Appleton and Company, 1902), 94.

9. Jay Monaghan, *Diplomat in Carpet Slippers: Abraham Lincoln Deals with Foreign Affairs* (Indianapolis, IN: Charter Books, 1945), 105.

10. George Francis Train, *Train's Union Speeches. Delivered in England During the Present American War* (Philadelphia: T. B. Peterson & Brothers, 1862).

11. *London American,* July 3, 1861.

12. *London American,* July 10, 1861.

13. Train, *Train's Union Speeches,* 27.

14. *London American* [Supplement], June 19, 1861. A full account of the dinner's proceedings can also be found in Train, *Train's Union Speeches,* 38–45.

15. Ibid., 46–47.

16. Ibid., 21.

17. George Francis Train, *The Downfall of England by George Francis Train* (Philadelphia: T. B. Peterson & Brothers, 1862), 20. Emphasis in original.

18. Ibid., 21. Emphasis in original.

19. Ibid., 26.

20. *London American,* 19 June 1861.

21. George Francis Train, *Train's Speech to the Fenians* (Philadelphia: T. B. Peterson & Brothers, 1865), 31.

22. Ibid., 34.

23. George Francis Train, *Spread-Eagleism* (New York: Derby & Jackson, 1860), 39.

24. *London American,* April 2, 1862.

25. Train, *Train's Union Speeches,* 29.

26. March 28, 1861, *The Journal of Benjamin Moran, 1857–1865,* ed. Sarah Agnes Wallace and Frances Elma Gillespie (Chicago: University of Chicago Press, 1947), II:793; see also May 15, 1862, Ibid., I:1005.

27. "The American War in London," *The Saturday Review,* August 2, 1862.

28. Seward quoted in Jay Sexton, *Debtor Diplomacy: Finance and Foreign Relations in the Civil War Era* (Oxford: Oxford University Press, 2005), 94.

29. Train, *Downfall of England*, 21.

30. For more detail on the pamphlets published by Hotze see Robert Bonner, "Slavery, Confederate Diplomacy, and the Racialist Mission of Henry Hotze," *Civil War History* 51, no. 3 (2005): 307–9.

31. Henry Hotze to Judah P. Benjamin, December 31, 1864, Hotze Papers, LoC.

32. "Our name," *Index*, May 1, 1862.

33. "A Historical Parallel," *Index*, June 5, 1862.

34. Free trade was central to many slaveholders' view of the South's centrality to world affairs; see Matthew Karp, *This Vast Southern Empire: Slaveholders at the Helm of American Foreign Policy* (Cambridge, MA: Harvard University Press, 2016); Robert E. May, "The Irony of Confederate Diplomacy: Visions of Empire, the Monroe Doctrine, and the Quest for Nationhood," *Journal of Southern History* 83, no. 1 (2017): 69–106.

35. "The South as a Literary Market," *Index*, June 5, 1862.

36. "Federal and Confederate Finances," *Index*, August 21, 1862. See also "Federal and Confederate Resources," *Index*, August 28, 1862.

37. "Southern feeling towards England," *Index*, May 15, 1862.

38. James Williams, *The South Vindicated* (London: Longman, Green, Longman, Roberts & Green, 1862), 215–16.

39. Matthew Karp, "King Cotton, Emperor Slavery: Antebellum Slaveholders and the World Economy," in *The Civil War as Global Conflict: Transnational Meanings of the American Civil War*, ed. David T. Gleeson and Simon Lewis (Columbia: University of South Carolina Press, 2014), 37–55.

40. "The Cotton Famine," *Index*, July 3, 1862; "Continued insults to the British flag," *Index*, May 22, 1862.

41. "The Supply of American Cotton," *Index*, May 29, 1862.

42. "Cotton still King," *Index*, December 10, 1863.

43. "The cotton trade," *Index*, October 28, 1863.

44. Ibid.

45. "The South in the Social Science Congress," *Index*, June 12, 1862. See also "The Productiveness of the South," *Index*, June 12, 1862.

46. "A Word on the Negro," *Index*, February 12, 1863.

47. Karp, *This Vast Southern Empire*, 169. See also Anthony E. Kaye, "The Second Slavery: Modernity in the Nineteenth Century South and the Atlantic World," *Journal of Southern History* 75, no. 3 (2009): 627–50.

48. "Southern Feeling Towards England," *Index*, May 15, 1862. See also "The advocacy of the Southern Cause," *Index*, November 26, 1863. Paul Quigley makes a powerful case that Southern nationalism was consistently framed along European lines in his excellent study of Confederate nationalism, *Shifting Grounds: Nationalism and the American South, 1848–1865* (Oxford: Oxford University Press, 2012). For more on Confederate invocation of transatlantic racial affinity, see Richie Devon Watson, *Normans and Saxons: Southern Race Mythology and the Intellectual History of the American Civil War* (Baton Rouge: Louisiana State University Press, 2008); Robert Bonner, "Roundheaded Cavaliers? The Context and Limits of a Confederate Racial Project," *Civil War History* 48, no. 1 (2002): 34–59; Hugh Dubrulle, "'We Are Threatened with . . .

Anarchy and Ruin': Fear of Americanization and the Emergence of an Anglo-Saxon Confederacy in England during the American Civil War," *Albion* 33, no. 4 (2001): 583–613.

49. "The Supply of American Cotton," May 29, 1862.

50. For an excellent summary of the extent and diversity of that knowledge see Huzzey, *Freedom Burning*, 21–40; Howard Jones, *Union in Peril: The Crisis over British Intervention in the Civil War* (Chapel Hill: University of North Carolina Press, 1992), 33.

51. Williams, *South Vindicated*, 15, emphasis in original; Yonatan Eyal, "A Romantic Realist: George Nicholas Sanders and the Dilemmas of Southern International Engagement," *Journal of Southern History* 78, no. 1 (2012): 107–30.

52. Clare Anderson, "After Emancipation: Empires and Imperial Formations," in *Emancipation and the Remaking of the British Imperial World*, ed. Catherine Hall, Nicholas Draper, and Keith McClelland (Manchester, UK: Manchester University Press, 2014), 117.

53. Huzzey, "Manifest Dominion," 85.

54. Quoted in Ousmane K. Power-Greene, *Against Wind and Tide: the African-American Struggle Against the Colonization Movement* (New York: New York University Press, 2014), 170.

55. "West India Emancipation Celebration in Leeds, England," *Douglass' Monthly*, October 1861.

56. "The American Crisis and Slavery," *Birmingham Gazette*, December 14, 1861; Richard J. M. Blackett, *Beating Against the Barriers: Biographical Essays in Nineteenth-Century Afro-History* (Baton Rouge: Louisiana State University Press, 1986), 322.

57. Blackett, *Beating Against the Barriers*, 150–53, 107–20, 151–55, 193–97, 314–15, 319–23; Manisha Sinha, *The Slave's Cause: A History of Abolition* (New Haven: Yale University Press, 2016), 371–80, 574–80. On free produce see Carol Faulkner, "The Root of the Evil: Free Produce and Radical Antislavery, 1820–1860," *Journal of the Early Republic* 27, no. 3 (2007): 377–405.

58. Hotze to Benjamin, September 26, 1863, Hotze Papers, LoC.

59. See, for example, *Punch*, October 18, 1862; *The Times*, January 16, 1863.

60. "A Word for the Negro," *Index*, February 12, 1863; see also "Abolitionism and the Negro," *Index*, October 20, 1864.

61. "The Negro's Place in Nature," *Index*, December 10, 1863.

62. "The Negro in the Southern Armies," *Index*, November 10, 1864.

63. Bonner, "Racialist Mission of Henry Hotze," 288–316.

64. Henry Hotze to Judah P. Benjamin, August 27, 1863, *Official Records of the Union and Confederate Navies in the War of the Rebellion* (Washington, DC: Government Printing Office, 1894–1922), II:878.

65. Henry Hotze to Judah P. Benjamin, September 17, 1864, Ibid., II.1207. Bledsoe's activities are recounted in Terry A. Barnhart, *Alfred Taylor Bledsoe: Defender of the Old South and Architect of the Lost Cause* (Baton Rouge: Louisiana State University Press, 2011).

66. George McHenry, *The African Race in America, North and South: Being a Correspondence on that Subject Between two Pennsylvanians* (London:

Bradbury and Evans, 1861), 9. Among McHenry's publications are *Visits to Slave-Ships* (London: British and Foreign Anti-Slavery Society, 1862); *A Familiar Epistle to Robert J. Walker* (London: Saunders, Otley, and Co., 1863); and *The Southern Confederacy and the African Slave Trade* (Dublin: McGlashan & Gill, 1863). For a brief overview of his career see Charles Francis Adams, "James McHenry on the Cotton Crisis, 1865," *Proceedings of the Massachusetts Historical Society* 47 (1914): 279–87.

67. McHenry, *African Race in America*, 9–10.

68. George McHenry, *The Cotton Trade: Its Bearing Upon the Prosperity of Great Britain and Commerce of the American Republics* (London: Saunders, Otley and Co., 1863), 255–56.

69. Huzzey, *Freedom Burning*, 177–86.

70. Hugh Dubrulle, "'If it is still impossible . . . to advocate slavery . . . . It has . . . become a habit persistently to write down freedom': Britain, the Civil War, and Race," in *The American Civil War as Global Conflict: Transnational Meanings of the American Civil War*, ed. David T. Gleason and Simon Lewis (Columbia: University of South Carolina Press, 2014), 56–85.

71. "Dr. Hunt on the Negro's Place in Nature," *Index*, November 26, 1863.

72. Bonner, *Mastering America*, 302.

73. George Francis Train, *The Facts: Or, At Whose Door Does the Sin (?) Lie? Who Profits by Slave Labor? Who Initiated the Slave Trade? What Have the Philanthropist Done? These Questions Answered* (New York: R. M. DeWitt, 1860), 6.

74. Hotze to Benjamin, August 27, 1863, in *Official Records of the Union and Confederate Navies*, III:1117. See also "The Distinctions of Race," *Index*, October 23, 1862.

75. *London American*, March 19, 1862; Train, *Union Speeches*, 66.

76. Ibid., 69. Emphasis in original. The importance Train attached to his pseudo-scientific race-based gradualism can be garnered from the fact that he chose to republish this speech in the United States in a separate pamphlet titled *Train's Speeches in England on Slavery and Emancipation* (Philadelphia: T. B. Peterson and Brothers, 1862). Train was also the author of *Young America on Slavery* (Liverpool: Griffin McGhie, 1859).

77. Samuel Roberts Wells, *How To Read Character: A New Illustrated Hand-Book of Phrenology and Physiognomy for Students and Examiners* (New York: Fowler and Wells, 1869), explored the cranial differences between "Caucasians" and "Negros"; see vii, 31, 33, 63.

78. Hotze to Benjamin, May 7, 1864, in *Official Records of the Union and Confederate Navies*, III:878.

79. Reginald Horsman, *Race and Manifest Destiny: The Origins of American Racial Anglo-Saxonism* (Cambridge, MA: Harvard University Press, 1981), 157; Bonner, "Racialist Mission of Henry Hotze," 315.

80. The idea of transnational approaches "thickening" the context of US history was put forward in Tom Bender's clarion call to internationalize the study of the US past; see Thomas Bender, "Introduction: Historians, Nation, and the Plenitude of Narratives," in *Rethinking American History in a Global Age*, ed. Thomas Bender (Berkeley: University of California Press, 2002), 12.

81. Robert Bremner, *The Public Good: Philanthropy and Welfare in the Civil War Era* (New York: Knopf, 1980); J. Matthew Gallman, "Voluntarism in Wartime: Philadelphia's Great Central Fair," in *Toward a Social History of the Civil War: Exploratory Essays,* ed. Maris A. Vinovskis (Cambridge, UK: Cambridge University Press, 1990), 93–116.

82. Judith Ann Giesberg, *Civil War Sisterhood: The U.S. Sanitary Commission and Women's Politics in Transition* (Boston: Northeastern University Press, 2000).

83. John Duffy, *The Sanitarians: A History of American Public Health* (Urbana: University of Illinois Press, 1997); John Harley Warner, *Against the Spirit of the System: The French Impulse in Nineteenth-Century Medicine* (Baltimore: Johns Hopkins University Press, 2003).

84. Jane E. Schultz, "Nurse as Icon: Florence Nightingale's Impact on Women in the American Civil War," in Gleeson and Lewis, eds., *Civil War as Global Conflict,* 235–252.

85. Margaret Humphreys, *Marrow of Tragedy: The Health Crisis of the American Civil War* (Baltimore: Johns Hopkins University Press, 2013), 9, 46, 63.

86. Lawrence Goldman, "Exceptionalism and Internationalism: The Origins of American Social Science Reconsidered," *Journal of Historical Sociology* 11, no. 1 (1998): 1–36.

87. Edmund Crisp Fisher, *The English Branch of the United States Sanitary Commission. Motive of its Establishment and Results of Its Work* (London: William Ridgway, 1865), 4; *Report of Charles S.P. Bowles upon the International Congress of Geneva Convened at Geneva, 8 August 1864* (London: R. Clay, Son, and Taylor, 1864); Stephen Tuffnell, "Expatriate Foreign Relations: Britain's American Community and Transnational Approaches to the U.S. Civil War," *Diplomatic History* 40, no. 3 (2016): 635–63.

88. February 20, 1864, Journal of E.C. Fisher, Folder 1, Box 2, EBA.

89. Ibid.

90. Fisher, *English Branch,* 5; William Maxwell, *Lincoln's Fifth Wheel: The Political History of the United States Sanitary Commission* (New York: Longman, Green & Co., 1956), 228–29.

91. Fisher, *English Branch,* 17.

92. March 3, 1864, Journal of E.C. Fisher, Folder 1, Box 2, EBA.

93. Benjamin Moran to Thomas H. Dudley, October 4, 1864, Box 22, Thomas Haines Dudley Papers, HuL.

94. September 20, 1864, Journal of E.C. Fisher, Folder 1, Box 2, EBA.

95. *Penny Illustrated Newspaper,* November 5, 1864.

96. September 2, 1864, *Journal of Benjamin Moran,* II:1320.

97. Ezekiel B. Elliot to Edmund Fisher, October 5, 1864, Folder 2, Box 1, EBA. Emphasis in original.

98. "Appeal of the United States Sanitary Commission to Americans at Home and Abroad," Journal of E.C. Fisher, EBA.

99. Valerie H. Ziegler, *The Advocates of Peace in Antebellum America* (Bloomington: Indiana University Press, 1992), 150.

100. Thomas Bailey Potter to Fisher, September 13, 1864, Folder 1, Box 1, EBA.

101. Fisher to Henry Bellows, December 31, 1864, Letter Press Books, EBA.

102. Fisher to J. Foster Jenkins, December 31, 1864, Letter Press Books, EBA.

103. Jonathan Woods to Fisher, September 9, 1864, Folder 1, Box 1, EBA.

104. February 18, 1865, *Journal of Benjamin Moran,* II:1380.

105. Jonathan Woods to Fisher, April 4, 1865, Folder 11, Box 1, EBA.

106. Elliott also lectured at the International Statistical Congress in Berlin in late 1863, subsequently published in pamphlet form as *Military Statistics of the United States of America* (Berlin, 1863) and distributed to foreign dignitaries in London, Europe, and as far away as St. Petersburg. See Frances M. Clarke, *War Stories: Suffering and Sacrifice in the Civil War North* (Chicago: University of Chicago Press, 2011), 134.

107. Edmund Crisp Fisher, *Military Discipline and Volunteer Philanthropy: A Paper Read before the Social Science Congress Held in the City of York, September 1864* (London: William Ridgway, 1864); Clarke, *War Stories,* 135.

108. Fisher, *English Branch,* 8.

109. Fisher to Jenkins, February 26, 1865, Letter Press Books, EBA. Emphasis in original.

110. *The Index,* December 3, 1863, December 31, 1863, December 22, 1864; see also James M. Mason to A. Coolidge, January 25, 1865, in *The Public Life and Diplomatic Correspondence of James M. Mason, with Some Personal History,* ed. Virginia Mason (New York: Neale, 1906), 532–39; Benjamin to Hotze, March 30, 1863, *Official Records of the Union and Confederate Navies,* II:732.

111. Blackett, *Divided Hearts,* 161.

112. Ibid., 161–62.

113. *The Times,* October 7, 1864. See also *Index,* October 20 & 27, 1864.

114. Quoted in Amanda Foreman, *World on Fire: An Epic History of Two Nations Divided* (London: Allen Lane, 2010), 595.

115. *Liverpool Mercury,* October 19 & 20, 1864; *Standard,* October 19, 1864.

116. Blackett, *Divided Hearts,* 184–85.

117. *Leeds Mercury,* October 28, 1864; *Penny Illustrated Newspaper,* November 5, 1864. See also *Standard,* February 8, 1865.

118. The best accounts are Christine Bolt, *The Anti-Slavery Movement and Reconstruction: A Study in Anglo-American Co-Operation, 1833–77* (London: Oxford University Press, 1969), and Clare Midgley, *Women Against Slavery: The British Campaigns, 1700–1870* (London: Routledge, 1992), 185–190.

119. Bolt, *Anti-Slavery Movement and Reconstruction,* 61.

120. John Sella Martin to Michale E. Strieby, June 4, 1865, ProQuest Black Abolitionist Papers Online.

121. "The Emancipated Slaves of America," *Liberator,* November 3, 1865.

122. Midgley, *Women Against Slavery,* 190; Bolt, *Anti-Slavery Movement and Reconstruction,* 61.

123. Blackett, *Beating Against the Barriers,* 226.

124. James E. Smith (consul, Dundee) to Thomas Dudley, February 14, 1865, Box 24, Thomas Haines Dudley Papers, HuL; Sanitary Commission, *Narrative of Privations and Sufferings of United States Officers and Soldiers*

While Prisoner of War in the Hands of the Rebel Armies (Philadelphia: King & Baird, 1864).

125. Dudley to Fisher, December 1, 1864, Folder 6, Box 1, EBA.

126. Dudley to Fisher, December 5, 1864, Journal of E. C. Fisher, EBA.

127. Ibid. Emphasis in original. Union and Confederate prison camps featured in the graphic imagery of the war too, one of the primary ways in which British readers received news of the conflict; see *Illustrated London News,* March 29, 1862 & March 18, 1865.

128. Dudley to Fisher, February 17, 1865; Fisher to Jenkins, February 26, 1865, Letter Press Books, EBA.

129. Fisher to Jenkins, March 11, 1865, Letter Press Books, EBA; October 19, 1864, Journal of E. C. Fisher, EBA.

130. May 12, 1865, Journal of E. C. Fisher, EBA.

131. "Treatment of Prisoners in the South," *Glasgow Herald,* September 10, 1864; "Prisoners in the South," *Leeds Mercury,* November 5, 1864; "Horrors of Prison Life in the South," *Glasgow Herald,* November 28, 1864; "The Treatment of War Prisoners in America," *Daily News,* December 17, 1864; "Confederate Cruelties to Federal Prisoners," *Leeds Mercury* December 14, 1864; "The Treatment of War Prisoners in America," *Daily News,* December 27, 1864; "Federal Prisoners in the Confederate States," *Birmingham Daily Post,* January 28, 1865.

132. Fisher, *English Branch,* 30.

133. S. Dunne to Edmund Fisher, February 21, 1865, Folder 10, Box 1, EBA.

134. Fisher, *English Branch,* 8.

135. "Circular to all Known Americans in Britain," September 20, 1864, Journal of E. C. Fisher, EBA.

136. *The Times,* July 11, 1862.

137. George Peabody to John P. Kennedy, enclosed in Kennedy to Strong, May 30, 1864, Box 31, New York Standing Committee Correspondence, USSC.

138. Merle Curti, *American Philanthropy Abroad: a History* (New Brunswick, NJ: Rutgers University Press, 1963), 179–182.

139. William P. Bowles to J. Foster Jenkins, April 19, 1864, Box 30, New York Standing Committee Correspondence, USSC.

140. Detailed lists of all contributors, from which these details were compiled, can be found in Accounts and Vouchers Series (hereafter: Accounts), Folders 2–4, Box 16, USSC.

141. Henry Darwin Rogers to Thomas Dudley, June 15, 1864, Box 19, Thomas Haines Dudley Papers, HuL.

142. Summary of Receipts, Folder 1, Box 15, Accounts, USSC.

143. Charles Lush Wilson to Dudley, January 8, 1864, Box 17; Fisher to Dudley, October 27, 1864, Box 22, Dudley Papers, HuL; Dudley to Henry Bellows, April 15, 19 & 22, 1865, Box 44, Folder 9, New York Standing Committee Correspondence, USSC.

144. Huzzey, *Freedom Burning,* 36–37; Frank Prochaska, "Charity Bazaars in Nineteenth Century England," *Journal of British Studies* 16, no. 2 (1977): 62–84.

145. Edward Middelton to Thomas Dudley, April 2, 1864, Box 18, Thomas Haines Dudley Papers, HuL; Thomas Dudley to Henry Bellows, 25 April 1865,

Folder 10, Box 44, New York Standing Committee Correspondence, USSC. See also Philip S. Justice to Dudley, May 11, 1864 & John H. Eastcourt to Thomas Dudley, May 13, 1864, Box 19, Thomas Haines Dudley Papers, HuL.

146. Dudley to Bellows, May 2, 1865, Folder 11, Box 44, New York Standing Committee Correspondence, USSC; *New York Times,* November 8, 1864.

147. Treasurer's Accounts, Volume 3, International Relief Committee Records, NYHS. See also John A. Carpenter, "The New York International Relief Committee: A Chapter in the Diplomatic History of the Civil War," *New York Historical Society Quarterly* 56 (1972): 239–52.

148. Daniel James to William E. Dodge, February 7, 1863, Box 16, Phelps Dodge & Co. Records, NYPL; Daniel James, Stephen Guion, and Benjamin Babcock to International Relief Committee, 14 August 1863, Volume 1, International Relief Committee Records, NYHS. Guion's hand was undoubtedly behind the ACC's gift of £1,000, in November 1862 to help relieve the impoverished textile workers in Manchester; see W.O. Henderson, "The American Chamber of Commerce for the Port of Liverpool," *Transactions of the Historic Society of Lancashire and Cheshire* 85 (1933), 10.

149. Daniel James to William E. Dodge, February 14, 1863, Box 16, Phelps Dodge & Co. Records, NYPL.

150. Treasurer's Accounts, Volume 3, International Relief Committee Records, NYHS. A further $30,000 was raised by the Produce Exchange Committee and $62,000 by a Philadelphia Committee.

151. *Report of the American International Relief Committee, for the Suffering Operatives of Great Britain, 1862-'63* (New York: C.A. Alvord, 1864), 8.

152. *Freedmen's-Aid Reporter,* June 1866, 17.

153. Andrew Porter, "Trusteeship, Anti-slavery, and Humanitarianism," in *The Oxford History of the British Empire Volume 3: The Nineteenth Century,* ed. Andrew Porter (Oxford: Oxford University Press. 1991), 198–221; David Kennedy, *The Dark Side of Virtue: Reassessing International Humanitarianism* (Princeton, NJ: Princeton University Press, 2004); Alan Lester and Fae Dussart, *Colonization and the Origins of Humanitarian Governance: Protecting Aborigines Across the Nineteenth-Century British Empire* (Cambridge, UK: Cambridge University Press, 2014).

CHAPTER FIVE. AMERICAN INVASIONS

1. "Americans in Europe," *Saturday Review,* August 2, 1873, 140.

2. Hiram Fuller, *Grand Transformation Scenes in the United States, or, Glimpses of Home After Thirteen Years Abroad* (New York: G.W. Carleton & Co., 1875), 7.

3. Carlos Martyn, "Un-American Tendencies," *Arena,* September 1891, 432.

4. "Indications of a Closer Intercourse between England and America," *Anglo-American Times,* September 15, 1866.

5. Frederick MacKenzie, *The American Invaders* (London: Grant Richards, 1902), 9.

6. *London American,* August 9, 1895.

7. "American Diplomacy," *Atlantic Monthly,* September 1868, 348–49; "Republicans Abroad," *Harper's Bazaar,* January 13, 1872, 18; Leslie Butler, *Critical Americans: Victorian Intellectuals and Transatlantic Liberal Reform* (Chapel Hill: University of North Carolina Press, 2007); Frank Ninkovich, *Global Dawn: The Cultural Foundations of American Internationalism, 1865–1890* (Cambridge, MA: Harvard University Press, 2009), 72–76.

8. "American Diplomacy," *Atlantic Monthly,* September 1868, 349–50.

9. "Our Diplomatists," *The Nation,* March 28, 1878, 209.

10. Kristin Hoganson, *Fighting for American Manhood: How Gender Politics Provoked the Spanish-American and Philippine-American Wars* (New Haven, CT: Yale University Press, 1998), 21–22.

11. "Lady Travellers," *The Albion,* June 14, 1873, 378.

12. John Sherwood, "Why do American Girls Wish to Marry Abroad?," *Harper's Bazaar,* December 13, 1900, 982.

13. John Darwin, *The Empire Project: the Rise and Fall of the British World-System, 1830–1970* (Cambridge, UK: Cambridge University Press, 2009), 117.

14. Dolores Greenberg, "Yankee Financiers and the Establishment of Trans-Atlantic Partnerships: A Re-Examination," *Business History* 16, no. 1 (1974), 28, 30.

15. Lance E. Davis and Robert E. Gallman, *Evolving Financial Markets and International Capital Flows: Britain, the Americas, and Australia, 1865–1914* (Cambridge, UK: Cambridge University Press, 2001), 324.

16. Gary Magee and Andrew S. Thompson, *Empire and Globalisation: Networks of People, Goods, and Capital in the British World* (Cambridge, UK: Cambridge University Press, 2010), 173.

17. Edward P. Crapol, *America for the Americans: Economic Nationalism and Anglophobia in the Late Nineteenth Century* (Westport, CT: Greenwood Press, 1973).

18. Henry Carey, *The Way to Outdo England Without Fighting Her* (Philadelphia: H. C. Baird, 1865), 49.

19. Ibid., 68, 108. Emphasis in original.

20. A. G. Hopkins, *American Empire: A Global History* (Princeton, NJ: Princeton University Press, 2017), 309.

21. Constance Smedley, "The Expatriates. III. The American Colony in London," *Bookman,* July 1907, 484.

22. "Americans Abroad," *Harper's Bazaar,* May 16, 1868, 458.

23. *The Morning Post,* July 5, 1895.

24. "The Tide of Travel from America," *Anglo-American Times,* June 2, 1866.

25. Henry Morford, *Over-Sea; or, England, France and Scotland as Seen by a Live American* (New York: Hilton & Company, 1867), 65. See also Parsons Brainerd Cogswell, *Glints from Over the Water* (Concord, NH: Republican Press Association, 1880), 2.

26. John Forney, *Letters from Europe* (Philadelphia: Peterson, 1867), 36–37. See also Noble L. Prentis, *A Kansan Abroad* (Topeka, KS: Martin, 1878), 15; Morford, *Over-Sea,* 71.

27. Prentis, *Kansan Abroad,* 13–14.

28. "Liverpool: Port, Docks and City," *Illustrated London News,* May 15, 1886.

29. Foster Rhea Dulles, *Americans Abroad: Two Centuries of European Travel* (Ann Arbor: University of Michigan Press, 1964), 102–5, and Christopher Endy, "Travel and World Power: Americans in Europe, 1890–1917," *Diplomatic History* 22, no. 4 (1998): 567.

30. Nancy Ritchie-Noakes, *Liverpool's Historic Waterfront: The World's First Mercantile Dock System* (London: HM Stationary Office, 1984), 12–13.

31. Alison Lockwood, *Passionate Pilgrims: the American Traveler in Great Britain, 1800–1904* (London: Cornwall Books, 1981), 297; Julie Husband and Jim O'Loughlin, *Daily Life in the Industrial United States, 1870–1900* (Westport, CT: Greenwood Press, 2004), 2.

32. Sarah Palmer, "Ports," in *Cambridge Urban History of Britain,* ed. Peter Clark and D. M. Palliser (Cambridge, UK: Cambridge University Press, 2000), III:142.

33. Graeme J. Milne, *Trade and Traders in Mid-Victorian Liverpool: Mercantile Business and the Making of a World Port* (Liverpool, UK: Liverpool University Press, 2000), 75.

34. Joel Cook, *A Holiday Tour in Europe* (Philadelphia: David McKay, 1889), 25.

35. William H. Rideing, "The Ferry Across the Atlantic," *Frank Leslie's Popular Monthly,* June 1880, 3.

36. Ella W. Thompson, *Beaten Paths; or, A Woman's Vacation* (Boston: Lee and Shepard, 1874), 11.

37. Endy, "Travel and World Power," 567. Enterprising Britons began publishing seasonal travel guides for American tourists; see, for example, Frank C. Higgins, *America Abroad. A Handbook for the American Traveller* (London: E. Forster Groom, 1891).

38. Curtis Guild, *Britons and Muscovites, or Traits of Two Empires* (Boston: Lee & Shepherd, 1888), 1.

39. James Belich, *Replenishing the Earth: The Settler Revolution and the Rise of the Anglo-American World, 1783–1939* (Oxford: Oxford University Press, 2009), 449.

40. Ritchie-Noakes, *Liverpool's Historic Waterfront,* 7.

41. Morford, *Over-Sea,* 62.

42. For Liverpool as a diasporic city, see John Herson, "'Stirring Spectacles of Cosmopolitan Animation': Liverpool as a Diasporic City, 1825–1913," in *The Empire in One City? Liverpool's Inconvenient Imperial Past,* ed. Sheryllynne Haggerty, Anthony Webster, and Nicholas J. White (Manchester, UK: Manchester University Press, 2008), 55–78.

43. "Americans in Liverpool," *Liverpool Critic,* January 13, 1877.

44. Cook, *Holiday Tour,* 26.

45. Milne, *Trade and Traders,* 36.

46. "The Success of Anglo-American Telegraphy," *Anglo-American Times,* July 28, 1866.

47. "The Anglo-American Telegraph," *Anglo-American Times*, August 4, 1866; Simone M. Müller and Heidi J. S. Tworek, "'The telegraph and the bank': on the Interdependence of Global Communications and Capitalism," *Journal of Global History* 10, no. 2 (2015): 259–83.

48. Alexander Nabach, "'Poisoned at the Source'? Telegraphic New Services and Big Business in the Nineteenth Century," *Business History Review* 77, no. 4 (2003): 577–610; Julian Roche, *The International Cotton Trade* (Cambridge, UK: Woodhead Publishing, 1994), 10; on prices see Müller and Tworek, "'The telegraph and the bank,'" 275.

49. Roland Wenzlhuemer, *Connecting the Nineteenth-Century World: The Telegraph and Globalization* (Cambridge, UK: Cambridge University Press, 2013), 132.

50. The imaginations of nineteenth-century observers were fired by its impact on time and space; the best treatment is Simone M. Müller, *Wiring the World: the Social and Cultural Creation of Global Telegraph Networks* (New York: Columbia University Press, 2016), 83–118.

51. "Fourth of July in Liverpool," *Anglo-American Times*, July 7, 1866.

52. Thompson, *Beaten Paths*, 13.

53. James B. Converse, *A Summer Vacation: Sketches and Thoughts Abroad in the Summer of 1877* (Louisville, KY: Converse & Co., 1878), 76.

54. Elizabeth Blackwell to Henry Brown Blackwell, June 1, 1872, Reel 50, Henry Brown Blackwell Papers, LoC.

55. Edward P. Thwing, *Outdoor Life in Europe, or, Sketches of Seven Summers Abroad* (New York: Hurst & Co., 1888), 63.

56. *Anglo-American Times*, August 25, 1866.

57. William Pembroke Fetridge, *The American Traveller's Guide: Harper's Hand-book for Travellers in Europe*, 12th Edn. (New York: Harper's, 1873), 64.

58. Prentis, *Kansan Abroad*, 49; William Augustus Croffut, *A Midsummer Lark* (New York: H. Holt and Company, 1883), 78.

59. Lynda Nead, *Victorian Babylon: People, Streets, and Images in Nineteenth-Century London* (New Haven, CT: Yale University Press, 2000), 14.

60. Rudolph Williams, *Europe from May to December* (Chicago: Weeks, 1895), 61.

61. Theron C. Crawford, *English Life* (New York: Lovell, 1889), 167.

62. July 20, 1870, vol. 26, BMJ. See also "Americans in Europe," *Saturday Review*, August 2, 1873.

63. June 19, 1861, vol. 29; August 29, 1872, vol. 36, BMJ.

64. August 29, 1872, vol. 36, BMJ.

65. "Americans in Europe," *Saturday Review*, April 1, 1882.

66. "Fair Americans Abroad," *London American*, November 1, 1895.

67. Sydney Brooks, "Through American England," *Harper's Weekly*, July 4, 1903, 1114. See also Fred Gilbert Blakeslee, "Hints on London for American Tourists," *Overland Monthly*, March 1907, 221–25.

68. See Kenneth O. Morgan, "The Future at Work: Anglo-American Progressivism, 1890–1917," in *Contrast and Connection: Bicentennial Essays in*

Anglo-American History, ed. Harry C. Allen and Roger Thompson (London: G. Bell & Sons, 1976), 245–71.

69. For an excellent overview see Ian Tyrrell, *Reforming the World: The Creation of America's Moral Empire* (Princeton, NJ: Princeton University Press, 2010), 19–25.

70. Alfred Maurice Low, "Foreign Affairs," *Forum,* October 1906, 176.

71. Daniel T. Rodgers, *Atlantic Crossings: Social Politics in a Progressive Age* (Cambridge, MA: Harvard University Press, 1998), 4.

72. Booker T. Washington to the Editor of the Indianapolis *Freeman,* July 15, 1899, in *Booker T. Washington Papers,* ed. Louis R. Harlan and Raymond Smock (Urbana: University of Illinois Press, 1972–1985), 5:154.

73. Marilyn Lake and Henry Reynolds, *Drawing the Global Colour Line: White Men's Countries and the International Challenge of Racial Equality* (Cambridge, UK: Cambridge University Press, 2008), 245.

74. Guild, *Britons and Muscovites,* 2.

75. *London American,* March 27, 1896.

76. *London American,* April 10, 1896; "In the reading room at the bankers," *Harper's Weekly,* March 15, 1890.

77. The *Times* was founded in 1865, the *Register* in 1868.

78. On Cooke's London branch see Ellis Paxson Oberholtzer, *Jay Cooke: Financier of the Civil War* (Philadelphia: George W. Jacobs, 1907), II:206–9.

79. *London American,* July 26, 1895.

80. Richard H. Heindel, *The American Impact on Great Britain, 1898–1914: A Study of the United States in World History* (Philadelphia, 1940), 16; *London American,* June 21, 1895.

81. Henry Adams to Henry Cabot Lodge, July 9, 1880, in *Letters of Henry Adams,* ed. Chauncey Worthington Ford (Boston: Houghton, Mifflin, 1930), I:325.

82. Ehrman Syme Nadal, *Notes of a Professional Exile* (New York: Century, 1895); William J. Hoppin to Anna Hoppin, November 22, 1877; Hoppin to Sallie and Hattie Hoppin, November 24, 1877, *Journal of a Residence in London* Vol. II, Papers of William J. Hoppin, HL.

83. July 4, 1873, vol. 35; June 19, 1874, vol. 39; November 29, 1865, January 5, 1866, February 14, 1866, vol. 16; January 15, 1868, vol. 19; January 18, 1870, vol. 24; September 18 and 23, 1872, vol. 33, BMJ; "Destitute Americans in England," *Anglo-American Times,* May 26, 1866; July 24, 1876, Minute Book of William J. Hoppin; Hoppin to Anna Hoppin, November 20, 1876, *Journal of Residence* in London Vol. I, Papers of William J. Hoppin, HL.

84. "Indications of a Closer Intercourse between England and America," *Anglo-American Times,* September 15, 1866.

85. "European Travel," *Scribner's Monthly,* September 1879, 783.

86. "Wasting Money Abroad: The Growth of American Colonies in Europe and the Evils of American Emigration," *Michigan Farmer,* June 27, 1887. See also "Americans Abroad," *Lippincott's,* October 1880, 473; Ehrman Syme Nadal, *Impressions of London Social Life* (New York: Scribner, Armstrong & Company, 1875), 191–92.

87. "What is an American?," *Atlantic Monthly,* May 1875, 565. Emphasis in original.

88. "An American Invasion of Europe," *Anglo-American Times,* July 7, 1866.

89. "Denationalized Americans," *Harper's Bazaar,* August 1, 1885, 490.

90. Carlos Martyn, "Un-American Tendencies," *Arena,* September 1891, 437.

91. Margherita Arlina Hamm, "Women as Travelers. The American Woman in Action—VIII," *Frank Leslie's Popular Monthly,* June 1899, 13.

92. Jane S. Gabin, *American Women in Gilded Age London: Expatriates Rediscovered* (Gainesville: University Press of Florida, 2006).

93. "Seeing Europe on $200," *Ladies' Home Journal,* June 1887; A. R. Ramsey, "How to go Abroad," *Ladies' Home Journal,* May and June 1889; "How we went Abroad," *Ladies' Home Journal,* August 1889; H. Mott, "The Art of Travelling Abroad," *Ladies' Home Journal,* May 1895; E. I. Stevenson, "Tips of Travel," *Harper's Bazaar,* July, August, and September 1899; "The Secret of Profitable Travel," *Ladies' Home Journal,* February 1900, 16.

94. Kristin L. Hoganson, *Consumer's Imperium: The Global Production of American Domesticity* (Chapel Hill: University of North Carolina Press, 2007), especially chapter 1.

95. L. H. Hooper, "American Women Abroad," *The Galaxy,* June 1876, 818.

96. M. E. W. Sherwood, "American Girls in Europe," *North American Review* 150 (June 1890), 687–88.

97. Sherwood, "American Girls in Europe," 686–87; "American Women Abroad," *Washington Post,* March 20, 1903. See also Mildred Stapley, "Is Paris Wise for the Average American Girl?," *Ladies' Home Journal* 23 (April 1906), 16–17; Hooper, "American Women Abroad," 820.

98. A. Gore, "Americans Abroad," *Lippincott's,* October 28, 1880, 31; Nadal, *Impressions,* 110.

99. Gore, "Americans Abroad," 31.

100. "Denationalized Americans," *Harper's Bazaar,* August 1, 1885, 490.

101. Lodge, "Colonialism in the United States," *Atlantic Monthly,* May 1883, 614.

102. Margaret MacFadden, *Golden Cables of Sympathy: The Transatlantic Sources of Nineteenth Century Feminism* (Lexington, KY: University Press of Kentucky, 1999); Christine Bolt, *The Women's Movements in the United States and Britain from the 1790s to the 1920s* (Amherst: University of Massachusetts Press, 1993); Tyrrell, *Reforming the World,* 74, 80.

103. Tyrrell, *Reforming the World,* 20–21.

104. Blackwell's career is covered closely in Nancy Ann Sahli, "Elizabeth Blackwell, MD (1821–1910): A Biography" (Ph.D. diss., University of Pennsylvania, 1974).

105. Elizabeth Blackwell to Alice Stone Blackwell, undated, Reel 4, Alice Stone Blackwell Papers, LoC.

106. Elizabeth Blackwell to Alice Stone Blackwell, June 18, 1877, Reel 4, Alice Stone Blackwell Papers, LoC.

107. Sarah L. Silkey, *Black Woman Reformer: Ida B. Wells, Lynching, and Transatlantic Activism* (Athens: University of Georgia Press, 2015), 60–63.

108. Douglas A. Lorimer, *Science, Race Relations, and Resistance: Britain, 1870–1914* (Manchester, UK: Manchester University Press, 2013), 276, 281. Wells's indebtedness to British co-religionists, philanthropists, radicals, and newspaper editors were well documented in her autobiography; see Ida B. Wells, *Crusade for Justice: The Autobiography of Ida B. Wells,* ed. Alfreda Duster (Chicago: University of Chicago Press, 1970), 216.

109. Caroline Bressey, *Empire, Race and the Politics of Anti-Caste* (London: Bloomsbury Academic, 2013), 107–27.

110. Noaquia N. Callahan, "A Rare Colored Bird: Mary Church Terrell, *Die Firtschritte der Farbigen Frauen,* and the International Council of Women's Congress in Berlin, Germany, 1904," *German Historical Institute Bulletin Supplement* 13 (2017), 102. For a broad overview of African-American women's transnationalism see Michelle Rief, "Thinking Locally, Acting Globally: The International Agenda of African American Clubwomen, 1880–1940," *Journal of African American Women's History* 89, no. 3 (2004): 203–22.

111. "Ida B. Wells Abroad," *Daily Inter-Ocean,* April 9, 1894.

112. "Ida B. Wells Abroad," *Daily Inter-Ocean,* June 25, 1894.

113. "Lynch Law in the United States," *Liverpool Mercury,* March 19, 1894.

114. "Lynch Law in the United States," *Birmingham Daily Post,* May 16, 1893.

115. "Ida B. Wells Abroad," *Daily Inter-Ocean,* June 25, 1894.

116. Gail Bederman, *Manliness & Civilization: A Cultural History of Gender and Race in the United States, 1880–1917* (Chicago: University of Chicago Press, 1995), 60–67.

117. "Lynch Law in America," *Reynold's Newspaper,* June 3, 1894.

118. Wells, *Crusade for Justice,* 189.

119. Cited in Ibid.

120. Ian Tyrrell, *Woman's World—Woman's Empire: the Woman's Christian Temperance Union in International Perspective, 1880–1930* (Chapel Hill: University of North Carolina Press, 1991), 63.

121. Quoted in Tyrrell, *Woman's World/Woman's Empire,* 28.

122. "A World League of English-Speaking Women," *Review of Reviews,* January 1892, 65.

123. See the early novels of Henry James; Frances Hodgson Burnett, *Little Lord Fauntleroy* (New York: Scribner's, 1886) and *The Shuttle* (London: William Heineman, 1906); Burton Harrison, *The Anglomaniacs* (New York: Century, 1890).

124. *Daily News,* April 19, 1895.

125. *New York Times,* July 30, 1878.

126. Maureen Montgomery, *Gilded Prostitution: Status, Money, and Transatlantic Marriages, 1870–1914* (London: Routledge, 1989), 73; Kathleen Burk, *Old World New World: The Story of Britain and America* (London: Little, Brown, 2007), 545.

127. David Cannadine, *The Decline and Fall of the British Aristocracy* (New Haven: Yale University Press, 1990), 342.

128. "American Fools," *Washington Post,* August 31, 1880.

129. *Daily News,* April 19, 1895.

130. Montgomery, *Gilded Prostitution,* 249–57; Cannadine, *Decline and Fall,* 347.

131. Paul Woolf, "Special Relationships: Anglo-American Love Affairs, Courtships, and Marriages in Fiction, 1821–1914" (D.Phil Thesis, University of Birmingham, 2007), 160.

132. Elizabeth Banks, *Campaigns of Curiosity: Journalistic Adventures of an American Girl in London* (New York: F. Tennyson Neely, 1894), 184.

133. Cannadine, *Decline and Fall,* 346.

134. Lady Randolph Spencer Churchill, *The Reminiscences of Lady Randolph Churchill* (London: E. Arnold, 1908), 47.

135. Colonial, "Titled Colonials v. Titled Americans," *Contemporary Review,* June 1905, 869.

136. Thomas H. S. Escott, *Society in London by a Foreign Resident* (London: Chatto & Windus, 1885), 98.

137. *New York Times,* July 11, 1880; Gore, "Americans Abroad," 468–69.

138. William T. Stead, *The Americanisation of the World, or, the Trend of the Twentieth Century* (London: Review of Reviews, 1902), 123.

139. Endy, "Travel and World Power," 573–74.

140. *London American,* October 11, 1895.

141. Anglo-American, "The American Colony in London," *Harper's Magazine,* July 30, 1904.

142. Stapley, "Is Paris Wise," 16.

143. Stead, *Americanisation of the World,* 123; George W. Smalley, *London Letters and Some Others* (New York: Harper & Brothers, 1891), II:106–10.

144. A. G. Baker, "International Marriages," *Independent,* October 1908, 757; Paul Kramer, "Empires, Exceptions, and Anglo-Saxons: Race and Rule Between the British and United States Empires, 1880–1910," *Journal of American History* 88, no. 2 (2002): 1327. The best and most comprehensive treatment of this subject can be found in Dana Cooper, *Informal Ambassadors: American Women, Transatlantic Marriages, and Anglo-American Relations, 1865–1945* (Kent, OH: Kent State University Press, 2014).

145. Charles Waldstein, *The Expansion of Western Ideals and the World's Peace* (New York: Lane, 1899), 158.

146. Stead, *Americanisation of the World,* 124.

147. *London American,* May 1, 1895.

148. Chalmers Roberts, "At the Court of St James," *Harper's Weekly,* March 10, 1900, 226.

149. *London American,* September 13, 1895.

150. Frederick S. Daniel, "Going Abroad," *Frank Leslie's Popular Monthly,* May 1891, 541.

151. *London American,* January 3, 1896.

152. *London American,* September 13, 1895.

153. "Our Raison D'être," *London American,* April 3, 1895.

154. *London American,* May 1, 1895.

155. "The American Society in London," loose circular in Vol. 161, Thomas F. Bayard Papers, 1780–1899, LoC; *London American,* April 10, 1895; Henry

S. Wellcome to H. B. Chamberlin, April 4, 1895 and April 24, 1895, WA/HSW /CO/IND/B.3, Papers of Henry S. Wellcome, WL.

156. "The American Society in London," *London American,* April 10, 1895.

157. *London American,* April 25, 1895.

158. Ibid.

159. *Society of American Women in London, Constitution, By-Laws, Standing Rules* (London: privately printed, 1899), 5.

160. Mrs. Hirst Alexander, "The Society of American Women in London," *Strand Magazine* (US Edition), June 1900, 521.

161. "American Women in London," *London American,* July 21, 1899.

162. Ibid.

163. *Milwaukee Sentinel,* March 26, 1899 (repr. from the *New York World*).

164. Angela Woolacott, *To Try Her Fortune in London: Australian Women, Colonialism, and Modernity* (Oxford: Oxford University Press, 2001), 100.

165. Sheila E. Braine, "London's Clubs for Women," in G. R. Sims, ed., *Living London* (London: Cassell and Company, 1902), I:114; Erika Rappaport, *Shopping for Pleasure: Women in the Making of London's West End* (Princeton, NJ: Princeton University Press), 74.

166. Quoted in Ralph Nevill, *London Clubs: their History and Treasures* (London: Chatto & Windus, 1911), 135.

167. Leila J. Rupp, "Constructing Internationalism: The Case of Transnational Women's Organizations, 1888–1945," *American Historical Review* 99, no. 5 (1994): 1573.

168. "American Women in London," *London American,* July 21, 1899.

169. *New York Times,* July 4, 1899.

170. Leila J. Rupp, *Worlds of Women: The Making of an International Women's Movement* (Princeton, NJ: Princeton University Press, 1997), 159–79.

171. Hirst Alexander, "The Society of American Women in London," *Strand Magazine* (US Edition), June 1900, 521.

172. Ibid.

173. "Society of American Women in London," *London American,* July 7, 1899.

174. *London American,* 27 December 1895; *London American,* January 3, 1896.

175. Charles Robinson, "Our Underpaid Officials," *American Journal of Politics,* December 1893, 636.

176. "Ambassadors and Their Pay," *Harper's Weekly,* April 15, 1893, 342. See also *Life,* April 13, 1893, 234.

177. Robinson, "Our Underpaid Officials," 636.

178. Constance Smedley, "The Expatriates. III. The American Colony in London," *The Bookman,* August 1907, 628.

179. *London American,* July 10, 1896.

180. Ibid.

181. Paul Laity, *The British Peace Movement, 1870–1914* (Oxford: Oxford University Press, 2001).

182. "Bayard Correspondence" File, WA/HSW/CO/GEN/M.1, Papers of Henry S. Wellcome. Bayard's diplomatic arts were not as appreciated by the US Congress who passed a resolution censuring his conduct in January 1896 after he made speeches criticising protectionism, see Charles C. Tansil, *The Foreign Policy of Thomas F. Bayard, 1885–1897* (New York: Fordham University Press, 1940), 721.

183. *London American,* 4 December 1896.

184. Ibid.

185. William T. Stead, *Always Arbitrate Before You Fight: An Appeal to All English-Speaking Folk* (London: Review of Reviews, 1896); Laity, *British Peace Movement,* 131–33. Stead also directly lobbied members of the American diplomatic circle for support; see William T. Stead to Thomas F. Bayard, February 28, 1896, Vol. 164, Bayard Papers, LoC.

186. Frederick C. Van Duzer to Thomas F. Bayard, October 23, 1895, Vol. 161, Bayard Papers, LoC; "Fourth of July Abroad," *New York Times,* July 6, 1897.

187. Peter Clarke, "The English-Speaking Peoples before Churchill," *Britain and the World* 4, no. 2 (2011): 202.

188. Kramer, "Empires, Exceptions, and Anglo-Saxons," 1323; Clarke, "The English-Speaking Peoples before Churchill," 224.

189. For an overview of these ideas see Duncan Bell, *Reordering the World: Essays on Liberalism and Empire* (Princeton, NJ: Princeton University Press, 2016), 182–207.

190. Stuart Anderson, *Race and Rapprochement: Anglo-Saxonism and Anglo-American Relations, 1895–1904* (London: Associated University Presses, 1981); Charles S. Campbell, Jr., *Anglo-American Understanding, 1898–1903* (Baltimore: Johns Hopkins University Press, 1957).

191. Kramer, "Empires, Exceptions, and Anglo-Saxons," 1315–53; Stephen Tuffnell, "'The International Siamese Twins': The Iconography of Anglo-American Inter-Imperialism," in *Comic Empires,* ed. Andrekos Varnava and Richard Scully (Manchester: Manchester University Press, 2020).

192. Edward Dicey, "The New American Imperialism," *Nineteenth Century,* September 1898, 499, 501.

193. Duncan Bell, *The Idea of Greater Britain: Empire and the Future of World Order, 1860–1900* (Princeton, NJ: Princeton University Press, 2007), 254–55.

194. *London American,* July 8, 1898.

195. *London American,* March 11, 1897.

196. *London American,* July 10, 1898.

197. *London American,* July 8, 1898.

198. Ibid.

199. William T. Stead, "Why not a British Celebration of the Fourth of July?" *Review of Reviews,* June 1898, 600.

200. Ninkovich, *Global Dawn,* 257–61; Kramer, "Empires, Exceptions, and Anglo-Saxons," 1315–30.

201. "Anglo-American League," *The Times,* July 14, 1898.

202. "Anglo-American Relations," *The Cyclopedic Review of Current History,* July 1, 1898, 569. For more, see Campbell, *Anglo-American Understanding,* 44; Stead, "Why not a British Celebration of the Fourth of July?," 600.

203. Heindel, *The American Impact on Great Britain,* 39.

204. Anne P. Baker, *The Pilgrims of Great Britain: A Centennial History* (London: Profile Books, 2002), 11.

205. John M. MacKenzie, "Empire and Metropolitan Cultures," in *The Oxford History of the British Empire, Volume 3, The Nineteenth Century,* ed. Andrew Porter (Oxford: Oxford University Press, 1999), 287.

206. Robert Rhodes James, *Henry Wellcome* (London: Hodder & Stoughton, 1994), 135.

207. Robert A. Stafford, "Scientific Exploration and Empire," in *The Oxford History of the British Empire: The Nineteenth Century,* ed. Andrew Porter (Oxford: Oxford University Press, 1999), 299.

208. *London American,* November 10 & 24, 1899; "American Women in London Act," *New York Times,* October 27, 1899.

209. "In aid of the Sufferers," *Morning Post,* November 6, 1899. The *Maine*'s sister ship, the *Missouri,* was similarly refitted and lent to the US to support actions in Cuba.

210. "The Queen and the American Hospital Ship," *The Times,* December 5, 1899; "American Ladies and the War," *Daily News* (London), November 24, 1899.

211. "American Ladies and the War," *Daily News,* November 24, 1899.

212. Rhodes, *Henry Wellcome,* 219.

213. Ibid., 234–36. For more on the importance of transatlantic gestures in this period, see Mike Sewell, "'All the English-Speaking Race is in Mourning': The Assassination of President Garfield and Anglo-American Relations," *Historical Journal* 34, no. 3 (1991): 665–86.

214. For studies of late-Victorian London as a site of colonial diaspora more broadly see Jonathan Schneer, *London 1900: the Imperial Metropolis* (New Haven, CT: Yale University Press, 2001); Antoinette Burton, *At the Heart of Empire: Indians and the Colonial Encounter in Late-Victorian Britain* (Berkeley: University of California Press, 1998), chapter 4; David Killingray, "Significant Black South Africans in Britain before 1912: Pan-African Organisations and the Emergence of South Africa's First Black Lawyers," *South African Historical Journal* 64, no. 3 (2012): 393–417. For the twentieth century history of black London and anti-colonial struggle see Marc Matera, *Black London: The Imperial Metropolis and Decolonization in the Twentieth Century* (Oakland: University of California Press, 2015); Kennetta Hammond Perry, *London is the Place for Me: Black Britons, Citizenship, and the Politics of Race* (New York: Oxford University Press, 2015).

215. Henry Sylvester Williams, *The British Negro: A Factor in the Empire, "The Ethiopian Eunuch". Two Lectures Delivered Before Many Distinguished Clubs and Associations in the United Kingdom of Great Britain, at the Request of Several British Friends, Interested in the Progress of the "Negro Race"* (Brighton: W. T. Moulton, 1902), 16

216. Williams's career is briefly outlined in John La Guerre, "Henry Sylvester Williams," *Dictionary of Caribbean and Afro-Latin American Biography*, ed. Franklin W. Knight and Henry Louis Gates Jr. (New York: Oxford University Press, 2008), available at Oxford African American Studies Center, http://www.oxfordaasc.com/article/opr/t456/e22211.

217. Schneer, *London 1900*, 216–19.

218. Immanuel Geiss, *The Pan-African Movement* (London: Metuen, 1974), 176–92; Peter Olisanwuche Esedebe, *Pan-Africanism: the Idea and the Movement, 1776–1963* (Washington, DC: Howard University Press, 1982).

219. Henry Sylvester Williams to Booker T. Washington, July 17, 1899, in Harlan and Smock, *Booker T. Washington Papers*, V:158; Lake and Reynolds, *Drawing the Global Colour Line*, 245.

220. "Pan-African Conference," *The Times*, July 26, 1900; "Across the Waters," *The Colored American*, August 11, 1900.

221. "Pan-African Conference," *The Times*, July 24, 1900.

222. Lorimer, *Science, Race Relations, and Resistance*, 289.

223. Ibid., 287; "The Pan African Conference," *Cleveland Gazette*, September 8, 1900.

224. W. E. B. Du Bois, "To the Nations of the World," in *The Oxford W. E. B. Du Bois Reader*, ed. Eric J. Sundquist (New York: Oxford University Press, 1996), 625–26.

225. Ibid., 626.

226. Susan D. Pennybacker, "The Universal Races Congress, London Political Culture, and Imperial Dissent, 1900–1939," *Radical History Review* 92 (2005): 103–17. Other conferences included the 1911 Universal Races Congress in London and the 1912 International Conference on the Negro, held at Booker T. Washington's Tuskegee Institute.

227. "England Observes the Glorious Fourth," *American Monthly Review of Reviews*, August 1898, 139.

228. Gary B. Magee and Andrew S. Thompson, *Empire and Globalisation: Networks of People, Goods and Capital in the British World, c.1850–1914* (Cambridge, UK: Cambridge University Press, 2010), 167.

229. *Anglo-American Times*, October 27, 1865.

230. F. A. MacKenzie, *The American Invaders* (London: Grant Richards, 1902), 25.

231. Ibid., 22. MacKenzie's hyperbolic claims were treated with healthy scepticism; see S. G. Hobson, "The Facts about American Competition," *Review of Reviews*, February 1902, 204–5.

232. MacKenzie, *American Invaders*, 240–1.

233. Carey, *The Way to Outdo England*, 102.

234. Christopher Furness, "The Old World and the American 'Invasion,'" *Pall Mall Magazine*, March 1902, 362.

235. Stead, *Americanization of the World*, 359.

236. Hopkins, *American Empire*, 309.

237. Frank Fayant, "A Commercial Invasion," *The Idler*, October 1902, 637.

238. Ibid.; see also "Americans Abroad," *Puck*, July 17, 1901.

239. Mona Domosh, *American Commodities in an Age of Empire* (London: Routledge, 2006); Nan Enstad, *Cigarettes, Inc.: An Intimate History of Corporate Imperialism* (Chicago: University of Chicago Press, 2018), 16–51; Hoganson, *Consumer's Imperium.*

240. Stead, *Americanisation of the World,* 381.

241. "The American Exhibition in London," *Morning Post,* January 7, 1887.

242. London American Exhibition, *Official Catalogue of the Exhibition* (New York: J.J. Garnett, 1887).

243. Buffalo Bill's show was perhaps the most prominent US cultural export in this period; see Robert W. Rydell and Rob Kroes, *Buffalo Bill in Bologna: The Americanization of the World, 1869–1922* (Chicago: University of Chicago Press, 2005). Cody and the Native Americans who travelled with him were quickly incorporated into visual culture; see, for example, "Buffalo Bill's Wild West Show at the American Exhibition, Earl's Court," *Graphic,* May 7, 1887.

244. Alfred Chandler, *Scale and Scope: the Dynamics of Industrial Capitalism* (Cambridge, MA: Harvard University Press, 1990), 157–61, 199–201.

245. MacKenzie, *American Invaders,* 78; "American Productions Abroad," *Scientific American,* June 8, 1878, 352; "American machine tools made in England," *Scientific American,* April 29, 1899, 261.

246. See Fred Carstensen, *American Enterprise in Foreign Markets: Studies of Singer and International Harvester in Imperial Russia* (Chapel Hill: University of North Carolina Press, 1984), 23–26.

247. "American Productions Abroad," *Scientific American,* June 8, 1878, 352; "American machine tools made in England," *Scientific American,* April 29, 1899, 261. Roy A. Church, "The Effect of the American Export Invasion on the British Boot and Shoe Industry, 1885–1914," *Journal of Economic History* 28, no. 2 (1968): 235; S.B. Saul, "The American Impact on British Industry, 1895–1914," *Business History* 3, no. 1 (1960): 19–38; S.J. Nicholas, "The American Export Invasion of Britain: The Case of the Engineering Industry, 1870–1914," *Technology and Culture* 21, no. 4 (1980): 570–88; Mathew Simon and David E. Novak, "Some Dimensions of the American Commercial Invasion of Europe, 1871–1914: An Introductory Essay," *Journal of Economic History* 24, no. 4 (1964): 591–605.

248. Stephen Tuffnell, "Anglo-American Inter-Imperialism: The American Invasion of Britain and the Empire, c. 1865–1914," *Britain and the World* 8, no. 2 (2013): 174–95. The best account of the broader global expansion of American business is Mira Wilkins, *Emergence of Multinational Enterprise: American Business Abroad from the Colonial Era to 1914* (Cambridge, MA: Harvard University Press, 1970), 35–70.

249. R.P. Porter, "An Anglo-American Experiment," *Review of Reviews,* September 1901, 322; "A Yankee Boss in England," *Review of Reviews,* December 1902, 53–57; An American in England, "More stories of the American Invasion of England," *World's Work,* January 1902, 1651; Fayant, "Commercial Invasion," 637–47.

250. Chandler, *Scale and Scope,* 199–201.

251. Wilkins, *Emergence of Multinational Enterprise,* 48–51.

252. Saul, "American Impact Upon British Industry," 31.

253. Lance E. Davies and Robert J. Cull, *International Capital Markets and American Economic Growth, 1820–1914* (Cambridge, UK: Cambridge University Press, 1994), 45; A. G. Kenwood and A. L. Lougheed, *The Growth of the International Economy, 1820–1990*, Third edition (London: Routledge 1992), 37.

254. *London American*, August 25, 1895.

255. Jackson Lears, *Fables of Abundance: A Cultural History of Advertising in America* (New York: Basic, 1994), 284.

256. Tuffnell, "Anglo-American Inter-Imperialism," 174–95.

257. Hopkins, *American Empire*, 310.

258. John Darwin, "Imperialism and the Victorians: Dynamics of Territorial Expansion," *English Historical Review* 112, no. 447 (1997): 642.

259. Darwin, *The Empire Project*, 116.

260. Müller, *Wiring the World*, 49.

261. Magee and Thompson, *Empire and Globalisation*, 136–37.

262. *Morning Post* (London), July 3, 1885.

263. *The American Club, Rules, Bye-Laws, Regulations, and List of Members* (London: privately printed, 1888), 11.

264. Darwin, *Empire Project*, 641; Magee and Thompson, *Empire and Globalisation*, 198–209.

265. Tuffnell, "Anglo-American Inter-Imperialism," 174–95.

266. See, for example, "Another Instance of Invasion," *Anglo-American Press*, February 1, 1902.

267. After its first edition the *Directory* became *Bancroft's Americans in London: A Handbook Regarding American Interests in Great Britain, Commercial and Social* (London: American Publishing Company, 1906).

268. Ibid., vii.

269. For an overview of American London see Banks, "American London," in Sims, *Living London*, II:107–13.

270. Genevieve C. Bancroft & Basil Bancroft, *The American Blue Book, Containing the List of Americans and American Firms in Great Britain* (London: The American Bureau, 1905), 3.

271. Ibid., 243.

272. Ibid.

273. "4 July 1901, Independence Day Speech," Folder 12, Box 25, Joseph Hodge Choate Papers, LoC.

274. Mira M. Wilkins, *The History of Foreign Investment in the United States to 1914* (Cambridge, MA: Harvard University Press, 1989), 142.

275. R. E. Lipsey, "U.S. Foreign Trade and the Balance of Payments, 1800–1913," *NBER Working Paper No. 4710* (April 1994): 5.

276. Magee and Thompson, *Empire and Globalisation*, 120; Edmund Rogers, "The United States and the Fiscal State in Britain," *Historical Journal* 50, no. 3 (2007): 593–622.

277. Vincent Carosso and Rose Carosso, *The Morgans: Private International Bankers, 1854–1913* (Cambridge, MA: Harvard University Press, 1987), 510–13.

278. Wilkins, *Foreign Investment in the United States,* 144; for an overview of foreign investment see 144–67.

279. Furness, "The Old World and the American 'Invasion,'" 366.

EPILOGUE

1. Thomas Burke, *London in My Time* (London: Rich & Cowan, 1934), 35.

2. *The Anglo-American Press,* December 7, 1901.

3. Ibid. The British press was more skeptical; see "American Exhibition at the Crystal Palace," *The Times,* June 2, 1902, 13.

4. *The Anglo-American Press,* December 7, 1901.

5. "Americans in London," *Town and Country,* July 15, 1905, 28; "Recent Social Triumphs for Americans Abroad," *Town and Country,* August 18, 1906, 26; "American Women Prominent in London," *Town and Country,* June 9, 1906, 30.

6. For example, "Americans Abroad: The London Season," *Town and Country,* May 27, 1911.

7. Ralph D. Blumenfeld, "American Diplomats in London," *Town and Country,* March 25, 1905, 17.

8. "American Women in English Society. 1. The Duchess of Marlborough," *Harper's Bazaar,* July 1905, 602.

9. Earl Mayo, "The Americanization of England," *Forum,* January 1902, 566.

10. Ibid., 568. Mayo was not alone in contrasting the mundane, everyday impact of American goods and customs with the grandiosity of "Americanization." For examples see Frederick MacKenzie, *The American Invaders* (London: Grant Richards, 1902), 142–43; Benjamin H. Thwaite, *The American Invasion* (London: Simpkin, Marshall, Hamilton, Kent & co., 1902), 21; William T. Stead, *The Americanisation of the World, or, the Trend of the Twentieth Century* (London: Review of Reviews, 1902), 342–59 ; J. Ellis Barker, *Drifting* (London: Grant Richards, 1901), 147–148; "How America Looks from Europe," *Harper's Weekly,* December 21, 1901, 1312.

11. Stephen Tuffnell, "'Uncle Sam is to be Sacrificed': Anglophobia in Late Nineteenth-Century Politics and Culture," *American Nineteenth Century History* 12, no. 1 (2011): 77–99.

12. *Congressional Globe,* February 8, 1853, 32nd Cong., 2nd Sess., 141.

13. Mayo, "Americanization of England," 566.

14. "The American Colony in London," *Harper's Weekly,* July 30, 1904.

15. Constance Smedley, "The Expatriates III: The American Colony in London in Two Parts. Part I. The Social Side," *The Bookman,* July 1907, 484.

16. Robert Franch, *Robber Baron: The Life of Charles Tyson Yerkes* (Urbana: University of Illinois Press, 2006), 279.

17. Sidney Low, "The Tangle of London Locomotion," *Fortnightly Review,* January 1902, 112.

18. Eric Banton, "Underground London," in *Living London: Its Work and its Play, its Humour and its Pathos, its Sights and its Scenes,* ed. G.R. Sims (London: Cassell and Company, 1902), II:127.

19. "American Construction of Rapid Transit in London," *World's Work*, December 1901, 221.

20. Lance E. Davies and Robert J. Cull, *International Capital Markets and American Economic Growth, 1820–1914* (Cambridge, UK: Cambridge University Press, 1994), 94, 289.

21. Ibid., 289–300; "American Who Built London Tubes," *The American Register*, April 17, 1910.

22. *The Cosmopolitan; a Monthly Illustrated Magazine*, August 1902, 414.

23. "Preface," *Punch*, June 26, 1901, iii.

24. John R. Day, *The Story of London's Underground* (London: London Transport, 1972), 91.

25. "The great London power station," *Scientific American*, December 17, 1904, 429.

26. Erika Rappaport, *Shopping for Pleasure: Women in the Making of London's West End* (Princeton, NJ: Princeton University Press, 2001), 146.

27. See the images accompanying Rupert Hughes, "The American Invasion of London," *Harper's Weekly*, June 15, 1901, 604–5.

28. Bradford Perkins, *The Great Rapprochement: England and the United States, 1895–1914* (New York: Athenuem, 1968), 124.

29. P. F. William Ryan, "Scenes from Shop and Store London," in *Living London*, III:143.

30. "An American Center in England," *Town and Country*, April 29, 1905, 43.

31. Elizabeth Banks, "American London," in *Living London*, II:111.

32. Mayo, "Americanization of England," 567. In the first decade of the twentieth century, an estimated two thousand American firms had opened offices in London, staffed by American managers, salesmen, and assistants. See Constance Smedley, "The Expatriates III.—The American Colony in London. Part II. Club Life, Literature, the Stage, and American Industry," *The Bookman*, August 1907, 629.

33. Ralph Blumenfeld, "Americans Crowding London," *Town and Country*, July 28, 1906, 15.

34. John Benson, *The Rise of Consumer Society in Britain, 1880–1980* (London: Longman, 1994), 143–63.

35. H. B. Marriott Watson, "The Deleterious Effect of Americanisation upon Woman," *Nineteenth Century*, November 1903, 787, 789.

36. Mayo, "Americanization of England," 568.

37. John Foster Carr, "Anglo-American unity fast coming," *World's Work*, October 1903, 4018.

38. Herbert W. Horwill, "Is England being Americanized?" *Forum*, April 1902, 235.

39. See for instance, Jean-Jacques Servan-Schreiber, *The American Challenge* (London: Atheneum, 1968). Historical accounts include David W. Ellwood, *The Shock of America: Europe and the Challenge of the Century* (Oxford: Oxford University Press, 2012); Alfred Eckes and Thomas Zeiler, *Globalization and the American Century* (Cambridge, UK: Cambridge University Press, 2003); Anne Orde, *The Eclipse of Great Britain: The United States and British Imperial Decline, 1895–1956* (Basingstoke, UK: Macmillan, 1996).

40. Piers Brendon, *The Decline and Fall of the British Empire, 1781–1997* (London: Vintage, 2008), 225–27; G. Searle, *The Quest for National Efficiency: A Study in British Politics and Political Thought, 1899–1914* (Oxford: Basil Blackwell, 1971); Keith T. Surridge, *Managing the South African War, 1899–1902: Politicians v. Generals* (Woodridge, UK: Boydell Press, 1998), 181–82.

41. Bernard Porter, *The Lion's Share: A History of British Imperialism 1850 to the Present,* 5th edition (Harlow, UK: Pearson, 2012), 105–31; Frank Trentmann, *Free Trade Nation: Commerce, Consumption, and Civil Society in Modern Britain* (Oxford: Oxford University Press, 2008).

42. Vaclav Smil, *Made in the USA: The Rise and Retreat of American Manufacturing* (Cambridge, MA: MIT Press, 2013), 31.

43. David A. Yerxa, *Admirals and Empire: The United States Navy and the Caribbean, 1898–1945* (Columbia: University of South Carolina Press, 1991).

44. "Two Presidents and the Limits of American Supremacy," *Fortnightly Review,* October 1, 1901, 570.

45. Marc-William Palen, "Protection, Federation and Union: The Global Impact of the McKinley Tariff upon the British Empire, 1890–94," *Journal of Imperial and Commonwealth History* 38, no. 3 (2010): 395–418.

46. "Lord Rosebery on National Culture," *The Times,* October 16, 1901.

47. John Darwin, *The Empire Project: The Rise and Fall of the British World-System, 1830–1970* (New York: Cambridge University Press, 2009), 274.

48. Barney Warf, *Time-Space Compression: Historical Geographies* (Abingdon, UK: Routledge, 2008), 113; Darwin, *Empire Project,* 274.

49. Darwin, *Empire Project,* 274.

50. Marilyn Lake and Henry Reynolds, *Drawing the Global Colour Line: White Men's Countries and the International Challenge of Racial Equality* (Cambridge, UK: Cambridge University Press, 2008).

51. The best works on this are Duncan Bell, *The Idea of Greater Britain: Empire and the Future of World Order, 1860–1900* (Princeton, NJ: Princeton University Press), and *Reordering the World: Essays on Liberalism and Empire* (Princeton, NJ: Princeton University Press, 2016). During this period, many Americans also began to speak of the "Greater United States"—but few sought to annex the British Empire into that geo-political imaginary. See Daniel Immerwahr, "The Greater United States: Territory and Empire in U.S. History," *Diplomatic History* 40, no. 3 (2016): 373–91.

52. Stead, *Americanisation of the World,* 2.

53. J. M. Campbell, "Our Yearly Exodus to Europe," *The World To-Day,* January 1907, 64.

54. *Harper's Weekly,* June 27, 1857.

Bibliography

MANUSCRIPT COLLECTIONS

Great Britain

The Baring Archive, ING Barings, 60 London Wall, London
    Diary of Joshua Bates
Liverpool Maritime Archive, Liverpool
    Business Records of Fraser, Trenholm & Co.
Liverpool Public Record Office, Liverpool
    Minute Books of the American Chamber of Commerce, 1801–1908
    Minute Books of the Liverpool Cotton Brokers' Association
Wellcome Library, Wellcome Institute, Euston Road, London
    Papers of Henry S. Wellcome
    Papers of Silas M. Burroughs

United States

Butler Library, Columbia University, New York, NY
    Moncure D. Conway Papers
Houghton Library, Harvard University, Cambridge, MA
    Abbott Lawrence Papers
    Adam Badeau Papers, 1831–1895
    William J. Hoppin Papers, 1813–1895
Huntington Library, San Marino, CA
    Thomas Haines Dudley Papers
    Letters from Benjamin Moran to Adam Badeau
    Papers of Charles Sumner

Library of Congress, Washington, DC
  Bancroft-Bliss Family Papers
  Benjamin Moran Papers
  Blackwell Family Papers
  Henry Hotze Papers, 1861–1865
  James M. Mason Papers, 1838–1870
  Joseph Hodge Choate Papers
  Judah P. Benjamin Papers
  Pennell-Whistler Correspondence
  Samuel Finley Breese Morse Papers
  Thomas F. Bayard Papers, 1780–1899
  Whitelaw Reid Papers, 1795–1970
  W. W. Corcoran Papers
Massachusetts Historical Society, Boston, MA
  Appleton Family Papers
  Edward Everett Papers
  Joseph Tuckerman Papers
  Thomas Wren Ward Papers
Morgan Library, The Morgan Library & Museum, New York, NY
  Papers of John Pierpont Morgan
  Papers of Junius Spencer Morgan
New Britain Public Library, New Britain, CT
  Elihu Burritt Collection
New York Historical Society, New York, NY
  Brown Brothers-Harriman Papers
  International Relief Committee Records, 1862–1863
New York Public Library, New York, NY
  Phelps, Dodge & Co. Records
  United States Sanitary Commission Papers, English Branch Archives
Phillips Library, Peabody Essex Institute, Salem, MA
  George Peabody, 1795–1865, Correspondence
  Papers of George Augustus Peabody
  Remond Family Papers, 1823–1869
Rhode Island Historical Society, Providence, RI
  John Talbot Pitman Papers
Vermont Historical Society, Barre, VT
  Henry Stevens Family Correspondence, 1841–1862

NEWSPAPERS AND JOURNALS

The Albion
The American Journal of Politics
The American Register
American Review of Reviews
American Whig Review
The Anglo-American Press
Anglo-American Times

The Anti-Slavery Reporter
Appleton's Journal of Literature, Science, and Art
Arena
The Atlantic Monthly
Ballou's Pictorial Drawing-Room Companion

Birmingham Daily Post
Birmingham Gazette
The Bookman
Boston Daily Advertiser
Boston Daily Atlas
Boston Post
Charleston Mercury (Charleston, SC)
The Chautauquan: A Weekly
    Newsmagazine
Chicago Daily Tribune
Christian Reflector
Cleveland Gazette
Cleveland Herald
The Colored American (Washington,
    DC)
Contemporary Review
Daily Herald and Gazette
    (Cleveland, OH)
Daily National Intelligencer
    (Washington, DC)
Daily News (London)
Daily Register (Raleigh, NC)
De Bow's Review
Dollar Magazine
Douglass' Monthly
The Edinburgh Review
The Examiner
Fortnightly Review
Frank Leslie's Popular Monthly
The Galaxy
The Globe (Washington, DC)
The Graphic
Hampshire Advertiser
Harper's Bazaar
Harper's Weekly
Home Journal
The Idler
Illustrated London News
The Independent
The Index
The Ladies' Home Journal
The Liberator
Life
Lippincott's Magazine
Literary Souvenir
Littell's Living Age
Liverpool Critic

Liverpool Mercury
The London American
The Merchants' Magazine and
    Commercial Review
The Milwaukee Sentinel
Monthly Supplement of the Penny
    Magazine
The Morning Chronicle (London)
The Morning Post (London)
The Morning Star (London)
Nash's Pall Mall Magazine
The National Era
New England Galaxy
The New York Herald
New York Observer and Chronicle
New York Spectator
The New York Times
The New York World
The Nineteenth Century and After: A
    Monthly Review
North American and Daily Adver-
    tiser (Philadelphia, PA)
The North American Review
Overland Monthly
Puck
Punch
Review of Reviews
Reynold's Newspaper
San Francisco Argonaut
The Saturday Review
Saturday Evening Post (US)
Scientific American
Scribner's Magazine
Scribner's Monthly
Southern Cultivator
Southern Literary Messenger
The Standard (London)
Strand Magazine (US Edition)
Town and Country
The United States Magazine and
    Democratic Review
Vanity Fair
The Washington Post
Washington Sentinel
The Weekly Herald (New York)
The World To-Day
World's Work

GOVERNMENT PUBLICATIONS

Annals of Congress

Congressional Globe

Foreign Relations of the United States (FRUS)

Minutes of Evidence, upon taking into consideration several petitions, presented to the House of Commons, respecting the orders in council. London: HMSO, 1808.

Official Opinions of the Attorneys General of the United States. 43 vols. Washington, DC: Government Printing Office, 1791–1982.

Official Records of the Union and Confederate Navies in the War of the Rebellion. 31 vols. Washington, DC: Government Printing Office, 1894–1927.

PRINTED PRIMARY SOURCES

Allen, Zachariah. *The Practical Tourist, or, Sketches of the State of the Useful Art, and of Society, Scenery, &c. &c. in Great Britain, France, and Holland.* 2 vols. Providence, RI: A. S. Beckwith, 1832.

The American Club: Rules, Bye-Laws, Regulations, and List of Members. London: privately printed, 1888.

An Account of the Proceedings of the Dinner Given by Mr. George Peabody to the Americans Connected with the Great Exhibition at the London Coffee House, Ludgate Hill, on the 27th October 1851. London: William Pickering, 1851.

Austin, William. *Letters from London, Written During the Years 1802 & 1803.* Boston: W. Pelham, 1804.

Baines, Thomas. *Liverpool in 1859: The Port & Town of Liverpool, and the Harbour, Docks, and Commerce of the Mersey in 1859.* London: Longman, 1859.

Bancroft, Elizabeth Davis. *Letters from England, 1846–1849.* New York: Charles Scribner's Sons, 1904.

Bancroft, Basil, and Genevieve C. Bancroft. *The American Blue Book, Containing the List of Americans and American Firms in Great Britain.* London: The American Bureau, 1905.

Bancroft's Americans in London: A Handbook Regarding American Interests in Great Britain, Commercial and Social. 6th Edn. London: American Publishing Company, 1906.

Banks, Elizabeth. *Campaigns of Curiosity: Journalistic Adventures of an American Girl in London.* New York: F. Tennyson Neely, 1894.

Barker, J. Ellis. *Drifting.* London: Grant Richards, 1901.

Bartlett, David W. *What I Saw in London: Or, Men and Things in the Great Metropolis.* Auburn, NY: Derby and Miller, 1852.

Beecher, Henry Ward. *Patriotic Addresses in England and America, 1850–1885: On Slavery, the Civil War, and the Development of Civil Liberty in the United States.* New York: Fords, Howard & Hulbert, 1888.

Bennett, Lonnie A., ed. *Henry Hotze, Confederate Propagandist: Selected Writings on Revolution, Recognition, and Race.* Tuscaloosa: University of Alabama Press, 2008.

Bishop, J. Leander. *A History of American Manufactures from 1608 to 1860.* 3 vols. Philadelphia: Edward Young & Co., 1866.

Booker T. Washington Papers. Edited by Louis R. Harlan and Raymond Smock. 14 vols. Urbana: University of Illinois Press, 1972–1985.

Bowles, Charles S. P. *Report of Charles S. P. Bowles upon the International Congress of Geneva Convened at Geneva, 8 August 1864.* London: R. Clay, Son, and Taylor, 1864.

Braine, Sheila E. "London's Clubs for Women." In *Living London: Its Work and its Play, its Humour and its Pathos, its Sights and its Scenes,* edited by G. R. Sims, 114–18. London: Cassell and Company, 1902.

Brown, William Wells. *The American Fugitive in Europe: Sketches of Places and People Abroad.* Boston: Jewett, 1855.

Buchloh, Paul G., and Walter T. Rix. *The American Colony in Göttingen: Historical and Other Data Collected Between the Years 1855 and 1888.* Göttingen, Germany: Vandenhoeck & Ruprecht, 1976.

Burke, Edmund. "Letter II. On the Genius and Character of the French Revolution as it Regards Other Nations." In *The Works of the Right Honourable Edmund Burke,* V:342–383. London: J. C. Nimmo, 1887.

Butterfield, Lyman Henry, Marc Friedlaender, and Richard Alan Ryerson, eds. *Adams Family Correspondence.* 12 vols. Cambridge, MA: Harvard University Press, 1963.

Carey, Henry C. *The Harmony of Interests, Agricultural, Manufacturing, and Commercial.* Philadelphia: J. S. Skinner, 1851.

———. *How to Outdo England Without Fighting Her.* Philadelphia: H. C. Baird, 1865.

———. *Principles of Social Science.* 3 vols. Philadelphia: J. B. Lippincott, 1853–1859.

Carey, Matthew. *A View of the Ruinous Consequences of a Dependence on Foreign Markets.* Philadelphia: M. Carey & Son, 1820.

Carter, Nathaniel Hazeltine. *Letters from Europe, comprising the Journal of a Tour through Ireland, England, Scotland, France, Italy and Switzerland in the Years 1825, '26, and '27.* 2 vols. New York: G. & C. Carvill, 1827.

Choules, John Overton. *The Cruise of the Yacht* North Star: *A Narrative of Mr. Vanderbilt's Party to England, Russia, Denmark, France, Spain, Italy, Malta, Turkey, Madeira, Etc.* New York: Evans and Dickerson, 1854.

Churchill, Lady Randolph Spencer. *The Reminiscences of Lady Randolph Churchill.* London: E. Arnold, 1908.

Citizen of Massachusetts. *The Times: Or, The Pressure and its Causes Examined; An Address to the People.* Boston: privately printed, 1837.

Clarke, James F. *Eleven Weeks in Europe; and What May be Seen in that Time.* Boston: Ticknor, Reid & Fields, 1852.

Cogswell, Parsons Brainerd. *Glints from Over the Water.* Concord, NH: Republican Press Association, 1880.

Colton, Calvin ed. *The Life, Correspondence, and Speeches of Henry Clay.* 6 vols. New York: A. S. Barnes & Co., 1857.

Converse, James B. *A Summer Vacation: Sketches and Thoughts Abroad in the Summer of 1877*. Louisville, KY: Converse & Co., 1878.

Cook, Joel. *A Holiday Tour in Europe*. Philadelphia: David McKay, 1889.

Cooper, James Fenimore. *Gleanings from Europe: England*. 2 vols. Philadelphia: Carey, Lea and Blanchard, 1837.

Corson, John W. *Loiterings in Europe: or, Sketches of Travel in France, Belgium, Switzerland, Italy, Austria, Prussia, Great Britain, and Ireland*. New York: Harper & Brothers, 1848.

Cox, Samuel Sullivan. *A Buckeye Abroad; or, Wanderings in Europe, and in the Orient*. New York: G. P. Putnam, 1852.

Crawford, Theron C. *English Life*. New York: Lovell, 1889.

Croffut, William Augustus. *A Midsummer Lark*. New York: H. Holt and Company, 1883.

Curtis, G. W., ed. *The Correspondence of John Lothrop Motley*. 2 vols. New York: Harper and Brothers, 1889.

Dewey, Orville. *The Old World and the New: Or, A Journal of Reflections and Observations Made on a Tour in Europe*. 2 vols. New York: Harper & Brothers, 1836.

Douglass, Frederick. *The Frederick Douglass Papers. Series One: Speeches, Debates, and Interviews,* edited by John W. Blassingame and John R. McKivigan. 5 vols. New Haven: Yale University Press, 1979–92.

———. *My Bondage and My Freedom*. New York: Miller, Orton & Mulligan, 1855.

Drew, William A. *Glimpses and Gatherings During a Voyage and Visit to London and the Great Exhibition in the Summer of 1851*. Augusta, ME: Homan & Manley, 1851.

Du Bois, W. E. B. "To the Nations of the World." In *The Oxford W. E. B. Du Bois Reader,* edited by Eric J. Sundquist, 624–27. New York: Oxford University Press, 1996.

Escott, Thomas H. S. *Society in London by a Foreign Resident*. London: Chatto & Windus, 1885.

Evans, David Morier. *The City; Or, The Physiology of London Business; with Sketches on 'Change and at the London Coffee Houses*. London: Baily Brothers, 1845.

Everett, Edward. *Speech at the Dinner Given in Honor of George Peabody, Esq., of London*. Boston: Henry W. Dutton & Son, 1857.

Fetridge, William Pembroke. *The American Traveller's Guide: Harper's Handbook for Travellers in Europe*. 12th edition. New York: Harper's, 1873.

Fisher, Edmund Crisp. *The English Branch of the United States Sanitary Commission: Motive of its Establishment and Results of Its Work*. London: William Ridgway, 1865.

———. *Military Discipline and Volunteer Philanthropy: A Paper Read before the Social Science Congress Held in the City of York, September 1864*. London: William Ridgway, 1864.

Fiske, Samuel. *Mr. Dunn Browne's Experiences in Foreign Parts*. Boston: Jewett, 1857.

Ford, Worthington Chauncey, ed. *A Cycle of Adams Letters, 1861–1865.* 2 vols. London: Constable, 1921.

Forney, John W. *Letters from Europe.* Philadelphia: Peterson, 1867.

Fuller, Hiram. *Grand Transformation Scenes in the United States, or, Glimpses of Home After Thirteen Years Abroad.* New York: G. W. Carleton & Co., 1875.

Gillespie, Frances Elma, and Sarah Agnes Wallace, eds. *The Journal of Benjamin Moran, 1857–1865.* 2 vols. Chicago: University of Chicago Press, 1947.

Grattan, Thomas Colley. *England and the Disrupted States of America.* London: Ridgway, 1862.

Greeley, Horace. *Glances at Europe: in a series of letters from Great Britain, France, Switzerland, etc., during the summer of 1851; including notices of the Great Exhibition, or World's Fair.* New York: Dewitt & Davenport, 1851.

Guild, Curtis. *Britons and Muscovites, or Traits of Two Empires.* Boston: Lee & Shepherd, 1888.

Hawthorne, Nathaniel. *The English Notebooks, 1853–1856.* Vol XXI, *The Centenary Works of Nathaniel Hawthorne,* edited by Bill Ellis and Thomas Woodson. Columbus: Ohio State University Press, 1997.

Higgins, Frank C. *America Abroad: A Handbook for the American Traveller.* London: E. Forster Groom, 1891.

Hopkinson, Joseph. *Lecture upon the Principles of Commercial Integrity, and the Duties Subsisting between a Debtor and His Creditors.* Philadelphia: Carey and Lea, 1832.

Howe, Anthony, and Simon Morgan, ed. *The Letters of Richard Cobden, 1860–1865.* 4 vols. Oxford: Oxford University Press, 2015.

Howe, Mark Antony DeWolfe. *The Life and Letters of George Bancroft.* 2 vols. New York: C. Scribner's Sons, 1908.

Kerr, William Schomberg Robert. *The Confederate Secession.* London: W. Blackwood and Sons, 1864.

Levenson, Jacob Clavner, ed. *The Letters of Henry Adams, Volume I: 1858–1868.* Cambridge, MA: Harvard University Press, 1982.

London American Exhibition. *Official Catalogue of the Exhibition.* New York: J. J. Garnett, 1887.

MacKenzie, Frederick. *The American Invaders.* London: Grant Richards, 1902.

Mason, Virginia, ed. *The Public Life and Diplomatic Correspondence of James M. Mason, With Some Personal History.* New York: Neale, 1906.

McClellan, Henry B. *Journal of a Residence in Scotland, and Tour Through England, France, Germany, Switzerland, and Italy.* Boston: Allen and Ticknor, 1834.

McHenry, George. *The African Race in America, North and South.* London: Bradbury and Evans, 1861.

———. *The Cotton Trade: Its Bearing Upon the Prosperity of Great Britain and Commerce of the American Republics.* London: Saunders, Otley and Co., 1863.

———. *A Familiar Epistle to Robert J. Walker.* London: Saunders, Otley, and Co., 1863.

————. *The Southern Confederacy and the African Slave Trade*. Dublin: McGlashan & Gill, 1863.

————. *Visits to Slave-Ships*. London: British and Foreign Anti-Slavery Society, 1862.

Melville, Herman. *Redburn*. London: Penguin, 1976 [1849].

Moore, John Bassett, ed. *The Works of James Buchanan Comprising his Speeches, State Papers, and Private Correspondence*. 12 vols. New York: Antiquarian Press, 1908–11.

Morford, Edmund. *An Inquiry into the Present State of the Foreign Relations of the Union: As Affected by the Late Measures of Administration*. Philadelphia: Samuel F. Bradford, 1806.

Morford, Henry. *Over-Sea; or, England, France and Scotland as Seen by a Live American*. New York: Hilton & Company, 1867.

Morgan, James Morris. *Recollections of a Rebel Reefer*. Boston, MA: Houghton Mifflin Company, 1917.

Nadal, Ehrman Syme. *Impressions of London Social Life*. New York: Scribner, Armstrong & Company, 1875.

————. *Notes of a Professional Exile*. New York: Century, 1895.

Nevill, Ralph. *London Clubs: Their History and Treasures*. London: Chatto & Windus, 1911.

Noah, Mordecai. *Travels in England, France, Spain, and the Barbary States in the Years 1813–14 and 15*. New York: Kirk and Mercein, 1819.

Oliver, Andrew, ed. *The Journal of Samuel Curwen Loyalist*. 2 vols. Cambridge, MA: Harvard University Press, 1972.

Pierce, Edward L, ed. *Memoirs and Letters of Charles Sumner*. 4 vols. Boston: Roberts Brothers, 1894.

Prentis, Noble L. *A Kansan Abroad*. Topeka, KS: Martin, 1878.

Report of the American International Relief Committee, for the Suffering Operatives of Great Britain, 1862–'63. New York, 1864.

Sanitary Commission. *Narrative of Privations and Sufferings of United States Officers and Soldiers While Prisoner of War in the Hands of the Rebel Armies*. Philadelphia: King & Baird, 1864.

Schurz, Carl. *The Reminiscences of Carl Schurz*. New York: The McLure Company, 1907.

Semmes, Raphael. *Memoirs of Service Afloat: During the War Between the States*. Baltimore: Kelly, Piet & Co., 1869.

Silliman, Benjamin. *A Journal of Travels in England, Holland, and Scotland, and of the Two Passages over the Atlantic*. 3 vols. Boston: T. B. Wait & Co., 1810.

Simond, Louis. *Journal of a Tour and Residence in Great Britain During the Years 1810 and 1811*. Edinburgh: George Ramsay and Company, 1815.

Sims, George Robert, ed. *Living London: Its Work and its Play, its Humour and its Pathos, its Sights and its Scenes*. 2 vols. London: Cassell and Company, 1903.

Smalley, George W. *London Letters and Some Others*. 2 vols. New York: Harper & Brothers, 1891.

Smith, Goldwin. *Letter to a Whig Member of the Southern Independence Association*. Boston: Ticknor and Fields, 1864.

Smith, John Jay. *A Summer's Jaunt Across the Water*. Philadelphia: J. W. Moore, 1846.

Smithers, Henry. *Liverpool, Its Commerce, Statistics, and Institutions with a History of the Cotton Trade*. Liverpool, UK: T. Kaye, 1825.

Society of American Women in London: Constitution, By-Laws, Standing Rules. London: privately printed, 1899.

Spence, James. *The American Union*. London: Richard Bentley, 1861.

Stead, William T. *Always Arbitrate Before You Fight: An Appeal to All English-Speaking Folk*. London: Review of Reviews, 1896.

———. *The Americanisation of the World, or, the Trend of the Twentieth Century*. London: Review of Reviews, 1902.

Stevens, Henry. *Henry Stevens—His Autobiography & Noviomagus Club*. Larchmont, NY: Sons & Stiles, 1978.

Stewart, Charles S. *Sketches of Society in Great Britain and Ireland*. Philadelphia: Carey, Lea, & Blanchard, 1834.

Stowe, Harriet Beecher. *Sunny Memories of Foreign Lands*. 2 vols. Boston: Phillips, Sampson & Company, 1854.

The Stranger in Liverpool; or, An Historical and Descriptive View. 12th edition. Liverpool: Thomas Kaye, 1841.

Swan, William Graham. *Foreign Relations: Speech of Hon. W. G. Swan, of Tennessee, Delivered in the House of Representatives of the Confederate States, February 5, 1863*. Richmond, VA: Smith, Bailey & Co., 1863.

Tallis, John. *History and Description of the Crystal Palace and the Exhibition of the World's Industry in 1851*. 3 vols. London: John Tallis & Co., 1852.

Taylor, Bayard. *Views A-Foot: or, Europe Seen with Knapsack and Staff*. New York: Wiley & Putnam, 1846.

Taylor, Thomas E. *Running the Blockade: A Personal Narrative of the Adventures, Risks and Escapes During the American Civil War*. London: John Murray, 1897.

Thompson, Arthur Bailey. *The Visitor's Universal New Pocket Guide to London*. London: Ward and Lock, 1861.

Thompson, Ella W. *Beaten Paths; or, A Woman's Vacation*. Boston: Lee and Shepard, 1874.

Thwaite, Benjamin H. *The American Invasion*. London: Simpkin, Marshall, Hamilton, Kent & Co., 1902.

Thwing, Edward P. *Outdoor Life in Europe, or, Sketches of Seven Summers Abroad*. New York: Hurst & Co., 1888.

Train, George Francis. *The Downfall of England by George Francis Train*. Philadelphia: T. B. Peterson & Brothers, 1862.

———. *The Facts: Or, At Whose Door Does the Sin (?) Lie? Who Profits by Slave Labor? Who Initiated the Slave Trade? What Have the Philanthropists Done? These Questions Answered*. New York: R. M. DeWitt, 1860.

———. *My Life in Many States and Foreign Lands*. New York: D. Appleton and Company, 1902.

———. *Spread-Eagleism*. New York: Derby & Jackson, 1860.

———. *Train's Speech to the Fenians*. Philadelphia: T. B. Peterson & Brothers, 1865.

———. *Train's Speeches in England on Slavery and Emancipation*. Philadelphia: T. B. Peterson and Brothers, 1862.

———. *Train's Union Speeches. Delivered in England During the Present American War*. Philadelphia: T. B. Peterson & Brothers, 1862.

———. *Young America Abroad*. London: Seth Low, 1857.

———. *Young America on Slavery*. Liverpool: Griffin McGhie, 1859.

Trevelyan, George M. *The Life of John Bright*. London: Constable, 1913.

Trimble, Robert. *The Negro North and South: The Status of the Coloured Population in the Northern and Southern States Compared*. London: Whittaker & Co., 1863.

———. *Popular Fallacies Relating to the American Question*. London: Whittaker & Co., 1863.

———. *Slavery in the United States of North America*. London: Henry Young, 1863.

Tuckerman, Henry T. *The Italian Sketch Book*. New York: J. C. Riker, 1848.

———. *A Month in England*. New York: Redfield, 1853.

———. *Rambles and Reveries*. New York: James P. Giffing, 1841.

Vanderlip, Frank A. *The American Commercial Invasion of Europe*. New York: Scribner's, 1902.

Vincent, John, ed. *Disraeli, Derby and the Conservative Party: Journals and Memoirs of Edward Henry, Lord Stanley, 1848–69*. Hassocks, UK: Harvester Press, 1978.

Waldstein, Charles. *The Expansion of Western Ideals and the World's Peace*. New York: Lane, 1899.

Ward, Matthew Flournoy. *Letters from Three Continents, By M., The Arkansas Correspondent of the Louisville Journal*. New York: D. Appleton, 1851.

Watts, Isaac. *The Cotton Supply Association: Its Origin and Progress*. Manchester, UK: Tubbs & Brook, 1871.

Weed, Thurlow. *Letters from Europe and the West Indies, 1843–1862*. Albany, NY: Weed, Parsons, and Company, 1866.

Wells, Ida B. *Crusade for Justice: The Autobiography of Ida B. Wells*. Edited by Alfreda Duster. Chicago: University of Chicago Press, 1970.

Wells, Samuel Roberts. *How To Read Character: A New Illustrated Hand-Book of Phrenology and Physiognomy for Students and Examiners*. New York: Fowler and Wells, 1869.

Wheaton, Nathaniel S. *A Journal of a Residence during Several Months in London*. Hartford, CT: H. & F. J. Huntington, 1830.

White, Joshua. *Letters on England*. Philadelphia: M. Carey, 1816.

Wilkes, George. *Europe in a Hurry*. New York: H. Long & Brother, 1853.

Williams, Henry Sylvester. *The British Negro: A Factor in the Empire, "The Ethiopian Eunuch." Two Lectures Delivered Before Many Distinguished Clubs and Associations in the United Kingdom of Great Britain, at the Request of Several British Friends, Interested in the Progress of the "Negro Race."* Brighton: W. T. Moulton, 1902.

Williams, James. *The South Vindicated*. London: Longman, Green, Longman, Roberts & Green, 1862.

Williams, Rudolph. *Europe from May to December*. Chicago: Weeks, 1895.

Willington, Aaron Smith. *A Summer's Tour in Europe, in 1851: In a Series of Letters Addressed to the Editors of the Charleston Courier.* Charleston, SC: Walker & James, 1852.

Witmer, Theodore. *Wild Oats, Sown Abroad. Or, On and Off Soundings; Being Leaves from a Private Journal by a Gentleman of Leisure.* Philadelphia: T.B. Peterson, 1853.

SECONDARY SOURCES

Adams, Bluford. "World Conquerors or a Dying People? Racial Theory, Regional Anxiety, and the Brahmin Anglo-Saxonists." *Journal of the Gilded Age and Progressive Era* 8, no. 2 (2009): 189–215.

Adams, Charles Francis. "James McHenry on the Cotton Crisis, 1865." *Proceedings of the Massachusetts Historical Society* 47 (1914): 279–87.

"African Americans and Transatlantic Abolition, 1845–1865." *Slavery & Abolition* 33, no. 2 (2012): 181–336.

Albion, Robert Greenhalgh. *The Rise of New York Port, 1815–1860.* New York: Charles Scribner's Sons, 1939.

———. *Square-Riggers On Schedule: The New York Packets to England, France, and the Cotton Ports.* Princeton, NJ: Princeton University Press, 1983.

Allen, Harry C. "Civil War, Reconstruction, and Great Britain." In *Heard Round the World: The Impact Abroad of the Civil War,* edited by Harold M. Hyam, 3–96. New York: Knopf, 1969.

Allgor, Catherine. "'A Republican in a Monarchy': Louisa Catherine Adams in Russia." *Diplomatic History* 21, no. 1 (1997): 15–43.

———. *Parlor Politics: In Which the Ladies of Washington Help Build a City and a Government.* Charlottesville: University Press of Virginia, 2000.

Anderson, Clare. "After Emancipation: Empires and Imperial Formations." In *Emancipation and the Remaking of the British Imperial World,* edited by Catherine Hall, Nicholas Draper, and Keith McClelland, 113–27. Manchester, UK: Manchester University Press, 2014.

Anderson, Stuart. *Race and Rapprochement: Anglo-Saxonism and Anglo-American Relations, 1895–1904.* London: Associated University Presses, 1981.

Arkle, A.H. "The Early Coffee Houses of Liverpool." *Transactions of the Historical Society of Lancashire and Cheshire* 64 (1912): 1–16.

Asaka, Ikuko. "'Our Brethren in the West Indies': Self-Emancipated People in Canada and the Antebellum Politics of Diaspora and Empire." *Journal of African American History* 97, no. 3 (2012): 219–39.

Auerbach, Jeffrey A., ed. *Britain, the Empire, and the World at the Great Exhibition of 1851.* Abingdon, UK: Routledge, 2008.

Austin, Peter E. *Baring Brothers and the Birth of Modern Finance.* London: Pickering & Chatto, 2015.

Bailyn, Bernard. *The Peopling of British North America: An Introduction.* New York: Knopf, 1988.

Baker, Anne P. *The Pilgrims of Great Britain: A Centennial History.* London: Profile Books, 2002.

Ball, Douglas B. *Financial Failure and Confederate Defeat.* Urbana: University of Illinois Press, 1991.

Balogh, Brian. *A Government Out of Sight: The Mystery of National Authority in Nineteenth Century America.* Cambridge, UK: Cambridge University Press, 2009.

Banton, Michael. *The Coloured Quarter: Negro Immigrants in an English City.* London: Jonathan Cope, 1955.

Barker, Anthony. *The African Link: British Attitudes to the Negro in the Era of the Atlantic Slave Trade, 1550–1807.* London: Cass, 1978.

Barnhart, Terry A. *Alfred Taylor Bledsoe: Defender of the Old South and Architect of the Lost Cause.* Baton Rouge: Louisiana State University Press, 2011.

Bayly, Christopher A. *The Birth of the Modern World, 1780–1914: Global Connections and Comparisons.* Oxford: Blackwell, 2004.

Beckert, Sven. "Emancipation and Empire: Reconstructing the Worldwide Web of Cotton in the Age of the American Civil War." *American Historical Review* 190, no. 5 (2004): 1405–39.

———. *Empire of Cotton: A New History of Global Capitalism.* London: Allen Lane, 2014.

———. *Monied Metropolis: New York City and the Consolidation of the American Bourgeoisie, 1850–1896.* New York: Cambridge University Press, 2001.

Bederman, Gail. *Manliness & Civilization: A Cultural History of Gender and Race in the United States, 1880–1917.* Chicago: University of Chicago Press, 1995.

Bedwell, C. E. A. "American Middle Templars." *The American Historical Review* 25, no. 4 (1920): 680–89.

Belich, James. *Replenishing the Earth: The Settler Revolution and the Rise of the Anglo-World, 1783–1939.* Oxford: Oxford University Press, 2009.

Bell, Duncan. *The Idea of Greater Britain: Empire and the Future of World Order, 1860–1900.* Princeton, NJ: Princeton University Press, 2007.

———. *Reordering the World: Essays on Liberalism and Empire.* Princeton, NJ: Princeton University Press, 2016.

Bender, Thomas. *A Nation Among Nations: America's Place in World History.* New York: Hill and Wang, 2006.

———, ed. *Rethinking American History in a Global Age.* Berkeley: University of California Press, 2002.

Bendixen, Alfred. "Travel Books about Europe before the Civil War." In *The Cambridge Companion to American Travel Writing,* edited by Alfred Bendixen and Judith Hamera, 103–27. Cambridge, UK: Cambridge University Press, 2009.

Bennett, John D. *London Confederates: The Officials, Clergy, Businessmen, and Journalists who Backed the American South During the Civil War.* London: McFarland, 2007.

Benson, John. *The Rise of Consumer Society in Britain, 1880–1980.* London: Longman, 1994.

Biagini, Eugenio F. *Liberty, Retrenchment and Reform: Popular Liberalism in the Age of Gladstone, 1860–1880.* Cambridge, UK: Cambridge University Press, 1992.

Bickers, Robert, ed. *Settlers and Expatriates: Britons over the Seas.* Oxford: Oxford University Press, 2010.

Black, Jeremy. *British Diplomats and Diplomacy, 1688–1800.* Exeter, UK: University of Exeter Press, 2001.

———. *The British Abroad: The Grand Tour in the Eighteenth Century.* New York: St Martin's, 1992.

Blackett, Richard J. M. "African Americans, British Public Opinion, and Civil War Diplomacy." In *The Union, The Confederacy, and the Atlantic Rim,* edited by Robert E. May, 69–101. West Lafayette, ID: Purdue University Press, 1995.

———. "African Americans, the British Working Class, and the American Civil War." *Slavery and Abolition* 17, no. 2 (1996): 51–67.

———. *Beating Against the Barriers: Biographical Essays in Nineteenth-Century Afro-History.* Baton Rouge: Louisiana State University Press, 1986.

———. *Building an Antislavery Wall: Black Americans in the Atlantic Abolitionist Movement, 1830–1860.* Baton Rouge: Louisiana State University Press, 1983.

———. *Divided Hearts: Britain and the American Civil War.* Baton Rouge: Louisiana State University Press, 2001.

Blower, Brooke L. *Becoming Americans in Paris: Transatlantic Politics and Culture Between the World Wars.* New York: Oxford University Press, 2011.

———. "Nation of Outposts: Forts, Factories, Bases, and the Making of American Power." *Diplomatic History* 41, no. 3 (2017): 439–59.

Blume, Kenneth. "The Mid-Atlantic Arena: The United States, the Confederacy, and the British West Indies, 1861–1865." Ph.D. diss., State University of New York at Binghamton, 1984.

Bolster, W. Jeffrey. *Black Jacks: African American Seamen in the Age of Sail.* Cambridge, MA: Harvard University Press, 1997.

Bolt, Christine. *The Anti-Slavery Movement and Reconstruction: a Study in Anglo-American Co-Operation, 1833–77.* London: Oxford University Press, 1969.

———. *The Women's Movements in the United States and Britain from the 1790s to the 1920s.* Amherst: University of Massachusetts Press, 1993.

Bonner, Robert. *Mastering America: Southern Slaveholders and the Crisis of American Nationhood.* Cambridge, UK: Cambridge University Press, 2009.

———. "Roundheaded Cavaliers? The Context and Limits of a Confederate Racial Project." *Civil War History* 48, no.1 (2002): 34–59.

———. "Slavery, Confederate Diplomacy, and the Racialist Mission of Henry Hotze." *Civil War History* 51, no. 3 (2005): 288–316.

Boodry, Kathryn. "August Belmont and the World the Slaves Made." In *Slavery's Capitalism: A New History of American Economic Development,* edited by Sven Beckert and Seth Rockman, 163–79. Philadelphia: University of Pennsylvania Press, 2016.

Bowley, Arthur L. *Wages in the Nineteenth Century United Kingdom.* Cambridge, UK: Cambridge University Press, 1900.

Bradburn, Douglas. *The Citizenship Revolution: Politics and the Creation of the American Union, 1774–1804.* Charlottesville: University of Virginia Press, 2009.

Braidwood, Stephen J. *Black Poor and White Philanthropists: London's Blacks and the Foundation of the Sierra Leone Settlement, 1786–1791*. Liverpool: Liverpool University Press, 1994.

Breen, T. H. *Tobacco Culture: The Mentality of the Great Tidewater Planters on the Eve of the Revolution*. Princeton, NJ: Princeton University Press, 2001.

Bremner, G. A. "The Metropolis: Imperial Buildings and Landscapes in Britain." In *Architecture and Urbanism in the British Empire*, edited by G. A. Bremner, 1–15. Oxford: Oxford University Press, 2016.

Bremner, Robert. *The Public Good: Philanthropy and Welfare in the Civil War Era*. New York: Knopf, 1980.

Brendon, Piers. *The Decline and Fall of the British Empire, 1781–1997*. London: Vintage, 2008.

Bressey, Caroline. *Empire, Race and the Politics of Anti-Caste*. London: Bloomsbury Academic, 2013.

Brown, Donna. "Travel Books." In *A History of the Book in America, Vol. 2: An Extensive Republic: Print, Culture, and Society in the New Nation, 1790–1840*, edited by Robert A. Gross and Mary Kelley, 449–58. Chapel Hill: University of North Carolina Press, 2010.

Buck, Norman Stanley. *The Development of the Organisation of Anglo-American Trade, 1800–1850*. New Haven, CT: Yale University Press, 1925.

Buonomo, Leonardo. *Backward Glances: Exploring Italy, Reinterpreting America*. Madison, NJ: Fairleigh Dickinson University Press, 1996.

Burk, Kathleen. *Old World New World: The Story of Britain and America*. London: Little, Brown, 2007.

Burns, Emily. "Puritan Parisians: American Art Students in Late Nineteenth-Century Paris." In *A Seamless Web: Transatlantic Art in the Nineteenth Century*, edited by Cheryll May and Marian Wardle, 123–47. Newcastle upon Tyne: Cambridge Scholars, 2014.

Burton, Antoinette, ed. *After the Imperial Turn: Thinking with and Through the Nation*. Durham, NC: Duke University Press, 2003.

———. *At the Heart of Empire: Indians and the Colonial Encounter in Late-Victorian Britain*. Berkeley: University of California Press, 1998.

Butler, Leslie. *Critical Americans: Victorian Intellectuals and Transatlantic Liberal Reform*. Chapel Hill: University of North Carolina Press, 2007.

Callahan, Noaquia N. "A Rare Colored Bird: Mary Church Terrell, *Die Firtschritte der Farbigen Frauen*, and the International Council of Women's Congress in Berlin, Germany, 1904." *German Historical Institute Bulletin Supplement* 13 (2017): 93–107.

Campbell, Charles Jr. *Anglo-American Understanding, 1898–1903*. Baltimore: Johns Hopkins University Press, 1957.

Campbell, Duncan Andrew. *English Public Opinion and the American Civil War*. London: Boydell Press, 2003.

Cannadine, David. *The Decline and Fall of the British Aristocracy*. New Haven, CT: Yale University Press, 1990.

Cannadine, David, and Simon Price, eds. *Rituals of Royalty: Power and Ceremonial in Traditional Societies*. Cambridge, UK: Cambridge University Press, 1987.

Carosso, Vincent, and Rose Carosso. *The Morgans: Private International Bankers, 1854–1913*. Cambridge, MA: Harvard University Press, 1987.

Carpenter, John A. "The New York International Relief Committee: A Chapter in the Diplomatic History of the Civil War." *New York Historical Society Quarterly* 56 (1972): 239–52.

Carstensen, Fred. *American Enterprise in Foreign Markets: Studies of Singer and International Harvester in Imperial Russia*. Chapel Hill: University of North Carolina Press, 1984.

Carwardine, Richard. *Transatlantic Revivalism: Popular Evangelicalism in Britain and America, 1790–1865*. Westport, CT: Greenwood Press, 1978.

Chandler, Alfred. *Scale and Scope: The Dynamics of Industrial Capitalism*. Cambridge, MA: Harvard University Press, 1990.

Chapman, Stanley S. *Merchant Enterprise in Britain: From the Industrial Revolution to World War One*. Cambridge, UK: Cambridge University Press, 1992.

———. *The Rise of Merchant Banking*. London: Allen & Unwin, 1984.

Checkland, Sydney George. *The Gladstones: A Family Biography, 1764–1851*. Cambridge, UK: Cambridge University Press, 1971.

Chernow, Ron. *The House of Morgan*. London: Simon & Schuster, 1990.

Church, Roy A. "The Effect of the American Export Invasion on the British Boot and Shoe Industry, 1885–1914." *Journal of Economic History* 28, no. 2 (1968): 223–54.

Clarke, Frances M. *War Stories: Suffering and Sacrifice in the Civil War North*. Chicago: University of Chicago Press, 2011.

Clarke, Peter. "The English-Speaking Peoples before Churchill." *Britain and the World* 4, no. 2 (2011): 199–231.

Cohen, Joanna. *Luxurious Citizens: The Politics of Consumption in Nineteenth-Century America*. Philadelphia: University of Pennsylvania Press, 2017.

Colby, Jason. *Business of Empire: United Fruit, Race, and U.S. Expansion in Central America*. Ithaca, NY: Cornell University Press, 2011.

Colley, Linda. *Britons: Forging the Nation, 1707–1837*. New Haven, CT: Yale University Press, 1992.

Colum, Giles, and Bob Hawkins. *Storehouses of Empire: Liverpool's Historic Warehouses*. Liverpool, UK: English Heritage, 2004.

Commager, Henry Steele. *Britain Through American Eyes*. New York: McGraw & Hill, 1974.

Cooper, Dana. *Informal Ambassadors: American Women, Transatlantic Marriages, and Anglo-American Relations, 1865–1945*. Kent, OH: The Kent State University Press, 2014.

Corton, Christine. *London Fog: The Biography*. Cambridge, MA: Harvard University Press, 2015.

Costello, Ray. *Black Salt: Seafarers of African Descent on British Ships*. Liverpool, UK: Liverpool University Press, 2012.

Cottrell, P. L. *British Overseas Investment in the Nineteenth Century*. London: Macmillan, 1975.

Crapol, Edward P. *America for the Americans: Economic Nationalism and Anglophobia in the Late Nineteenth Century*. Westport, CT: Greenwood Press, 1973.

Crawford, Martin. *The Anglo-American Crisis of the Mid-Nineteenth Century: The Times and America, 1850–1862*. Athens: University of Georgia Press, 1987.

Crook, David Paul. *The North, The South, and the Powers, 1861–1865*. New York: Wiley, 1974.

Croucher, Sheila. "Americans Abroad: A Global Diaspora?" *Journal of Transnational American Studies* 4, no. 2 (2012): 1–33.

Cull, Nicholas J. "International Capital Movements, Domestic Capital Markets, and American Economic Growth, 1820–1914." In *The Cambridge Economic History of the United States: The Long Nineteenth Century*, edited by Stanley Engerman and Robert Gallman, 733–812. Cambridge, UK: Cambridge University Press, 2000.

———. "Public Diplomacy: Taxonomies and Histories." *Annals of the American Academy of Political and Social Science* 616 (2008): 31–54.

Cull, Nicholas J. and Lance E. Davies. *International Capital Markets and American Economic Growth, 1820–1914*. Cambridge, UK: Cambridge University Press, 1994.

Cunningham, H. "Leisure and Culture," in *The Cambridge Social History of Britain, 1750–1950. Volume 2: People and their Environment*, edited by F.M.L Thompson, 279–339. Cambridge, UK: Cambridge University Press, 1990.

Curti, Merle. *American Philanthropy Abroad*. New Brunswick, NJ: Rutgers University Press, 1963.

D'Entrement, John. *Southern Emancipator: Moncure Conway, The American Years, 1832–1865*. New York: Oxford University Press, 1987.

Dalzell, Robert F. *American Participation in the Great Exhibition of 1851*. Amherst, MA: Amherst College Press, 1960.

Darwin, John. *The Empire Project: The Rise and Fall of the British World-System, 1830–1970*. Cambridge, UK: Cambridge University Press, 2009.

———. "Imperialism and the Victorians: Dynamics of Territorial Expansion." *English Historical Review* 112, no. 447 (1997): 614–42.

———. *Unfinished Empire: The Global Expansion of Britain*. London: Allen Lane, 2012.

David, Huw. *Trade, Politics, and Revolution: South Carolina and Britain's Atlantic Commerce, 1730–1790*. Columbia: University of South Carolina Press, 2018.

Davidoff, Leonore. *The Best Circles: Society, Etiquette and the Season*. London: Cresset Library, 1973.

Davis, Carl L. *Arming the Union: Small Arms in the Civil War*. Port Washington, NY: Kennikat Press, 1973.

Davis, Lance E., and Robert E. Gallman. *Evolving Financial Markets and International Capital Flows: Britain, the Americas, and Australia, 1865–1914*. Cambridge, UK: Cambridge University Press, 2001.

Davis, Robert. "Diplomatic Plumage: American Court Dress in the Early National Period." American Quarterly 20, no. 2 (1968): 164–79.

Day, John R. The Story of London's Underground. London: London Transport, 1972.

Dickerson, Vanessa D. *Dark Victorians*. Urbana: University of Illinois Press, 2008.

Diehl, Carl. *Americans and German Scholarship, 1770–1870*. New Haven, CT: Yale University Press, 1978.

Dierks, Konstantin. "Americans Overseas in the Early Republic." *Diplomatic History* 42, no. 1 (2018): 1–16.

Dingwall, Helen. "The Importance of Being Edinburgh." In *Centres of Medical Excellence? Medical Travel and Education in Europe, 1500–1789*, edited by Ole Peter Grell, Andrew Cunningham, and Jon Arrizabalaga, 305–24. Farnham, UK: Ashgate, 2010.

Domosh, Mona. *American Commodities in an Age of Empire*. London: Routledge, 2006.

Donald, David Herbert. *Charles Sumner and the Coming of Civil War*. Chicago: University of Chicago Press, 1981 [1960].

Downs, Jacques M. *The Golden Ghetto: The American Commercial Community at Canton and the Shaping of American China Policy, 1784-1844*. Hong Kong: Hong Kong University Press, 2015.

Doyle, Don H. *The Cause of All Nations: An International History of the American Civil War*. New York: Basic Books, 2015.

———. *Nations Divided: America, Italy, and the Southern Question*. Athens: University of Georgia Press, 2002.

Dubrulle, Hugh. "'If it is still impossible . . . to advocate slavery . . . . It has . . . become a habit persistently to write down freedom': Britain, the Civil War, and Race." In *The American Civil War as Global Conflict: Transnational Meanings of the American Civil War*, edited by David T. Gleason and Simon Lewis, 56–85. Columbia: University of South Carolina Press, 2014.

———. "'We Are Threatened with . . . Anarchy and Ruin': Fear of Americanization and the Emergence of an Anglo-Saxon Confederacy in England during the American Civil War." *Albion* 33, no. 4 (2001): 583–613.

Duffy, John. *The Sanitarians: A History of American Public Health*. Urbana: University of Illinois Press, 1997.

Dulles, Foster Rhea. *Americans Abroad: Two Centuries of European Travel*. Ann Arbor: University of Michigan Press, 1964.

Dupont, Brandon, Alka Ghandi, and Thomas Weiss. "The Long-term Rise in Overseas Travel by Americans, 1820–2000." *Economic History Review* 65, no. 1 (2012): 144–67.

Dupont, Brandon, Drew Keeling, and Thomas Weiss. "First Cabin Fares from New York to the British Isles, 1826–1914." NBER Working Paper 22426. https://www.nber.org/papers/w22426.pdf.

Dyer, Brainerd. "Thomas H. Dudley." *Civil War History* 1, no. 4 (1955): 401–13.

Earnest, Ernest P. *Expatriates and Patriots: American Artists, Scholars, and Writers in Europe*. Durham, NC: Duke University Press, 1968.

Eckes, Alfred E., Jr., and Thomas W. Zeiler. *Globalization and the American Century*. Cambridge, UK: Cambridge University Press, 2003.

Edling, Max. *A Hercules in the Cradle: War, Money, and the American State, 1783–1867*. Chicago: University of Chicago Press, 2014.

Ellis, Aytoun. *Heir of Adventure: The Story of Brown, Shipley & Co. Merchant Bankers, 1810–1960*. London: Brown, Shipley, 1960.

Ellwood, David W. *The Shock of America: Europe and the Challenge of the Century*. Oxford: Oxford University Press, 2012.

Elsden, Annamaria. *Roman Fever: Domesticity and Nationalism in Nineteenth-Century American Women's Writing*. Columbus: Ohio State University Press, 2004.

Endy, Christopher. "Travel and World Power: Americans in Europe, 1890–1917." *Diplomatic History* 22, no. 4 (1998): 565–94.

Enstad, Nan. *Cigarettes, Inc.: An Intimate History of Corporate Imperialism*. Chicago: University of Chicago Press, 2018.

Esedebe, Peter Olisanwuche. *Pan-Africanism: The Idea and the Movement, 1776–1963*. Washington, DC: Howard University Press, 1982.

Eyal, Yonatan. "A Romantic Realist: George Nicholas Sanders and the Dilemmas of Southern International Engagement." *Journal of Southern History* 78, no. 1 (2012): 107–30.

———. *The Young America Movement and the Transformation of the Democratic Party, 1821–61*. Cambridge, UK: Cambridge University Press, 2007.

Faulkner, Carol. "The Root of the Evil: Free Produce and Radical Antislavery, 1820–1860." *Journal of the Early Republic* 27, no. 3 (2007): 377–405.

Fedorowich, Kent, and Andrew S. Thompson. *Empire, Migration and Identity in the British World*. Manchester, UK: Manchester University Press, 2013.

Ferris, Norman. *Desperate Diplomacy: William H. Seward's Foreign Policy, 1861*. Knoxville: University of Tennessee Press, 1976.

Finn, Margot. *After Chartism: Class and Nation in English Reform Politics, 1848–1874*. Cambridge, UK: Cambridge University Press, 1993.

Fladeland, Betty. *Men and Brothers: Anglo-American Antislavery Cooperation*. Urbana: University of Illinois Press, 1972.

Flavell, Julie. *When London Was Capital of America*. New Haven, CT: Yale University Press, 2010.

Fogelman, Aaron S. "From Slaves, Convicts and Servants to Free Passengers: The Transformation of Immigration in the Era of the American Revolution." *Journal of American History* 85, no. 1 (1998): 43–76.

Foreman, Amanda. *A World on Fire: An Epic Story of Two Nations Divided*. London: Allen Lane, 2010.

Fowler, William M., Jr. *Steam Titans: Cunard, Collins, and the Epic Battle for Commerce on the North Atlantic*. New York: Bloomsbury, 2017.

Franch, Robert. *Robber Baron: The Life of Charles Tyson Yerkes*. Urbana: University of Illinois Press, 2006.

Gabaccia, Donna. *Foreign Relations: American Immigration in Global Perspective*. Princeton, NJ: Princeton University Press, 2012.

Gabin, Jane S. *American Women in Gilded Age London: Expatriates Rediscovered*. Gainesville: University Press of Florida, 2006.

Gallman, J. Matthew. "Voluntarism in Wartime: Philadelphia's Great Central Fair." In *Toward a Social History of the Civil War: Exploratory Essays*, edited by Maris A. Vinovskis, 93–116. Cambridge, UK: Cambridge University Press, 1990.

Games, Alison. "Migration." In *The British Atlantic World, 1500–1800*, edited by David Armitage and Michael J. Braddick, 33–52. Basingstoke, UK: Palgrave Macmillan, 2009.

Geiss, Immanuel. *The Pan-African Movement*. London: Metuen, 1974.

Gerstle, Gary. "Theodore Roosevelt and the Divided Character of American Nationalism." *Journal of American History* 86, no. 3 (1999): 1280–1307.

Ghosh, Peter. "Gladstone and Peel." In *Politics and Culture in Victorian Britain: Essays in Memory of Colin Matthew*, edited by Peter Ghosh and Lawrence Goldman, 46–73. Oxford: Oxford University Press, 2006.

Giesberg, Judith Ann. *Civil War Sisterhood: The U.S. Sanitary Commission and Women's Politics in Transition*. Boston: Northeastern University Press, 2000.

Gilje, Paul A. *Liberty on the Waterfront: American Maritime Culture in the Age of Revolution*. Philadelphia: University of Pennsylvania Press, 2004.

Gilroy, Paul. *The Black Atlantic: Modernity and Double Consciousness*. London: Verso, 1993.

Goldman, Lawrence. "Exceptionalism and Internationalism: The Origins of American Social Science Reconsidered." *Journal of Historical Sociology* 11, no. 1 (1998): 1–36.

Gould, Eliga H. *Among the Powers of the Earth: The American Revolution and the Making of a New World Empire*. Cambridge, MA: Harvard University Press, 2012.

———. "Independence and Interdependence: The American Revolution and the Problem of Postcolonial Nationhood, circa 1802." *William and Mary Quarterly* 74, no. 4 (2017): 729–52.

Gosse, Van. "'As a nation, the English are our friends': The Emergence of African American Politics in the British Atlantic World, 1772–1861." *American Historical Review* 113, no. 4 (2008): 1003–28.

Grant, Alfred. *The American Civil War and the British Press*. London: McFarland & Co., 2000.

Green, Nancy. "Expatriation, Expatriates, and Expats: The American Transformation of a Concept." *American Historical Review* 114, no. 2 (2009): 307–28.

———. *The Other Americans in Paris: Businessmen, Countesses, and Wayward Youth, 1880–1941*. Chicago: University of Chicago University, 2014.

Greenberg, Dolores. "Yankee Financiers and the Establishment of Trans-Atlantic Partnerships: A Re-Examination." *Business History* 16, no. 1 (1974): 17–35.

Greenhalgh, Paul. *Ephemeral Vistas: The Expositions Universelles, Great Exhibition, and World's Fairs, 1851–1939*. Rochester, NY: University of Rochester Press, 2005.

Guenther, Louise H. *British Merchants in Nineteenth-Century Brazil: Business, Culture, and Identity in Bahia, 1808–1850*. Oxford: Centre for Brazilian Studies, University of Oxford, 2004.

Gruesser, John. "Travel Writing." In *The Oxford Companion to African American Literature*, edited by William L. Andrews, Frances Smith Foster, and Trudier Harris, 735–36. New York: Oxford University Press, 1997.

Guterl, Matthew Pratt. *American Mediterranean: Southern Slaveholders in the Age of Emancipation.* Cambridge, MA: Harvard University Press, 2008.

Guyatt, Nicholas. *Providence and the Invention of the United States, 1607–1876.* Cambridge, UK: Cambridge University Press, 2007.

Haggerty, Sheryllynne. *The British Atlantic Trading Community, 1760–1810: Men, Women, and the Distribution of Goods.* Leiden: Brill, 2006.

Hahn, Steven. *A Nation Without Borders: The United States and its World in the Age of Civil Wars, 1830–1910.* New York: Viking, 2016.

Hall, Catherine. *Civilising Subjects: Colony and Metropole in the English Imagination, 1830–1867.* Chicago: University of Chicago Press, 2002.

———, Keith McClelland, and Jane Rendall, eds. *Defining the Victorian Nation: Class, Race, Gender, and the British Reform Act of 1867.* Cambridge, UK: Cambridge University Press, 2000.

Hall, Julie E. "'Coming to Europe,' Coming to Authorship: Sophia Hawthorne and her *Notes in England and Italy*." *Legacy* 19, no. 2 (2002): 137–51.

Hamilton, J. G. de Roulhac. "Southern Members of the Inns of Court." *North Carolina Historical Review* 10 (1933): 273–80.

Hancock, David. *Citizens of the World: London Merchants and the Integration of the British Atlantic Community, 1735–1785.* Cambridge, UK: Cambridge University Press, 1995.

Hart, John M. *Empire and Revolution: The Americans in Mexico Since the Civil War.* Berkeley: University of California Press, 2002.

Haskell, Thomas. "Capitalism and the Origins of the Humanitarian Sensibility, Part 1," in *The Antislavery Debate: Capitalism and Abolitionism as a Problem of Historical Interpretation,* edited by Thomas Bender, 107–35. Berkeley: University of California Press, 1992.

Hawkins, Angus. *Victorian Political Culture: "Habits of Heart and Mind."* Oxford: Oxford University Press, 2015.

Haynes, Sam W. *Unfinished Revolution: The Early American Republic in a British World.* Charlottesville: University of Virginia Press, 2010.

Heindel, Richard H. *The American Impact on Great Britain, 1898–1914: A Study of the United States in World History.* Philadelphia: University of Pennsylvania Press, 1940.

Henderson, W. O. "The American Chamber of Commerce for the Port of Liverpool." *Transactions of the Historic Society of Lancashire and Cheshire* 85 (1933): 1–61.

Herson, John. "'Stirring Spectacles of Cosmopolitan Animation': Liverpool as a Diasporic City, 1825–1913." In *The Empire in One City? Liverpool's Inconvenient Imperial Past,* edited by Sheryllynne Haggerty, Anthony Webster, and Nicholas J. White, 55–78. Manchester, UK: Manchester University Press, 2008.

Herzog, Ben. *Revoking Citizenship: Expatriation in America from the Colonial Era to the War on Terror.* New York: New York University Press, 2015.

Hidy, Ralph W. *The House of Baring in American Trade and Finance: English Merchant Bankers at Work, 1763–1861.* Cambridge, MA: Harvard University Press, 1949.

———. "The Organization and Function of Anglo-American Merchant Bankers, 1815–1860." *The Journal of Economic History* 1, no. 1 (1941): 53–66.

Hirota, Hidetaka. *Expelling the Poor: Atlantic Seaboard States and the Nineteenth Century Origins of American Immigration Policy.* New York: Oxford University Press, 2017.

Hobsbawm, Eric. *Nations and Nationalism since 1780: Programme, Myth Reality.* Cambridge, UK: Cambridge University Press, 1991.

Hoganson, Kristin L. *Consumer's Imperium: The Global Production of American Domesticity.* Chapel Hill: University of North Carolina Press, 2007.

———. *Fighting for American Manhood: How Gender Politics Provoked the Spanish-American and Philippine-American Wars.* New Haven, CT: Yale University Press, 1998.

Hopkins, A. G. *American Empire: A Global History.* Princeton, NJ: Princeton University Press, 2018.

———. "The United States, 1783–1861: Britain's Honorary Dominion?" *Britain and the World* 4, no. 1 (2011): 232–46.

Horn, James, and Philip D. Morgan. "Settlers and Slaves: European and African Migrations to Early Modern British America." In *The Creation of the British Atlantic World,* edited by Carole Shammas and Elizabeth Mancke, 19–44. Baltimore, MD: Johns Hopkins University Press, 2005.

Horne, Gerald. *The Deepest South: The United States, Brazil, and the African Slave Trade.* New York: New York University Press, 2007.

Horsman, Reginald. *Race and Manifest Destiny: The Origins of American Racial Anglo-Saxonism.* Cambridge, MA: Harvard University Press, 1981.

Howe, Daniel Walker. *The Political Culture of the American Whigs.* Chicago: University of Chicago Press, 1979.

Howman, Brian. "Abolitionism in Liverpool." In *Liverpool and Transatlantic Slavery,* edited by David Richardson, Anthony Tibbles, and Suzanne Schwartz, 277–96. Liverpool, UK: Liverpool University Press, 2007.

Hubbard, Charles. *The Burden of Confederate Diplomacy.* Knoxville: University of Tennessee Press, 1998.

Hughes, Francis. "Liverpool and the Confederate States: Fraser Trenholm and Company Operations During the American Civil War." Ph.D. diss., Keele University, 1996.

Humphreys, Margaret. *Marrow of Tragedy: The Health Crisis of the American Civil War.* Baltimore: Johns Hopkins University Press, 2013.

Hunt, Alfred N. *Haiti's Influence on Antebellum America: Slumbering Volcano in the Caribbean.* Baton Rouge: Louisiana State University Press, 1988.

Husband Julie, and Jim O'Loughlin. *Daily Life in the Industrial United States, 1870–1900.* Westport, CT: Greenwood Press, 2004.

Huzzey, Richard. "The British Empire and the Crises of the Americas in the 1860s." In *American Civil Wars: The United States, Latin America, Europe, and the Crisis of the 1860s,* edited by Don Doyle, 82–100. Chapel Hill: University of North Carolina Press, 2017.

———. *Freedom Burning: Anti-Slavery and Empire in Victorian Britain.* Ithaca, NY: Cornell University Press, 2012.

Hyde, Francis Edwin. *Liverpool and the Mersey: An Economic History of a Port, 1700–1970.* Newton Abbott, UK: David and Charles, 1971.

Immerwahr, Daniel. "The Greater United States: Territory and Empire in U.S. History." *Diplomatic History* 40, no. 3 (2016): 373–91.

"Interchange: Nationalism and Internationalism in the Era of the Civil War." *Journal of American History* 98, no. 2 (2011): 455–89.

Jackson, Patrick. *Education Act Forster: A Political Biography of W. E. Forster.* Madison, NJ: Fairleigh Dickinson University Press, 1997.

James, Robert Rhodes. *Henry Wellcome.* London: Hodder & Stoughton, 1994.

James, Scott D., and David A. Lake. "The Second Face of Hegemony: Britain's Repeal of the Corn Laws and the American Walker Tariff of 1846." *International Organization* 43, no. 1 (1989): 1–29.

James, Winston. "The Black Experience in Twentieth-Century Britain." In *Black Experience and the Empire,* edited by Philip D. Morgan and Sean Hawkins, 347–86. Oxford: Oxford University Press, 2004.

Jasanoff, Maya. *Liberty's Exiles: The Loss of America and the Remaking of the British Empire.* London: Harper Press, 2011.

———. "Revolutionary Exiles: The American Loyalist and French Émigré Diasporas." In *The Age of Revolutions in Global Context, c. 1760–1840,* edited by David Armitage and Sanjay Subrahmanyam, 37–58. Basingstoke, UK: Palgrave Macmillan, 2010.

John, Richard. "Recasting the Information Infrastructure for the Industrial Age." In *A Nation Transformed by Information: How Information Has Shaped the United States from Colonial Times to the Present,* edited by Alfred D. Chandler Jr. and James W. Cortada, 68–86. New York: Oxford University Press, 2000.

Johnson, Walter. *River of Dark Dreams: Slavery and Empire in the Cotton Kingdom.* Cambridge, MA: Harvard University Press, 2013.

Jones, Charles A. *International Business in the Nineteenth Century: The Rise and Fall of a Cosmopolitan Bourgeoisie.* New York: New York University Press, 1987.

Jones, Howard. *Blue and Grey Diplomacy: A History of Union and Confederate Foreign Relations.* Chapel Hill: University of North Carolina Press, 2010.

———. *Union in Peril: The Crisis Over British Intervention in the Civil War.* Chapel Hill: University of North Carolina Press, 1992.

Kaplan, Amy. *The Anarchy of Empire in the Making of U.S. Culture.* Cambridge, MA: Harvard University Press, 2002.

Karp, Matthew. "King Cotton, Emperor Slavery: Antebellum Slaveholders and the World Economy." In *The Civil War as Global Conflict: Transnational Meanings of the American Civil War,* edited by David T. Gleeson and Simon Lewis, 37–55. Columbia: University of South Carolina Press, 2014.

———. *This Vast Southern Empire: Slaveholders at the Helm of American Foreign Policy.* Cambridge, MA: Harvard University Press, 2016.

Kaye, Anthony E. "The Second Slavery: Modernity in the Nineteenth Century South and the Atlantic World." *Journal of Southern History* 75, no. 3 (2009): 627–50.

Kelly, Patrick J. "The Cat's Paw: Confederate Ambitions in Latin America." In *American Civil Wars: The United States, Latin America, Europe, and the*

Crisis of the 1860s, edited by Don Doyle, 58–81. Chapel Hill: University of North Carolina Press, 2017.

Keene, Edward. "The Treaty-Making Revolution of the Nineteenth Century." *International History Review* 34, no. 3 (2012): 475–500.

Kennedy, David. *The Dark Side of Virtue: Reassessing International Humanitarianism.* Princeton, NJ: Princeton University Press, 2004.

Kenwood, A. G., and A. L. Lougheed. *The Growth of the International Economy, 1820–1990.* Third edition. London: Routledge, 1992.

Kenin, Richard. *Return to Albion: Americans in England, 1760–1940.* New York: Holt, Rinehart and Winston, 1979.

Kerrigan, W. T. "'Young America!': Romantic Nationalism in Literature and Politics, 1843–1861." Ph.D. diss., University of Michigan, 1997.

Kilbride, Daniel. *Being American in Europe, 1750–1860.* Baltimore: Johns Hopkins University Press, 2013.

———. "Travel, Ritual, and National Identity: Planters on the European Tour, 1820–1860." *Journal of Southern History* 69, no. 3 (2003): 549–84.

Kilingray, David. "'A Good West Indian, a Good African, and in Short, a Good Britisher': Black and British in a Colour-Conscious Empire, 1760–1950." *Journal of Imperial and Commonwealth History* 36, no. 3 (2008): 368–81.

———. "Significant Black South Africans in Britain before 1912: Pan-African Organisations and the Emergence of South Africa's First Black Lawyers." *South African Historical Journal* 64, no. 3 (2012): 393–417.

Killick, John. "The Cotton Operations of Alexander Brown and Sons in the Deep South, 1820–1860." *Journal of Southern History* 43, no. 2 (1977): 169–94.

———. "An Early Nineteenth-Century Shipping Line: The Cope Line of Philadelphia and Liverpool Packets, 1822–1872." *International Journal of Maritime History* 22, no. 1 (2000): 61–87.

Kinser, Brent E. *The American Civil War in the Shaping of British Democracy.* London: Routledge, 2016.

Klein, Philip Shriver. *President James Buchanan: A Biography.* University Park: Pennsylvania State University Press, 1962.

Kramer, Paul A. "Empires, Exceptions, and Anglo-Saxons: Race and Rule between the British and United States Empires, 1880–1910." *Journal of American History* 88, no. 4 (2002): 1315–53.

Kulikoff, Alan. "Uprooted Peoples: Black Migrants in the Age of the American Revolution." In *Slavery and Freedom in the Age of the American Revolution,* edited by Ira Berlin and Ronald Hoffman, 143–71. Charlottesville: University Press of Virginia, 1983.

La Guerre, John. "Henry Sylvester Williams." In *Dictionary of Caribbean and Afro-Latin American Biography,* edited by Franklin W. Knight and Henry Louis Gates Jr. New York: Oxford University Press, 2008.

Lahiri, Shompa. "Contested Relations: The East India Company and Lascars in London." In *The Worlds of the East India Company,* edited by Huw V. Bowen, Margarette Lincoln, and Nigel Rigby, 169–81. Woodbridge, UK: Boydell Press, 2002.

Laity, Paul. *The British Peace Movement, 1870–1914*. Oxford: Oxford University Press, 2001.

Lake, Marilyn, and Henry Reynolds. *Drawing the Global Colour Line: White Men's Countries and the International Challenge of Racial Equality*. Cambridge, UK: Cambridge University Press, 2008.

Lears, Jackson. *Fables of Abundance: A Cultural History of Advertising in America*. New York: Basic, 1994.

Lee, Robert, ed. *Commerce and Culture: Nineteenth-Century Business Elites*. Farnham, UK: Ashgate, 2011.

Lepler, Jessica M. *The Many Panics of 1837: People, Politics, and the Creation of a Transatlantic Financial Crisis*. New York: Cambridge University Press, 2013.

Lester, Alan and Fae Dussart. *Colonization and the Origins of Humanitarian Governance: Protecting Aborigines Across the Nineteenth-Century British Empire*. Cambridge, UK: Cambridge University Press, 2014.

Levenstein, Harvey A. *Seductive Journey: American Tourists in France from Jefferson to the Jazz Age*. Chicago: University of Chicago Press, 1998.

Lewis, Samuel. "List of the American Graduates in Medicine in the University of Edinburgh." *New England Historical and Genealogical Review* 42 (1988): 159–65.

Lipsey, R. E. "U. S. Foreign Trade and the Balance of Payments, 1800–1913." *NBER Working Paper No. 4710* (April 1994).

Lockwood, Alison. *Passionate Pilgrims: The American Traveler in Great Britain, 1800–1904*. London: Cornwall Books, 1981.

Loeffler, Jane C. *Architecture of Diplomacy: Building America's Embassies*. New York: Princeton Architectural Press, 1998.

Lorimer, Douglas A. *Colour, Class, and the Victorians: English Attitudes to the Negro in the Mid-Nineteenth Century*. Leicester: Leicester University Press, 1978.

———. *Science, Race Relations, and Resistance: Britain, 1870–1914*. Manchester, UK: Manchester University Press, 2013.

MacFadden, Margaret. *Golden Cables of Sympathy: The Transatlantic Sources of Nineteenth Century Feminism*. Lexington, KY: University Press of Kentucky, 1999.

MacKenzie, John M. "Empire and Metropolitan Cultures." In *The Oxford History of the British Empire, Volume 3, The Nineteenth Century*, edited by Andrew Porter, 270–93. Oxford: Oxford University Press, 1999.

Maclear, J. F. "The Evangelical Alliance and the Antislavery Crusade." *Huntington Library Quarterly* 42, no. 2 (1979): 141–64.

Magee, Gary, and Andrew S. Thompson. *Empire and Globalisation: Networks of People, Goods, and Capital in the British World*. Cambridge, UK: Cambridge University Press, 2010.

Maischak, Lars. *German Merchants in the Nineteenth-Century Atlantic*. Cambridge, UK: Cambridge University Press, 2013.

Marler, Scott. *The Merchants' Capital: New Orleans and the Political Economy of the Nineteenth Century South*. Cambridge, UK: Cambridge University Press, 2013.

Marshall, Peter J. "Britain Without America: A Second Empire?" In *The Oxford History of the British Empire. Volume 2, The Eighteenth Century,* edited by Peter J. Marshall, 576–95. Oxford: Oxford University Press, 1998.

———. "Britain and the World in the Eighteenth Century: II, Britons and Americans." *Transactions of the Royal Historical Society* 9 (December 1999): 1–16.

———. *The Making and Unmaking of Empires: Britain, India, and America c. 1750–1783.* Oxford: Oxford University Press, 2007.

———. *Remaking the British Atlantic: The United States and the British Empire after American Independence.* Oxford: Oxford University Press, 2012.

Mason, Matthew. "'A World Safe for Modernity': Antebellum Southern Proslavery Intellectuals Confront Great Britain." In *The Old South's Modern Worlds: Slavery, Region, and Nation in the Age of Progress,* edited by L. Diane Barnes, Brian Schoen, and Frank Towers, 47–65. New York: Oxford University Press, 2011.

Matera, Marc. *Black London: The Imperial Metropolis and Decolonization in the Twentieth Century.* Oakland: University of California Press, 2015.

Matson, Cathy D., and Peter S. Onuf. *A Union of Interests: Political and Economic Thought in Revolutionary America.* Lawrence: University Press of Kansas, 1990.

May, Robert E. "The Irony of Confederate Diplomacy: Visions of Empire, the Monroe Doctrine, and the Quest for Nationhood." *Journal of Southern History* 83, no. 1 (2017): 69–106.

———. *The Southern Dream of a Caribbean Empire, 1854–1861.* Baton Rouge: Louisiana State University Press, 1973.

Maynard, Douglas H. "The Forbes Aspinwall Mission." *Mississippi Valley Historical Review* 45, no. 1 (1958): 67–89.

Maxwell, William. *Lincoln's Fifth Wheel: The Political History of the United States Sanitary Commission.* New York: Longman, Green & Co., 1956.

McCoy, Drew R. *The Elusive Republic: Political Economy in Jeffersonian America.* Chapel Hill: University of North Carolina Press, 1980.

McCusker, John J. "The Demise of Distance: The Business Press and the Origins of the Information Revolution in the Early Modern Atlantic World." *American Historical Review* 110, no. 2 (2005): 295–321.

McDaniel, Caleb. *The Problem of Democracy in the Age of Slavery: Garrisonian Abolitionists & Transatlantic Reform.* Baton Rouge: Louisiana State University Press, 2013.

McFadden, Margaret. *Golden Cables of Sympathy: The Transatlantic Sources of Nineteenth-Century Feminism.* Lexington: University Press of Kentucky, 2009.

Meardon, Stephen. "Richard Cobden's American Quandary: Negotiating Peace, Free Trade, and Anti-Slavery." In *Rethinking Nineteenth Century Liberalism: Richard Cobden Bicentenary Essays,* edited by Anthony Howe and Simon Morgan, 208–29. Aldershot, UK: Ashgate, 2006.

Meer, Sarah. *Uncle Tom Mania: Slavery, Minstrelsy, and Transatlantic Culture in the 1850s.* Athens: University of Georgia Press, 2005.

Mehrlander, Andrea. *The Germans of Charleston, Richmond, and New Orleans During the Civil War Period, 1850–1870: A Study and Research Compendium.* Berlin: De Gruyter, 2011.

Michie, Ranald. *The City of London: Continuity and Change Since 1850*. London: MacMillan, 1992.

Midgley, Clare. *Women Against Slavery: The British Campaigns, 1700–1870*. London: Routledge, 1992.

Mills, Karen M. "Americans Overseas in U.S. Consulates." U.S. Department of Commerce, Bureau of the Census Technical Paper 62. Washington, DC: Government Printing Office, 1993.

Milne, Graeme J. *Trade and Traders in Mid-Victorian Liverpool: Mercantile Business and the Making of a World Port*. Liverpool, UK: Liverpool University Press, 2000.

Milton, David Hepburn. *Lincoln's Spymaster: Thomas Haines Dudley and the Liverpool Network*. Mechanicsburg, PA: Stackpole Books, 2003.

Mitchell, Brian R. *British Historical Statistics*. Cambridge, UK: Cambridge University Press, 1988.

Monaghan, Jay. *Diplomat in Carpet Slippers: Abraham Lincoln Deals with Foreign Affairs*. Indianapolis, IN: Charter Books, 1945.

Montgomery, Maureen E. *Gilded Prostitution: Status, Money, and Transatlantic Marriages, 1870–1914*. London: Routledge, 1989.

———. "'Natural Distinction': The American Bourgeois Search for Distinctive Signs in Europe." In *The American Bourgeoisie: Distinction and Identity in the Nineteenth Century*, edited by Sven Beckert and Julia B. Rosenbaum, 27–44. New York: Palgrave Macmillan, 2010.

Morgan, Kenneth. "Business Networks." In *The Early Modern Atlantic Economy*, edited by John McCusker and Kenneth Morgan, 36–62. Cambridge, UK: Cambridge University Press, 2000.

———. "Liverpool's Dominance in the Transatlantic Slave Trade, 1740–1807." In *Liverpool and Transatlantic Slavery*, edited by D. Richardson, S. Schwarz, and A. Tibbles, 14–42. Liverpool, UK: Liverpool University Press, 2007.

Morgan, Kenneth O. "The Future at Work: Anglo-American Progressivism, 1890–1917." In *Contrast and Connection: Bicentennial Essays in Anglo-American History*, edited by Harry C. Allen and Roger Thompson, 245–71. London: G. Bell & Sons, 1976.

Mössland, Markus, and Torsten Riotte. "Introduction: The Diplomats' World." In *The Diplomats' World: A Cultural History of Diplomacy, 1815–1914*, edited by Markus Mössland and Torsten Riotte, 1–20. New York: Oxford University Press, 2008.

Mowat, Robert Balmain. *Americans in England*. London: George G. Harrao & Co., 1935.

Moya, Jose C. "Modernization, Modernity, and the Trans/formation of the Atlantic World in the Nineteenth Century." In *The Atlantic in Global History, 1500–2000*, edited by Jorge Calizares-Esguerra and Erik R. Seeman, 179–97. London: Routledge, 2016.

Müller, Simone M. *Wiring the World: The Social and Cultural Creation of Global Telegraph Networks*. New York: Columbia University Press, 2016.

———, and Heidi J. S. Tworek. "'The telegraph and the bank': On the Interdependence of Global Communications and Capitalism." *Journal of Global History* 10, no. 2 (2015): 259–83.

Munck, Ronaldo. *Reinventing the City? Liverpool in Comparative Perspective.* Liverpool, UK: Liverpool University Press, 2003.

Murphy, Brian Phillips. *Building the Empire State: Political Economy in the Early Republic.* Philadelphia: University of Pennsylvania Press, 2015.

Murphy, Kevin C. *The American Merchant Experience in Nineteenth-Century Japan.* London: Routledge Curzon, 2002.

Murray, Hannah-Rose. "'With almost electric speed': Mapping African American Abolitionists in Britain and Ireland, 1838–1847." *Slavery & Abolition* 40, no. 3 (2019): 522–42.

Mustafa, Sam A. *Merchants and Migrations: Germans and Americans in Connection, 1776–1835.* Aldershot, UK: Ashgate, 2001.

Myers, Norma. *Reconstructing the Black Past: Blacks in Britain, 1780–1830.* London: Frank Cass, 1996.

Nabach, Alexander. "'Poisoned at the Source'? Telegraphic New Services and Big Business in the Nineteenth Century." *Business History Review* 77, no. 4 (2003): 577–610.

Nagel, Joane. "Masculinity and Nationalism: Gender and Sexuality in the Making of Nations." *Ethnic and Racial Studies* 21, no. 2 (2010): 242–69.

Nagel, Paul C. *One Nation Indivisible: The Union in American Thought, 1776–1861.* New York: Oxford University Press, 1964.

Ngai, Mae M. *Impossible Subjects: Illegal Aliens and the Making of Modern America.* Princeton, NJ: Princeton University Press, 2004.

Nead, Lynda. *Victorian Babylon: People, Streets and Images in Nineteenth-Century London.* New Haven, CT: Yale University Press, 2000.

Nicholas, S. J. "The American Export Invasion of Britain: The Case of the Engineering Industry, 1870–1914." *Technology and Culture* 21, no. 4 (1980): 570–88.

Ninkovich, Frank. *Global Dawn: The Cultural Foundation of American Internationalism, 1865–1890.* Cambridge, MA: Harvard University Press, 2009.

Norwood, Dael A. "What Counts? Political Economy, or Ways to Make Early America Add Up." *Journal of the Early Republic* 36, no. 4 (2016): 753–81.

Norton, Mary Beth. *The British-Americans: The Loyalist Exiles in England, 1774–1789.* London: Constable, 1974.

Oberholtzer, Ellis Paxson. *Jay Cooke: Financier of the Civil War.* 2 vols. Philadelphia: George W. Jacobs, 1907.

O'Brien, Michael. *Conjectures of Order: Intellectual Life and the American South, 1810–1860.* 2 vols. Chapel Hill: University of North Carolina Press, 2004.

O'Brien, Susan. "A Transatlantic Community of Saints: The Great Awakening and the First Evangelical Network, 1735–1755." *American Historical Review* 91, no. 4 (1986): 811–32.

Olegario, Rowena. *Culture of Credit: Embedding Trust and Transparency in American Business.* Cambridge, MA: Harvard University Press, 2006.

Olson, Alison. *Making the Empire Work: London and American Interest Groups, 1690–1790.* Cambridge, MA: Harvard University Press, 1992.

Orde, Anne. *The Eclipse of Great Britain: The United States and British Imperial Decline, 1895–1956.* Basingstoke, UK: Macmillan, 1996.

Otte, Thomas. *The Foreign Office Mind: The Making of British Foreign Policy, 1865–1914.* Cambridge, UK: Cambridge University Press, 2011.

Owsley, H. C. "Henry Shelton Sanford and Federal Surveillance Abroad, 1861–1865." *Mississippi Valley Historical Review* 48, no. 2 (1961): 211–28.

Palen, Marc-William. "The Civil War's Forgotten Transatlantic Tariff Debate and the Confederacy's Free Trade Diplomacy." *Journal of the Civil War Era* 3, no. 1 (2013): 35–61.

———. "Protection, Federation and Union: The Global Impact of the McKinley Tariff upon the British Empire, 1890–94." *Journal of Imperial and Commonwealth History* 38, no. 3 (2010): 395–418.

Palmer, Sarah. "Ports." In *The Cambridge Urban History of Britain. Volume 3: 1840–1950*, edited by Peter Clark and D. M. Palliser, 133–50. Cambridge, UK: Cambridge University Press, 2000.

Parker, Franklin. *George Peabody: A Biography.* Nashville, TN: Vanderbilt University Press, 1971.

Parker, Wyman W. *Henry Stevens of Vermont: American Rare Book Dealer in London, 1845–1886.* Amsterdam: N. Israel, 1963.

Pennybacker, Susan D. "The Universal Races Congress, London Political Culture, and Imperial Dissent, 1900–1939." *Radical History Review* 92 (2005): 103–17.

Perkins, Bradford. *The Great Rapprochement: England and the United States, 1895–1914.* New York: Atheneum, 1968.

Perkins, Edwin J. *Financing Anglo-American Trade: The House of Brown, 1800–1880.* Cambridge, MA: Harvard University Press, 1975.

———. "Tourists and Bankers: Travelers' Credits and the Rise of American Tourism, 1840–1900." *Business and Economic History*, 2nd ser., 8 (1979): 16–28.

Perl-Rosenthal, Nathan. *Citizen Sailors: Becoming American in the Age of Revolution.* Cambridge, MA: Harvard University Press, 2015.

Perry, Kennetta Hammond. *London is the Place for Me: Black Britons, Citizenship, and the Politics of Race.* New York: Oxford University Press, 2015.

Phelps, Nicole. *U.S.-Habsburg Relations from 1815 to the Paris Peace Conference: Sovereignty Transformed.* Cambridge, UK: Cambridge University Press, 2015.

Picard, Liza. *Victorian London: The Life of a City, 1840–1870.* London: Weidenfeld & Nicolson, 2005.

Pietsch, Tamson. "Rethinking the British World." *Journal of British Studies* 52, no. 2 (2013): 441–63.

Pooley, Colin G. "Living in Liverpool: The Modern City." In *Liverpool 800: Culture, Character & History*, edited by John Belchem, 174–95. Liverpool, UK: Liverpool University Press, 2008.

Porter, Andrew. "Trusteeship, Anti-slavery, and Humanitarianism." In *The Oxford History of the British Empire Volume 3: The Nineteenth Century*, edited by Andrew Porter, 198–221. Oxford: Oxford University Press, 1991.

Porter, Bernard. *The Lion's Share: a History of British Imperialism 1850 to the Present.* 5th edition. Harlow, UK: Pearson, 2012.

Potter, Jim. "Atlantic Economy, 1815–1860: The USA and the Industrial Revolution in Britain." In *Studies in the Industrial Revolution: Presented* to T.S. Ashton, edited by L.S. Pressnell, 236–81. London: Athlone Press, 1960.

Potter, Simon, and Jonathan Saha. "Global History, Connected History and Connected Histories of Empire." *Journal of Colonialism and Colonial History* 16, no. 1 (2015).

Power-Greene, Ousmane K. *Against Wind and Tide: The African-American Struggle Against the Colonization Movement.* New York: New York University Press, 2014.

Price, Jacob M. "What Did Merchants Do? Reflections on British Overseas Trade, 1660–1790." *Journal of Economic History* 49, no. 2 (1989): 267–84.

Prochaska, Frank. "Charity Bazaars in Nineteenth Century England." *Journal of British Studies* 16, no. 2 (1977): 62–84.

Pryor, Elizabeth Stordeur. *Colored Travelers: Mobility and the Fight for Citizenship before the Civil War.* Chapel Hill: University of North Carolina Press, 2016.

Quarles, Benjamin. "Ministers without Portfolio." *Journal of Negro History* 39, no. 1 (1954): 27–42.

Quigley, Paul. *Shifting Grounds: Nationalism and the American South, 1848–1865.* New York: Oxford University Press, 2012.

Rafferty, Matthew. *The Republic Afloat: Law, Honor, and Citizenship in Maritime America.* Chicago: University of Chicago Press, 2013.

Rappaport, Erika. *Shopping for Pleasure: Women in the Making of London's West End.* Princeton, NJ: Princeton University Press, 2000.

Reber, Vera Blinn. *British Mercantile Houses in Buenos Aires, 1810–1880.* Cambridge, MA: Harvard University Press, 1979.

Reynolds, K.D. *Aristocratic Women and Political Society in Victorian Britain.* Oxford: Clarendon, 1998.

Rhoden, Nancy L. "The American Revolution: The Paradox of Atlantic Integration." In *British North America in the Seventeenth and Eighteenth Centuries,* edited by Stephen Foster, 256–88. Oxford: Oxford University Press, 2013.

Richards, Thomas. *The Commodity Culture of Victorian England: Advertising and Spectacle, 1851–1914.* Stanford, CA: Stanford University Press, 1990.

Rief, Michelle. "Thinking Locally, Acting Globally: The International Agenda of African American Clubwomen, 1880–1940." *Journal of African American Women's History* 89, no. 3 (2004): 203–22.

Riello, Giorgio. *Cotton: The Fabric that Made the Modern World.* Cambridge, UK: Cambridge University Press, 2013.

Ritcheson, Charles R. *Aftermath of Revolution: British Policy Toward the United States, 1783–1795.* Dallas, TX: Southern Methodist University Press, 1969.

Ritchie-Noakes, Nancy. *Liverpool's Historic Waterfront: The World's First Mercantile Dock System.* London: HM Stationary Office, 1984.

Roberson, Susan L. "American Women and Travel Writing." In *The Cambridge Companion to American Travel Writing,* edited by Alfred Bendixen and Judith Hamera, 214–27. Cambridge, UK: Cambridge University Press, 2008.

Roberts, Timothy Mason. *Distant Revolutions: 1848 and the Challenge to American Exceptionalism.* Charlottesville: University of Virginia Press, 2009.

Robertson, Craig. *The Passport in America: The History of a Document.* New York: Oxford University Press, 2010.

Robin, Ron. *Enclaves of America: The Rhetoric of American Political Architecture Abroad, 1900–1965*. Princeton, NJ: Princeton University Press, 1992.

Roche, Julian. *The International Cotton Trade*. Cambridge, UK: Woodhead Publishing, 1994.

Rockman, Seth. "What Makes the History of Capitalism Newsworthy?" *Journal of the Early Republic* 34, no. 3 (2014): 439–66.

Rodgers, Daniel T. *Atlantic Crossings: Social Politics in a Progressive Age*. Cambridge, MA: Harvard University Press, 1998.

Rogers, Edmund. "The United States and the Fiscal State in Britain." *Historical Journal* 50, no. 3 (2007): 593–622.

Rogers, George C. *Evolution of a Federalist: William Loughton Smith of Charleston (1758–1812)*. Columbia: University of South Carolina Press, 1962.

Rosner, Lisa. "Thistle on the Delaware: Edinburgh Medical Education and Philadelphia Practice, 1800–1825." *Social History of Medicine* 5, no. 1 (1992): 19–42.

Rothbard, Murray Newton. *Panic of 1819: Reactions and Policies*. New York: Columbia University Press, 1962.

Rouleau, Brian. *With Sails Whitening Every Sea: Mariners and the Making of an American Maritime Empire*. Ithaca, NY: Cornell University Press, 2014.

Rugemer, Edward B. *The Problem of Emancipation: The Caribbean Roots of the American Civil War*. Baton Rouge: Louisiana State University Press, 2008.

———. "Slave Rebels and Abolitionists: The Black Atlantic and the Coming of the Civil War." *Journal of the Civil War Era* 2, no. 2 (2012): 179–202.

Rupp, Leila J. "Constructing Internationalism: The Case of Transnational Women's Organizations, 1888–1945." *American Historical Review* 99, no. 5 (1994): 1571–1600.

———. *Worlds of Women: The Making of an International Women's Movement*. Princeton, NJ: Princeton University Press, 1997.

Rydell, Robert W. *All the World's a Fair: Visions of Empire at American International Expositions, 1876–1916*. Chicago: University of Chicago Press, 1984.

———, and Rob Kroes. *Buffalo Bill in Bologna: The Americanization of the World, 1869–1922*. Chicago: University of Chicago Press, 2005.

Sahli, Nancy Ann. "Elizabeth Blackwell, MD (1821–1910): A Biography." Ph.D. diss., University of Pennsylvania, 1974.

Saul, S.B. "The American Impact on British Industry, 1895–1914." *Business History* 3, no. 1 (1960): 19–38.

Saunders, Robert. "Lord John Russell and Parliamentary Reform, 1848–67." *English Historical Review* 120, no. 489 (2005): 1289–1315.

Saunier, Pierre-Yves. *Transnational History: Theory and History*. Basingstoke, UK: Palgrave Macmillan, 2013.

Schell, William. *Integral Outsiders: The American Colony in Mexico City, 1876–1911*. Wilmington, DE: SR Books, 2001.

Schermerhorn, Calvin. *The Business of Slavery and the Rise of American Capitalism, 1815–1860*. New Haven, CT: Yale University Press, 2015.

Schlereth, Eric. "Privileges of Locomotion: Expatriation and the Politics of Southwestern Border Crossing." *Journal of American History* 100, no. 4 (2014): 995–1020.

Schneer, Jonathan. *London 1900: The Imperial Metropolis.* New Haven, CT: Yale University Press, 2001.

Schoen, Brian. *The Fragile Fabric of Union: Cotton, Federal Politics, and the Global Origins of the Civil War.* Baltimore: Johns Hopkins University Press, 2009.

Schoeppner, Michael A. *Moral Contagion: Black Atlantic Sailors, Citizenship, and Diplomacy in Antebellum America.* Cambridge, UK: Cambridge University Press, 2019.

Schoonover, Thomas. "Napoleon is Coming! Maximilian is Coming? The International History of the Civil War in the Caribbean Basin." In *The Union, The Confederacy, and the Atlantic Rim,* edited by Robert E. May, 101–30. West Lafayette, IN: Purdue University Press, 1995.

Schulten, Susan. *Mapping the Nation: History and Cartography in Nineteenth-Century America.* Chicago: University of Chicago Press, 2012.

Schultz, Jane E. "Nurse as Icon: Florence Nightingale's Impact on Women in the American Civil War." In *The American Civil War as Global Conflict: Transnational Meanings of the American Civil War,* edited by David T. Gleason and Simon Lewis, 235–52. Columbia: University of South Carolina Press, 2014.

Schulzinger, Robert D. *The Making of the Diplomatic Mind: The Training, Outlook, and Style of United States Foreign Service Officers, 1908–1931.* Middletown, CT: Wesleyan University Press, 1975.

Scobie, Edward. *Black Britannia: A History of Blacks in Britain.* Chicago: Johnson Publishing Company, 1972.

Scully, Eileen P. *Bargaining with the State from Afar: American Citizenship in Treaty Port China, 1844–1942.* New York: Columbia University Press, 2001.

Searle, G. *The Quest for National Efficiency: A Study in British Politics and Political Thought, 1899–1914.* London: Basil Blackwell, 1971.

Servan-Schreiber, Jean-Jacques. *The American Challenge.* London: Atheneum, 1968.

Sewell, Mike. "'All the English-Speaking Race is in Mourning': The Assassination of President Garfield and Anglo-American Relations." *Historical Journal* 34, no. 3 (1991): 665–86.

Sexton, Jay. *Debtor Diplomacy: Finance and Foreign Relations in the Civil War Era.* Oxford: Oxford University Press, 2005.

———. "Epilogue." In *British North America in the Seventeenth and Eighteenth Centuries,* edited by Stephen Foster, 318–48. Oxford: Oxford University Press, 2013.

———. *The Monroe Doctrine: Empire and Nation in Nineteenth-Century America.* New York: Hill & Wang, 2011.

Sharkey, Heather. *American Evangelicals in Egypt: Missionary Encounters in the Age of Empire.* Princeton, NJ: Princeton University Press, 2008.

Shepherd, James F., and Gary M. Walton. "Economic Change after the American Revolution: Pre- and Post-War Comparisons of Maritime Shipping and Trade." *Explorations in Economic History* 13, no. 4 (1976): 397–422.

Shoemaker, Nancy. "The Extraterritorial United States to 1860." *Diplomatic History* 42, no. 1 (2018): 36–55.

Shumway, Daniel B. "The American Students of Gottingen." *German American Studies Annals* 8 (1910): 171–254.

Silkey, Sarah L. *Black Woman Reformer: Ida B. Wells, Lynching, and Transatlantic Activism.* Athens: University of Georgia Press, 2015.

Simon, Mathew, and David E. Novak. "Some Dimensions of the American Commercial Invasion of Europe, 1871–1914: An Introductory Essay." *Journal of Economic History* 24, no. 4 (1964): 591–605.

Sinha, Manisha. *The Slave's Cause: A History of Abolition.* New Haven, CT: Yale University Press, 2016.

Smil, Vaclav. *Made in the USA: The Rise and Retreat of American Manufacturing.* Cambridge, MA: MIT Press, 2013.

Smith, Anthony. *The Nation in History: Historiographical Debates about Ethnicity and Nationalism.* Hanover, NH: University Press of New England, 2000.

Smith, Walter B. *America's Diplomats and Consuls of 1776–1865.* Arlington, VA: Foreign Service Institute, US Department of State, 1986.

Snyder, Jennifer K. "Revolutionary Refugees: Black Flight in the Age of Revolution." In *The American South and the Atlantic World,* edited by Brian Ward, Martyn Bone, and William A. Link, 81–103. Gainesville: University Press of Florida, 2013.

Sosin, Jack M. *Agents and Merchants: British Colonial Policy and the Origins of the American Revolution, 1763–1775.* Lincoln: University of Nebraska Press, 1965.

Stafford, Robert A. "Scientific Exploration and Empire." In *The Oxford History of the British Empire: The Nineteenth Century,* edited by Andrew Porter, 294–319. Oxford: Oxford University Press, 1999.

Stebbins, Theodore E. *The Lure of Italy: American Artists and the Italian Experience, 1760–1914.* New York: N.H. Abrams, 1992.

Stephanson, Anders. *Manifest Destiny: American Expansion and the Empire of the Right.* New York: Hill & Wang, 1996.

Surridge, Keith T. *Managing the South African War, 1899–1902: Politicians v. Generals.* Woodridge, UK: Boydell Press, 1998.

Swanberg, William A. *Sickles the Incredible.* New York: C. Scribner's Sons, 1956.

Tansil, Charles C. *The Foreign Policy of Thomas F. Bayard, 1885–1897.* New York: Fordham University Press, 1940.

Taylor, George R. *The Transportation Revolution, 1815–1860.* New York: Reinhart, 1951.

Thistlethwaite, Frank. *Anglo-American Connection in the Early Nineteenth Century.* Philadelphia: University of Pennsylvania Press, 1959.

Thornton, Tamara Plakins. "Capitalist Aesthetics: Americans Look at the London and Liverpool Docks." In *Capitalism Takes Command: The Social Transformation of Nineteenth-Century America,* edited by Michael Zakim and Gary J. Kornblith, 169–98. Chicago: University of Chicago Press, 2012.

Torpey, John. *The Invention of the Passport: Surveillance, Citizenship, and the State.* Cambridge, UK: Cambridge University Press, 2000.

Trentmann, Frank. *Empire of Things: How We Became a World of Consumers, From the Fifteenth Century to the Twenty-First.* London: Allen Lane, 2016.

———. *Free Trade Nation: Commerce, Consumption, and Civil Society in Modern Britain.* Oxford: Oxford University Press, 2008.

Tsiang, I-mien. *The Question of Expatriation in America Prior to 1907*. Baltimore, MD: Johns Hopkins Press, 1942.

Tuffnell, Stephen. "Anglo-American Inter-Imperialism: The American Invasion of Britain and the Empire, c. 1865–1914." *Britain and the World* 8, no. 2 (2013): 174–95.

———. "Expatriate Foreign Relations: Britain's American Community and Transnational Approaches to the U.S. Civil War." *Diplomatic History* 40, no. 3 (2016): 635–63.

———. "'The International Siamese Twins': The Iconography of Anglo-American Inter-Imperialism." In *Comic Empires*, edited by Andrekos Varnava and Richard Scully. Manchester, UK: Manchester University Press, 2020.

———. "'Uncle Sam is to be Sacrificed': Anglophobia in Late Nineteenth-Century Politics and Culture." *American Nineteenth Century History* 12, no. 1 (2011): 77–99.

Tyrrell, Ian. *Reforming the World: The Creation of America's Moral Empire*. Princeton, NJ: Princeton University Press, 2010.

———. *Transnational Nation: United States History in Global Perspective Since 1789*. Basingstoke, UK: Palgrave Macmillan, 2007.

———. *Woman's World—Woman's Empire: The Woman's Christian Temperance Union in International Perspective, 1880–1930*. Chapel Hill: University of North Carolina Press, 1991.

Unterman, Katherine. *Uncle Sam's Policemen: The Pursuit of Fugitives Across Borders*. Cambridge, MA: Harvard University Press, 2015.

Van Riper, Robert. *A Life Divided: George Peabody, Pivotal Figure in Anglo-American Finance, Philanthropy and Diplomacy*. London: Lightning Source, 2000.

Vance, William L. "The Sidelong Glance: Victorian Americans and Baroque Rome." *New England Quarterly* 58, no. 4 (1985): 501–30.

Vincent, John. *The Formation of the Liberal Party, 1857–1868*. London: Constable, 1966.

Walvin, James. *Black and White: The Negro and English Society, 1555–1945*. London: Penguin, 1973.

Warf, Barney. *Time-Space Compression: Historical Geographies*. Abingdon, UK: Routledge, 2008.

Warner, John Harley. *Against the Spirit of the System: The French Impulse in Nineteenth-Century Medicine*. Baltimore, MD: Johns Hopkins University Press, 2003

Watson, Richie Devon. *Normans and Saxons: Southern Race Mythology and the Intellectual History of the American Civil War*. Baton Rouge: Louisiana State University Press, 2008.

Wattenberg, J. *Statistical History of the United States: From Colonial Times to the Present*. New York: Basic Books, 1976.

Wenzlhuemer, Roland. *Connecting the Nineteenth-Century World: The Telegraph and Globalization*. Cambridge, UK: Cambridge University Press, 2013.

Widmer, Edward L. *Young America: The Flowering of Democracy in New York City*. New York: Oxford University Press, 1999.

Wilkins, Mira. *Emergence of Multinational Enterprise: American Business Abroad from the Colonial Era to 1914*. Cambridge, MA: Harvard University Press, 1970.

———. *The History of Foreign Investment in the United States to 1914*. Cambridge, MA: Harvard University Press, 1998.

Williams, D.M. "Liverpool Merchants and the Cotton Trade, 1820–1850." In *Liverpool and Merseyside: Essays in the Economic and Social History of the Port and its Hinterland,* edited by John R. Harris, 182–211. London: Cass, 1969.

Willson, Beckles. *America's Ambassadors to England (1785–1928): A Narrative of Anglo-American Diplomatic Relations*. London: John Murray, 1928.

Wilson, Harold S. *Confederate Industry: Manufacturers and Quartermasters in the Civil War*. Jackson: University Press of Mississippi, 2005.

Winsboro, Irvin D.S., and Joe Knetsch. "Florida Slaves, the 'Saltwater Railroad' to the Bahamas, and Anglo-American Diplomacy." *Journal of Southern History* 79, no. 1 (2013): 51–78.

Wise, Stephen R. *Lifeline of the Confederacy: Blockade Running During the Civil War*. Columbia: University of South Carolina Press, 1991.

Wong, Edlie L. *Neither Fugitive nor Free: Atlantic Slavery, Freedom Suits, and the Legal Culture of Travel*. New York: New York University Press, 2009.

Woolacott, Angela. *To Try Her Fortune in London: Australian Women, Colonialism, and Modernity*. Oxford: Oxford University Press, 2001.

Woolf, Paul. "Special Relationships: Anglo-American Love Affairs, Courtships, and Marriages in Fiction, 1821–1914." D.Phil thesis, University of Birmingham, 2007.

Yerxa, David A. *Admirals and Empire: The United States Navy and the Caribbean, 1898–1945*. Columbia: University of South Carolina Press, 1991.

Yokota, Kariann Anemi. *Unbecoming British: How Revolutionary American Became a Postcolonial Nation*. New York: Oxford University Press, 2011.

Zakim, Michael. *Accounting for Capitalism: The World the Clerk Made*. Chicago: University of Chicago Press, 2018.

Zelinsky, Wilbur. *Nation into State: The Shifting Symbolic Foundations of American Nationalism*. Chapel Hill: University of North Carolina Press, 1988.

Ziegler, Philip. *The Sixth Great Power: Barings, 1762–1929*. London: Collins, 1988.

Ziegler, Valerie H. *The Advocates of Peace in Antebellum America*. Bloomington: Indiana University Press, 1992.

Ziesche, Philipp. *Cosmopolitan Patriots: Americans in Paris in the Age of Revolution*. Charlottesville: University of Virginia Press, 2010.

Ziff, Larzer. *Return Passages: Great American Travel Writing, 1780–1910*. New Haven, CT: Yale University Press, 2000.

Zolberg, Aristide R. "The Exit Revolution." In *Citizenship and Those Who Leave: The Politics of Emigration and Expatriation,* edited by Nancy L. Green and François Weil, 33–63. Urbana: University of Illinois Press, 2007.

Index

Founded in 1893,
UNIVERSITY OF CALIFORNIA PRESS
publishes bold, progressive books and journals
on topics in the arts, humanities, social sciences,
and natural sciences—with a focus on social
justice issues—that inspire thought and action
among readers worldwide.

The UC PRESS FOUNDATION
raises funds to uphold the press's vital role
as an independent, nonprofit publisher, and
receives philanthropic support from a wide
range of individuals and institutions—and from
committed readers like you. To learn more, visit
ucpress.edu/supportus.